W9-DBN-022

Sport in the Classroom

Sport in the Classroom

Teaching Sport-Related Courses in the Humanities

EDITED BY
David L. Vanderwerken

Rutherford • Madison • Teaneck
Fairleigh Dickinson University Press
London and Toronto: Associated University Presses

Associated University Presses
440 Forsgate Drive
Cranbury, NJ 08512

Associated University Presses
25 Sicilian Avenue
London WC1A 2QH, England

Associated University Presses
P.O. Box 488, Port Credit
Mississauga, Ontario
Canada L5G 4M2

The paper used in this publication meets the requirements of the American National Standard for Permanence of Paper for Printed Library Materials Z39.48-1984.

Library of Congress Cataloging-in-Publication Data

Sport in the classroom: teaching sport-related courses in the humanities/edited by David L. Vanderwerken.
p. cm.
Includes bibliographies.
Includes index.
ISBN 0-8386-3354-4 (alk. paper)
1. Sport sciences. 2. Sports—Social aspects—Great Britain. 3. Sports—Social aspects—Canada. 4. Sports—Social aspects—United States. I. Vanderwerken, David L.
GV558.S68 1990
306.4′83—dc20 88-46148
CIP

PRINTED IN THE UNITED STATES OF AMERICA

To the memory of my father
Leon Edgar Vanderwerken (1920–1967)

"not held fast in earth but free in earth and not in earth but of earth"
—William Faulkner

Contents

Acknowledgments

Steve Moore, "In the Bleachers." Reprinted by permission of Tribune Media Services.

An earlier version of "On the Teaching of American Sport Literature," by David L. Vanderwerken, appeared in the 1987 issue of *CCTE Studies*. Reprinted by permission of the Conference of College Teachers of English of Texas, Dallas Lacy, Executive Secretary.

By Way of Preface and Introduction: The Stabilizing of Sport Studies

DAVID L. VANDERWERKEN

The spring 1986 issue of *PROTEUS: A Journal of Ideas* is devoted to sports. The editor, Angelo Costanzo, writes a prefatory "Editor's Remarks" in which he expresses his surprise at having received sixty manuscripts in response to his call for papers. In winnowing the submissions, Costanzo says he "came away with a new awareness and deep appreciation of the richness and complexity of sports experiences," and he goes on to wonder "why our universities and colleges have done relatively little with the disciplined study of sports in the various subjects taught across the curriculum." Indeed, he continues, "There is a need for courses in sports literature, psychology, sociology, history, education, and economics, to name a few. It is not enough to relegate the study of sport to the physical and health departments of universities. This idea can be supported by the fact that most of our contributions came from professors in the schools of arts and sciences and that many of these educators have designed rigorous courses in sports subjects at their institutions."

The foregoing remarks are touchingly uninformed, of course, and seem downright quaint given the year in which Costanzo is writing. Considerably more than sixty faculty teach sport-related courses. The Sport Literature Association has more than six hundred members, and equivalent numbers belong to thriving sport-related professional associations in philosophy, sociology, anthropology, psychology, and history. It is a rare college or university catalog that does not have sport-related listings in its arts and sciences curricula. Sport studies are legitimate. They have arrived. It's probably time to stop being apologetic and defensive. I don't think I'll ever again justify in print the legitimacy of what I do as a student of sport studies. Such is no longer necessary.

This collection is only a sampling—certainly an elite sampling—of some of the sport-related offerings in the United Kingdom, Canada, and the United States, taught by some of the world's leaders in sport studies who are willing to share their techniques and wisdom, their trials and errors, their thrills of classroom victories and poignant agonies of defeats. Most have been offering their respective courses for several years. Along with the twelve essays in specific disciplines, the volume features six pieces on interdisciplinary courses. All chapters include helpful appendixes consisting of syllabi, assignment guidelines, bibliographies, and sample tests or test questions. Informal in style, conversational in tone, and ready in wit, the essays reveal imaginative uses of course material and innovative teaching strategies and course requirements along with more traditional and time-tested methods. The emphasis throughout is "hands on," practical rather than theoretical, a pedagogical companion to Robert J. Higgs's *Sports: A Reference Guide* (Westport, Conn.: Greenwood Press, 1982). The audience for the text is international: faculty in humanities, social sciences, and Health, Physical Education, and Recreation (HPER) who are currently teaching or wishing to propose sport-related classes. The book is intended to be a resource, an aid, a forum for ideas and information between colleagues engaged in sport studies. While the primary focus of most chapters is on the undergraduate classroom, those graduate faculty who are training academic successors in universities around the globe may find the material useful as well. The contributors to this volume can be viewed as part of the pioneering generation, those who tried out sport-related courses in the sixties and seventies—no doubt impressionistically conceived—feeling isolated and regarded with suspicion if not outright derision, and who refined and modified their courses into the sophisticated, methodologically valid, pedagogically sound, and intellectually challenging classes described herein. In a sense this collection becomes a chronicle, almost a social history, of sport-related studies in our time. Perhaps, as well, the volume is a legacy for the next generation.

The collection's arrangement divides into three broad categories: humanities, social sciences, and interdisciplinary approaches. The intent is to roughly parallel the development of intellectual history in the Western world. Humanities breaks into four subheadings: history, literature, philosophy, and religion. The need for historical grounding mandates that that section lead off, followed by the expression of human dreams and desires and ultimate concerns in literature, philosophy, and religion. Correspondingly, it is fitting that anthropology, the broadest and most historically based of the social sciences, begins that unit, leading into sociology and psychology. The sequence of the six interdisciplinary chapters forms a kind of hour glass shape with a broad top, tapering in as the chapters narrow in focus, then expanding again in outlook and intention.

Essays on teaching U.S., Canadian, and British sport history comprise "History of Sport." Donald J. Mrozek, in his "American Sport History" course, describes several "history labs" in which students eat a turn-of-the-century training meal and hit feather-stuffed leather golf balls. Mrozek also has some wise words concerning the differing notions held by students and instructors of what, and how much, documentation is necessary for persuasiveness in historical study. Don Morrow challenges faculty members to rethink our assumptions about teaching in his piece on both undergraduate and graduate courses in "Canadian Sport History." Morrow has had his undergraduates devise a version of the game show *Jeopardy*, using Canadian sport history data, and he has invited them to ride his nineteenth-century bicycle during their study of the impact of the bicycle in Canadian society and its consequent impact on sport. In his graduate seminars, Morrow offers students the opportunity of writing an applied professional assignment, a grant proposal—as an alternative to a research paper. J. A. Mangan offers an overview of the emerging discipline of British sport history, which has lagged behind its New World counterparts, and shares four active learning methods he uses to involve and immerse his students in the material: (1) sequential self-instructional seminars; (2) rotating commentators; (3) evocative literature and art seminars; (4) local historical studies. Mangan includes an Appendix that details three sport history courses he has taught, including "British" and "World," with an aggressive emphasis on sport history as a subdiscipline of social history.

In my own retrospective piece on teaching American sport literature, I survey the brief history of the entire endeavor, from its impoverished origins to the flush times of the present. I also recount my experience of teaching the course to a nontraditional audience—Air Force personnel at a SAC base—with its special demands and rewards.

The "Philosophy of Sport" section features one piece on teaching the material from the analytic tradition by Spencer K. Wertz, and a complementary view from the phenomenological/existential tradition written by Klaus V. Meier. Wertz's comprehensive description of a three-module class narrates his rewarding yet frustrating experience in having his students invent a platonic dialogue in lieu of the more standard paper assignment. In an equally comprehensive essay, Meier discusses his use of "creative disturbances" in his undergraduate classes, in which he plays the devil's advocate, for example, in arguing that drug use for performance enhancement should be encouraged by the sports establishment.

Charles S. Prebish, in teaching "Religion of Sport," tells us how he coaxes his students toward precision in definitions, while leading them to accept the very notion of the affinities between sport and religion as a valid idea worthy of serious inquiry. Prebish introduces his undergraduates to—for them—startling and provocative ways of thinking about both sport and religion.

Andrew W. Miracle and Kendall A. Blanchard collaborate in describing their teaching of classes in the anthropology of sport, a very recently emerging field. Students hooked into Miracle's and Blanchard's courses by titles alone eventually discover that they have absorbed many principles and methodologies of classical and traditional anthropology for their tuition outlay.

In one of the two chapters on teaching sociology of sport, Jay J. Coakley explains his stimulating use of panels in his class, including one in which a group of young children talk about their experiences in both organized and sandlot sports, and another in which varsity hockey players discuss their perceptions of aggression and violence. Professor Coakley also shares his method of having students prepare their own essay questions and provides several examples of the results. In complementary contrast, Mary McElroy discusses her teaching classes in the sociology of sport within a department once called "Physical Education," but now the Department of Physical Education, Dance, and Leisure Studies. This restyling of her workplace has led McElroy to retool her courses to meet the needs and interests of a different kind of student audience. While Coakley uses panels, McElroy uses the debate as a major pedagogical strategy, making the issues she examines come alive for her students as they play roles and articulate perspectives that, at first, are foreign to their experience and previous knowledge. In addition, McElroy often weaves a novel into her syllabus so that students may experience the happy blending of the factual and the imagination's use of the factual in a work of sport-centered fiction. She provides detailed appendixes for both the debate project and the writing assignment for the novel, in this case a critique of *A Separate Peace* by John Knowles.

Two essays describing different but complementary approaches to teaching psychology of sport constitute that section. Jeffrey H. Goldstein takes a humanistic orientation in his course, showing the evolution within the discipline from a narrow focus on performance enhancement of the elite athlete toward broader considerations such as the psychological well-being of all athletes and the causes and effects of spectator behavior. A recognized authority on violence in sports, Goldstein highlights that unit in his course. He also gives us some insight into the kinds of students who take Psychology 546 at Temple University. Wayne A. Burroughs emphasizes the application of theory in his sport psychology class at Central Florida, focusing in particular on performance enhancement of all athletes, not only those labeled "elite." Burroughs's syllabus shows how closely he ties the theoretical and the practical in his classroom. One finds a pleasing balance of lecture days and workshop days. When students have mastered relaxation theories, for instance, the class spends a day or two practicing relaxation techniques. For class projects, individuals or small teams make presentations based on research and field work on such topics as "motion analysis and hurdling" and "imagery and free throw shooting."

Six essays on interdisciplinary offerings round out the volume. Allen Guttmann narrates the genesis and gestation of his course, "Sport and Society," or how an American Studies Ph.D. ended up teaching Sociology 22. Joan M. Chandler describes how she uses the small-group method effectively in having her class respond to the readings, and her handling of an assignment in which students analyze a live or televised sports event in "Sport and U.S. Society." Gregory S. Sojka chronicles the development of his class on U.S. sports culture, in his "Teaching an American Sports Culture Class: A Paradigmatic Approach." Sojka uses the methodology and resources of American Studies in his multidisciplinary class, in which novels, films, and guest speakers figure prominently. As a structural principle for his course, Professor Sojka has adopted the "paradigm drama"—an important event in American sport history that integrates and focuses a range of cultural issues, such as the Nazi Olympics of 1936 or the Billie Jean King–Bobby Riggs tennis clash in 1973. Frank Cosentino relates his strategies for battling Canada's "cultural amnesia" in his course, "Sports in Canadian Life." He sends his students immediately to the library where they learn how to run the microfilm reader, which they employ in looking up the sports section of a newspaper published on the day they were born. The point is that students discover that not only did life exist nineteen or so years ago, but also that Canadian sporting life existed. As the semester continues, they learn that theirs is a rich heritage of which they are largely oblivious. Cosentino uses collaborative projects, creative projects and presentations, and innovative lecture methods to reanimate Canadian sport history for his classes. One lecture is colorfully presented in the form of a letter to the popular novelist Arthur Hailey, trying to interest Hailey in a book idea about distance swimmer Marilyn Bell, who crossed Lake Ontario in 1954. Susan Birrell documents the origin and evolution of the syllabus for her course in sociology of women and sport in "Teaching 'Women in Sport' from a Feminist Perspective." Birrell's essay reminds academics that the best pedagogy results in a shared enterprise: students and instructor learning together through discussion and dialogue that transcend the arbitrary bounds of semesters and classrooms, leading to increased perception and awareness of received wisdoms. Birrell's piece describes—like the other chapters in this volume—the engaged intellect applied to sport studies and the energy and illumination that emerge. Finally, Neil D. Isaacs offers a sort of sporting spiritual autobiography in "Teaching at the Cutting Edge: Sports-Related Courses and Curricular Legitimacy," in which he describes the development of no less than five courses over a ten-year span and the books—both done and undone—that led to or derived from the various classes. Isaacs provides a model for the organic relationship between teaching and research. Curricular legitimacy, indeed.

Any collection is by definition a collective effort, and this one is no exception. The contributors, consummate professionals all, met their deadlines so I could meet mine and bore my editorial nitpicking with good humor. If the book has merit, the credit is all theirs. For helpful comments and suggestions, I am indebted to Professor Robert J. Higgs of East Tennessee State University. I appreciate the support of the administrators of Texas Christian University who granted me a leave of absence in Spring 1986 to work on the project. Moreover, I am grateful for the encouragement of Fred Erisman, Chair of the Department of English at TCU. And I am more than much obliged to the students in English 4503 and English 3523 in its various avatars since 1974. You know who you are.

Sport in the Classroom

PART 1
History of Sport

1

"It Ain't Nothin' Until I Call It": What Belongs in a Course in American Sport History?

DONALD J. MROZEK

Teaching American sport history recalls the quarrel between the baseball umpire and the base runner who slid into third. The umpire called, "Out."

The player argued: "What do you mean 'Out'? Look, you can see my mark on the bag. I was safe!"

To which the umpire replied serenely, "It ain't nothin' until I call it."

So it must be with the instructor in sport history—often locked in disagreement over the proper content of the course, partly because teacher and students often have different notions of what history is and what sport is. The first responsibility of the teacher is to play umpire and "call it"—explain in some detail the assumptions behind the course, the biases and special concerns of the instructor, the vision of how students may be changed through their coursework, and what the course will *not* seek to do, as well as what it has been designed to accomplish.

To illustrate, real "sports fans" find it hard to believe that their love of statistics and knowledge of trivia will give them no advantage. So, too, some athletes confuse talent on the playing field with knowledge in the classroom. Thus, fairness demands that they be given concrete cautionary guidance. For example, one may observe that knowing baseball statistics and records can spark casual conversation outside of class yet give no real benefit in classroom performance. On the other hand, appreciating how and why records and statistics came to be kept is crucial to the course—yet it requires no prior familiarity with those records or statistics. In general, then, those who suspect that their past personal familiarity with various sports (including their participation in them) will carry them through this course may be seriously disappointed and perform poorly. In such cases, the "instructor as umpire" must be able to say honestly that he "called it" clearly from the start but that the player just wasn't listening.

What the student "players" will listen to with great diligence are the reading and writing requirements for the course, as well as any special guidelines concerning test procedures. Students have proven generally receptive to Benjamin G. Rader's textbook *American Sports* (1983), finding Rader's emphasis on social history more satisfying than the more conventional narrative in John R. Betts, *America's Sporting Heritage* (1974) and less episodic than John Lucas and Ronald Smith, *Saga of American Sport* (1978). In the end, however, the apparent superiority of one text over another depends largely on its suitability to a course structure and not only on how the book has been written.

The anthology of primary and secondary materials on American sport edited by Steven A. Riess, *The American Sporting Experience* (1984), provides welcome sources. But a teacher is well advised to assign the work only if classroom lecture and discussion will draw frequently and explicitly on material from the collection. Students unfamiliar with how to use such sources may be in the majority; and, lacking help in how to use it, their frustration is likely to mount.

The choice of additional book-length readings is a roll of the dice—a pretense of skill and a reality of chance and luck. Here, too, the key is establishing clear teaching objectives. Is the purpose to cover topics not fully explored in class? Is it to expose students to different ways of thinking and writing about the history of sport? Is the goal to "humanize" the course by focusing on some of its heroes and stars? Depending on one's specific purposes, biographical studies such as Randy Roberts's study of Jack Dempsey (1979) or Peter Levine's appraisal of Albert Spalding (1985) may be in order; or, with different goals in mind, Richard Crepeau's *America's Diamond Mind, 1919–1941* (1980), drawing broadly on a wide range of literary and other sources, could serve quite effectively.

It is difficult to conceive of a history course that lacked essay questions on regular tests. Broad themes lend themselves to this format, such as the relationship between colonial cultures and religious traditions on the one hand with the emergence of different patterns in leisure, games, and sport. But certain kinds of short-answer questions may also be used profitably. One kind looks, at first glance, like a conventional multiple-choice question. So, for example, one might ask: "Which colony offered the greatest opportunities for the development of a sporting culture: (A) Massachusetts, (B) New York, (C) Virginia." But no credit would be given simply for picking a colony. Instead, the student must explain briefly *why* this choice seems better than the alternatives. In this way, what seems to be a simple multiple-choice question actually starts to look like the rough outline of an essay. Students enjoy a sense of being in command—able to explain themselves a bit without being strait-jacketed by a mere "True" or "False" or letter in a space. Teachers enjoy the fact that they have asked the historically more difficult question "why" rather than only "what."

Whether to assign a paper may be a matter of time, work-load, and logistics. Few college and university libraries lack resources sufficient for such an undertaking, regardless of the number of students enrolled. But some sources might be made useful only with a degree of teacher involvement not feasible when enrollment is very high. For example, various nineteenth-century sports periodicals are accessible on microfilm; but the medium is unfamiliar to most students, adding an additional challenge. Even here, however, an alternative device may be worth considering. Each student can be encouraged to keep a diary of his or her participation in the course. At the end of each class, the student may write down how the material discussed that day relates to contemporary issues and their own personal concerns. The diary may serve as a medium through which the student comes to understand why the instructor considered the material worth presenting to the class. Also, if the student fails to see why the instructor saw the material as important and pertinent, there is a basis on which to ask pertinent questions.

Clear signals from the outset will enhance student-teacher relations. So, too, the insistence of high standards from the very beginning may play to surprisingly strong positive response from the students. Jose Ortega y Gasset's defense of rigorous thinking and careful discourse, *Mission of the University* (1966), becomes readily understandable, partly because he uses analogies from athletic training and competition. Setting rigorous guidelines is like establishing the rules of a game; and requiring reading and writing is like demanding practice and personal discipline of those who want to be on the starting team. If used in other courses, such analogies might seem merely corny. In sport history, they may still be corny, but they are persuasive nonetheless.

DEFINING SPORT AND ITS PART IN HISTORY

The truism on shaping a lecture also applies to designing a whole course—"tell them what you're going to tell them, tell them, and then tell them what you told them." This is especially crucial when the content of the course will run counter to the expectations of many students. Students who enter the course thinking that late-twentieth century sporting institutions and ethos typify what sport has been like in earlier times need to have this assumption challenged and broken. Students who assume that people engage in sport because it is fun not only fail to see the diversity of justifications offered on behalf of sport over the centuries; they also beg basic questions of what "fun" is, why sport should be considered fun, and who thought so, when, and for how long? Although it is often said that history is the study of "change over time," too many students of sport act as if it were an unchanging conceptual absolute—and as if one studied sport's history to judge the extent to which different eras measured up to it. This disposition clearly violates the central dynamics of historical research and teaching, and it is the first and most insidious enemy.

A sensible first goal to keeping teacher and student on common ground is to define the term "sport," or really to discuss the shifts in meaning the term has had in different cultures and the eventual development of sport as an autonomous institution, taken for granted as readily as religion or education. Distinguishing among such terms as "sport," "play," "games," "recreation," and "leisure" leads directly into why and how sport, as we have come to think of it, is a comparatively recent or "modern" social invention. Depending on the length of the course and the sophistication of the students enrolled, Allen Guttmann's *From Ritual to Record* (1978) can be an extremely useful assigned reading—especially if there is sufficient opportunity to discuss Guttmann's arguments with the students. Failing that, *From Ritual to Record* provides a useful base for introductory lectures dealing with definition of several basic issues. Similarly, Roger Caillois's *Man, Play, and Games* (1961) explores the anthropological and cultural meanings of different forms of play and games. Caillois suggests how one culture may be inclined to games emphasizing chance while another leaned toward skill, one toward disorientation and another toward routine. Meanwhile, Johan Huizinga's *Homo Ludens: A Study of the Play Element in Culture* (1955) makes clear the pervasiveness of play and the diversity of its expressions, suggesting by contrast the contingency of sport on special societal conditions and choices.

The subject matter of the course—and the interpretation that unifies it—has been divided into three phases (that also correspond to three written examinations). The first deals with "pre-modern" play, games, and other physical activities that served as the forerunners of modern sport—in essence, a presentation of definitions and theory followed by study of the European origins of American sport and of colonial and early national sporting experience. The second phase concentrates on the period from the early nineteenth century through the early years of the twentieth century, exploring the transformation in attitudes toward the body and toward the social worth of various physical activities. The third phase extends through the twentieth century and traces the emergence of sport as a major part of American life and mass culture. The conceptual concerns in the course's various phases may differ considerably, allowing for the use not only of different data but different methods of presentation.

HOW MUCH IS ENOUGH?

Finding the right balance among readings and classroom presentations can be difficult. In one semester, for example, I assigned my own *Sport and American Mentality* (1983) so as to cut back on classroom lectures over the same material. This also permitted greater reliance on new research, such as sport's relationship to mass culture between 1910 and 1945. Review of the end-of-semester forms with students' reactions to the course, however, suggests that one can offer "too much of a good thing"—in this case, perhaps, too much research focused on a particular area of concern. Of course, students will have differing opinions based on their own backgrounds, interests, and levels of preparation. One "just loved" the book, while others "couldn't understand it." Another thought it "not as bad as my friend thought," and sometimes a wayward soul would wonder "what book?" One must reason through such moments, trying to determine if it is a case of too much research offered to students with too little need for it.

This problem clearly appears regardless of the authors and the kind of books one assigns. This in itself hints that the problem is not that a specific book may have been poorly written. A key to the problem appears to be attention span. Books such as *Sport and American Mentality* (1983)—or even Roberts's *Jack Dempsey* (1979)—may tell many times more about their subjects than undergraduate students have been conditioned to care about. To some extent, this must reflect a deficiency among students—an unpreparedness to do the more demanding work of scholarship at the college level as well as the tendency to restrict their efforts to whatever work has the most immediate and obvious payoff. But it also reflects what may be the central issue—the central source of difficulty—in meshing research in sport history with teaching sport history to undergraduates. That issue is to identify the target audience with unfamiliar precision—and, as a corollary, to accept them as they are now as the basis for what you wish them to be when the course is at an end. The rule of reason, as distinct from theory, may lie with Bertolt Brecht, who once said, "The house will be built with the bricks that are there." It is hardly surprising that a culture so given to short thought-units—six-minute segments of situation comedy, half-minute television commercials, three-minute popular songs (whose lyrics, parenthetically, pose views without developing them)—should have produced students ill-disposed to read a fully developed argument.

Still, a second problem deserves admission—the instructor needs much more information and argument to accept an author's thesis than will prove necessary or useful in the classroom. Thus, most research findings—let alone the data upon which they are based—must be radically compressed and synthesized for worthwhile application in the classroom. In this sense, there is a canyon of difference between "how much is enough" to justify an instructor's remarks in a lecture and "how much is enough" when the student reads supplementary material. When asked a simple question, the academic's first impulse is to give a complex answer. The first remark is usually: "Well, it's not nearly so simple as that. You can't make it a simple 'Yes' or 'No.' And for that matter, there's a good book on that subject you ought to read." Sometimes, it is better to violate this habit and give a plain, short answer. Students sometimes do not comprehend the answers we give—in spoken words or readings assigned—because they have not yet personally come to see the pertinence of the questions with which they are coupled. Sometimes, we approach the study of sport with such complex apparatus and so many interrelated issues in mind that we feel confronted with problems that have no solutions—virtually no essay or book can go on too long or give us too much information and argument. And it is this level of conviction that allows academics to use such arguments in a lecture. But for our students, such levels of detail are mere solutions that have no problem.

WHAT CAN ACADEMICS GIVE OF THEMSELVES?

Still, teachers must be able to give something of themselves and of their own research and special insights. So they must consider examples of what might work, setting out some broad rules of fair and appropriate use. And a first lesson that I relearned is rooted in the old saying, "Tell them what you know, not what you don't know." Despite great reluctance to talk much about one's own experiences and thus to turn a college classroom into kindergarten show and tell, teachers may reap a harvest of interest by using their own experiences as grist for lectures or discussion. For example, during some of my own time in the Arctic, I have used some techniques of anthropology as well as oral history to develop material for future projects—one of which I was writing at the same time I used the material in the classroom. Talking in a matter-of-fact way about one's time in the Arctic sparked curiosity; and it was clear that the students regarded me as someone who had, in the Civil War era term, "seen the elephant." Whatever a teacher may think, when it comes to the reception a student will give him, the personal experience of that teacher may be more eloquent and more persuasive than all the apparatus learned in graduate study and methods courses. So, to the extent that the circumstances in which research was conducted have a certain theatrical appeal, they can be a great aid to communicating effectively in the classroom.

One may also gain brilliantly by taking advantage of guests who have made a relevant contribution to sport's historic development—that is, those who made history rather than those who write it. In this way, the teacher not only brings a visitor into the room, providing a welcome change of face and voice; he brings valuable primary sources directly into the classroom and, in the course of interviewing them, demonstrates to the assembled students how at least one form of research can be conducted. Peter Levine has had some extraordinarily good results in using this approach with such guests as Peter Gent, Robert Lipsyte, and Harry Edwards. Admittedly, this not only provides a chance to display oral history techniques—it lends a measure of authority and stature to the course itself, precisely because people of reputation and stature have chosen to visit it.

When one cannot bring such people into the room live, it may pay to bring them in on tape. In my sport history class, I use a videotaped segment from the program "Hard Road to Glory," produced by Arthur Ashe, in which Muhammad Ali recalls the sport heroes he used as models when he was a child and a young man. It would be simple to tell the students that he was captivated by Joe Louis and Sugar Ray Robinson. But letting Ali say it, as the tape rolls forward, lets them hear the slurs in his speech, see the drift in his eyes, and mourn over the puffy face growing prematurely heavy jowls. The videotape brings the personal, human Ali into the room—and the students are often suitably uncomfortable watching this remnant of a once truly great athlete. One might note, at least in passing, that the videotape seems to sway the student more effectively than does film. The mind knows that both media capture a candid scene or a live interview; but the look of the videotape recording conveys a far more persuasive feel of realism.

These techniques all aim at registering with the student less on the basis of the historical importance of the source exploited—although each is legitimate by that test—than on the students' own fixation on celebrity. This is no insult to the students—or, more precisely, it is not a disparagement restrictively applied to students. Our culture at large has grave difficulty distinguishing between fame and notoriety, between heroes and celebrities. So, too, the culture sanctifies the presumption that those who are known (even if only known for being known) are somehow superior to those who are not, no matter what things the obscure ones may have accomplished or what values they may exemplify. So, then, while the fact of celebrity cannot be the sufficient test of what one would include in an article or in preparing for a lecture, it must be among the necessary tests for including it in actual presentation in the classroom.

AUDIO-VISUALS AS CONTENT

It is customary to think of audio-visual aids as methods through which teachers may amplify their words and make concepts somewhat clearer and more concrete for our students. But it is also true that some sport historians use photographs, films, songs, and many other objects in material culture as crucial primary sources for their research. In this way, if the research carries over into the classroom, audio-visual materials actually govern the content of lectures to a considerable degree. For some historical perspectives, such as cultural history, the images seen and heard may even be the great bulk of the primary data under consideration.

Again, the nature of our culture makes for benefits and pitfalls in using audio and visual images. Ours has become an increasingly non-verbal culture—one in which repeated use of the phrase "you know" is a substitute for precision of vocabulary. It is a culture in which a highly-rated talk show host routinely asks his guests not "what do you think" about an issue but "how do you feel." The decline of precision has been much noted, and it is troubling. Still, one ought not forget that sport itself is a form of non-verbal communication—a reminder that such communication is not necessarily bad, as long as it does not simply cancel out the alternatives. When such imprecision of thought meets a flood of visual imagery, the results can be unsatisfactory. The saying that "a picture is worth a thousand words" is true; but we need to know, at any given moment, which one of the thousand possible words we are to have in mind. The effort to insure that the right word from among the thousand does come to the students' minds raises once again the critical role of appropriate method.

Visual images can have for many undergraduates a certain power of conviction that words possess for few of them. In part, this is because the vocabulary of so many students is so sparse, badly inhibiting their grasp of ideas spoken in conventional lectures. But the way in which photographic images are used is a key to their effectiveness in the classroom. So, for example, no matter the eloquence in talking of male dress reform in sporting attire, the power of photographic images can be overwhelming by comparison. It is one thing to say that Bernarr MacFadden advocated playing tennis while wearing swim trunks, and quite another to project an image of him (or a follower) dressed in that manner opposite an image of Bill Tilden, dressed in long-sleeved shirt and white flannel trousers. A picture that is worth a thousand words can be merely confusing when a student doesn't know which word a teacher has in mind at any given moment. But two photographs juxtaposed may provide comparison and contrast that make the pertinent words, from among the thousand, clear even to a functional illiterate.

Similarly, one may talk endlessly about how sport became a part of the mass popular culture in interwar America. But saying so in class leaves this observation as little more than a sentence uttered by an instructor that is prudent to remember as a possible test question. If one shows images of Charles Atlas and his successful student Tony Sansone in poses closely imitated by Johnny Weissmuller in the role of Tarzan, the student is far more prone to think it really happened. Similarly, many students hear claims that sport and entertainment industries dove-tailed and think these notions mere words. But showing Johnny Weissmuller giving Jack Dempsey an impromptu swimming lesson helps them believe it.

To illustrate the rather subtle point of how the sporting cultures of different eras may produce quite distinct sets of icons or ritually repeated images, one may compare athletes from the 1930s and 1960—both swimmers—and compare the attitudes imputed to those athletes and their coaches. In 1939, the swimming team of Mercersberg Academy in Pennsylvania was presented in *Look* magazine in a manner clearly exemplifying the concept of "strength through joy." But in 1964, an Indiana University swimmer was shown in *Life* magazine as a devotee of "all out agony" and was said to "train by torture" (Richards and Mrozek 1977). The words that distinguish 1939 and 1964 are quite accurate. Sometimes, students even remember them. But the force of the visual imagery clearly banishes doubt. Especially considering that swimmers in both eras surely gave great effort in their training and competition, what students witness in the photographs is a conscious choice of how athletes, coaches, and sport itself are to be presented. It is not an act of depiction but of definition—not a response to reality but the creation of a preferred version of reality. All of this is at the heart of research technique and methodology in cultural history—and, as long as one places more emphasis on visual images than words, one's research can be used with surprising success in the classroom.

But it is worth noting a common feature of the successful examples just mentioned—MacFadden and Tilden, Atlas and Sansone and Weissmuller, Mercersberg and Indiana. For their effectiveness, all of these cases depend not on illustration but on juxtaposition. In this way, students tolerate—and even enjoy—the visual images because students respond to them as statements of *new* information, displacing the words that one may deliver in advance of showing the photographs. What the undergraduates cannot stomach nearly so well (and what they seem to profit from somewhat less) are images used *essentially* for the purpose of illustrating some thought whose primary presentation and broad development come in spoken commentary. In these cases, the photographs seem to be taken as trivia and adornments, suggesting the fastidiousness and care of the instructor but not taken as a crucial source of historical insight. Without that bold juxtaposition, the photographs appear to be taken by many undergraduates as that most lethal of things—mere repetition. What the faculty member regards as enrichment of a basic idea by pursuing its complexities and implications, many undergraduates are likely to dismiss with a remark often heard among their candid, off-the-cuff comments to one another: "Oh, the instructor just kept saying the same thing over and over." The border between enrichment and boredom is defined by the question, "How much is enough?" But the border will be discovered and respected only by the corollary question, "Enough for whom?" The test of juxtaposition maximizes the chance that the visual imagery will be enough for the undergraduate student without being too much.

EXPERIENCE AS "OUR NEXT FEATURE"

One potentially useful tool in the classroom is what might be called "history lab"—carefully planned experiences in which students recreate past ways of acting, eating, training, and playing. A host of possibilities is available, such as the testing of old training regimens or past "training table" diets, experimenting with old training devices and medical gear (such as those using mild electrical current), and playing certain sports under their original rules or with equipment in something closer to its original form. (Consider, for example, playing golf with balls made out of leather stuffed with feathers. One may tell a student that golf was not quite the same game before the development of gutta-percha balls; but the student is apt to believe you after trying to drive a feather-ball down the fairway.) The same tendency to rely on "non-verbal communication," mentioned earlier, is pertinent here, too. For some students, there is an intrinsic appeal to learning by doing—learning in a way that seems concrete, while words too often strike them as abstract.

But there is a huge trapdoor in the midst of this busy stage of historical "research experiments"—the problem of perspective. What a historian may see as a heuristic for gaining insight into alternatives faced by people decades or centuries ago, some students may take merely as a form of entertainment. If this happens, then each such "lab experience" is just the "feature attraction" for the day, as in a motion picture theater; and the effort to establish a pattern of research results from a series of such "lab experiences" plays like little more than a diverting reel of coming attractions.

If there is a solution to this difference in perspective, it may lie in the degree and quality of preparation that the students receive prior to a "history lab" experience. One may adapt the old rule in lecturing—"Tell them what you're going to tell them. . . ." In such a "history lab," tell them what they should be looking for and why, and what it will imply. Then remind them of these things as they are occurring; and recapitulate and elaborate upon these points after the experience is done. Apart from spoken guidelines, a printed handout is usually desirable—partly because it gives the student psychological assurance that *you* have done your homework and are not just taking an easy alternative to preparing a formal lecture. In all, though, the preparation should be intense; and it should come several class periods before the "history lab" actually occurs.

CONCLUDING COMMENTS

The final choice of what to do and how to teach—how much of one's own or others' research clearly shapes a course, what methods one employs, what kind of readings to use—must depend on what one hopes to accomplish, what kind of students one may have to work with, and what limits on resources one must contend with. As for objectives in a course, various methods suggested above clearly aid in developing a student's sensitivity to change over time—to historical disjunction—to the relativity of values, fashion, personal style. These same methods would not necessarily be the most effective in promoting awareness of other historical themes and concerns. So, in theory, problems can result when there is a gap between desired goal and chosen method.

But the safety net that will break the fall as we reach such a gap is, quite simply, honesty. And it is this that I would suggest as the final means to temper our work in the classroom. As has been noted earlier, one must make unusually clear what it is that we intend to achieve by bringing various materials into a course—the students must feel themselves to be part of the whole process of discovering the meaning of these materials. But what if it doesn't work? Or what if the results are equivocal? The safety net of candor comes into play. Discuss the matter with the students, exploring the accomplishments and deficiencies in any experience you have arranged or in the use of any materials you have introduced. Discussing these matters with the students may not leave them with a complete or even a better understanding of some specific piece of research. But it may lead them to a better sense of how historians work and how history itself is meant to be a search for personally relevant truth—not just some abstract academic game and not rarified hot air teachers use to puff themselves up with. The final lesson may then be the most valuable one of all—that honesty is not only the best policy but the best history.

APPENDIX I: SYLLABUS

History of Sport
History 515 / EH 15 (TU 9:30–10:45 AM)
Fall 1985

Donald J. Mrozek

GENERAL REMARKS

This course concentrates on the emergence of sport as a significant, distinct institution in American life and culture. "Sport" and other terms such as play, games, recreation, and leisure will be defined and distinguished from one another, at least sufficiently to show why sport as we have come to think of it is a comparatively recent or "modern" social invention. How it emerged—and to some extent, at least, why it emerged—will be a major concern of the course. As also noted, the emphasis will be on sport in American life and culture. However, non-U.S. subjects and influences will be considered to the extent appropriate to understanding the American developments.

This course is open to and suitable for all students who have a genuine interest in following the development of a major American institution. It is not a course in which sports fans will do especially well; nor is it one in which a knowledge of sports trivia will prove particularly beneficial to the student. Prior knowledge of sports—even prior interest in them—will not necessarily give a student any special advantage. For example, knowing baseball statistics and records may be of interest in casual conversation outside of class; but it will not necessarily have any positive effect on one's performance in class. On the other hand, appreciating how and why records and statistics came to be kept is an important aspect of the course—but one which requires no prior familiarity with those records or statistics. In general, then, those who suspect that their past personal familiarity with various sports (including their participation in them) will carry them through this course will be seriously disappointed and may prove seriously deficient in performance.

COURSE DESIGN

This course has been conceived basically as a lecture course. However, the instructor will seek to reserve time for questions and for occasional in-class discussion. Moreover, students are welcome to raise questions during the course of a specific lecture when the material presented or the manner of presentation seems unclear. The objective is not to suppress discussion—far from it. But the course design is intended to guard against having "discussion" degenerate into expression of mere opinion unsupported by reading and careful thought.

The subject matter of the course—and the interpretation that unifies it—has been divided into three phases (which will correspond to the three written examinations that will be given). The first deals with "pre-modern" play, games, and other physical activities that served as the forerunners of modern sport. The second phase concentrates on the period from the early nineteenth century through the early years of the twentieth century, exploring the transformation in attitudes toward the body and toward the social worth of various physical activities. The third phase extends through the twentieth century and traces the emergence of sport as a major institution in American life and culture.

There will be two tests, or written examinations, held during the semester and a third test held at the end of the semester. Each test will deal with lecture and reading materials. In addition, the third test will include comprehensive questions extending over the material of the whole semester and designed to bring the material into a coherent whole for the student. As a result of the logic underlying the structure of these tests, all students will be expected to take all three of these tests. There will be no exemptions from the final examination, neither for senior status nor prior performance in tests nor other reasons.

The tests will consist of questions in a variety of multiple choice formats and also of essay-type questions. Although the instructor reserves the right to adjust the proportion as necessary, the present intention is to have approximately two-thirds of each test's point value in multiple-choice questions and the balance in essay-format questions. Grades will not be adjusted on a curve.

There will be no paper for this course. However, each student is encouraged to keep a diary of her or his participation in the course. A useful device is to ask, at the end of each class, how the material presented and considered may be made personally meaningful. Meaning and relevance are not external matters. They must be discovered and, in a sense, created by each individual. The diary may serve as a medium through which the student comes to understand why the instructor considered the material worth presenting to the class. Also, if the student does not figure out why the instructor saw the material as important and pertinent, he or she will have a basis on which to ask a pertinent question on the subject. There will also be occasional "lab experiences" outside the classroom, usually on an optional basis. The purpose of these "history labs" is to help you to understand fundamental changes in the nature of sport or in how different peoples have conducted it—how equipment may affect the feel of a game, what emotions are fostered and which are suppressed, and so on.

There will be no extra credit projects. There will be no substitutions of papers or book reports for other work (such as tests) not performed. There will be no blanket tolerance of nonappearance at scheduled tests, and makeup tests will be given only rarely and for demonstrated good reason. "Good reason" includes such things as a registered medical emergency; it does not include such things as needing to get a prescription for a minor ailment or irritation. "Good reason" includes what the military would call "compassionate leave," such as is required by a clear crisis in one's immediate family; but it does not include such things as a choice by the student to take advantage of a vacation or other travel opportunity. "Good reason" does not include having more than one test on the same day. Although some students may regard a course such as this one as secondary to their own purposes, it is primary to the purposes and interests of its instructor. Hence, the instructor suggests that any student facing a conflict in test scheduling negotiate with other instructors for relief. Even more, the student should so construct her or his schedule so as to avoid any such conflicts, or at least minimize them in the first place.

The firmness which the instructor intends to insist upon for such matters as test performance, is not a matter of whim but a matter of equity. In all candor, the large number of students seeking a rescheduling of a test tend to do so because they have used their time improperly or planned poorly and hence are not ready to take the tests and do as well as they would wish. At the same time, other students—the great majority of them—have scheduled their time as well as they could and then take tests and accept the results with considerable grace. It is manifestly and grossly unfair to students who have played by the rules to give special advantageous treatment to those who have not. In this course, such special treatment will not be accorded.

READINGS

Benjamin G. Rader, *American Sports*
Donald J. Mrozek, *Sport and American Mentality*
Donald J. Mrozek, *Sport in the West*
Peter Levine, *A. G. Spalding and the Rise of Baseball*
Steven Riess, *The American Sporting Experience*

SCHEDULE

27 August—Introductory meeting
29 August—Rader, 1–21; Riess, 10–14
3 September—Rader, 24–43; Riess, 15–34
5 September—Mrozek, *Sport/West*, 3–9, 37–43
10 September—Rader, 46–86; Riess, 35–57
12 September—Rader, 88–122, Riess, 58–79, 80–90
17 September—Mrozek, *Sport/West*, 10–29, 44–61
19 September—Rader, 124–69; Riess, 104–34
24 September—Mrozek, *Sport/West*, 30–36
26 September—Test No. 1
1 October—Mrozek, *Sport/Mentality*, 1–27
3 October—Mrozek, *Sport/Mentality*, 28–66
8 October—Mrozek, *Sport/Mentality*, 66–135; Riess, 138–63
10 October—Mrozek, *Sport/Mentality*, 136–88; Riess, 164–208
15 October—Mrozek, *Sport/Mentality*, 189–235
17 October—Rader, 176–215
22 October—Rader, 217–39
24 October—Rader, 241–63

29 October—Rader, 265–82
31 October—Rader, 283–99
5 November—Test No. 2
7 November—Rader, 301–21; Riess, 214–38
12 November—Rader, 324–44; Riess, 239–54
14 November—Rader, 345–60; Riess, 255–63
19 November—Mrozek, *Sport/West*, 62–69
21 November—Levine; Riess, 264–305
26 November—Levine; Riess, 306–24
28 November—Thanksgiving (holiday)
3 December—Levine; Riess, 330–64
5 December—Levine; Riess, 365–84
10 December—Riess, 385–97
12 December—Review
17 December—Final Examination (2:00–3:50 PM)

NOTE: This schedule is subject to adjustment if and as necessary, although no change will be made which would significantly alter the workload of students enrolled.

APPENDIX II: SAMPLE TEST

PART ONE: In each of the following, circle the letter identifying what you consider the best answer. Then, *briefly explain why you consider this the most effective answer*, also noting any major defects in the other options. Your *justification* of the choice is what determines points earned. Each is worth a maximum of 10 points. *Respond to all seven questions.*

1.) Which of the following characteristics described by Roger Caillois most fully describes such activities as tennis and chess?
   A) agon
   B) ilinx
   C) alea
   D) mimickry
2.) Among the following characteristics that Allen Guttmann includes in his list of what makes modern sport modern, which appears to have been *least* present in American sport before the nineteenth century?
   A) secularization
   B) quest for records
   C) equality of opportunity to compete
   D) specialization of roles
3.) Which of the following colonial experiences had the most significant long-term impact in shaping American sport?
   A) Virginia plantation culture
   B) New England Puritan culture
   C) the diverse Dutch and Germanic cultures of the middle colonies
   D) Hispanic culture
4.) In general, which of the following influences was strongest in the shaping of colonial American sport?
   A) religious belief
   B) folk traditions from the parent European cultures
   C) environmental conditions in America

D) persistence of rigid European class structure

5.) Which of the following was most important in molding the American sporting experience in the early and middle decades of the nineteenth century?
   A) muscular Christianity
   B) transcendentalism
   C) time thrift
   D) Jacksonian "popular" politics

6.) Which of the following best exemplified a drift toward some distinctively American approach in sport?
   A) blood sports
   B) urban sports clubs
   C) "pedestrianism" and prize fights
   D) college sports clubs

7.) Of the following groups of men and women, which represented the most important and influential tendencies in American sport and physical culture in the nineteenth century?
   A) John Cox Stevens, James Gordon Bennett, John Morissey
   B) Catharine Beecher, Rev. John Todd, Thomas Wentworth Higginson
   C) Dio Lewis, Horace Mann, the staff of Round Hill School
   D) Tom Molineaux, William Jackson, "Deerfoot"

PART TWO: Select only one of the following essay topics. Be sure your essay presents a thesis and supports it with argument and evidence. Plan your essay before beginning to write. Your essay may be worth up to a maximum of 30 points.

EITHER

1. What were the most important forces accounting for how the American colonists engaged in sport and games? Religion? Availability of spare time? Availability of money and other material resources? Other influences? What was their relative importance?

OR

2. Based on the writings and ideas of such people as Allen Guttmann, Roger Caillois, and Carl Diem; how can we define "sport" as distinct from play, games, or other terms? What are its key features, and what is *not* to be included within our understanding of the term "sport"? Make use of extensive examples from the early American experience in games, play, and sport to illustrate your argument.

WORKS CITED

Betts, John R. 1974. *America's Sporting Heritage: 1850–1950.* Reading, Mass.: Addison-Wesley.

Caillois, Roger. 1961. *Man, Play, and Games.* Translated by Meyer Barash. New York: Free Press.

Crepeau, Richard C. 1980. *America's Diamond Mind, 1919–1941.* Orlando: University Presses of Florida.

Guttmann, Allen. 1978. *From Ritual to Record: The Nature of Modern Sports.* New York: Columbia University Press.

Huizinga, Johan. 1955. *Homo Ludens: A Study of the Play Element in Culture.* Translated by R. F. C. Hull. Boston: Beacon Press.

Levine, Peter. 1985. *A. G. Spalding and the Rise of Baseball.* New York: Oxford University Press.

Lucas, John A., and Ronald A. Smith. 1978. *Saga of American Sport.* Philadelphia: Lea & Febiger.

Ortega y Gasset, Jose. 1966. *Mission of the University*. 1944. Translated and edited by Howard Lee Nostrand. New York: Norton.

Mrozek, Donald J. 1983. *Sport and American Mentality, 1880–1910.* Knoxville: University of Tennessee Press.

Rader, Benjamin G. 1983. *American Sports, From the Age of Folk Games to the Age of Spectators*. Englewood Cliffs, N.J.: Prentice-Hall.

Richards, Arne, and Donald J. Mrozek, eds. 1977. *Sports Periodicals.* Westport, Conn.: Greenwood Press.

Riess, Steven A. 1984. *The American Sporting Experience, A Historical Anthology of Sport in America.* New York: Leisure Press.

Roberts, Randy. 1979. *Jack Dempsey, The Manassa Mauler.* Baton Rouge: Louisiana State University Press.

2
Reflections on Teaching Canadian Sport History

DON MORROW

Canadian sport history as an academic area of inquiry and as a teaching subject area is not much older than the comparable facets of sport literature. In reality it has only been since 1970 that Canadian sport history has emerged as a serious field of scholarly and pedagogical endeavor. At present most physical education departments offer courses or portions of courses in this field to undergraduate students while some history departments have embraced selected aspects of Canadian sport history as teachable material with true historical relevance. After twelve years of university teaching in this area, I found the concerted introspection necessitated in writing this essay to be a useful self-inspection of my own teaching styles, methods, and structures. I trust that the product of this exercise triggers to some degree a heightened awareness of the significance of teaching in a university environment.

How do I teach my subject area? I don't. I really do not believe that in a university setting that this is the proper question. My conviction is that I teach students about Canadian sport history, and perhaps, in some cases, I might even teach them to think—using Canadian sport history as a backdrop. Idealistic? Maybe, but I cannot accept that knowledge, education, inquiry is so fragmented that educators can delude themselves into thinking they teach pure content to empty mental sponges who are highly motivated, somehow, to soak up facts, dates, and Canadiana in a mindless quest for marks. Similarly, it is sheer folly to presume that each student learns in exactly the same fashion, at the same rate, unhindered by external influences such as personal problems, financial considerations, other courses, and so forth. In short, Canadian sport history is not nearly so important as a teaching consideration to me as are the students who learn Canadian sport history.

Certain assumptions underlie everyone's teaching whether or not they all come to the surface. In my own case, the roots of my teaching perspective in Canadian sport history—very few university professors have ever been taught to teach—can be traced to a single question posed by my doctoral adviser:

What is worth knowing?

Extracted from Postman's and Weingartner's excellent education system critique, *Teaching As a Subversive Activity* (1969), the question incensed me. It was an interrogative cart-before-the-horse; no one had ever confronted me with a value-of-knowledge issue. Like most students, unwittingly, I had come to accept the empty jug theory of knowledge. New teachers kept pouring new material into my vessel and I retained some of it, never knew or used most of it, and certainly never questioned its worth. But, "What is worth knowing?" was and remains the most significant question anyone can ask about education.

The answer is not simple; the answers are dependent on so many sets of factors. For example:

How do you go about getting to know what is worth knowing?

From what perspective is the question being asked? As the teacher? As the student?

What prior knowledge can be assumed?

Why would someone want to know anything about Canadian sport history?

The global answer to "what is worth knowing?" is "something about something," but it depends on the individual, one's situation, and a host of other variables and questions. In essence, any knowledge given or taken must be meaningful or be made meaningful to the individual learner to be of any worth. Canadian sport history is not intrinsically meaningful to more than a very small number of students. As a teacher of the subject, I perceive that a greater part of my role is to *make* Canadian sport history meaningful in some way to as many students taking the courses offered as possible. I have accepted it, and I believe that the subject is worth knowing; the university has accepted it, and every undergraduate physical education major at my institution must take it.

How do I go about making Canadian sport history meaningful? The dilemma I face from day one is the Canadian environment and our attitude, in general terms, to our own history. As the Canadian poet, Alden Nowlan, has stated so succinctly:

My country has no history, only a past.

Students in Canada, for the most part, are living products of a sort of national ahistoricism. The richness and excitement of Canada's history is rarely or poorly conveyed to students because of a teaching emphasis on chronological facts, dates, wars, and politics—a sort of system history rather than a people history. My first overhead in class, as a result, is adapted from C. Ware, *The Cultural Approach to History* (1940):

> I know history isn't true Hennessy because it ain't like what I see every day in Haisted Street. If anyone comes along with a history for Greece or Rome that will show me the people fighting, getting drunk, making love, getting married, owing the grocery man and being without hard coal, I'll believe there was a Greece or Rome, but not before. . . . History is a post-mortem examination. It tells you what a country died for. But I'd like to know what it lived for.

The point I try to make is that sport history is social history; it does tell you something meaningful about what Canadians lived for, what they elected to do by choice, what was meaningful to them. With a brief, highly selective and biased collection of slides, I proceed to show them some of the sporting life of Canadians, and I play the salesman and use every ounce of enthusiasm I can muster to persuade a captive audience that Canadian sport history and my course is meaningful, interesting, and challenging in different ways to different people. I perform on the first day of class; I do very little teaching. The hype is to whet their appetite, and I view it as absolutely necessary and no injustice to either history or academia.

Next class, I try to convey three basic elements to provide a foundation or starting point for the class as a group: an approach to historical thinking; the significance of the concept of time; and *doing* history by asking questions. In the use of the last element, I convey my bias about the study of history:

History is what historians say it is.

I borrow extensively and with latitude from Berkhofer's *A Behavioral Approach to Historical Analysis* (1969) to try to show that history may well be everything that happened in the past, but that history can only be interpreted by the person, the historian, the student *doing* the history. Question-framing is paramount in the process. Who, what, when, and where are basic, all too often the only questions given in history classes. Their answers are important ingredients, but I expect students to probe more with how and why to gain significance and meaning in Canadian sport history. I even tease to hammer home the significance of asking good questions with the rhetorical, imponderable question, "Did Adam have a navel?" I don't mention Berkhofer; I use examples such as the case of Tom Longboat. An Onondaga (Iroquois) long-distance runner, Longboat was the odds-on-favorite to win the 1908 Olympic marathon. He collapsed at the nineteen-mile mark. Subsequent examination determined a drug overdose, likely strychnine. The issues became questions of who and why:

Who, possibly, might have done it?

Why did he, she, they do it?

Why is his case significant/meaningful in the perspective of Canadian sport history?

Since history focuses on change, the example is excellent for slicing into sport history, probing the facts, asking questions of the data, and otherwise playing historical detective.

Nonsporting examples—such as an embellished fantasy about a series of murders at mid-nineteenth century reportedly perpetrated by the Donnelly Family—juxtaposed with a good historical analysis of the same events, or the methods used to come to the conclusion over a century after his death that Napoleon Bonaparte was murdered; are used to convey the importance of students/people/historians doing history as opposed to absorbing it by osmosis. In the same fashion I talk about time as a historian's benchmark, as a location for setting events in context. Often, I put up an overhead or reveal a concealed blackboard filled with dates and tell the students to copy them all down because these are the most important dates in Canadian sport history. I do so not to belittle the historian's craft but because I have found that dates need not be emphasized or drilled into students. They learn them as a matter of course when they focus on how-and-why questions. We discuss chronological time as a concept, traditional dating of important benchmarks in Canadian history (minus sport), subjective time, time as change, "the times," periodization, and the meaning of sport "times." (What does it mean or how fast, in energy requirements, would a five minute, forty second mile time be in an 1871 Montreal snowshoe race?) Such concepts of time go hand-in-hand with a logical approach to history (not merely chronological) as one method of studying human behavior in the past.

In a technocracy that tugs its Canadian devotees further and further into ahistorical oblivion, the past compared to the future carries value-laden connotations. In an effort to induce their receptivity to the logic of doing Canadian sport history, I try to instill a different way of thinking about the past. To do so, I borrow from Robert Pirsig's *Zen and the Art of Motorcycle Maintenance* (1974):

> [The Greeks] saw the future as something that came upon them from behind their backs with the past receding away before their eyes.
>
> When you think about it, that's a more accurate metaphor than our present one. Who really *can* face the future? All you can do is project from the past, even when the past shows that such projections are often wrong. And who really can forget the past? What else is there to know?

The quality of each student's experience in the course depends upon the ability to perceive the interrelationships and patterns connecting past, present, and future in terms of change.

If, in this fashion, I can lay the groundwork for the course, I find students more open, more receptive, and above all, more perceptive about a course in Canadian sport history. Structural elements define the way in which I teach Canadian sport history, but they don't necessarily limit it. I consider teaching as important as my research, and I make every effort to dovetail the two. With classes of forty students, I lecture on topics in a roughly chronological framework of historical events and break the class into groups of ten for seminars on in-depth issues/persons/events/sports that relate to the lecture material. Readings are for seminar and lecture amplification and for doing-history purposes. Seminars do not work unless everyone does the assigned readings since historical interpretation is not derived by immaculate perception. Students respond well to seminars and, possibly as a carryover effect, they become more willing and able to provoke meaningful questions and discussions in lecture situations. The administration of undergraduate seminars is considerable. Students lead them and they need help in preparing, organizing, eliciting participation, and so forth. The results range from disastrous to exciting to amazing. I prefer the seminar approach at all levels. At the graduate level, all classes are three-hour, weekly seminars that I lead based upon a set of previously-assigned readings. Topics (see Appendix II) tend to be more issue-centered and more deeply approached. I don't believe in graduate students presenting seminars; my view is that graduate seminars should be informal discussions led by the professor. My graduate classes, then, are based on the assumption that everyone has done the readings. The format is socratic; I never lecture in a graduate class. Instead, I challenge, probe, question, offer interpretations, interrogate the readings and student's perceptions of the readings. Initially graduate students are intimidated, they tell me, by this method, but they report that it totally changes their approach to the readings, to studying, taking notes, and doing history, and that they prefer the method.

Before each graduate class, a written framework or general set of questions is handed out for the issue to be studied so that students can tackle the issue with perspective. Assignments at this level include the review of a book of the student's choosing, a research paper on an approved topic, or the full presentation of a research grant proposal (see Appendix II). The research grant proposal has proved to be an excellent, applied project to planning research and all of its inherent idiosyncrasies. I become the granting agency with a slight twist in that a mark is assigned rather than conferring approval or nonapproval. A final exam completes the course requirements.

At the undergraduate level, the Canadian sport history course is now a compulsory core course with two hundred students in a one-semester course each year. The luxury of the seminar approach is no longer a reality. Furthermore, the course is a "designated essay" course, meaning that the course must have an essay as a major grading component. In smaller courses, I have tried the "creative project" approach wherein students recreate a sport under original rules, do a painting or sculpture of a sport celebrity, and any number of other artistic pursuits. A sport history "Jeopardy" game based on the TV quiz show was probably the most academically useful project. While the projects were often excellent in artistic quality, I found it increasingly difficult to judge history vis-à-vis art. On the other hand, the essays allow unbridled doing of Canadian sport history. I grade each and every one, an unenviable but always enlightening task in both positive and negative respects.

In doing the essays, worth 40 percent of the final grade, students get caught up in primary sources. Newspaper microfilm lures them into unimagined interests in the past whether directly related to the essay topic or not. They interview famous former athletes and organizers. They form their own ideas, opinions, and interpretations of past events. In short, they do sport history first hand. I have been delighted with and surprised by the quality of their finished products. Over the years, some students have achieved 100 percent on their papers:

The Eddie Shore-Ace Bailey Incident of 1933

The Training Methods of an Elite Marathoner in the 1920s: A Case Study of Johnny C. Miles

The Concept of the 6-day Cycling Show-Circus in the 1930s: the Star Showman, 'Torchy' Peden

They weren't flawless, but they were the epitome of reasonable expectations of essay quality for undergraduate students. All papers have been published in the *Canadian Journal of History of Sport*.

Unlike the situation in the United States, there is no comprehensive textbook on Canadian sport history. In 1987, McClelland and Stewart released *Canada Learns to Play: The Emergence of Organized Sport 1807–1914* by Alan Metcalfe. The text is written as part of the publisher's social history series. Although useful for the first half of the course, it does not deal with twentieth-century sporting issues. Furthermore, it is better received by graduate rather than undergraduate students because it is jampacked with information, and because it presents a consistent theme that requires discussion and interpretation from a variety of different perspectives. My preference is to have students read into an issue or topic rather than read around the general flow of events. At both levels, undergraduate and graduate, readings are assigned topically or by unit (see Appendixes). Examples of primary sources are used—newspaper sporting ads, rules, acts, and so forth—in conjunction with overheads in undergraduate classes to encourage student discussion and interpretation. Even in classes of two hundred plus students, it is surprising how much discussion can take place. I tell students that it is a known fact that grades are most highly correlated with sitting in the first three rows of large classes—the correlation does not reveal the true variables for this finding—and I repeat all points and questions to the entire class. A huge screen makes overheads and slides larger than life, easy to view, and brings history's atmosphere into the classroom. As with the readings, slides are perceived as indispensable for undergraduate courses because of the ahistorical backgrounds of the students. Slides bring readings into focus and provide an anchor of awareness of subject matter, although care has to be taken in pointing out to students what is meaningful about the slides. In short, slides are shown as the lecture progresses, not as wrap up materials or illustrated shows. For me, that means walking with the forward/reverse/focus paddle in hand or pocket since I try to go up aisles and across the room while talking. Lecture material integrates the theme(s) or issue(s) of the readings but I do not cover the readings in detail unless students express difficulties with one of them in class.

As for style of teaching in undergraduate classes, aside from audio-visual aids such as slides and overheads, I operate from the premise that enthusiasm is infectious, and I try to capture their attention and interest. The latter increases as the course progresses once students begin to believe in doing history and once they become accustomed to (never comfortable with, I hope) the way I teach. Anecdotes, humour, case studies, asides, role-playing, and sarcasm go a long way in aiding the digestion of otherwise seemingly dry material to students who are used to being bombarded with all manner of colorful information in the media to which they attend. When we discuss the revolution in transport and sport initiated by the bicycle, I set aside time to have them try to ride a penny-farthing replica that I own. (Each student who rides signs a waiver first!) It does reinforce their appreciation for the contrivance and its usage a century ago. The significance is the social impact of the bicycle, and while there are other methods to cover the topic, the experience on the high wheeler works well for me.

Finally, examinations are the major grading component at both levels of my Canadian sport history courses. I have tried short-answer types—multiple choice, identification/significance, fill-in-the-blanks, matching, and true-false; but with little satisfaction that it suits my style of teaching since there is little opportunity for expression or interpretation. Therefore, essay questions comprise all examinations (see Appendix III). Grading in larger courses, once again, is a problem, but I cannot help in clinging to the belief that teaching subsumes extensive grading. Since tests and exams are really performance-pressure not learning-demonstration experiences, grading is a very important aspect of teaching and in the final analysis, the grade carries its own meaning on transcripts and grade reports.

Teaching is an art and it is a skill that is person-specific and not easily acquired. It's also an attitude more than it is a physical experience. Still, in an information age, "high tech and high touch," as Naisbitt interprets these terms in *Megatrends* (1982), can be combined. The potential for computer use in doing Canadian sport history is exciting and limited only by the imagination. Readings, documents, learning games, review questions, essay topic suggestions, case studies, and many other functions can be applied to this important teaching tool so long as the tool does not become the teacher. Self-centered learning that proceeds at each student's pace and abilities and interests seem to be wedded to a computer future. The process of teaching has few boundaries and ought to be given at least equal consideration, for students' sakes, with course content and with academe's emphasis on research.

APPENDIX I: SYLLABUS (UNDERGRADUATE)

The University of Western Ontario
Faculty of Physical Education
Canadian Sport History
P.E. 263F
1987–88
Dr. Don Morrow
Room 115B, Thames Hall
679-2111 Ext. 8385
Office Hours: M W 1:30–3:30 PM or by appointment

CALENDAR COURSE DESCRIPTION

A historical analysis of the development of sport in Canada. Topics include methodology, recreation in French Canada, native sport, industrialization and the growth of organized sport, issues in sport, mass participation, and government involvement.

PURPOSES AND OBJECTIVES

> Ignorance is the first requisite of the historian—ignorance which simplifies and clarifies, which selects and omits, with a placid perfection unattainable by the highest art.
>
> —Lytton Strachey, *Eminent Victorians*, 8.

> My country has no history, only a past.
>
> —Canadian poet Alden Nowlan.

> What are the qualities that make a historian? Obviously these three—a capacity for absorbing facts, a capacity for stating them, and a point of view. Without the latter, history is sawdust.
>
> —Lytton Strachey, "Hume" in *The Shorter Strachey*.

Physical Education 263F is designed as a history course that focuses upon one aspect of Canadian social history—sport. Students will be provided with:

1. A general introduction to the historical analysis of sport.

2. An appreciation of Canada's cultural, sporting heritage.
3. An understanding of the application of historical inquiry to the evolution of Canadian sport.
4. An analysis of persistent, historical, sporting issues as they were manifested in Canada.
5. An opportunity to develop writing skills through an essay assignment that stresses independent research.

COURSE FORMAT

Lecture/discussion.

COURSE TEXT

Metcalfe, Alan. 1987. *Canada Learns to Play: The Emergence of Organized Sport, 1807–1914*. Toronto: McClelland & Stewart.

For background, supplementary information, the following texts have been placed on reserve in Weldon Library:

Howell, M., and N. Howell. 1969. *Sport and Games in Canadian Life: 1700 to the Present.* Toronto: Macmillan.

Roxborough, H. 1966. *One Hundred-Not Out: The Story of Nineteenth Century Canadian Sport.* Toronto: The Ryerson Press.

Wise, S. F., and D. Fisher. 1974. *Canada's Sporting Heroes: Their Lives and Times.* Don Mills: General Publishing Co.

Cosentino, F., and G. Leyshon. 1975. *Olympic Gold.* Toronto: Holt, Rinehart & Winston.

REQUIRED READINGS

Required readings are listed and highlighted in the Topical Outline section of the course outline. Readings are intended to *complement* lecture material and to provide a knowledge-base for class discussions. Readings are contained in the reserve file for this course at the main circulation desk, D. B. Weldon Library. Students are advised to keep one week ahead of the class schedule in doing the readings since there is a considerable number of articles and a considerable number of pages of reading to be done.

EVALUATION, EXAMINATIONS AND ASSIGNMENTS

First Examination—30 percent, *Friday*, 23 October, 3:30–5:30 PM, Natural Sciences Room 1

Final Examination—30 percent, during Christmas Examination Period, 2 hours

Essay Assignment—40 percent, *due date*, Friday, 13 November 1987.

The essay assignment description is attached to the course outline. READ IT CAREFULLY *before* beginning the paper. We will be having a representative in to speak to the class from both the Weldon Library Reference section and from the Department of Effective Writing to assist you in the preparation for and planning of the research and writing processes. Also, please note the "Useful Sources" listings appended to the course outline. Each essay is graded by the course instructor. Both exams are short-answer/essay format.

COURSE FORMAT

The class meets three times per week, for fifty minutes each time. The teaching style used will be lecture/discussion format, respecting the limitations of 225 students in one room. Slides will be used frequently since I believe that history is something you *do*, not something you absorb by osmosis. (In short, a picture is worth a thousand words.)

TOPIC OUTLINE

Week 1. *Introduction and Basic Concepts*

—concepts and frameworks
—facts, dates and questions in history
—lessons and constants in history/sport history
—DOING history and the fundamental concept of change
—history/biography
—Canadian history/Canadian sport history

Required Readings

Tuchman, Barbara W. "History by the Ounce" in *Practicing History*. New York: Alfred A. Knopf, 1981 (Reserve).

Week 2. *Foundations for Canadian Sport to 1860*

—indigenous games and recreations
—physical activity in French Canada
—British heritage: *Tom Brown's School-days* and the transplanted games ethic
—societal influence and first modern sports

Required Readings

Lindsay, P. L. "The Impact of the Military Garrisons on the Development of Sport in British North America," *Canadian Journal of History of Sport* 1, no. 1 (May 1970): 33–43 (*Reserve*).
Rules and Regulations of the Montreal Curling Club, 1807; the Montreal Games, 1844; The Lord's Day Act, 1845 (all three in *Reserve*, Newspaper Clippings File)
Text, Chap. 1, 15–31

Weeks 3 and 4. *Industrialization and the Growth of Organized Sport, 1850–1900*

—changes in sport interrelated with changes in transportation, communications, equipment and facilities
—sport standardization
—rise of commercialism
—the amateur ideology
—the bicycle and female "emancipation"

Required Readings

Text, Chap. 3, 47–98.
Humber, W. "Cheering for the Home Team: Baseball and Town Life in 19th Century Ontario, 1854–1869." *Proceedings of the 5th Canadian Symposium on the History of Sport and Physical Education*, Toronto, 1982, 189–198 (*Reserve*).
1873 Ottawa Snow Show Race ad (*Reserve*).
1882 Lucknow Caledonian Games article of agreement (*Reserve*).

Week 5 *Urbanization, Social Class, and Ethnicity*

—concepts of class and stratification
—case studies of Toronto and Montreal
—ethnohistory and the Scots in sport

Required Readings

Text, Chap. 2, 32–46.

Morrow, D. "The Powerhouse of Canadian Sport: The Montreal Amateur Athletic Association, Inception to 1909," *Journal of Sport History* 8, no. 3 (Winter 1981): 20–39 (*Reserve*).

"Montreal," *Canada's Sporting Heroes*, 13–26 (*Reserve*).

Week 6. *Impact Champions: Selected Sports in the Nineteenth Century*

—champions and heroes/heroines in sport history
—nationalism and sport
—the institutionalization of sport

Required Readings

Cosentino, F. "Ned Hanalan—Canada's Premier Oarsman: A Case Study in 19th Century Professionalism" in *Canadian Journal of History of Sport* 5, No. 2 (December 1974): 5–17 (*Reserve*).

Lindsay, P. L. "George Beers and the National Game Concept: A Behavioral Approach," *Proceedings of the Second Canadian Symposium on the History of Sport and Physical Education*, Windsor, 1972, 27–44 (*Reserve*).

1878 Hanlan vs. Courtney ad; 1880 Victoria Skating Rink List of Figures (*Reserve*).

Text, Chap. 6, 181–218.

First Exam—October 23, 1987 4–6 PM

Week 7. *The Amateur Ideology*

—the dominance of exclusivity
—definitions, non-definitions and problems
—the ethnic twist in Canadian amateur policies
—the professional as prostitute

Required Readings

Text, Chap. 4, 99–132.

Morrow, D. "A Case Study in Amateur conflict: The Athletic War in Canada 1906–1909," *The British Journal of Sports History* (September 1986): 173–190 (*Reserve*).

Week 8. *The Growth of Team and Spectator Sport to 1910*

—commercialism and entrepreneurship
—control and power shifts
—the rise of mass sport, mass spectatorship

Required Readings

Text, Chap. 5, 133–80.

Kidd, Bruce. "In Defense of Tom Longboat," *Canadian Journal of History of Sport* 14, No. 1 (May 1983): 34–63 (*Reserve*).

1897 Ontario Hockey Association Rules; 1910 National Hockey Association contract (*Reserve*).

Weeks 9 and 10. *Sport Promotion, People and Problems Between the Wars*

—the geographical dilemma
—media promotion
—sport journalism
—militarism vs. sport in physical education

Required Readings

Lappage, R. S. "Sport as an Expression of Western and Maritime Discontent Between the Wars," *Canadian Journal of History of Sport* 8, no. 1 (May 1977): 50–71 (*Reserve*).

Lenskyj, H. "Femininity First: Sport and Physical Education for Ontario Girls, 1890–1930," *Canadian Journal of History of Sport* 8, no. 2 (December 1982), (*Reserve*).

Morrow, D. "Lionel Pretoria Conacher," in *Journal of Sport History* 6, no. 1 (Spring 1979): 5–37, (*Reserve*).

Week 11. *New Images: Women's Sport in 20th Century Canada*

—the 'female' image in sport
—the Edmonton Commerical High School Graduates
—Cook, Rosenfeld and promotion of the image
—sweetheart sport: the feats and legacies of Marilyn Bell and Barbara Ann Scott

Required Readings

Nicol, R. "The Edmonton Grads" (unpublished paper) (*Reserve*).

Morrow, D. "Sweetheart Sport: Barbara Ann Scott and the Post World War Two Image of the Female Athlete in Canada" (unpublished paper) (*Reserve*).

Hall, M. A. "Women's Sport in Canada Prior to 1914" in *Proceedings of the First Canadian Symposium in the History of Sport*, Edmonton, 1970, 69–90 (*Reserve*).

Week 12. *The Olympic Movement in Canada Prior to 1940*

—Olympism and international sport
—the Matchless Six
—the Nazi Olympics

Required Readings

Kidd, B. "Canadian Opposition to the 1936 Olympics in Germany," in *Canadian Journal of History of Sport* 9, no. 2, (December 1978), 20–40 (*Reserve*).

Cosentino, F. and G. Leyshon. *Olympic Gold* (Toronto: Holt, Rinehart and Winston, 1975), 80–94. (*Reserve*).

Week 13. *Government Involvement in Sport and the Fitness Movement*

—war and fitness: the National Physical Fitness Act
—government control: the 1968 Task Force

—university sport: sport in higher education
—PARTICIPaction

Required Readings

Schrodt, B. "Changes in the Governance of Amateur Sport in Canada," *Canadian Journal of History of Sport* 14, no. 1 (May 1983): 1–20 (*Reserve*).
Outline history of PARTICIPaction, (unpublished paper) (*Reserve*).

ESSAY ASSIGNMENT

Physical Education 263F is one of two DESIGNATED ESSAY courses in the second year of the Physical Education program. The essay assignment tests the student's ability of write clearly and correctly as well as to carry out research in an academic area of inquiry. The 1987–88 *Western Calendar*, page 17, states:

> Students must demonstrate the ability to write clearly and correctly. Work presented in English in any subject, at any level, which shows a lack of proficiency in English and is therefore unacceptable for academic credit, will either be failed or, at the discretion of the instructor, returned to the student for revision to a literate level. To foster competence in the use of the English language within their own discipline, all instructors will take proficiency in English into account in the assignment of grades.

Thus, the essay assignment is regarded as a significant component of this course. The following material is presented to provide guidelines for the satisfactory completion of the essay assignment.

The *purpose* of DOING a history essay is to present coherently an *argument*, *thesis*, *question*, or *point of view* that is based upon research. An essay should *not* simply restate the theories or findings of other historians. Adding facts to a massive pile of other facts is somewhat akin to adding another brick to a huge mound of bricks; it simply brings chaos to the brickyard, rather than a significant structure to the bricks. In doing the essay, you are doing history. In studying history, one examines the *behavior* of the people in the past, not merely past events.

Identifying a Topic

An endless list of topics could be prepared, but it is my belief that the choice of a topic should be energized and directed by student interest in some general topic about sport history. To use an example: a student might be interested in figure skating as a sport. From parents, that student has heard about Barbara Ann Scott, Canada's world and Olympic figure skating champion of the late 1940s. The student decides that a biographical study of Scott would be an interesting topic. In checking out library resources, the student finds that Scott wrote at least three books and that three or four books have been written about her. Completely deflated, the student might decide that EVERYTHING has been done, Scott's biography is exhausted. In fact, the student has just completed stage 1 of identifying a topic, that is finding out something about a general topic.

Stage 2 involves narrowing the general topic down to *essay* size. No one in P.E. 263F is going to do a definitive, life-long biography of any sports figure in three months' time. To carry on the example of Scott, the student needs to decide on some aspect of Scott's behaviour to provide a scope and framework for writing an essay. In short, the student needs a *research question*: what is worth knowing about Barbara Ann Scott, to the student. The identification of a legitimate, bite-size question is the most critical component of writing an essay in history or any discipline. These questions do *not* come from dreams, nor are they immaculately perceived. Often a great deal of reading or scanning *secondary* and *primary* sources must be done before an appropriate question can be framed. In pursuing the case of Barbara Ann Scott, the student finds a number of periodicals with articles written about Scott, then and now. Further, the student finds that the media coverage of Scott between 1946 and 1951 was extremely extensive; the sports pages of every Canadian newspaper (almost) contain lengthy articles on her. Questions, conscious and subconscious arise in the student's mind:

How did she train?
What figures did they use?
How was she funded?
Who promoted her?
How did she get to be the world's best?
What was judging like in her era?
How would her skating differ from today's?
Why did she receive so much press coverage?
Why does the newspaper coverage focus so much on her femininity rather than her athleticism?

At this juncture, the student must choose some direction for the research and frame a question for the essay. As an example:

> What was the image portrayed to the public by the media about the female athlete in the 1940s, using Barbara Ann Scott as a case study?

There are many other questions about technique in skating, training for skating, etc. that are just as viable as the example question above. The important element is that the student has identified a research question.

It is at this point that each student should make an appointment to discuss the essay with me. *Please*, do not come to me with, "What do you think of an essay on the history of ice hockey in Canada, I just can't think of anything else to write about!?" Once the research topic and question are approved, the processes of gathering data and writing the paper can be engaged in earnest.

Gathering Data for the Essay—The Principle of Selection

As you carry out intensive investigation of sources, keep your research question in mind and be certain the material you collect is specific to your topic and question. That is, gather information only directly pertinent to your thesis or question (the principle of selection). *Examine* the sources; *sift* the appropriate information; *collect* it by *classifying* it into subgroups or subtopics. This process is the most time-consuming, but if it is done in organized fashion, the actual writing of the paper is facilitated greatly. Be critical of all sources of information; just because something is in print does not mean it is completely accurate or without bias. You have to judge your sources through logic, comparison, verification, and weighing evidence; that is the essence of *doing* as opposed to *absorbing* history. Thinking logically is as important in history as it is in any other subject. Try to carry in mind your own contemporary biases; for example, in researching the image of Barbara Ann Scott, your immediate response might be that the image was grounded in extreme chauvinism *by today's standards*. Was it chauvinistic in the 1940s?

Identifying library resources is critical. Once the topic is identified, the student needs to use the *finding aids* to best advantage. For Canadian sport history, the main index system is a good general source. The *Periodical Index*, the *Union List of Serials* and the reference guides save a great deal of time. The University of Oregon microfilm collection in the Spencer Room contains many theses and dissertations on Canadian sport history. Bibliographies in these sources and in books provide further possibilities for information retrieval. Most Canadian newspapers are contained on microfilm in the Spencer Room. The reference librarians are there for your convenience; when in doubt, ask for help. A reference librarian will be coming into class on 17 October.

Composing the Paper

Before actually writing a rough draft of the paper, make a one-page or two-page outline as a BLUEPRINT for the essay. This should *sketch* the main areas of your paper, from title page to bibliography. Most important, the blueprint should list the main points of the paper and/or the major headings. Once you're satisfied with the blueprint (coherency of information and logic of your argument, for example), frame the essay by doing the *bibliography* and the *title page*. Type or print your major question or point of view or argument, on one sheet of paper, in block letters. Post it above your desk and ECHO THE QUESTION throughout the paper to remind both yourself and the reader that the information or argument being written is, in fact, pertinent to your research question. With dictionary at close hand and with style manual (APA, or Turabian) available, prepare to write the paper.

The Finished Product

Your paper in its final form should contain a *title page* that displays your name and I.D. number and the title. The title is NOT given as a question, it is stated positively, for example:

The Female Image of Sport in the 1940s:
A Case Study of Barbara Ann Scott

Be creative if you wish, but use the title as a *significant indicator* of the scope of the paper.

The *introduction* to the paper is probably the most important section of the paper. The entire paper is based on the question or point of view given in the introductory section. State the point of view and provide a *cognitive map* for the reader about to examine your essay. Once the argument is stated, briefly describe how you *did* the history, your assumptions, perceived limitations of your research, boundary dates and any introductory material pertinent to the topic. (For example, *briefly*, what did Barbara Ann Scott do?)

The *main body* of the essay is the longest section of the paper. In this section, you present evidence to support your point of view related to the question or the main point of your paper. Subheadings can be used if you wish. Build your argument brick by brick; proceed from strongest evidence to minor points, for example. Follow your blueprint.

The conclusion is the final section of the paper. In it, you should summarize your main argument or point of view. The conclusion(s) should provide *reasonable inferences* based upon the findings. The conclusion and the topical paragraph delineating your argument should coincide directly.

In summary your essay should be organized in the following fashion:

1. title page
2. topical paragraph (main argument) and introduction
3. main body of the paper
4. conclusions
5. bibliography—include all sources *consulted*

Referencing material in the main body of the paper *must* be included consistently and *must* be based on a style manual (APA or Turabian, for example). Avoid *plagiarism*; acknowledge an author's idea even when it is paraphrased. *LENGTH OF PAPER*: excluding the title page and bibliography, the paper should be a MAXIMUM of *fifteen Pages*, *typed* in *double spacing*.

The paper is worth forty marks toward the final course grade. The course instructor will grade every paper in the course. *Proofread* your paper; faulty spelling and grammar are a waste of marks. Use a *dictionary* and a *style manual*. Read your paper out loud to your roommate, friend, or confidant. Writing has been described as the *art of compression*; do your best to compress. Grading is done by section according to the five areas:

1. title page—5 percent
2. introduction—15 percent
3. main body—55 percent
4. conclusions—10 percent
5. bibliography—15 percent

Finally, the best suggestion I can give for successful performance on the essay assignment is *PROOFREAD*:

1. *Proofread* your paper with the blueprint in hand.
2. *Proofread* the final copy *TWICE*.
3. Ask a friend to *proofread* the paper.
4. Check all words about which you have any doubt in the dictionary.
5. Don't put yourself in the situation of typing the paper yourself into the wee hours of the morning the night of the due date.

DUE DATE: Friday, 13 November 1986, 4:00 PM, Room 103 T.H. Assignments handed in after that date will be graded out of 20.

TOPIC APPROVAL: This is *not* mandatory, but is *very* highly recommended. I will meet with each student individually to discuss the essay, by appointment. The invitation is open to you.

GOOD WRITING!

NOTE: As examples of *outstanding* papers, two papers from previous courses have been placed on reserve in the 263F readings:

Calpin, C. "The Training Methods of an Elite Marathoner in the 1920s: A Case Study of Johnny C. Miles." (*Reserve*).

Browne, R. "The Concept of the 6-day Cycling Show-Circus in the 1930s, the Star Showman, 'Torchy' Peden." (*Reserve*).

Both papers have been published in the *Canadian Journal of History of Sport* (December 1986).

APPENDIX II: SYLLABUS (GRADUATE)

The University of Western Ontario
Faculty of Physical Education
Canadian Sport History
P.E. 561
1986–87
Dr. Don Morrow
Room 301A Som. House
679-2111 Ext. 5484

INTRODUCTION

This course uses the theoretical constructs and principles of the main discipline of history to focus upon and analyze the evolution of Canadian sport. Sport is construed by the instructor to be no different and no more or less special than art or music in that sport is just one form of human behavior in Canadian society. The interaction of the phenomenon of sport with Canadian society over the past 150 years is what makes the historical study of sport in this country unique. Thus, many of the general trends of sport history—amateurism, social class, urbanization—pertinent to the study of sport history in any western country will be examined with specific reference to Canada.

Rather than a chronological format, the course will be taught from a topical perspective using assigned readings as the basis for class discussions. Each class will be based upon these assigned readings and it is my expectation that each student will complete all assigned readings for each weekly topic prior to the class. My teaching style is one of question-framing and interpretation of material; I will not be lecturing in a formal sense or regurgitating written material. Similarly, I view my role as the instructor for the course, and I will not require seminar presentations from students in a formal sense, although every student will be asked to express points of view, arguments, criticisms, and interpretations of material.

If you have not had an undergraduate course in Canadian sport history, I strongly recommend that you read:

H. H. Roxborough, *One Hundred-Not Out; The Story of Nineteenth Century Canadian Sport*, 1966. (On reserve in Weldon Library, Reserve Reading List for P.E. 263F).

D. Morrow, "The Historical Development of Sport in Canada." Mimeographed paper in 561 Readings folder in Graduate Office.

Topics and readings can be altered with class interest and initiative. Similar to most history courses, the readings are not particularly difficult but they are time-consuming and demand some discipline on your part to read them critically. Sources for each reading are indicated in brackets.

GRADING

1. BOOK OR THESIS REVIEW—15 percent. In consultation with the instructor, each student will select and review one book OR thesis (M.A. or Ph.D.) pertaining to sport history in Canada. After thorough reading and analysis, the work will be analyzed with respect to content, style, methodology, significance, and contributions to sport history.
   DUE: 30 October 1986

2. RESEARCH PAPER—35 percent. The paper will concern itself with a specific topic approved by the instructor. A *suggested* list of broad topical areas and guidelines for the preparation of the paper will be distributed in class.
   DUE: 27 November 1986

OR

RESEARCH GRANT PROPOSAL—35 percent. This assignment entails the full preparation of a research grant proposal using the format of the Social Sciences and Humanities Research Council of Canada. Copies of the application form and guidebook will be distributed in class and discussed fully with anyone interested in this assignment. Papers are very common assignments; this research grant proposal assignment is viewed as an excellent applied opportunity for students to engage in the planning process for doing research instead of diving head first into information and literature on a topic. In essence, doing a grant proposal is akin to preparing a full blueprint for a building—the blueprint has to be detailed, complete, thorough, and a model for the construction of the building. This assignment is an excellent proving ground for your own research development. As the instructor, I act as the granting agency except that a mark is assigned to the proposal.

3. FINAL EXAM—50 percent. The exam is essay-format, written in class during the week of 8–12 December. It is three hours in length and is based upon readings assigned and class discussions. The exact date and time will be determined by student consensus in class.

CLASS SCHEDULE, COURSE ORGANIZATION AND READINGS

11 September—*Introduction and Organization*

—introduction to and overview of the course

—review and criticism of an *Audio-Visual History of Canadian Sports*

18 September—*Roots: The British Heritage*

—Hughes, Thomas. "Rugby and Football," *Tom Brown's School-days* (chapter 5, Part I) (561 Folder)

—McIntosh, Peter. "Athleticism I" and "Athleticism II" *Sport in Society*, 57–79 (561 Folder)

—Mangan, J. A. "Discipline in the Dominion: The Canuck and the Cult of Manliness," *The Games Ethic and Imperialism*, 142–67 (561 Folder)

Sport in Canada, it is suggested, is a derivative of the "revival" of modern sport in Britain. This section examines the values of sport and the cultural implications of the British sport system.

25 September—*Historiography*

—Eyler, Marvin H. "Some Reflections on Objectivity and Selectivity in Historical Inquiry" in *JSH* 1, no. 1 (May 1974): 63–76 (561 Folder and Library Periodicals)

—Tuchman, Barbara. "History by the Ounce," *Practising History* (1981), 35–50 (561 Folder).

—Fisher, David H. "Fallacies of Causation," *Historians' Fallacies: Toward a Logic of Historical Thought*, 164–86 (561 Folder)

—Berkhofer, R. F. "Conceptions of Time: Their Variety and Uses" and "Time and the Discipline of History," *A Behavioral Approach to Historical Analysis*, 211 to 269 (561 Folder)

History is: the sum total of everything that happened in the past?

OR

what historians say happened in the past?

> "What are the qualities that make a historian? Obviously these three—a capacity for absorbing facts, a capacity for stating them, and a point of view. Without the latter, history is sawdust."
>
> —Lytton Strachey, *The Shorter Strachey*

2 October—*Historiography and Sport History*

> "Ignorance is the first requisite of the historian . . ."
>
> Strachey, *Eminent Victorians*

—Berryman, J. W. "Sport History as Social History" in *Quest* 20 (Spring 1973): 65–72 (561 Folder)
—Adelman, M. "The Role of the Sports Historian" in *Quest* (May 1969): 61–65 (561 Folder)
—Park, Roberta J. "The Use of Hypotheses in Sport History," *Sport History Research Methodology* (1980): 25–36 (561 Folder)
—Morrow, D. "Canadian Sport History: A Critical Essay," *JSH* 10, no. 1, 67–79 (Weldon Library, Periodicals)

9 October—*Premodern or Preorganized Canadian Sport*

> My country has no history, only a past.
>
> —Alden Nowlan, Canadian poet

—Metcalfe, Alan. "Some Background Influences on 19th Century Canadian Sport and P.E." *CJHS* V, no. 1, (May 1974): 62–73 (Library Periodicals and 561 Folder)
—Lindsay, P. L. "Introduction" in "A History of Sport in Canada, 1807–1867" Ph.D. thesis (1969): 1–21 (561 Folder)
—Lindsay, P. L. "The Impact of the Military Garrisons on the Development of Sport in British North America" *CJHS* 1, no. 1 (May 1970): 33–44 (561 Folder)

16 October—*Organization and Technological Influence*
—Humber, W. "Cheering For the Home Team: Baseball and Town Life in 19th Century Ontario, 1854–1869," *5th Canadian Symposium Proceedings*, 1982, 189–198 (561 Folder)
—Cosentino, F. "Ned Hanlan—Canada's Premier Oarsman: A Case Study in 19th Century Professionalism," *CJHS*, 5, no. 2 (December 1974): 5–17 (Library Periodicals)
—Williams, T. "Cheap Rates, Special Trains and Canadian Sport in the 1850's" in *CJHS* 12, no. 2 (December 1981), 84–93 (Library Periodicals)

> If it moves, why not race it?
>
> —Morrow

23 October—*Organization, Urbanization, and Social Class*

Modern, industrial sport is very much a product of these three variables. How do they interact to establish patterns of sport in Canada?

—Metcalfe, Alan. "Sport and Social Stratification in Toronto, Canada, 1860–1920" Unpublished paper, 1972 (561 Folder)

—Mott, Morris. "Canadian Sports History: Some Comments to Urban Historians," *Urban History Review/Revue d'histoire urbaine* 12, no. 2 (October 1983), 25–29 (561 Folder and Library Periodicals)

—Mott, Morris. "One Solution to the Urban Crisis: Manly Sports and Winnipeggers, 1900–1914," *Urban History Review/Revue d'histoire urbaine* 12, no. 2 (October 1983): 57–70 (561 Folder and Library Periodicals)

—Morrow, D. "The Powerhouse of Canadian Sport: The Montreal Amateur Athletic Association" in *JSH*, 8, no. 3 (Winter 1981): 20–39 (Library Periodicals)

—Wise, S. F. and D. Fisher. "Montreal," *Canada's Sporting Heroes: Their Lives and Times*, 13–26 (561 Folder and P.E. 263F Reserve List)

30 October—*Amateurism/Professionalism*

The most pervasive thread in modern sport history is the conceptualization of the amateur ideology. It was a case of process, ideological change, and/or resistance to change and exclusion. (Who could engage in sport with whom and under what conditions?)

—Morrow, D. "A Case Study in Amateur Conflict. The Athletic War in Canada, 1906–1908," *The British Journal of Sports History* (September 1986) (561 Folder)

—Jones, Kevin. "Developments in Amateurism and Professionalism in Early 20th Century Canadian Sport," *JSH* 2, no. 1 (Spring 1975): 29–40. (Library Periodicals)

—Cosentino, F. "The Years of Transition, 1921–1932," in "A History of the Concept of Professionalism in Canadian Sport," Ph.D. thesis, 266–308 (561 Folder)

6 November—*Issues and Anomalies*

Sabbatarianism, the growth of team and spectator sport, entrepreneurship, and unusual circumstances and/or special people exerted considerable influence and change on Canadian sport.

—Morrow, D. "The Canadian Image Abroad: The Great Lacrosse Tours of 1876 and 1883," *5th Canadian Symposium Proceedings* (1982), 11–22 (561 Folder)

—Homel, G. H. "Sliders and Backsliders: Toronto's Sunday Tobogganing Controversey of 1912," *Urban History Review/Revue d'histoire urbaine* 10, no. 2 (October 1981): 25–34 (561 Folder and Library Periodicals)

—Betke, C. "Sports Promotion in the Western Canadian City: The Example of Early Edmonton," *Urban History Review/Revue d'histoire urbaine* 12, no. 2 (October 1983): 47–56 (561 Folder and Library Periodicals)

—MacDonald, C. "The Edmonton Grads: Canada's Most Successful Team—A History and Analysis of Their Success" M.H.K. thesis (1976), 1–5 and 159–181 (561 Folder)

13 November—*Mass Sport, Mass Physical Education*

—Lenskyj, H. "Moral Physiology in P.E. for Girls in Ontario 1890–1930," in *5th Canadian Symposium Proceedings* (1982), 139–49 (561 Folder)

—Kidd, B. "In Defence of Tom Longboat," *CJHS* 14, no. 1 (May 1983), 34–63 (Library Periodicals)

—Metcalfe, A. "The Urban Response to the Demand for Sporting Facilities: A Study of Ten Ontario Towns/Cities, 1919–1939," *Urban History Review/Revue d'histoire urbaine* 12, no. 2 (October 1983): 31–45 (561 Folder)

—Lappage, R.S. "Sport as an Expression of Maritime and Western Discontent in Canada Between the Wars," *CJHS* 8, no. 1 (May 1977): 50–71 (Library Periodicals)

—Morrow, D. "Lionel Pretoria Conacher" in *JSH*, 6, no. 1 (Spring 1979), 5–37 (Library Periodicals)

This section focuses upon the sprawl of sport in the transition from its nineteenth-century restrictions to an emphasis upon team sport and broader participatory and spectatorial groups.

20 November—*Sportswriting and Sport Journalism*

For the most part, newspapers are a vital primary source for historians. Very little work has been done in analyzing the interaction of sportswriting and sport.

—Waters, Janice. "A Content Analysis of the Sport Section in Selected Canadian Newspapers 1927 to 1935," M.A. thesis (1981), 15–49 (Library)

—Morrow, D. "Sweetheart Sport: Barbara Ann Scott and the Post World War Two Image of the Female Athlete in Canada," *CJHS* (forthcoming, May 1987) (561 Folder)

—Morrow, D. "Lou Marsh: The Pick and Shovel of Canadian Sporting Journalism," *CJHS* 14, no. 1 (May 1983), 21–33 (Library Periodicals)

Selected newspaper columnists/columns selected and assigned by the instructor.

27 November—*The Sport Hero*

> *Andrea*: Unhappy the land that has no heroes. *Galileo*: No, unhappy the land that needs heroes.
>
> —Bertolt Brecht, *Life of Galileo.*

—Key, J.W. "Socio-Cultural Characteristics and the Image of the Urban Anglo-Canadian Athletic Hero, 1920–1939," M.H.K. thesis (1982): 1–20, 114–31 (561 Folder)

—Norwood, D. R. "The Sport Hero Concept and Louis Cyr," M.H.K. thesis (1983): 1–26, 52–62 (561 Folder)

—Whitehead, Eric. *Cyclone Taylor: A Hockey Legend*, 1977 (copies available from instructor)

—Morrow, D. "Biographical Studies," *Sport History Research Methodology* (1980): 55–61 (561 Folder)

—Brown, A. "Edward Hanlan, The World Sculling Champion Visits Australia," *CJHS* 11, no. 2 (December 1980): 1–44 (Library Periodicals)

The study of individual sport figures is lionized by the term "hero." Biographical studies are often labeled in some category other than history. Is biography history? Have significant studies on sports figures been done in sport history?

4 December—*Odds and Ends*

The last class will be used to cover such topics as computer use in doing sport history, writing techniques, teaching sport history, and other topics you might wish to discuss.

BOOK REVIEW GUIDELINES

A book review should be thorough, concise, and critical. In most cases, a reviewer has to research certain aspects or topical areas concerning the content of a book. All too often, book reviews can be condensed into one line: "This book is truly a valuable addition to the field and should be in everyone's library." Among other topical areas of your own choosing, let me suggest that you consider:

1. Readership: at whom is the book aimed and does it fulfill its target objective?
2. Theme(s): is the book written for a specific purpose and does it show some thematic pattern(s)?
3. Sources: what *evidence* is used for drawing conclusions (primary, secondary, both)? What is the quality and quantity of the sources?
4. Style: consider chapter divisions, manner of presentation, use of language, for example, proper grammar, over/underuse of adverbs and adjectives; narrative and topical flow.
5. Content: what, really, is in the book?
6. Content: how does the book enhance either some genre of sport history and how does it contribute to the field of research?

Examples of good and weak book reviews can be found in the *Journal of Sport History*, the *Canadian Journal of History of Sport*, and the *Canadian Historical Review*.

For thesis review, the same topical areas of analysis might prove worthwhile, except for *readership* since a thesis is not normally written for trade publication.

The book or thesis selected must be approved by me, and it must relate to Canadian sport history or a topical area of 561 (for example, amateurism).

Maximum length: 5 pages, double spaced, type-written.

Suggested theses: Given your own situation as an M.A. student, I suggest an M.A. thesis rather than a doctoral dissertation. To that end, there are some fifteen to twenty M.A. theses in Canadian sport history completed at Western. University of Alberta, Windsor, and Dalhousie are the other three major universities with master's theses. In the Spencer Room at Weldon Library, there is an excellent collection of M.A. and Ph.D. theses in all areas of P.E. at the "University of Oregon Microcard Collection" for which there is an index.

Suggested books:

Redmond, G., *The Sporting Scots of the Nineteenth Century.*
Gzowski, P., *The Game of Our Lives.*
Dryden, K., *The Game.*
Batten, J., *The Leafs in Autumn.*
Carver, J. A., *The Vancouver Rowing Club.*
Robinson, D., *Howie Morenz.*
Isaacs, N. D., *Checking Back: A History of the N.H.L.*
Coleman, S., *A Hoofprint on My Heart.*
Flood, B., *Saint John: A Sporting Tradition.*
Cosentino, F., *Canadian Football: The Grey Cup Years.*
Whitehead, E., *The Patricks: Hockey's Royal Family.*
Gross, K., *Donald Jackson: King of Blades.*
Bull, W. P., *From Rattlesnake Hunt to Hockey: The History of Sports in Canada and of the Sportsmen of Peel, 1798 to 1934.*
Stevenson, J. A., *Curling in Ontario, 1846–1946.*
Gruneau, R., *Class, Sports and Social Development.*

Howell, N., and M. L. Howell, *Sports and Games in Canadian Life: 1700 to the Present.*
Humber, W., *Cheering for the Home Team.*
Selke, F., *Behind the Cheering.*
Ludwig, J., *Five Ring Circus.*
Backman B., and P. Backman, *The Bluenose.*
McGill, J., *The Joy of Effort.*

APPENDIX III: SAMPLE GRADUATE COURSE EXAM QUESTIONS IN CANADIAN SPORT HISTORY

Four questions constitute a complete paper. Everyone *must* answer question *ONE* plus *any three* questions from PART B. All questions are equally weighted (25 marks).

1. The method any historian uses to analyze his data can vary from "immaculate perception" on the one extreme to a rigidly controlled, quantitative model that ferrets out variables on the other. Barbara Tuchman, in *Practising History*, goes as far as to state that a rigid method (strict methodology, in general) reduces history from being an art to a science. Discuss, by comparison and contrast, the method(s) employed in at least 2 of the following works:

   Metcalfe, "Sport and Social Stratification in Toronto, Canada, 1860–1920."
   Waters, "A Content Analysis of the Sports Section in Selected Canadian Newspapers, 1927 to 1935."
   Macdonald, "The Edmonton Grads."

   In your answer, discuss the use of the method(s) in relation to the purpose(s) of the study, the findings, the historical value of the study, the strengths and weaknesses of the method itself, and so forth. Please DON'T just reiterate the method.

2. Explain the significance of the following events, persons or factors upon *change(s)* in Canadian sport history:
   a. *Tom Brown's School-days*
   b. technological innovations in the nineteenth century
   c. the M.A.A.A. (surprise!)
   d. Ned Hanlan

3. If we can make the analogy that Canadian sport has evolved dramatically like hundreds of ping pong balls bouncing and rebounding perpetually in a huge glass globe, then the glass boundary would be the forces of amateurism that encapsulated all forms of Canadian sport from about 1880 to the present. Explain the manner in which amateurism became the most significant force in Canadian sport between 1880 and 1930. (Significant does *not* merely imply positive significance.)

4. The concept of the sport hero is a nebulous one in Canadian society—that is, it is difficult to pinpoint. Nevertheless, certain individuals, leaders if you like, have exerted considerable influence through change in Canadian sport. Often the change(s) were made by example in sport or its related

fields. Discuss the various forms of leadership exerted by the following:
   a. Myrtle Cook
   b. Louis Rubenstein
   c. Cyclone Taylor or Louis Cyr
   d. Lou Marsh

5. In Canada, sport evolved in direct relationship to values associated with the British public school tradition while physical education emanated almost purely from militaristic roots. Explain the evolution of physical education in Ontario with respect to the Strathcone Trust and to the "moral physiology" incipient in girls' physical education.

6. The following research question has been posed and approved as a starting point for research and analysis in sport history:

   > How did the middle class value systems come to dominate Canadian sport between 1850 and 1900?

   In *detail*, list or describe the questions and processes that the researcher would face in researching the above question. (For example, what assumptions would have to be made? What definitions would be necessary? What data would be needed?) In short, I would like you to explain the process the researcher would go through, *not* the answer(s) to the question.

7. What is worth knowing in Canadian sport history?

WORKS CITED

Berkhofer, Robert F., Jr. 1969. *A Behavioral Approach to Historical Analysis*. New York: Free Press.

Metcalfe, Alan. 1987. *Canada Learns to Play: The Emergence of Organized Sport, 1807–1914*. Toronto: McClelland and Stewart.

Naisbitt, John. 1982. *Megatrends: Ten New Directions Transforming Our Lives*. New York: Warner Books.

Pirsig, Robert M. 1974. *Zen and the Art of Motorcycle Maintenance: An Inquiry into Values*. New York: William Morrow.

Postman, Neil, and Charles Weingartner. 1969. *Teaching as a Subversive Activity*. New York: Delta Books.

Ware, Caroline. 1940. *The Cultural Approach to History*. New York: Columbia University Press.

3
The Social History of Sport: Reflections on Some Recent British Developments in Research and Teaching

J. A. MANGAN

INTRODUCTION

In 1984 I addressed an audience in Melbourne on the topic of the academic study of sport in society and admitted to mixed emotions of continued exasperation and nascent optimism.

Ringing continually in my ears, I told it, were two quotations from Ernst Jokl:

> The categorical significance of the newly emerging science and philosophy of sport lies in the fact it represents a new effort at bridging the gap between intellectualism and those areas which are shared by all.
>
> Current humanistic theory does not yet admit that the body may be of equal dignity with the heart, the mind and the soul. Contemporary thinking is still permeated by philosophical thinking to thc effect that the body ranks low in the scale of values. In Western Society the body has for centuries been assailed on two fronts: it was anathemized as sinful and it was the target for contempt. Religious ethics, contemporary literature, the utilitarian ideology of mechanization and absolute scientific positivism, all have the disparagement of the body in common.

The source of my ambivalence was "opportunity lost, image demeaned and philistinism rampant." I continued in a pessimistic tone, and asked a number of uncomfortable questions of myself and others. Are the bony fingers of disciplinary inferiority nurtured on the tenets of puritanical Pauline Christianity, the ambitions of crude capitalism, the savage snobberies of nineteenth- and twentieth-century British education, and the harsh utilitarianism of amelioration, still clutching nervous shoulders? Has the unflattering image of the "Hearty," the "Jock," and "the PTI" quite disappeared amid piles of reference books, heaps of essays, and pages of scientific jargon? Is muscle still equated with mindlessness? I concluded that old prejudices unlike old soldiers seldom just fade away, and that there was little room for complacency.

Nevertheless, I wanted to be sanguine and offered my antipodean audience a vision of the future that had been a realized ambition of the past, namely the Graeco-Renaissance ideal of the individual developed in mind, emotions, and body. It was, of course, as I reminded them, a concept at the core of Western liberal education, but in the modern world would only be realized when the academic discipline of "sports sciences" or whatever title is considered apposite, respected for rigor, quality, and insight, was fully incorporated in its various branches in educational institutions at all levels. These sciences were, I argued, indispensable adjuncts of modern life, and should be part of every institutional curriculum. They serve intellectual, aesthetic, and pragmatic ends; they provide mental and physical health, extend life, ensure pleasure, permit understanding; they were at present underresearched, undertaught, and underestimated.

OVERVIEW

In the light of such remarks, what of the social history of sport in Britain as an academic field of inquiry in the late 1980s? I have grounds, I believe, for cautious optimism. Readers of the *Journal of Sport History* will recall that Professor William J. Baker reminded them in 1983 in a review of "The State of British Sports History" that prior to the 1970s, the works of Brailsford and McIntosh "stood as glaring exceptions to the rule that British sport was ignored by serious historians." Consideration of this significant aspect of social existence, he added, lay largely in the hands of amateurs. And Richard Holt has taken up the same refrain. "The histories of sport," he has written recently, "which have been written so far are not the work of historians but of popular journalists or important officials in the world of sport itself. In general, they take the form of commentaries on record-breaking performances interspersed with anecdotes evoking the great days of a particular club or a famous sportsman." In his view, this is scarcely good enough. The social history of sport has to explain how games move in step with society, analyzing "the relationship between changing material and cultural circumstances on the one hand, and the transformation of physical recreation on the other."

Since 1970 things have changed—quite dramatically. A subdiscipline of social historical studies dealing with sport in society has been established. Academic interest in the social history of sport has grown rapidly in Britain, stimulated in part by perceptive observations by distinguished historians such as Hobsbawm and in part by a general appreciation on the part of other social historians (and sociologists) of the significance of sport in society in terms of its hegemonic, ritualistic, and symbolic roles; its efficacy as an agent of control and cohesion; and its association with ethics, education, social class, religion, leisure, politics, and popular and elite culture. While the index of Lord Asa Briggs's *A Social History of England* (1983) may have omitted "sport" and "games"—a quite extraordinary omission; subsequently Lord Briggs has made handsome amends by joining the International Editorial Board of the *British Journal of Sports History* (Now *The International Journal of the History of Sport*)—a more than isolated symbolic gesture since the journal now has among its consultant editors some of the best known British social historians including Harold Perkin, David Rubinstein, and James Walvin. The creation of the *British Journal of Sports History* is in itself a sign of the times. Founded in 1983 with the purpose of "stimulating, promoting and coordinating interest in the history of sport, recreation and leisure with special but not exclusive reference to the British Isles," it aims to advance scholarship in, and provide a forum for, the study of these related aspects of social history. To this end it has encouraged contributions from the whole of the international academic community. It has included contributions from Australia, Canada, Eire, New Zealand, the United States, and West Germany as well as Britain and has expanded its executive editorial team, contents, and international editorial board in keeping with its policy of establishing itself as an international forum for discussion on the interrelated themes of the history of sport, leisure, and recreation throughout the world.

No less a sign of the times was the establishment in March 1983 of the British Society of Sports History. It speedily gathered to itself an enthusiastic group of professional and amateur historians who have met at four annual conferences in Keel, Chester, Glasgow, and Telford respectively. The 1986 conference was at North Staffordshire Polytechnic in July, and the conference theme was "Imperialism and Sport." This theme with various associated subthemes—"Sport and Nationalism"; "Sport and Ethics"; "Sport and Urbanization"; and "Sport, Recreation, and Leisure" also served as the focus for papers for the historical component of the 1986 Commonwealth Games Academic Congress held at Jordanhill College of Education, Glasgow, from 18–23 July. This Congress completed a notable double for Scotland. In the summer of 1985 Jordanhill was the venue for the eleventh HISPA (International Society for the History of Sport and Physical Education) World Congress. It drew some 125 delegates from thirty countries, the largest HISPA Congress in its thirteen year history, and in its way a tribute by the rest of the world to the energy, enthusiasm, effort, and quality of British historians of sport over the last fifteen years.

It is frequently suggested that emerging literature first establishes and then consolidates an academic discipline. The literature of British sport, recreation, and leisure history has made marked and pleasing advances in the last fifteen years. There is evidence of both fulfillment and promise.

Interesting and valuable works that have appeared since 1970 include: Robert W. Malcolmson, *Popular Recreations in English Society 1700–1850* (1973); James Walvin, *The Peoples' Game: The Social History of British Football* (1974); John Lowerson and John Myerscough, *Time to Spare in Victorian England* (1977); James Walvin, *Leisure and Society 1830–1950* (1978); Wray Vamplew, *The Turf: A Social and Economic History of Horse Racing* (1976); Hugh Cunningham, *Leisure in the Industrial Revolution 1780–1800* (1980); Tony Mason, *Association Football and English Society 1863–1915* (1980); J. A. Mangan, *Athleticism in the Victorian and Edwardian Public School* (1981); Robert Archer and Antoine Bouillon, *The South African Game: Sport and Racism* (1983); and J. A. Mangan, *The Games Ethic and Imperialism* (1985). Patriotism is not quite enough. In any discussion of sport in a British historical context, a quite outstanding book by an American should not escape our notice, namely Bruce Haley's *The Healthy Body and Victorian Culture* (1978). To depart further from insularity for a moment, notable British academics who have turned their attention to foreign fields include James Riordan, *Sport in Soviet Society* (1977), and Richard Holt, *Sport and Society in Modern France* (1981).

Journal articles on the history of British sport now proliferate and are to be found in a wide variety of academic journals including the *Journal of Sport History*, *British Journal of Sports History*, *Stadion*, *Canadian Journal of History of Sport and Physical Education*, *Quest*, *Journal of Educational Administration and History*, *History of Education*, *Journal of Social History*, *Labour History*, *Victorian Studies*, *Irish Historical Studies*, *Church Quarterly*, *Workshop History*, *Welsh History Review*, *Historical Studies*, *Albion*, *Scottish Educational Review*, and *Journal of British Studies*. A helpful set of source references can be found in Baker's article in the *Journal of Sport History* (1983, 10, 53–56) mentioned earlier, but inevitably such is the pace of progress that Baker's review is already dated and additional useful references are contained in the various bibliographies compiled by Richard Cox in the *British Journal of Sports History*, in 1984, 1985, and 1986.

So much for fulfillment. As regards promise, at least four forthcoming books are awaited with interest—Lowerson's study of sport, religion, and the middle classes in the Victorian era; Holt's survey of sport in British working class society since 1800; Brailsford's work on sport and the industrial revolution; and the final volume of Mangan's trilogy on ideology, education, and sport dealing with the games ethic and the ancient universities.

It is significant that the increasing quality of publications and the growing numbers of academic contributions to the area has attracted the interest of publishers. Perhaps the most active of them is the London publisher, Frank Cass. Cass publishes the *British Journal of Sports History* and has recently produced two works edited respectively by J. A. Mangan, and J. A. Mangan and Roberta J. Park entitled *Pleasure, Profit and Proselytism: British Culture and Sport at Home and Abroad, 1700–1914* (1986) and *From 'Fair Sex' to Feminism: Sport and the Socialization of Women in the Industrial and Post-Industrial Eras* (1987). Another academic publisher who has taken cognizance of the growth of sports history as an academic subject is Manchester University Press, which has incorporated sports history as a topic into its forthcoming series on the social history of imperialism and has published *Manliness and Morality: Images of the Male in the Old and New Worlds, 1800–1950* (1986), edited by J. A. Mangan and James Walvin. Here sport figures substantially. The book will place sport inter alia within the wider social, cultural, and political contexts of family and class pressures and processes, patterns of formal and informal education, and period military and imperial imperatives. In addition, Manchester University Press has recently commissioned a series on the history of sport entitled "International Studies in the Social History of Sport." It is envisaged that the early contributors will include Dennis Brailsford, Nicholas Fishwick, Arnd Kruger, Eric Halliday, John Lowerson, James Riordan, Neil Tranter, Wray Vamplew, Patricia Vertinsky, and Eric Williams.

The series is clearly an important milestone in the historical studies of sport in society.

British writers and publishers (among others) are exploring a more or less academic virgin territory that promises much. To echo Hobsbawm, far too little is known about "one of the most significant of the new social practices" of the Victorian and Edwardian eras, namely sport in society. Furthermore Hobsbawm remarks with complete veracity that the social history of upper and middle class sports in general remains to be written. And, it can be added with justification, so too does the social history of proletarian sport. And the whole process of geographical and cultural diffusion, assimilation, adaptation, (and rejection) of British sport throughout the Empire and the Commonwealth, across continental Europe, down the landmass of South America, and in even more exotic places above and below the equator, together with an analysis of the political, educational, economic, and recreational consequences; has barely begun to attract the attention it merits. Closer to home, as Baker notes, what of the struggle between native and imported sports for dominance in the Celtic Fringe? And what of the influence of competing Victorian ideologies such as Social Darwinism and Muscular Christianity on patterns of sport in the wider society beyond the educational system? What of sexual stereotyping, concepts of femininity, and the socialization of girls and women through sport? What of regional and local emphases and patterns? What of sport and the military? Much more regarding gaps and omissions could be added, and all within the confines of the Victorian and Edwardian eras—a fact that leaves a great deal of history to be investigated both inside and outside their chronological boundaries.

This brief article has concentrated on the growing subdiscipline of sport history in Britain. In passing it might be noted that in the United States, Canada, and Australia, of course; matters are relatively well advanced. Academics on the continent, notably the West Germans, also make a major contribution to the literature; and throughout the world but particularly in New Zealand, Japan, Brazil, and Nigeria, interest in the subdiscipline is steadily developing. Internationally the literature of the field is now sizeable and increases rapidly. As is well known, there are now two international associations for the study of the history of sport—HISPA (International Society for the History of Sport and Physical Education) and ICOSH (International Society for Sports History). Apart from the British Society of Sports History, there are also a number of regional and national academic societies in various parts of the world including the North American Society of Sport History, and the Australian Society of Sports History. In addition to the *Journal of Sport History*, the *British Journal of Sports History*, *Sporting Traditions*, and the *Canadian Journal of the History of Sport and Physical Education*, there is, of course, a well-established journal of sports history published in Germany under the title of *Stadion*, and new journals have just been created in Denmark, France, Italy, and Japan.

Gradually, the social history of sport is becoming part of the content of courses in history in Europe, the Commonwealth, the United States, and elsewhere. There is reason to believe that it will eventually be a popular and permanent part of social history courses in universities and colleges throughout the world. Developments in Britain mirror developments elsewhere in the world.

BRIEF REFLECTIONS ON METHODOLOGY

Self-evidently, if literature of high academic quality establishes a discipline, interesting and effective pedagogy maintains enthusiasm for it. Experimentation with a variety of methodological and thematic approaches over the last decade has produced a preference on my part for a mix of methods: a combination of active and passive learning techniques with a deliberate *imbalance* in favor of the former. Such an approach keeps faith with the extensive research into the learning of adults and the appropriate techniques to adopt to motivate such learners. There is nothing revolutionary or even original in what follows, but as a personal validation of the arguments of analysts such as Tight, Lewis, Howe, Evans, and others; it may prove of interest.

The four approaches discussed briefly below have been selected for their special value as active learning aids. They all give considerable responsibility to the learner, and they have proved most satisfying because they have produced enthusiastic, careful, and comprehensive reflections on the part of students on the issues under review.

SEQUENTIAL SELF-INSTRUCTIONAL SEMINARS

These take the shape of group learning sessions organized and led by the students in relatively small groups of no more than fifteen per group, chaired by a group-appointed student convener who collates and synopsizes the main conclusions of each meeting. The course director is *never* present. There are usually three sessions of one hour's duration in which a selected item or topic is *progressively* analyzed so that a full and comprehensive analysis is ultimately achieved. The initial theme or topic is chosen from a group of themes or topics selected by the course director, linked directly to his or her lecture program and introduced to the students by the director in a briefing seminar. Progress from the first to the last seminar is assisted by evaluative comments by the director on the conclusions reached at the end of each self-instructional seminar and by suggestions by the director for subsequent considerations by the group. Evaluation and recommendation occur immediately prior to each student self-directed seminar and last for thirty minutes. The points made, of course, are nonprescriptive and may be completely ignored. If useful, they are utilized.

There seems to be several advantages to this technique: the emphasis on student self-reliance appears to promote wide involvement in the group; the mixture of structured and unstructured discussion ensures some direction but permits divergent reflection; as a corollary, the partial absence of the "expert" reduces student inhibition, stimulates a cross-section of views, and so helps ensure a quite subtle and full consideration of the topic. Most important of all, perhaps, is that sophistication of analysis is promoted both by the seminar postmortems and a sequence of seminars in which one builds upon the next—deliberately and systematically.

The self-instructional seminars conclude with a summarizing seminar in which the student convener draws together the main conclusions (by use of handout, board, overhead, or slide) and at which the course director acts as an observer commenting judiciously, if necessary, on the conclusions reached.

ROTATING COMMENTATORS

This approach makes use of appropriate commentators who shed helpful light on matters under consideration. The commentators are chosen by the course director for their *differing* perspectives on the *same* topic and "interrogated" by the students divided into groups of between twelve and twenty. The commentators, in short, rotate around the groups and are generally interviewed for thirty minutes. (Of course, the amount of time will depend on the total size of the course group and the number of commentators: generally the total group is not more than eighty and the commentators not more than four.) The groups decide upon the main questions to be put to the visitors in a self-instructed group session prior to the visit. This rotational technique has been found especially valuable for bringing home to students the interpretive nature of historical analysis. It also provides an excellent opportunity for placing topics in an interdisciplinary context. For example, a visiting group of commentators on "muscular Christianity," comprising a sociologist, a theologian, and a historian offers an intriguing set of diverse opinions on the essential nature of that too-often glibly and superficially analyzed phenomenon.

"EVOCATIVE" LITERATURE AND ART SEMINARS

Introductory course seminars utilizing "evocative" pictorial and literary material as a means of establishing period atmosphere and as a tool for arousing an emotional interest in historical eras have proved a stimulating and valuable learning approach. The propagandizing art of the Third Reich, the mystical Arthurian paintings of the Victorian period, the complacent photographs and cartoons of the Victorian and Edwardian "bloods," the class-biased rural "huntin', shootin', and fishin'" prints of eighteenth-century England, the poetry of Newbolt with its theme of the sacrificial warrior, the jaunty philathletic doggerel of *Punch* give an immediacy to period values that quickly arouses interest and comment. And such material has proved superior in some respects to videos and films in that it can be much more easily scrutinized and discussed *simultaneously*; and, of course, it captures attitudes and activities sometimes inadequately covered by cinema and television.

Images initially selected by the course director can be augmented, extended, contradicted by student reaction to each selection; the choice of appropriate clusters of descriptive adjectives by students can establish a comprehension of underlying ideological values; inquiry into the origins of a particular painting, print, or poem can throw light on period predilections and imperatives. In these ways or others, the student plays an active part in the exploratory process.

LOCAL HISTORICAL STUDIES

Here the concern is less with methodology and more with thematic emphasis. The investigation with students of local historical material has found increasing favor with me over the last few years. I once tended to steer clear of such inquiries considering them especially prone to the sins of parochialism and antiquarianism. Clearly, they need not be so, and certainly concentration on such material, in my experience, greatly interests students. They bring personal associations to the studies, and relate quickly to the topic under scrutiny. Singly or in groups, they are able to gain access, cheaply and extensively, to a wide range of primary and secondary literature and oral information through the utilization of obvious and easily available sources such as local newspapers; church records; local club minutes; university, city, and regional libraries; and county and city record offices. It is important, of course, that the material unearthed is set in a national context and related to wider movements and fashions, that the approach is always analytical and never simply descriptive, and that surveys undertaken have a coherence that comes from a clear purpose and an intelligent set of questions.

In my experience, there can be attractive by-products of local historical inquiries. There are opportunities, on occasion, for students to lecture on their findings to schools, local clubs, and societies. Again, specialist inputs can be a distinct possibility with students who have individual interests and skills in map design, interviewing, archival investigation, and report writing assuming specific responsibilities in a group inquiry and thus producing a high quality report. It is also possible to established a continuous record of neglected local events covering a substantial period of time by means of group concentration on particular historical periods and then dovetailing and integrating the findings. Finally, the opportunity, certainly among undergraduates, to be original and to unearth new information is undoubtedly greater in local studies than in national or international inquiries.

In conclusion, the four approaches briefly outlined above reflect a clear but not exclusive predilection on my part for active learning techniques. They constitute methods and approaches that have produced interest, enthusiasm, comprehension, and not infrequently, excellence on the part of students—clearly essential criteria for both retention and development.

APPENDIX I: A CULTURAL, SOCIAL, AND POLITICAL HISTORY OF SPORT IN SOCIETY

The module is divided into three parts, each with a distinct emphasis:

Part 1 is concerned with the relationship between social class, culture, leisure, and sport in the preindustrial and industrial world of the eighteenth and nineteenth centuries.

Part 2 traces the evolution of the so-called games ethic in British education, the diffusion of the ethic throughout the empire and beyond and both the intended and unintended consequences of this significant and potent moralistic ideology.

Part 3 concentrates on the association between sport and political (and religious) ideologies in the twentieth century and on the uses to which democracy, fascism and communism have put sport in continental Europe.

APPENDIX II: THEY TAUGHT THE WORLD TO PLAY

The module presents a case study of a cultural revolution: the games ethic and its dissemination throughout Britain, the Commonwealth, and the New World.

Attitudes and actions of the past have significant lessons for the present. This course sheds light on the influence of idealism, pragmatism, and casuistry on educational and social systems and holds a mirror up to the present.

Through the medium of this largely influential ideological exemplar this course deals with the impact and impermanence of belief systems, their intentional and unintentional consequences, and their overt and covert purposes. The course is based substantially on archival sources from Britain, the Commonwealth and the New World. Much of the material is both dramatic and fascinating and many of the characters encountered are both forceful and colorful. And their actions have influenced cultural, social, and educational systems throughout the world.

PART 1.
Emergence and Dissemination

1. Eton, Harrow and others: the public schools and games for status, discipline and survival.
2. Evolutionists and inspirationalists: schoolmaster ideologues, Thring, Almond, Temple, and Hart—the autocratic innovators.
3. Oxford and Cambridge: the matrix of a revolution and the home of muscular Christians.

State Imitation

Emulators, status-seekers, and holy hearties—the spread of the games ethic into British middle-class schools and society.

Diffusion into Empire

Aspects of the dissemination of an idea—Eton in India, Gentleman Galore in Nigeria, John Browns in South Africa, "Blues and blacks" in the Sudan, and Muscular Missionaries everywhere.

PART 2.
Obeisance to Idealism and Idolatry: the techniques of indoctrination, persuasion and coercion

The motivating power of the word: the language of morality, patriotism, esprit de corps and sexual identity.

The crushing force of ritualism and symbolism: "bloods," blues, badges, and beatings.

PART 3.
"The Game is played by Decent Chaps"

Late Victorian and Edwardian Britain, Dominions and "Empire": a world replete with muscular Christians and healthy Hedonists.

Symbols of Ideological Purity—some notable heroes of the Victorian and Edwardian games field.

PART 4.
Ripples in the Wider World

Tom Brown in the New World; Yanks in the Old World; England's Thomas Hughes in the United States and American Rhodes Scholars at Oxford.

APPENDIX III: WESTERN CIVILIZATION AND SPORT

From "ritual to record": the evolution of sport in Western Society in relation to its social, economic, intellectual and political significance.

TEXTS

Basic: W. J. Baker, *Sports in the Western World*, 1982 and John A. Lucas and Ronald A. Smith, *Saga of American Sport*, 1978.

Supplementary: A. Guttmann, *From Ritual to Record*, 1978. Donald J. Mrozek, *Sport and American Mentality 1880–1910*, 1983. Richard Mandell, *Sport: A Cultural History*, 1984.

COURSE OUTLINE

Overview: Ideology, society, and sport.

Greece: City states, national games, and philosophers: Athens and Sparta, Plato, the Pan-Hellenic festivals and xenophen.

Rome: Pragmatism, militarism, and hedonism: fitness for domination and mass spectator sport.

Interlude: Christianity and chivalry: repression and deceit. Liberalism, humanism, and classicism: the inspirationalists. Feltre, Vergerius, Elyot, Ascham, Mercurialis.

Renaissance and the Reformation: Lutherism, Calvinism and Presbyterianism, religion, and dogmatism. Reaction and Realism: the reformers-Montaigne, Mulcaster, Comenius, Fenelon.

Enlightenment: The Return to Nature: Rousseau and Emile. Naturalism and German Assimilation: Basedown, Guts Muths. Medical Reinforcement: Fuller, Frank, Tissot (S. A.), and Tissot (C. S.). Educational Adaptation and Development: Pestalozzi and Froebel.

Nationalism: Germany—a Case Study: Jahn to National Socialism.

Imperialism: Britain—a Case Study: Victorian upper-class education for imperial duty.

America: The saga of American sport: colonial period. Pre–Civil War. Post–Civil War. Rise of college athletics. Sport and "the American Way of Life." Issues in modern American sport.

REFERENCES

Baker, William J. 1982. *Sports in the Western World*. Totowa: Rowman and Littlefield.

Baker, William J., and J. A. Mangan. 1987. *Sport in Africa: Essays in Social History*. New York: Africana Publishing Co.

Bailey, Peter. 1978. *Leisure and Class in Victorian England*. London: Routledge and Kegan Paul.

Bottomley, Frank. 1979. *Attitudes to the Body in Western Christendom*. London: Lepus Books.

Briggs, Asa. 1984. *A Social History of England*. London: Weidenfeld and Nicolson.

Burke, Peter. 1978. *Popular Culture in Early Modern Europe*. London: Temple Smith.

Cantelon, Hart, and Richard Gruneau. 1982. *Sport, Culture and the Modern State*. Toronto: University at Toronto Press.

de Grazia, Victoria. *The Culture of Consent: Mass Organisation of Leisure in Fascist Italy*. 1981. New York: Cambridge University Press.

Guttmann, Allen. 1978. *From Ritual to Record: The Nature of Modern Sports*. New York: Columbia University Press.

Haley, Bruce E. *The Healthy Body and Victorian Culture*. 1978. Cambridge: Harvard University Press.

Hoberman, John M. 1984. *Sport and Political Ideology*. London: Heinemann: Educational.

Holt, Richard. 1981. *Sport and Society in Modern France*. London: Macmillan in Association with St. Antony's College.

Honey, John. 1977. *Tom Brown's Universe: The Development of the English Public School in the Nineteenth Century*. New York: Quadrangle.

Malcolmson, Robert W. 1973. *Popular Recreations in the English Society, 1700–1800*. Cambridge: Cambridge University Press.

Mandell, Richard D. 1984. *Sport: A Cultural History*. New York: Columbia University Press.

Mangan, J. A. 1981. *Athleticism in the Victorian and Edwardian Public School: the Emergence and Consolidation of an Education Ideology*. Cambridge: Cambridge University Press.

———. 1985. *The Games Ethic and Imperialism: Aspects of the Diffusion of an Ideal*. New York: Viking.

Marrus, Michael R. 1974. *The Rise of Leisure in Industrial Society*. St. Charles: Forum Press.

Mason, Tony. 1980. *Association Football and English Society, 1863–1915*. Brighton: Harvester Press.

Mrozek, Donald J. 1983. *Sport and American Mentality, 1890–1910*, Knoxville: University of Tennessee Press.

Murray, Bill. 1984. *The Old Firm: Sectarianism, Sport and Society in Scotland*. Edinburgh: N.P.

Samuel, Raphael, and Gareth Stedman Jones. 1983. *Culture, Ideology and Politics: Essays for Eric Hobsbawm*. London: Routledge and Kegan Paul.

Storch, Robert B., ed. 1982. *Popular Culture and Custom in Nineteenth Century England*. London: Croom Helm.

Walvin, James. 1975. *The People's Game: A Social History of British Football*. London: Allen Lane.

Yeo, Eileen and Stephen. 1981. *Popular Culture and Class Conflict*. Brighton: Harvester Press.

PART 2
Literature of Sport

4

On the Teaching of American Sport Literature

DAVID L. VANDERWERKEN

Ten years have passed since I first wrote about my class in a piece called "English 4503: Sports in Modern American Literature," *College Literature* 3, no. 2 (1976): 130–38. At the time, such a course was a novelty, a bit suspect—so much so that the editor, Bernard Oldsey, felt moved to write a rare justificatory headnote for the article so that leery readers of the young journal might give the essay the benefit of the doubt. The status of both *College Literature*—one of the truly useful publications in our profession—and of sport literature has advanced significantly.

Just how far sport studies have come is indicated by Wiley Lee Umphlett's "The Literature of American Sport Culture: The Emergence of a Productive Field of Study and Research," *PROTEUS: A Journal of Ideas* 3, no. 2 (Sping 1986): 28–33. In this special issue devoted to "The Sports Experience," Umphlett surveys an impressive body of work in all the humanistic disciplines and coins a useful phrase to label it: The Literature of American Sport Culture. When I first offered Sports in Modern American Literature in Spring 1974, there was no Literature of American Sport Culture, no anthologies of sport-centered creative writing, no critical studies, not much in the way of social analysis. I possessed the hubris of the pioneer. By 1980 I had learned that I was but one of many pioneers, that an underground of sport studies courses in many fields existed. The books started to appear; the organizations began to form; and the rest, as they say, is history. I spend nearly two hundred dollars a year in dues, and I can hardly keep up with current work. Sport studies is taking on the cottage industry quality of Faulkner scholarship. Teaching and writing about sport-centered literature is legitimate, institutionalized, promotable, and tenurable. And *Aethlon: The Journal of Sport Literature*, sitting on a "Current Periodicals," shelf looks every bit as proud as *ELH*.

Certainly the founding of the Sport Literature Association (SLA) in 1984 has been the most significant pedagogical development for teachers of sport-centered literature. We now know who we are and how and what we teach. The annual meeting and *Aethlon* provide a forum for both critical analysis and pedagogical exchange. To the master spirit of the SLA—Professor Lyle I. Olsen, Department of Physical Education, San Diego State University—the membership owes a debt of gratitude that can never be repaid. He brought the whole endeavor up from underground into the light of day. Many SLAers belong jointly to the professional associations in sport philosophy, history, sociology, anthropology, psychology, and physical education. Such cross-pollination increases knowledge and enriches all. Sessions on sport literature are cropping up on the most unlikely of conference programs. And workshops for secondary school faculty in sport literature are a new permanent feature at National Council of Teachers of English meetings. While sport literature enthusiasts haven't yet set up card tables at airports, we are no longer bashful about where we live and move and have our being.

A second major development in the teaching of sport literature is the exponential growth of quality primary material and secondary tools in the last ten years. Lyle Olsen has compiled and distributed to SLA members a selective bibliography just from the Eighties containing 112 items. Texts that have been unavailable for years have been reprinted, such as Mark Harris's *Bang the Drum Slowly* by Nebraska-Bison (1984) and Jason Miller's *That Championship Season* by Viking Penguin (1983). Strong anthologies exist that meet the needs of convenience and price: Higgs and Isaacs (1977), Dodge (1980), Vanderwerken and Wertz (1985). All three contain useful bibliographies, as do the critical studies by Umphlett (1975), Messenger (1981), Berman (1981), Higgs (1981), and Oriard (1982). For background readings from other disciplines, Higgs's *Sports: A Reference Guide* (1982) is the starting point. While in 1974 locating enough texts to run a decent course was a serious problem, so many choices now confront the instructor that it's no easier than making selections for a survey course. But it's a nice problem to have.

Having offered my course every two years since 1974, I now have a fine-tuned syllabus of material that wins most of the time (see Appendix). The course breaks into four units: baseball, football, basketball, and the future of sport. The rhythm of this is especially effective in the fall semester since it follows that of the several sports. The class has been around long enough to be a known quantity, so I don't have much trouble anymore with a bunch of folk enrolling with the wrong assumptions and expectations. I send every new academic coordinator hired by the Department of Athletics a copy of the course description and syllabus. On opening day, after the usual housekeeping chores, I launch into a keynote lecture called "Pens and Jocks" in which I try to account for the appeal that sport has for the American writer and identify some of the key issues that the course will take up (see my *College Literature* piece, especially 131–36). The units on the literature of the major American team sports follow the pattern of a day or two of lecture/discussion based on poems and essays to establish the unique features of the game, then extended discussion of two full-length works for a week or so each. Also, the class covers the more realistic work first, followed by the more complex or fantastic or surreal piece. Easing students into Coover's *Universal Baseball Association* (1968) after *Bang the Drum Slowly* (1956) lessens students' bewilderment—at least partially. While certain texts have taken on the aura of official classics, I do work in recent material. In the baseball unit, eventually, I intend to experiment with W. P. Kinsella's *Shoeless Joe* (1982), Donald Hays's *The Dixie Association* (1984), David Carkeet's *The Greatest Slump of All Time* (1984), and Eric Rolfe Greenberg's *The Celebrant* (1983). Since most everything I teach has been filmed, I find it fruitful to spend a day discussing the adaptations, especially of the radically altered Hollywood versions of *The Natural* (released 1984) and *North Dallas Forty* (released 1979). With the VCR explosion, plus premium cable, chances are that students will have seen these movies without an arranged showing. I suggest that the triumphal Redford/Hobbs ending is truer to the spirit of baseball than that of the novel. (Judging from the Malamud obituaries, one surmises that the author may have thought so, too.)

Since creative writing on baseball must outstrip that on other sports by about ten to one, selecting the readings for that unit continues to be the most difficult. Understandably, several teachers of sport literature have designed courses on baseball alone because of its riches. Using essays by Angell, Grella, and Schrag as well as poems by Francis, Wallace, Moore, Updike, Humphries, and Goodman; the class and I determine what special characteristics of baseball have generated so much good work by so many writers (see Appendix for titles). The list includes the special nature of time and space in baseball (Angell, Grella, Schrag, Humphries); its inherent zaniness, tolerance of eccentricity, caprice, and whimsy (Angell, Grella, Francis) that accounts for the enormous amount of fantasy and magical realism in baseball-centered fiction; its richness of history, event, and legend, becoming like mythic "matter" (Angell, Goodman); its exacting skill level and maddening difficulty (Angell, Schrag); its relaxed, pastoral rhythms that are inconsistent with modern culture (Grella, Schrag, Humphries); its aesthetic, poetic, proportional—even religious—qualities (Angell, Wallace, Moore, Updike); its following of the seasons like the seasons of mankind (Grella, Humphries); and its offering rare glimpses of perfection (Angell, Goodman). This discussion of the confluence of baseball elements and literary motifs prepares the class for the novels. Students are able to discern how appropriate a milieu baseball is for Malamud's exploration of redemption, maturation, and responsibility in *The Natural*; for Harris's treatment of mortality and human behavior in *Bang the Drum Slowly*; for Coover's meditation on the glory and the peril of the human imagination in *The Universal Baseball Association*; for Kinsella's examination of human dreams, resurrection, and fulfillment in *Shoeless Joe*.

Our study of football also begins with some short pieces to identify its mythos. King's essay, Shaw's modern classic, and Dickey's subtle analysis of Lombardi point up some dramatic contrasts with baseball literature (see Appendix for titles). The most obvious of these, of course, is that football is governed by a clock. Contemporary students, especially the Texans in my classes, are more intensely involved in the mystique of football since the game seems to more accurately reflect modern life than baseball. Indeed, my students are sometimes impatient with the baseball material. Novak, Ross, and many others have written eloquently on the differences between football and baseball. Football writing tends to be considerably less playful, creating a world of sophistication, technology, corporate bureaucracy, and rigid organization. In contrast, the pastoral world of baseball seems naive and sentimental. Discipline, pain, sacrifice—these are the words that spring to mind regarding football. Indeed, football seems worked instead of played. While baseball fiction tends to isolate its world from external reality, football literature tends to equate the sport with modern American life. The violence and the values of the one reflect the other. For several years in recent history, playing or following football was automatically patriotic. The White House mixed mythoi, playing "hardball" and rooting for the 'Skins. After the class establishes these qualities of football and its literature, students read *North Dallas Forty* (1973) and one other—*End Zone* (1972), *Joiner* (1971), or *A Fan's Notes* (1968). Students usually respond most strongly to Gent's novel, one that I firmly believe has emerged as the best football-centered novel. And it's the most teachable. *Joiner* and *A Fan's Notes* present difficulties of length, style, structure, and mode; I have to teach my buns off with those books. Students will warm to *End Zone* after they see what DeLillo is doing with language, epistemology, and teleology (two words best left unused in class).

While basketball-centered writing lags far behind that of baseball and football, the choices have increased in recent years. Yet, I must confess that basketball receives short shrift in the course, a condition I would like to rectify. Currently, the class reads a few poems and Miller's drama, *That Championship Season* (1972). In previous years, I have used Neugeboren's *Big Man* (1966) and Shainberg's *One on One* (1970), depending on availability, with mixed success. The experience of teaching *One on One* is similar to that of teaching Coover or DeLillo. Berman's book, especially, provides teachable help in confronting all three of these rich and complex texts.

The prefatory poems (see Appendix for titles) by Vincent, Updike, Trudell, and Hilton capture that sport's mass appeal, part of which is its "cost effectiveness"—all one needs is a hoop and a ball—accounting for its popularity as both the city game and the rural game. Basketball is improvisational (Vincent), expressive (Hilton), therapeutic (Trudell), and legendizing (Updike). And it's a game where rules violations, the good foul, are strategic—which separates basketball from the other two sports. Indeed, the central McGuffin, as Hitchcock would say, of *That Championship Season* is Coach's instructions to Martin to foul the opposing center, get him off the court. The foul underlies the play's conflicts, Martin's absence, the quality of the championship—pure or tainted—and helps students understand the foul lives of these men since their hour of glory twenty-five years before. *That Championship Season* provides an excellent closing full-length work in the course since it synthesizes and reprises all of the major issues examined throughout. Students don't necessarily like this play, but they do find it compelling in its dramatization of the social ethos of sport, its perversion of the play spirit, its examination of the American coach/priest, and its celebration of youth and innocence. In many ways, *That Championship Season* hits us where we live as much as *Death of a Salesman* does.

The final unit of the course is loose by design to cover some issues vital to sport in America and to speculate on the future (see Appendix for titles). Students usually enjoy this more relaxed capstone to the semester's labors. The essays by Tunis and Rafferty generate lively discussions of how culture uses sport for its own ends, to perpetuate its own social mythology. The pieces by Lipsyte, Weiss, and Boslooper and Hayes focus on the status of women in sports and the conventional wisdom on that issue. The deepest beliefs of some students will emerge during discussion here. Greenberg and Hoch have wise things to say about spectator participation, beyond that of Morganna. Moreover, Hoch's essay introduces students to the Marxist critique of sport in capitalist societies, a critique few students are aware of and one they find disturbing. The class reaches the final gun by looking at two very different prophecies on the future of sport: the optimistic notion on the part of Leonard that the play spirit will return to SportsWorld; the equally compelling argument that things will get worse and worse until gladiatorial bloodsport becomes the order of the day in Harrison's powerful story, "Roller Ball Murder." My "Roller Ball: Sport and Society in the Future," *Arete: The Journal of Sport Literature* 2, no. 2 (1985): 39–45, offers my own conjectures on the issue.

The foregoing describes my American sport literature course in its most frequent form as an advanced, undergraduate offering. However, the course has several other avatars: as a graduate seminar, as part of Texas Christian University's Master of Liberal Arts enrichment degree within Extended Education, and as the off-campus variant of the same program housed at Carswell Air Force Base, a SAC installation. These audiences require certain modifications. M.A. and Ph.D. students in English in some ways are more traditional in their perception of the literary canon than other audiences—understandably so, perhaps, since they face monstrous comprehensive examinations in literary history. For these skeptics, I prepare a considerably more elaborate opening lecture of justification that, I hope, convinces them that more will emerge from the course than the vision of Dr. V. riding his hobby horse. Befitting a graduate seminar, the class reads more primary work as well as a healthy chunk of critical and bibliographical material. The selected checklist I prepare fully convinces the dubious. On library reserve, I place the major texts of what Umphlett calls the Literature of American Sport Culture, requiring the class to read around extensively in humanistic sport studies. Course requirements consist of critical reports, a book review, two exams, and the usual substantial paper.

While I enjoy doing the class at all levels, I am especially fond of the Master of Liberal Arts version, an audience of bright, post-baccalaureates with some living behind them. I tailor this course to a generalist audience since the backgrounds and training are so disparate—physicians, public school teachers, business professionals, law enforcement people, and retirees. This course is the least literary in focus, the most topical in material since the class reads a bit more nonfiction. The discussions are very lively. These folk are here because they want to be. Have I already said that I enjoy this group immensely?

The least traditional—all right, the wildest—form of the course is the one I do at the air base. In the classroom, it is tacitly understood that rank doesn't exist, so the enlisted man can disagree with the colonel's comment with impunity. Air Force personnel live intense lives, to say the least—lives lived on the edge, not unlike those of professional athletes. To paraphrase Dr. Johnson, flying B-1 and B-52 bombers carrying nukes wonderfully concentrates the mind. Sometimes flight crews come to class, which meets at a nonprime 5:30–8:15 PM time slot, in full gear after a ten-hour mission. A segment of the class may be on alert. Fighters may scramble in midclass. Beepers constantly beep. If the red phone in the classroom rings, I was told, don't *you* answer it. Blackouts, with accompanying sirens, occur in midsentence, effectively ending the evening's session. And sometime during the semester, half the enrollment is apt to be ordered to Guam on one day's notice. Somebody is always on temporary duty asignment. The key to a successful teaching experience at the base is to remain very, very flexible. These men don't find the style of life depicted in *North Dallas Forty* particularly abnormal. Not surprising. Teaching in a hangar where the Coke machines are full of Bud, Coors, and Miller—for rehydration I'm told—restores perspective to the whole endeavor.

With the support resources now available and its legitimacy established, sport literature studies are in a strong curricular position. The late A. Bartlett Giamatti, former president of Yale and Commissioner of Baseball, wrote movingly of baseball. The titles keep pouring forth. I can't keep up with W. P. Kinsella's work. Workshops for high school teachers at professional meetings have not been empty exercises since many are experimenting with sport literature in their classes. Texas, for example, requires four credits in English for a high school diploma, and teachers are seeking ideas for new courses and fresh material. Eventually, college faculty will be the beneficiaries, receiving students who have already read "The Eighty-Yard Run" and "For the Death of Vince Lombardi." Upon this foundation, we can build even more sophisticated courses. Let me end out on a limb: ten years from now, look for Sport Literature listed in *PMLA* as a division, right up there with Film and Literature and the Milton Society.

APPENDIX: SYLLABUS

English 3523-45
Sports in Modern American Literature
Fall 1984

Vanderwerken

COURSE DESCRIPTION
In 1932 John Dos Passos wrote: "We write today for the first American generation not brought up on the Bible, and nothing as yet has taken its place as a literary discipline." In recent years American writers seem to have discovered a possible "discipline" in sports. The proliferation in the 1960s, 1970s, and 1980s of works that focus primarily or tangentially upon sports might indicate that American writers are increasingly using sports as: (1) a ready-made source of allusion, metaphor, and symbol; (2) a pervasive context in which to explore American values and beliefs; (3) a cultural phenomenon expressing the best and the worst in the national character. Sports provide American writers (as well as Presidents) with something to "plug into" out there in television land since, unless one lives in a cave, all Americans have at least some rudimentary familiarity with sports. This course will focus on the literary uses of sports and will attempt to discover why American writers find them so congenial for their creative purposes. The class will be discussion oriented. The final grade will result from three exams and a six- to eight-page paper on a topic of your own choosing that grows out of the course.
Texts:

1. Malamud, Bernard, *The Natural* (1952).
2. Harris, Mark, *Bang the Drum Slowly* (1956).
3. Gent, Peter, *North Dallas Forty* (1973).
4. DeLillo, Don, *End Zone* (1972).
5. Miller, Jason, *That Championship Season* (1972).
6. Vanderwerken, David L., and Spencer K. Wertz, *Sport Inside Out* (1985).
7. Assorted handouts.

SCHEDULE

23 August Introduction and Pre-game Warmup. Lecture: Pens and Jocks.

Baseball: The Summer Game

28 August Roger Angell, "The Interior Stadium." George Grella, "Baseball and the American Dream." Peter Schrag, "The Age of Willie Mays" (handout).

30 August Robert Francis, "Pitcher." Robert Wallace, "The Double Play." Marianne Moore, "Baseball and Writing." John Updike, "Tao in the Yankee Stadium Bleachers." Rolfe Humphries, "Polo Grounds." Paul Goodman, "Don Larsen's Perfect Game."

4, 6, 11, 13 September Bernard Malamud, *The Natural.*

18, 20, 25, 27 September Mark Harris, *Bang the Drum Slowly*

2 October FIRST EXAM.

Football: Autumn Madness

4 October Larry L. King, "Getting 'em Ready for Darrell." Irwin Shaw, "The Eighty-Yard Run." James Dickey, "For the Death of Vince Lombardi."

9, 11, 16, 18 October Peter Gent, *North Dallas Forty.*

23, 25, 30 October and 1 November. Don DeLillo, *End Zone.*

1 November PAPER PROSPECTUS DUE.

6 November SECOND EXAM.

Basketball: The City Game

8 November Stephen Vincent, "Basketball." John Updike, "Ex-Basketball Player." Dennis Trudell, "The Jump Shooter." David Hilton, "The Poet Tries to Turn in His Jock."

13, 15 November Jason Miller, *That Championship Season.*

The Future of Sport

20 November PAPER DUE. John R. Tunis, "The Great American Sports Myth." Max Rafferty, "Interscholastic Athletics: The Gathering Storm."

THANKSGIVING BREAK

27 November Robert Lipsyte, "Designated Heroes, Ranking Gods, All-Star Holy Persons." Paul Weiss, "Women Athletes." Thomas Boslooper and Marcia Hayes, "The Feminine Physique."

29 November Peter S. Greenberg, "Wild in the Stands." Paul Hoch, "Coliseums and Gladiators."

4 December George Leonard, "The Dance Within the Game." William Harrison, "Roller Ball Murder."

11 December FINAL EXAM.

WORKS CITED

Berman, Neil D. 1981. *Playful Fictions and Fictional Players: Game, Sport, and Survival in Contemporary American Fiction.* Port Washington, N.Y.: Kennikat Press.

Dodge, Tom, ed. 1980. *A Literature of Sports.* Lexington, Mass: Heath.

Higgs, Robert J. 1981. *Laurel & Thorn: The Athlete in American Literature.* Lexington: University Press of Kentucky.

———. 1982. *Sports: A Reference Guide*. Westport, Conn: Greenwood.

Higgs, Robert J., and Neil D. Isaacs, eds. 1977. *The Sporting Spirit: Athletes in Literature and Life*. New York: Harcourt.

Messenger, Christian K. 1981. *Sport and the Spirit of Play in American Fiction: Hawthorne to Faulkner*. New York: Columbia University Press.

Novak, Michael. 1976. *The Joy of Sports*. New York: Basic Books.

Oriard, Michael. 1982. *Dreaming of Heroes: American Sports Fiction, 1868–1980*. Chicago: Nelson-Hall.

Ross, Murray. "Football Red and Baseball Green." *Chicago Review* 22, no. 22–23 (1971). Rev. 1982. Reprinted in Vanderwerken and Wertz, 716–25.

Umphlett, Wiley Lee. 1975. *The Sporting Myth and the American Experience*. Lewisburg, Pa: Bucknell University Press.

Vanderwerken, David L., and Spencer K. Wertz, eds. 1985. *Sport Inside Out: Readings in Literature and Philosophy*. Fort Worth: Texas Christian University Press.

PART 3
Philosophy of Sport

Origins of sports terminology.

5
"Time Out": Teaching Sport and Philosophical Analysis

SPENCER K. WERTZ

A recent cartoon of *In the Bleachers* by Steve Moore features an episode titled "Origins of sports terminology" in which a caveman with raised club, standing over a helpless comrade, says to an onlooker: "'Time out'? What he mean 'Time out'?" Here, the cartoonist has captured pictorially the fundamental question about the nature of language in sports; that is, the saying creates the situation—a foul called by an official makes it a foul. The magical power of language to shape reality has been preserved in sports (see Martland 1985). Sports viewed as cultural institutions have a sufficient amount of language and critical argumentation embodied in them for educators to teach the skills and techniques of philosophical analysis. I have a rather liberal interpretation of "philosophical analysis," by which I mean a method for handling philosophical problems and questions that is almost, but not quite, Rortyean in design. (A few of Richard Rorty's writings are listed in Works Cited.) I will explain this quasi-Rortyean conception in the pages below.

Appendix II reveals that I include more than just readings that are the product of ordinary language philosophers or logicians, but their techniques and methods are ones I bring to the sports world and into the classroom. Critical thinking about sports has been my goal, so whatever serves this purpose I have adopted in one form or another. I have done this with limited success, which is better than none, and so have continued over the years. Perhaps the time out I take here to describe my courses will be of assistance to the reader. To this end, I have included course outlines and tests in the appendixes.

Much debate surrounds sports, and a great deal is claimed of them. Do sports build character? Do they contribute to human knowledge or understanding? These questions and the arguments they generate have important pragmatic consequences because athletics passes for a part of the curriculum in Texas as elsewhere. Should they? What is the justification for their inclusion? These are just a few questions prompted by sports when an inquisitive mind turns and looks reflectively upon them. Indeed, an abundant supply of philosophic literature pursuing answers to these and other questions has evolved over the past twenty years. See my essay "Teaching Sport Philosophy Analytically" (1986, especially section III). In this chapter, I shall select what I think is the most useful available material for classroom use, but due to space I shall discuss primarily my junior level course and the first module in a series of three—each of which lasts five weeks.

Only a few analytically trained philosophers—like Aspin, Best, Carr, Lenk, Simon, Suits, and Ziff—took the initiative and began to contribute to this relatively new area. This is a rare opportunity for philosophers, since most issues and their corresponding literature have a two thousand year history that usually has to be taken into account. But not the area of sport philosophy, except with perhaps Plato (Ardley 1967). Within this area, the selections at the moment are rather limited, thus allowing for a review. But before turning to the analytic literature, let me give a brief characterization of "sport."

"Sport" isn't just the sports we normally associate with the term. "Sport" (in the generic sense that includes all kinds of human movement activities, dance, and the less institutionalized forms of play) has, since 1972, become the focus of research for the Philosophic Society for the Study of Sport (Fraleigh 1983). A few years after its founding, I heard of the group and its journal. Simultaneously I began to look for course ideas that would intrigue a student body no longer interested in the humanities. My research in the region of Sport took me into inquiries I though I would never pursue, such as dance and the martial arts. This was tough for a guy who is rather shy of dance floors, and who takes falls about as gracefully as a rhino.

Also, David Best's *Expression in Movement and the Arts* (1974), *Philosophy and Human Movement* (1978), and *Feeling and Reason in the Arts* (1985) took me into directions I initially didn't expect to go. I once developed a course on the topic human movement and spent a large part of it discussing dance. (See Appendix I for a course outline on Human Movement.) Journals devoted to this topic are: *Momentum* and the *Journal of Human Movement Studies*, both British publications that are interdisciplinary in nature. David Carr, the English—not the Canadian—philosopher has an excellent series of articles on this topic that should be taught in upper level courses: "Practical Reasoning and Knowing How" (1978); "The Language of Action, Ability and Skill: Part I—The Language of Action" (1980); and "The Language of Action, Ability and Skill: Part II—The Language of Ability and Skill" (1980). The best place to begin is with Carr's Part I on the language of action, which surveys the mind-body problem, among others. This ties in nicely with Best's opening chapters on the mind-body problem in both *Philosophy and Human Movement* and *Expression in Movement and the Arts*. A discussion of dualism helps students see the need for the kind of criticism Best develops of theories found in physical education. The Best readings, I have discovered with my students, should follow Carr's studies on the language of action, ability, and skill, although the Best-Carr order may be more in keeping with traditional exposition. Best exposes what he thinks is wrong with the established theories in physical education, and Carr supplants these with new improved theories. I tried teaching the Best-Carr literature this latter way, but the students found Best too difficult, so it became necessary to weave Carr into the discussion of each problem or topic for things to run more smoothly. Students are able to understand Carr's more ambitious piece on practical reasoning and knowing after having read Best's essay.

Carr keeps his discussion as general as possible to cover all that is included under the term "human movement." I have spent class time applying this material to specific sports and instances of the concepts he introduces. My students have found this difficult, but rewarding. An instructor must supply numerous examples familiar to the students to bring Carr's and Best's analyses to life. This is not easy, given our student population. In my junior lever course, Thinking about Sport, students have had three hours of freshman or sophomore introductory philosophy; they know how to recognize arguments and assumptions, raise critical questions, and develop argumentative responses. This doesn't always go as planned, to say the very least. There have been Best headaches that needed Aspins.

Let me sketch my use of Carr's work. He begins his study with a discussion of the language we use to describe our actions: "the best way by far to proceed with questions about actions is by attending closely to our ordinary uses of action idioms—by considering and inquiring into the structure of our language about action" (1980a, 76). The cardinal tenet of philosophical analysis is that language is our repository of human wisdom; that is, the things that remain in our language have survived one of the most critical tests of all human history. It follows that focusing our attention on language should be the primary, initial step in critical thinking. But it must not end there. Alvin Goldman gives us good advice when he says in the preface of *A Theory of Human Action* (1970, vi):

> It is also my purpose to develop a set of sharp conceptual tools that will be useful for studying action in a systematic way. The achievement of this goal demands that we look beyond the ideas embedded in common sense wisdom. . . . Common sense wisdom does not provide a clear conceptual scheme for analyzing these relationships. At this point the theoretician must introduce novel concepts, the justification for which should ultimately be assessed by their contribution to further investigation and analysis.

Carr has followed Goldman's enterprise and has skillfully adapted it to human movement studies.

Carr follows his analysis of human action with a discussion of intentionality and extensional (truth-functional) languages in which he concludes (1980a, 82–83):

> The debate, then, continues, but it is reasonably safe to claim so far it has not been shown conclusively that it is possible to eliminate intensional idioms from our discourse about human mental life. Moreover, in a recent work, von Wright (1974) has persuasively argued that the concept of *causation* which surely no physical scientist would dream of trying to dispense with, cannot be satisfactorily interpreted either, within a purely extensional language. If this is so then it seems likely that the phenomenon of intensionality [and intentionality] is just something with which logically we have to live.

This conclusion leads Carr to explore answers given to the question: are reports of intentional actions, intensional constructions, then? Several action theorists, like Anscombe (1963), Danto (1973), Davidson (1980), von Wright (1974; 1983), are discussed and divided into two camps: the agent causationist who says "A brings it about that q" and the event causationist who reports "p causes it to be the case that q." For q, I substitute sport actions like A, an agent, throwing a pass in football, A serving a tennis ball, A kicking a soccer ball, and so on.

The students are led to a discussion of the nature of sport action. For a bodily movement to be a human action, it must meet a pair of requirements: (a) that A be conscious, that is, have some mental grasp of A's environment and A's place within it; and (2) that A have moderate control over the body moving. Now, over and above these requirements, what else is needed for us to have a *sport action*? One particular proposal (Jeu 1972, especially 157) is that sport actions are actions of protagonists who confront one another and that they struggle to defeat each other. (Here "opponent" is a broad enough term to include nature or records.) Jeu adds: "It is necessary to possess a definite technique and to use it with determination." This last condition implies some *mastery* over the move or act in question. Certain things must happen in order for a move or act to become a sport action; in sum, they are:

1. A is to be conscious of the act.
2. A has some mastery over the act.
3. A is a protagonist who confronts another protagonist.
4. They struggle to defeat each other.
5. The struggle exemplifies technique and its use, in willful determination.

The above paragraph comprised a handout used to facilitate a discussion of each requirement. For instance, the practice of some swimming coaches in America is to *eliminate* consciousness in their swimmers. Is this a good practice? Is this just one more way that sport is threatened? I argue that it is—by the loss of the first article on the list; hence, it no longer qualifies as a sport action. This list generated many good discussions as the weeks passed by. Carr's last two articles were helpful in dealing with the remaining items on the list. I suggested to my students that they use philosophy to express their hopes and aspirations for sport and not merely to justify current practices in the realm of sport. Some institutions or practices *threaten* the realm of sport, and philosophy aids us in seeing these for what they are. Hans Lenk's essay on action theory and the social scientific analysis of sport actions is an additional reliable guide to the literature in action theory and its relation to sport. For more of this topic, see my presidential address on choking—something my tennis buddies have deemed me an expert on, so I decided to write about it within the context of action theory.

In my first module, "What Is Sport?" (see Appendix II), I asked the class to write a dialogue—using Plato's *Euthyphro* and Wittgenstein's language games as exemplars or models—to facilitate the process of actually *engaging* them in the activity of philosophy. One can take a Rortyean view of philosophy when it comes to teaching, without feeling that one has sold out entirely. Philosophy, according to Rorty, is a conversation that has no limits and no purpose, except those set by a free or voluntary agreement of the participants in the dialogue. Agreement of scope and method was derived from the readings. The students' only requirement lay somewhere in the dialogues they were to compose. I encouraged them to raise philosophical questions (like "What is sport?"), to attempt some answers, and to back them up with reasons or arguments.

The students were asked to be playful with sport because, after all, play is what sport and philosophy have in common if we view the latter along the lines of Gadamer and Rorty, not to mention Plato (Ardley 1967). While the students complained bitterly about the lack of direction, they ultimately enjoyed the freedom to be creative. On the faculty evaluation form, one student commented: "At first I thought that he had not prepared us for the dialogue, but leaving us as much free room as possible made it easier to write the paper." Conversely, another student remarked: "The dialogue was a pretty neat idea. The problem with it though is that I have *never* written one before and to have 50 percent of your grade determined by it is pretty scary"; to which I felt compelled to reply: "I hope not. This assignment is novel in that its purpose is to get you to do something different with your writing skills." My admittedly vague instructions for the assignment generated a stupor; my students just stared back at me with puzzled looks on their faces. It became quite clear that the students would have to learn by example. So I would commence at the beginning again: what is sport? Is it a matter of life and death or is it entertainment and amusement? Why is it important for Americans? Does it speak to our collective unconscious? How? Why? I just went on and on to puzzle and to create a state of wonder. This much I *did* succeed in doing.

One hurdle I never made with the class was their preconception that there must be one way or "right" way to compose a dialogue. As an alternative to Plato's dialogues, I suggested examining Wittgenstein on language games as a clue to writing a dialogue. I thought it would be fun to imagine a conversation or an interview one would have with Howard Cosell. Only one student wrote such a dialogue. An undergraduate from the one-way camp said:

> I enjoyed doing the dialogue because it was very thought-provoking. My only concern is if what I wrote was correct. Even if it wasn't, the idea of the dialogue made me more involved in the class.

Some lower classmen found the involvement a source of frustration:

> Writing the dialogue was *very* difficult. Maybe it should be changed just to a formal paper. I had five different papers but could not make a dialogue from any of them. I finally had to talk to a friend and record our conversation. It didn't go as deep as I would have liked, but at least it sounded like a dialogue.

I struck out on this one.

I have taught the remaining material in both upper- and lower-level courses, focusing primarily on informal logic, especially theories of meaning and definition. In addition to the categories of Human Movement and Sport, the literature of analytic sport philosophy also divides into a realm of Play. Play has the longest intellectual history—dating back to Plato (Ardley 1967). Yet not until the Thirties did the idea of play become a major historiographical tool and philosophical concept. In *Homo Ludens: A Study of the Play Element in Culture* (1955, 13), Johan Huizinga defines "play" in the following way:

> Summing up the formal characteristics of play we might call it a free activity standing quite consciously outside "ordinary" life as being "not serious," but at the same time absorbing the player intensely and utterly. It is an activity connected with no material interest, and no profit can be gained by it. It proceeds within its own proper boundaries of time and space according to fixed rules and in an orderly manner. It promotes the formation of social groupings which tend to surround themselves with secrecy and to stress their difference from the common world by disguise or other means.

This definition reflects the doctrine of essentialism. The debate between essentialists and nonessentialists is one I cover in some detail. An *essentialist* is one who thinks that terms, like "play," "game," or "sport," have necessary and sufficient conditions that each and every member of the class must satisfy. This philosophical position goes back as far as Plato, and I illustrate it with the dialogue *Euthyphro*, who thought that all important terms had an essence. Huizinga apparently shared this belief with Plato, for it is seen in the above definition by calling the definiens "formal characteristics."

Definitions like Huizinga's were criticized by the nonessentialists. A *nonessentialist* is one who holds that most concepts admit of borderline cases. I use Wittgenstein's investigations (1958, especially paragraphs 66–76) to illustrate this position. It is most interesting to compare Wittgenstein and Huizinga. Anthony Manser's "Games and Family Resemblances" (1967) is particularly helpful with this comparison. Wittgenstein is difficult for students to understand by himself, so if Huizinga's *Homo Ludens* (the first three chapters) is read along with Wittgenstein, his ideas come easier for them. It is also interesting historically because Huizinga was lecturing in Austria and England during the times Wittgenstein was there, so perhaps he was conversant with the Dutch historian. His ideas may play a larger part in Wittgenstein's thinking than we expect. (See my address on the philosophical genesis of the term *Lebensform*, [1982].)

Bernard Suits tries to rescue essentialism from its critics, especially Wittgenstein. I devote a third of the semester-long course to Suits's book, and sometimes I spend more class time on it if I use other related material. His dialogue, *The Grasshopper*, is a sustained attempt to adequately define "game-playing." After much deliberation with Skepticus and Prudence, the Grasshopper presents the following definition (1978, 41):

> To play a game is to attempt to achieve a specific state of affairs (prelusory goal), using only means permitted by rules (lusory means), where the rules prohibit use of more efficient means (constitutive rules), and where the rules are accepted just because they make possible such activity (lusory attitude). I also offer the following simpler and, so to speak, more portable version of the above: playing a game is the attempt to overcome unnecessary obstacles.

Suits has his critics. They argue that the definition is both too broad (covers committee meetings and *Robert's Rules of Order*) and too narrow (omits animals—e.g., stags and insects—who engage in game playing, as well as omitting some human activities that should be included under "game-playing"). Is Zen a game the masters play with their students? The editors, Robert Sohl and Audrey Carr, of *Games Zen Masters Play* (1976), think so. They describe Zen as "the game of insight, the game of discovering who you are beneath the social masks." Zen is viewed as a goal, a basic strategy (chap. 1), and plays and maneuvers (chap. 2). Is this a corruption of Zen? Is this a misuse of "games" and "play," or are these legitimate uses? If they are the latter, then there is trouble for Suits's definition. Wittgensteinians, like Frank McBride (1975) and Robert Paddick (1979), have argued that because of criticism like the above, Suits's definition is inadequate. Suits offers a defense of his definition in "McBride and Paddick on *The Grasshopper*" (1981). Hans Lenk also offers criticism of the Wittgensteinians in his "Prolegomena" (1985). This debate gives us a chance to talk about the rules and roles definitions play in critical thinking and philosophizing.

In *This Book Needs No Title: A Budget of Living Paradoxes*, Raymond Smullyan briefly explains why there is a need for people to argue over a definition (1980; 127):

> I believe it is sometimes very important that one *should* argue about a definition. This is far from a merely pedantic enterprise. The words we choose for our own use have a major effect in coloring our thinking and in determining our emotional attitudes toward things.

Each semester, one or two skeptics always demand that I address the reasons why one should spend the time arguing over definitions. Again, imparting this knowledge is usually achieved through play. For example Suits's question, is sex sport? Hmmm. Or, we might wonder whether the sexual act must be considered a type of game. (See Suits's query 1981, 72–73, complete with a drawing.) This topic always gets the skeptics' attention if all else fails. (The drawing helps a lot!) Suits argues for a negative answer (1981, 80–81), but a plausible affirmative answer can be developed, especially if one pays attention to Oriental, non-Western sexual practices (Chang 1977). A discussion of this sort usually demonstrates how narrow their belief systems are. Smullyan is right! This is a good way to end.

I frequently have students write argumentative responses pertaining to philosophical or conceptual issues in sport (although usually not on whether sex is sport), and Clark's piece on writing papers for philosophy classes in his *Introduction to Moral Reasoning* (1986) helps students prepare their responses. A dialogue between the Grasshopper and the student is sometimes suggested if not required, especially when I get a class that is particularly excited about Suits's dialogue. I have students trade off reading parts of *The Grasshopper* in class, and then the class discusses some of the ideas and arguments raised in the story. With the better student dialogues, I do the same.

The essentialism and nonessentialism debate in recent mid-twentieth century philosophy enables one to discuss Rorty's ideas about the nature of philosophy and to contrast these with the more traditional views, such as Plato's. Rorty sees the importance of nonessentialism or antiessentialism as the way in which one can blend these ideas with other tendencies to produce a gradual move away from scientism and positivism ("From Logic to Language to Play" [1986], 749). He adds that "this development has made possible a more playful, more cosmopolitan, less professional tone in which to philosophize" (748). Philosophy of sport is perhaps best conducted in an atmosphere like the one that Rorty describes if it is to have any impact on the type of student body teachers must educate today. Pedagogically, Rorty's metaphilosophical views are liberating, and they enable one to conceive of "philosophical analysis" without dogmatic beliefs tied to its historical development. In fact, if there is an area of applied philosophy where teachers would *expect* it to be playful-seriousness, it would be the philosophy of sport. As I have stated at the opening of this chapter, critical thinking about sport *is* my goal, and whatever contributes to that end—even being playful with my subject and discipline—I will try, at least once, in the spirit of Sport.

APPENDIX I: SYLLABUS

The Philosophy Department announces a new course to be offered in the summer semester (1983, first five-week term).
3973.30 Philosophical Studies: Human Movement
6263.30 Seminar in contemporary Philosophy: Human Movement
Spencer K. Wertz

COURSE OUTLINE
The course may be taken for either undergraduate or graduate credit. Limited enrollment and permission of the instructor are necessary. The class will meet at 11:00 AM daily in Reed Hall 203. The seminar is designed for students interested in dance, kinesiological studies, the martial arts, and philosophy. Interdisciplinary projects will be encouraged. The topics for discussion are:

philosophy and human movement
the meaning and use of "movement"
rhythm in movement
movement and the intellect
"kinesthetic intelligence"
the empirical and conceptual aspects of movement
the aesthetic dimension of human movement
the essence of movement
meaning in movement
communication in movement
thinking in movement
expressive movement and intentional action
representation in movement
the nature of action
the language of ability
the concept of skill

PARTIAL LIST OF READINGS

David Best, *Expression in Movement and the Arts: A Philosophical Enquiry.*

David Best. *Philosophy and Human Movement.*

David Carr. "Practical Reasoning and Knowing How." *Journal of Human Movement Studies* 4 (1978): 3–20.

David Carr. "The Language of Action, Ability and Skill: Part I—The Language of Action." *Journal of Human Movement Studies* 6 (1980): 75–94.

———. "The Language of Action, Ability and Skill: Part II—The Language of Ability and Skill." *Journal of Human Studies* 6 (1980): 111–26.

Roger Copeland and Marshall Cohen, Eds. *What is Dance? Readings in Theory and Criticism.* New York: Oxford University Press, 1983.

Maxine Sheets-Johnstone, "Thinking in Movement." *Journal of Aesthetics and Art Criticism* 39 (1981): 399–407.

Joseph Margolis, "The Autographic Nature of Dance." Ibid., 419–27.

Mary Sirridge and Adina Armelagos, "The Role of 'Natural Expressiveness' in Explaining Dance." Ibid. 41 (1983): 301–7.

APPENDIX II: SYLLABUS

Philosophy 1701—Spring 1986
What Is Sport? Module (1 hour)
Spencer K. Wertz.
MB-164S

COURSE REQUIREMENTS:

Read Harper's essay, Plato's *Euthyphro*, and the readings on sport assigned below. Then I want you to think up a contemporary dialogue evolving around sport—very much like the dialogue Euthyphro and Socrates had about piety or holiness. This is an exercise in analogical reasoning—using the Platonic dialogue as a model. My lectures will show you ways to do this. Your dialogue must be a minimum of four *typed* pages, and the maximum is ten pages. This is the "creative" part of your work, one half of your grade. The other half of your grade comes from a test at the end of the five weeks (19 February 1986). This test will be designed in such a way for you to demonstrate to me that you have read and understood the literature assigned and discussed in class.

Harper. "The Philosopher in Us." In *Sport inside out*, part III, sec. 3.

Plato. *Euthyphro* (handout).

Wittgenstein. Selections on meaning and language (handout).

Heinegg. "Philosopher in the Playground: Notes on the Meaning of Sport." In *Sport inside out*, part III, sec. 3.

Jeu. "What Is Sport?" (handout).

Gilbert and Twyman. "Violence: Out of Hand in the Stands." In *Sport inside out*, part I, sec. 2.

Belaief. "Meanings of the Body." In *Sport inside out*, part III, sec. 2.

Lenk. "Herculean 'Myth' Aspects of Athletics." In *Sport inside out*, part III, sec. 2.

Kuntz. "Aesthetics Applies to Sport as Well as to the Arts." In *Sport inside out*, part III, sec. 4.

Martland. "Not Art and Play, Mind You, nor Art and Games, but Art and Sports" (handout).

Wertz. "Artistic Creativity in Sport." In *Sport inside out*, part III, sec. 4.
Galvin. "Aesthetic Incontinence in Sport." In *Sport inside out*, part III, sec. 4.
Wertz. "Comments on Galvin." In *Sport inside out*, part III, sec. 4.
Wertz. "Sport and the Artistic" (handout).

SCHEDULE

17 January. Introduction to the Module. Read Harper and Plato for next time.
20 January. Philosophy and Sport. The Philosopher In Us. Read "Writing Papers for Philosophy Classes" (handout).
22 January. Plato's *Euthyphro*. Read Wittgenstein.
24 January. Plato's *Euthyphro* and Wittgenstein. Read Heinegg and Jeu.
27 January. The Meaning of Sport. What Is Sport? Read Gilbert and Twyman.
29 January. What Is Sport? Violence: Out of Hand in the Stands. Read Belaief.
31 January. Violence. Meanings of the Body. Read Lenk.
3 February. Meanings of the Body. Herculean "Myth" Aspects of Athletics. Read Kuntz.
5 February. Aesthetics Applies to Sport as well as to the Arts. Read Martland.
7 February. Not Art and Play, Mind You, nor Art and Games, but Art and Sports. Read Wertz.
10 February. Artistic Creativity in Sport. Read Galvin and Wertz. Paper (dialogue) due.
12 February. Aesthetic Incontinence in Sport. Is Sport Art?
14 February. Sport and the Artistic. Conceptual Change.
17 February. Paradigm shift in Sport. Review.
19 February. Exam (over meetings 1–15).

EXAM

Directions

You have fifteen minutes per short-essay question: select one from each of the three areas. Be sure to answer the question that is asked and to weave your understandings of the assigned readings into your discussion. Take a total of forty-five minutes for the exam and five minutes to review your test.

Part I: Informal Logic. Select one.

1. From your reading of William Harper's essay, "The Philosopher in Us," what does Harper mean by the phrase *sport inside out*?
2. Euthyphro defines "piety" as "doing what is pleasing to the gods." Give Socrates' critiques of this definition and comment on them.
3. Describe and explain the importance of "language-games" in Wittgenstein's *Philosophical Investigations*.
4. Discuss Bernard Jeu's answer to the philosophical question, "What is sport?" Do you think he has adequately captured the notion of sport? If so, give reasons why you think so. (This question is answered either negatively or affirmatively, so be prepared to substantiate your position.)

Part II: Social Philosophy. Select one.

1. How does violence in sport pose problems for our understanding of our concept of sport? (Be careful: stay within the context of the readings.)

2. Discuss Lenk's Hercules-Prometheus "Myth" aspects of the athlete. Does it suggest a revision or reformation of our conception of the athlete?

3. Discuss Lynne Belaief's positive, "The Good Me" meaning of the body and its implications for sport? Does this view seem a promising, viable alternate to what we see operating in today's society?

Part III. Aesthetics. Select one.

1. Discuss Martland's claim that art has no fans. Give the background distinctions and analysis, plus reasons why you agree or disagree.

2. Discuss the presence of artistic creativity in sport and its implications (i.e., what do Kuntz, Wertz, and others make of it).

3. Discuss the comic/tragic distinction in the sport as art analogy.

APPENDIX III: SYLLABUS

Philosophy 1711
Sport and Philosophy module
Spencer K. Wertz
MB-164S

READINGS AND TOPICS: SECOND MODULE

"Is Sport a Metaphor of Life?" This module leads off with the above question, and we shall examine several proposed answers given by sport philosophers. Gent, Michalos, and McMurtry selections will help us to probe the relationships between *sport and life* (more *social philosophy*). Drew Hyland's piece leads us into *moral issues*, (*ethics*) dealt with in the Hemingway, Pearson, Fraleigh, and Lehman selections. Next we deal with the nature of sport language, and this section will be introduced by way of Hans Lenk's "Prolegomena Toward an Analytic Philosophy of Sport." *Theory of Knowledge* (epistemology) follows with Adam Smith's essay and those by Margaret Steel and Scott Kretchmar. The last section is *metaphysics*—here we ponder the ontic elements of the game with Angell, Memmott, VanderZwaag; plus Roland Garrett's metaphysics of baseball; Michael Novak's sacred space, sacred time; and end (appropriately enough) with Slusher's and Ermler's selections in the section on death.

Readings (all selections from the text):
Gent, Michalos, McMurtry, 225–45.
Hyland, 280–89.
Hemingway, 43–62.
Pearson, Fraleigh, Lehman, 459–73.
Lenk, 474–80.
Martin, Fraleigh, Martin, Hecht, 592–610.
Smith, Steel, Kretchmar, 63–103.
Angell, Memmott, VanderZwaag, 725–32.
Novak, 725–32.
Slusher, 752–61.
Ermler, 761–65.

SCHEDULE

21 February. Is Sport a Metaphor of Life? Football through the eyes of Gent, Michalos, and McMurtry. Read Drew Hyland.
24 February. Playing to Win: How much should it hurt? Read Hemingway and Pearson.
26 February. "Fifty Grand" and Deception. Read Fraleigh and Lehman.
28 February. Why the Good Foul Is Not Good. Can Cheaters Paly the Game? Read Lenk's Prolegomena and the Martin-Fraleigh exchange.
3 March. The Language of Sport. Read Hecht.
5 March. The Nature of Sports Language. Read Smith, Steel, Kretchmar.
7 March. The Knowing in Playing. Read Angell and Memmott.
10 March. The Interior Stadium. Read VanderZwaag and Novak.
12 March. The Inner Seals of Sport. Read Garrett.
14 March. The Metaphysics of Baseball. Read Slusher.
24 March. Sport and Death. Read Ermler. Paper due.
26 March. Failure in Sport. Emergence of a New Paradigm in Sport.
31 March. Review.
2 April. Exam.

NOTE: The paper is due the day after spring break. Use one of your experiences in sport to discuss several of the issues brought out in the above readings. Here again we use Harper's article and his distinction between contemplative and discursive acts of philosophy. Your contact (the contemplative) will be your sport experience; then you should analyze it along the lines of the above readings and topics. (I will pass out some samples of this kind of expository writing). Minimum length is four typed pages. Review Clark's essay on writing papers for philosophy classes that I passed out at the beginning of the first module.

EXAM

Directions

The duration of the exam is forty-five minutes with five minutes to review your test. There are fifteen minutes per part, so budget your time carefully. Be sure to answer the question asked and make every sentence count toward reflecting your understanding of the texts you have studied. Select one from each part.

Part I. Ethics and moral issues.

1. Discuss cheating. Why is it a philosophical problem to be dealt with in philosophy of sport classes? And how is it dealt with by the various authors we have examined?

2. Discuss the morality and immorality of football. Gent describes professional football's total disregard for human values, whereas Michalos extols the game's virtues. McMurtry sides with Gent. Briefly summarize this debate and then tell me who you side with and why.

3. Should players play at all costs? Who is to decide: players, doctors, or coaches? What are the "ethical ambiguities" which Drew Hyland speaks of and how does he resolve them?

Part II. Philosophy of language and the nature of sports language.

1. What are the attempts at defining "a good clutch hitter"? What does the

Martin-Fraleigh exchange teach us about ordinary sports language and what we can expect of it?

2. What does Hans Lenk find presently wrong with analytic philosophy of sport and how does he propose to correct it?

Part III. Metaphysics and the theory of knowledge.

1. Explain what Adam Smith means by "Sport is a Western Yoga." What are its implications for sport?

2. Explain the metaphysics of baseball, and contrast Garrett's study with that of Slusher and Ermler.

3. Roger Angell claims that baseball is THE GAME, that is, it is superior to any other game. What are his reasons for thinking this, and do you agree or not? (Be sure to give your own reasons for thinking so.) The Memmott and VanderZwaag pieces should be helpful to you here.

4. Explain Margaret Steel's position in regard to what we know when we know a game.

APPENDIX IV: SYLLABUS

(My colleague, Richard F. Galvin, taught the third module and his syllabus and two tests are below.)

Philosophy 1721
Sport and Social Values
10 MWF Moudy 164S
Richard F. Galvin
Reed 215B

GENERAL OUTLINE:

This is the third in the "Sport Module" series. We will read Bob Simon's book, *Sport and Social Values*, in pretty much its entirety, as well as some material from *Sport inside out* and a few handouts. Since 1701 and 1711 are prerequisites, I assume that you are not total neophytes, although I will presume little about your knowledge of ethics and value theory.

REQUIREMENTS:

Two exams; in class, on April 21 and May 7. No make-up exams—only official university excuses will be honored. The exams will be objective, short-essay type exams, each counting for 50 percent of the final grade. Attendance at lectures is mandatory.

COURSE OUTLINE:

This is somewhat tentative, since it's difficult to forecast how long it will take to get through the material. Assigned readings follow dates.

4 April.
7, 9, 11 April. Paul Taylor, "Nature vs. Convention (handout). Simon, chaps. 1–2.
14, 16, 18 April. Simon, chap. 3.
21 April. Exam.
23, 25 April. Simon, chap. 6, and Peter S. Wenz, "Human Equality in Sports," in *Sport inside out*, 208–21.

28, 30 April, 2 May. Simon, chap. 7.
5 May. Simon, chap. 4.
7 May. Exam.

FIRST EXAM

Answer five of the following questions by writing clear, coherent analytic essays in handwriting that would make an IBM Selectric blush.

1. "Relativism promotes progress." Discuss.
2. "All and only those statements that can be verified or falsified by using the Scientific Method are objective. All others are subjective." Discuss.
3. "The moral relativist cannot consistently hold any moral beliefs of his own." Discuss.
4. Explain Dworkin's distinction between alleged rights to "equal treatment" and "treatment by equals," and explain how this applies to the issue of equality in competitive sport.
5. Does Simon believe that competition is a source of value or disvalue in sport? Explain his argument on this issue.
6. Thoroughly explain Mill's "Harm Principle" and explain how it applies to arguments against boxing.

SECOND EXAM

Answer five of the following questions by writing clear, coherent, critical analytic essays in handwriting that would please Sister Marianne Joseph, my third-grade teacher.

1. Thoroughly explain Simon's "Vulnerability Principle," and explain how it relates to arguments concerning the justifiability of violence in sport.
2. Thoroughly explain *both* of Simon's arguments concerning how violent sports like boxing might cause harm to society.
3. Thoroughly explain *both* (a) the assimilationist *and* pluralist models for Sex Equality in sport, and (b) discuss *one* serious difficulty faced by each.
4. "If one accepts the assimilationist model as the standard for justice and equality in the political and economic spheres, one must apply it as well to the social sphere." Discuss.
5. Present and evaluate *two* arguments designed to show that athletics are "educational," and hence desirable, within a university setting.
6. Should there be (a) athletic scholarships and (b) minimum entrance and grade requirements for athletes? Why or why not?

WORKS CITED

Anscombe, G. E. M. 1963. *Intention*. 2d. ed. Ithaca, N.Y.: Cornell University Press.

Ardley, Gavin. 1967. "The Role of Play in the Philosophy of Plato." *Philosophy* 42, no. 161, 226–44.

Aspin, D. N. 1977. "Kinds of Knowledge, Physical Education and the Curriculum." *Journal of Human Movement Studies* 3: 21–37.

———. 1983. "On Human Movement Studies." *Momentum* 8: 2–11.

Best, David. 1974. *Expression in Movement and the Arts: A Philosophical Enquiry*. London: Lepus Books.

———. 1978. *Philosophy and Human Movement*. London: George Allen & Unwin.

———. 1985. *Feeling and Reason in the Arts*. London: George Allen & Unwin. See especially chaps. 6, 11, and 12.

Carr, David. 1978. "Practical Reasoning and Knowing How." *Journal of Human Movement Studies* 4: 3–20.

———. 1980a. "The Language of Action, Ability and Skill: Part I—The Language of Action." *Journal of Human Movement Studies* 6: 75–94.

———. 1980b. "The Language of Action, Ability and Skill: Part II—The Language of Ability and Skill," *Journal of Human Movement Studies* 6: 111–26.

Chang, Jolan. 1977. *The Tao of Love and Sex: The Ancient Chinese Way to Ecstasy*. New York: E. P. Dutton.

Clark, Ralph W. 1986. "Writing Papers for Philosophy Classes." *Introduction to Moral Reasoning*. Belmont, Calif.: Wadsworth, xiii–xvii.

Danto, Arthur C. 1973. *Analytical Philiosophy of Action*. Cambridge: Cambridge University Press.

Davidson, Donald. 1980. *Essays on Actions and Events*. Oxford: Clarendon Press.

Fraleigh, Warren. 1983. "The Philosophic Society for the Study of Sport: 1972–1983." *Journal of the Philosophy of Sport* 10: 3–7.

Gadamer, Hans-Georg. 1975. *Truth and Method*. English ed. London: The Seabury Press. 91–119 on play.

Goldman, Alvin I. 1970. *A Theory of Human Action*. Princeton: Princeton University Press.

Huizinga, Johan. 1955. *Homo Ludens: A Study of the Play Element in Culture*. Boston: Beacon Press.

Jeu, Bernard. 1972. "What Is Sport?" Trans. R. Blohm. *Diogenes* 80: 150–63.

Lenk, Hans. 1985a. "Prolegomena Toward an Analytic Philosophy of Sport." Reprinted in *Sport Inside Out: Readings in Literature and Philosophy*. David L. Vanderwerken and Spencer K. Wertz, Eds. Fort Worth: Texas Christian University Press, 474–80.

———. 1985b. "Action Theory and the Social Scientific Analysis of Sport Actions." Reprinted in *Sport Inside Out*. 480–86.

Manser, Anthony. 1967. "Games and Family Resemblances." *Philosophy* 42, no. 161: 210–25.

Martland, T. R. 1985. "Not Art and Play, Mind You, nor Art and Games, but Art and Sports." *Journal of Aesthetic Education* 19, no. 3: 65–74.

McBride, Frank. 1975. "Toward a Non-definition of Sport." *Journal of the Philosophy of Sport* 2: 4–11.

Paddick, Robert J. 1979. "Review Essay of *The Grasshopper* by Bernard Suits." *Journal of the Philosophy of Sport* 6: 73–78.

Rorty, Richard. 1979. *Philosophy and the Mirror of Nature*. Princeton: Princeton University Press.

———. 1982. *The Consequences of Pragmatism: Essays 1972–1980*. Minneapolis: University of Minnesota Press.

———. 1985. "Philosophy without Principles." *Critical Inquiry* 11, no. 3: 459–65. See the essays on each side of Rorty's.

———. 1986. "From Logic to Language to Play." *Proceedings & Addresses of the American Philosophical Association* 59, no. 5: 747–53.

Simon, Robert L. 1985. *Sports and Social Values*. Englewood Cliffs, N.J.: Prentice-Hall.

Smullyan, Raymond. 1980. *This Book Needs No Title: A Budget of Living Paradoxes*. Englewood Cliffs, N.J.: Prentice-Hall.

Sohl, Robert, and Audrey Carr, eds. 1976. *Games Zen Masters Play*. New York: Mentor.

Suits, Bernard. 1978. *The Grasshopper: Games, Life and Utopia*. Toronto: University of Toronto Press.

———. 1981. "McBride and Paddick on *The Grasshopper*." *Journal of the Philosophy of Sport* 8: 69–78.

Von Wright, G. H. 1974. *Causality and Determinism.* New York: Columbia University Press.

———. 1983. *Practical Reason.* Ithaca, N.Y.: Cornell University Press.

Wertz, S. K. 1982. "On the Philosophical Genesis of the Term 'Form of Life.'" *Southwest Philosophical Studies* 6: 1–16.

———. 1985. "Sport and the Artistic." *Philosophy* 60, no. 233: 392–93.

———. 1986a. "Is 'Choking' an Action?" *Journal of the Philosophy of Sport* 13: 95–107.

———. 1986b. "Teaching Sport Philosophy Analytically." *Teaching Philosophy* 9, no. 2: 121–46.

Wittgenstein, Ludwig. 1958. *Philosophical Investigations.* 3d. ed. Trans. G. E. M. Anscombe. New York: Macmillan.

Ziff, Paul. 1974. "A Fine Forehand." *Journal of the Philosophy of Sport* 1: 92–109. Reprinted in Ziff's *Antiaesthetics.* Boston: D. Reidel, 1984, 59–68.

6

"Time In": On Teaching Phenomenological Approaches to Sport and Meaning

KLAUS V. MEIER

First, and foremost, I am an educator retained to instruct students in the art and practice of philosophy. To accomplish this task, I have taught, for the past decade and one half, both undergraduate and graduate courses in the philosophy of sport. This particular realm of academic endeavor may be divided conveniently into two related, but somewhat diverse facets, namely: first, the utilization of sport as an exemplary vehicle to better teach and to understand numerous traditional philosophic issues; and second, the employment of the tools of philosophic inquiry to illuminate the phenomena of sport, games, and play. Whereas Spencer Wertz has largely employed the former orientation in the delineation of teaching the philosophy of sport from an analytic perspective contained in the chapter immediately preceding, I have herein chosen to concentrate on the latter.

It is, of course, frequently acknowledged that the primary purpose of all forms of education is to open man to the world and, conversely, to open the world for man. That is, education is charged with the task of encouraging, cultivating, enhancing, and directing man's awareness of himself and the nature of the human condition. The study and careful investigation of most, if not all, aspects of the physical, social, and cultural milieu are significant components of this important enterprise.

In addition, philosophy may appropriately be characterized as "the art of wondering." In fact, one noteworthy introductory text to the discipline utilizes this phrase in its title (Christian 1973). It takes to heart the Socratic assertion that for man, "the unexamined life is not worth living," and forwards invitations to question, to think, and to speculate in the pursuit of wisdom. Further, it is a probing, critical discipline that is comprised of careful description of, and systematic inquiry into, various aspects of man and the world in an effort to construct an accurate and well-grounded picture of reality, in which the numerous and diverse elements of human knowledge, experience, and aspirations will find their proper place.

The philosophy of sport, thus, ponders man's nearly universal and historically extended involvement in sport, play, and games. It is presumed that such an investigation—undertaken from the perspectives of varying contemporary philosophic orientations, positions, and investigative methodologies—facilitates the clarification and understanding of the nature, purpose, and significance of these phenomena.

1

In my courses on the philosophy of sport—although I address and emphasize the enterprise predominantly from the perspectives of phenomenological inquiry and existential philosophy—I have found it to be extremely productive to introduce the entire area of concern with a detailed analytic examination of the basic structures of sports, games, and play. However, since Wertz has already addressed himself at length to this facet of the philosophic project, I will presume that this end has been successfully attained and, thus, I will state little more about the matter herein. The reader interested in perusing my own reflections on this topic is referred to an early paper (Meier 1981) that was largely concerned with the clarification of the philosophic issues at stake in sociological definitions and concepts of sport. It is clear, however, that the provision of an adequate framework incorporating these three forms of human activity permits additional philosophic issues to be raised.

These introductory deliberations yield several noteworthy and beneficial consequences, most of which will not be specified at this point due to spatial limitations. However, one extremely significant factor does warrant mention. Clarification of the characteristics, qualities, and purposes that differentiate sport and games as play and nonplay makes it possible to discuss the necessary implications of these differing orientations for subsequent decisions concerning actions contained therein. In other words, the groundwork has been completed for a systematic and productive examination of the manner of conduct of specific sport, game, or play occasions to determine whether particular potentials are permitted to be manifested or, conversely, are precluded by certain structural orientations. It may be asserted, thus, that philosophy serves a more encompassing and synoptic function than solely that of analysis. Philosophy consists of more than the consideration of linguistic and logical issues; procedural clarity, thus is a means, not an end. Philosophy may, and indeed should, profitably address significant metaphysical, as well as axiological, problems. Indeed, to consider the latter momentarily, the domain of value theory may be richly harvested for recommendations as to how life in general, or specific avenues of human conduct in particular, ought to proceed, to be changed, or to be improved. Current interest in biomedical ethics, for example, clearly demonstrates the demand for, and necessity of, such ventures. The philosophy of sport is another such enterprise with rather large potentials.

An introduction to this area of concern may be provided readily by addressing, for instance, the question of the nature of competition and the appropriate role of winning in sport, games, and play. Despite the uncontested importance of this particular area of the philosophy of sport, since metaphysical not axiological inquiry is the main charge of this chapter, the interested reader is directed to Appendix I ("Competition, Sportsmanship, and Cheating") for a further consideration of this matter. However, it should be kept in mind that the pursuit of the second is inextricably based on the first (Meier 1985, especially 65–67, 74–75).

2

Before a philosophical investigation can be conducted into meaning in sport, play, or games, or any other human activity for that matter, it is necessary to understand man's embodied nature. This is not an easy undertaking: "As even a cursory glance at the history of philosophy attests, the significant task of elucidating and resolving the problem of the interdependence of mind and body presents a plethora of intriguing and intricate difficulties" (Meier 1985, 192). Although it is not possible, or desirable for present purposes, to engage in an extensive exploration of the "mind-body" problem, it is essential to provide students with at least an introductory historical survey of selected influential philosophical treatments of human corporeality, from Plato to Descartes, to behaviorism and, finally, to the phenomenology of the "lived-body."

Since the dualistic conception of man still prevails in Western theories of epistemology, behavior, education, and, of course, human movement forms such as sport, I have found it useful to begin this phase of the course with a brief excerpt from Plato's *Phaedo*, namely, "The Separation of Body and Soul." (Please note that all articles and excerpts discussed in this section on embodiment are reprinted in Morgan and Meier [1988]; for a list of the specific titles of the works referred to, see Section III, "Sport and the Body," of the reading outline provided in Appendix II.)

A rapid leap of roughly two thousand years—with a short detour to explore Christianity's influential, predominantly antiphysical, and even ascetic, doctrines in the intervening period of time—leads to a consideration of an important excerpt from Descartes' *Meditations on First Philosophy*. Descartes provides, in part, a preliminary restatement of Plato's dualistic structure in different guise and adds an extremely detailed and rigorous mechanistic position on the necessary interrelationships between the extended body and the immaterial mind. His extreme bifurcation of these two entities has provided philosophy with a conception of man with which it has struggled for more than three centuries. Not only has Cartesian dualism spawned such contemporary philosophical dependents as behaviorism, but it has also influenced certain significant modern philosophy of sport expositions (see, for example, the selection from Weiss).

At this point, I turn directly to contemporary phenomenological analyses that commence with a view of man as an incarnate subject, a unity, not a union of two discrete components. The study of the "body-subject" focuses upon man as an incarnate consciousness concerned with his continual unfolding in the world. Selections from the writings of Sartre, Marcel, Zaner, and Schrag are utilized to explore this aspect of human existence. My own article, "Embodiment, Sport, and Meaning" (1979), provides a culminating synthesis of some of this material, in addition to an extended exploration of Merleau-Ponty's enlightened and seminal phenomenological analysis of man's insertion into and centering in the world through the expressive body.

It is readily apparent, even from the very brief preceding description, that phenomenology provides an important balance to an enduring intellectual history of the deprecatory and mechanistic stereotypes inherent in dualistic philosophical positions. Thus, it may be asserted that (Morgan and Meier 1988, 197):

> If the radical shift from Cartesian to phenomenological conceptions of the nature of man is acknowledged and accepted, the distinctive potentialities of man's participation in sport may be vigorously and profitably explored. Rather than concentrating solely on the objectified, treadmill image of sport, predominantly centered upon the development and attainment of physical strength, motor skills, and technical efficiency, it appears to be legitimate, fruitful, and imperative to focus upon the full range of dynamic, lived experiences available therein.
>
> Through free, creative, and meaning-bestowing movement experiences, man becomes cognizant of the limits and potentials of his existence. His actions in sport represent, express, and affirm his capabilities, intentionality and mode of being. In short, sport may be characterized and extolled as the celebration of man as an open and expressive embodied being.

The next section of this chapter specifically addresses participation in sport as a meaningful experience and places the entire enterprise within the parameters of an existential analysis of the possibilities and limitations inherent in the human condition.

3

Undoubtedly, the topic best received by students in the entire course is that which may be termed "phenomenological analysis and metaphysical speculations" about human movement forms as meaningful experience; this is particularly the case for the investigation of the possibilities and significance of sport as a form of "authentic existence," as elucidated in, and ultimately derived from, the voluminous literature of existential philosophy.

An important qualifying note must be introduced at this point. The extensiveness and the sophistication of the philosophic materials to be assigned and discussed in a course of this nature, of necessity, are dependent upon both the available class time and the academic level and interests of the students concerned. The course content about to be described can be abbreviated to accommodate numerous component or term sizes; this may be achieved readily through selective reductions without seriously compromising the overall merit of the undertaking. I will commence by describing, in section 4, the materials suggested for a graduate or advanced undergraduate course experience and, subsequently, in section 5, indicate appropriate content for an introductory undergraduate course.

4

David Storey's *The Changing Room* (1972) introduces the question of the personal meaning of sports participation very nicely through the perspective of an English rugby club. Despite its large cast and, for North American students at least, somewhat foreign sports environment; the play works well in demonstrating, contrary to first appearances and expectations, how devastatingly little sport at times contributes to genuine human satisfaction. Storey also addresses this theme in an insightful manner in his more famous novel, *This Sporting Life* (1962). An effective alternative vehicle is Jason Miller's *That Championship Season* (1972); this drama provides illuminating, if bitter, reflections about the merit and consequences of sporting success for individual members of an American basketball team many years after winning a state championship title.

The previous introduction to the topic in general is followed by Samuel Beckett's play, *Waiting for Godot* (1954), a now classic exposition of the emptiness and, more significantly, the inherent possibilities of the human condition. With the aid of some enlightened discussion—the adjective "enlightened" is the operative term here; Beckett's play has also precipitated extremely inept efforts at interpretation and application to sport studies—the piece permits and invariably facilitates entrance into the literature of existential philosophy proper.

Although several additional works may be appropriate to present a basic exposition of the major components and tenets of this area of philosophical inquiry, I usually employ one of the following three texts to provide a basic introduction: Macquarrie's *Existentialism* (1973), Kaufman's *Existentialism from Dostoevsky to Sartre* (1970), or Schrader's more complex and rewarding, *Existential Philosophers: Kierkegaard to Merleau-Ponty* (1967). These sources set the stage and permit an exploration of the context of the twentieth century components of the movement. Included in this process is the asking of such questions as follow: what does existential philosophy react against; what new areas does it focus upon; and what new perspectives, orientations, and methods shape its pursuits?

With graduate students I continue the course with an extended scrutiny of the specific concept of "authenticity" as delineated in Martin Heidegger's monumental *Being and Time* (1962) and Karl Jasper's *Philosophy 2* (1970). The discussion is focused predominantly upon confrontation with ultimate limitations or "boundary situations" (particularly individual finitude), freedom and projective possibilities, personal responsibility, interpersonal communications (including the "loving struggle") and, finally, "authentic existence." For the study of Heidegger, and only with advanced students, I have found the following parts of *Being and Time* to be particularly useful: (1) "Dasein," being-in-the-world (secs. 4, 9, 12, 13, 15); (2) modes of being-in, falling (secs. 28, 29, 31, 38); (3) the "they," anxiety, care (secs. 25–27, 39–41); (4) death, conscience, authenticity (secs. 45–48, 50–53, 58, 60, 62, 64). For Jaspers, most parts of *Philosophy 2* may be explored profitably.

With this foundational exposition in hand, I once again turn directly towards a scrutiny of what sport literature suggests about the realities of participation. Such novels as Coover's *The Universal Baseball Association, Inc., J. Henry Waugh, Prop.* (1968), Gardner's *Fat City* (1969), Gent's *North Dallas Forty* (1974), and DeLillo's *End Zone* (1972) all "share the same startling vision of a world that is actively hostile to any manifestation of freedom, of play. Those forms of play it does pretend to allow, namely, sports, it manages to deaden, to transform into a grotesque parody of true play" (Berman 1981, 8).

However, all is not totally lost. In DeLillo's excellent novel about the personal meaning of football, there is a vibrant moment of athletic participation during an exuberant, impromptu scrimmage, when the players temporarily bracket the overbearing, mechanical, and utilitarian vision of life to luxuriate, openly and completely, in play as a joyful occurrence, an expression of freedom, potential, and self. In other words, the experience is perceived as an absorbing and delightful transcendence of everyday functionality, and is valued solely for its intrinsic rewards. This situation addresses a major theme directly; namely, that despite the conduct and mode of participation often or even mostly to be found, other possibilities and meanings await discovery in open sports and true play experiences.

Although there is, most assuredly, a great deal more which could be said about the utilization of sport literature for the introduction and exemplification of existential themes, I will not do so here. Obviously, the chapter by Vanderwerken, "On the Teaching of American Sport Literature," in this volume provides a great deal of insightful and helpful suggestions concerning the use of this material. In addition, Vanderwerken's and Wertz's anthology (1985) contains not only pertinent excerpts from the Gent, DeLillo, and Coover novels, but also provides additional literary writings that may be profitably perused.

5

As indicated at the end of section 3, the material described in the previous section requires both an extended period of time and an advanced class. If either or both of these requirements are absent, it is still possible to address adequately the state of affairs delineated in the penultimate paragraph of the preceding section by utilizing different readings. In fact, there is a considerable body of literature of brief, philosophically inclined works that provide introductory exposure to the pertinent issues at hand, including the following pieces: "Man, Nature and Sport" (Progen 1979); "Man Alone" (Harper 1969); "Freedom and Sport" (Coutts 1968); "To Test the Wave is to Test Life" (Slusher 1969); "'And That is the Best Part of Us': Human Beings and Play" (Hyland 1977); "Play Springs Eternal" (Caspar 1978); and "Play and Possibility" (Esposito in Morgan and Meier 1988).

I usually assign and discuss most of the previous readings en masse, and then proceed directly to a critical investigation of Jean-Paul Sartre's "Play and Sport" (Morgan and Meier 1988). The discussion of play and sport as appropriation contained in this excerpt is one of the few reasonably well developed expositions concerned with these activities to be found in the works of any major philosopher. (For graduate courses I usually assign the following material from *Being and Nothingness* (Sartre 1966): (1) the problem of nothingness, bad faith, and being-for-itself, (3–117); (2) Part Four—having, doing, being, (529–754); and (3) the conclusion, which summarizes much of the entire essay in fourteen pages, (755–69). In conjunction with this, three specific philosophic studies that comment upon or criticize Sartre's treatment of this topic also warrant discussion (Fell 1979; Keating 1978; Netzky 1974).

Further, Sartre's analysis of the art and purpose of skiing sets the stage for the consideration of a pertinent question that invariably arises, and whose answer is most significant to the topic at hand; namely, what is the enticement and attraction of risk sports? In other words, why deliberately place oneself in dangerous situations in sports?

The previous question leads quite readily into a serious consideration of the concept of death, and here there is indeed much from which to choose. Once again, I have found a literary introduction—say, Tolstoy's "The Death of Ivan Ilyitch" (1960)—to work quite well. Subsequently, Gorer's brief piece, "The Pornography of Death" (1976), addresses what may be termed inauthentic responses to human finitude; the positive aspects of this confrontation are delineated rather clearly in such works as Koestenbaum's *The Vitality of Death* (1971) and Keen's notes on personally planning one's own death (1970, 74–81).

At this point, I turn directly to a consideration of mountain climbing—one of the ultimate risk sports—which, because it often requires its participants to walk the "feather edge of danger," highlights the encounter with personal mortality rather dramatically. Perhaps the best source of an athlete's serious reflections on the enterprise is still Herzog's description of the devastating personal costs, yet overwhelming individual rewards, resulting from the 1950 French expedition to climb Annapurna in the Himalayas (1953). Other helpful sources, which provide both expansion and counterpoint, include Alvarez's very brief piece, "I Like to Risk My Life" (1967); Sayre's informative chapter entitled "Why Men Climb Mountains" (1964, 209–19); and Wyschogrod's "Sport, Death, and the Elemental" (1973). An extended discussion of these works usually culminates with the conclusion that, since "death is the question existence puts to us" (this, parenthetically, leads to a good examination question; see Appendix III), participation in risk sports, despite any contrary superficial appearances, provides the opportunity for developing a very individually meaningful response.

On a considerably less precipitous level, I utilize one of my own studies, "An Affair of Flutes: An Appreciation of Play" (Morgan and Meier 1988), to focus the inquiry directly upon an intensive study of the nature, requirements, and implications of the world of play. A deliberately provocative opening paragraph, celebrating the apparently "useless," usually catches my student's interest (1988, 24):

> In this paper, I wish to proclaim, to extol, to champion, and to celebrate the cause of frivolity, uselessness, unproductivity, inconsequentiality, nonachievement, gratuitousness, irrelevance, and irreverence. In short, I wish to offer an apology for, and an appreciation of, play.

Students are often puzzled and challenged by this stance—a not altogether unusual response in a culture permeated and dominated by the ideology of work and praise of economic instrumentality and prudent utilitarianism. Thus, the ground has been prepared for an intensive study of significant phenomenological and existential inquiries into the nature of play and sport by Fink (Morgan and Meier 1988), Ehrman (1968), Krell (1972), Novak (1976), and Hyland (1977), among others. These works all contend that play and sport both permit and facilitate—if one opens oneself to the possibilities inherent in responsive participation—the development of personal identity and authentic existence.

Thus, to utilize my own summary of some of the preceding material, it may be asserted that (1988, 37–38):

> Play is an intrinsically rewarding, purposeless activity which requires no external justification and is located at the center of life, not relegated to its distant perimeter. Indeed, it may be characterized as a rich and vital focal point of diverse lived meanings. It is a *joie de vivre*, an adventurous, festive undertaking which reduces man's provincialism and enlarges his experience by embracing, and penetrating to, the heart of life.
>
> Although it is impossible to delineate fully the diverse components, expressive possibilities, and multitude of infectious delights inherent in the sphere of play, it is readily apparent that it is a most extraordinary and commodious realm—a transubstantiated and wondrous world permeated with serenity, joy, happiness, as well as surprise.
>
> Ultimately, play is an essential, revelatory, liberating, most human enterprise. It is "an affair of flutes" wherein man is provided a grove in which he may listen to the fluid rhythms of inner music, cheerfully express all aspects of his being, including the affirmation of his sensual nature, and luxuriate in the intense, fully-lived release, if not explosion, of his subjectivity. And this is most worthy of praise and celebration, indeed.

6

The foregoing clearly indicates that entrance into the world of play, and sport conducted as a play form, affords the open and responsive participant the opportunity to luxuriate in heightened consciousness and to extend personal being. Thus, the title of this chapter may finally have become clear. Although on a minor level it was selected deliberately to complement that chosen by Wertz in the preceding essay, the major purpose was to emphasize the culminating insights to be derived from a phenomenological and existential analysis of sport and play. That is, these activities permit the participant to probe "beneath superficial surfaces and concerns to address the heart of the matter, thereby permitting revelational penetration into true being" (1988, 36). In other words, this is the real *time-in*; the rest of ordinary life is preparatory to admission to these ventures that put us in the presence of the meaning of life and the world.

7

There are, of course, numerous additional major themes and issues to be investigated and discussed in the area of the philosophy of sport. Beyond those matters already addressed in this chapter—and the analytic and epistemological concerns about sport skills acquisition and performance delineated by Wertz in the previous chapter—the following very brief listing will present some indication of both the range and the flavor of some of these topics:

1. *The Aesthetics of Sport*, including investigations of the beautiful, the technically excellent, the useful, the sentimental, the dramatic, the emotionally satisfying or cathartic, and the artistic in sports participation. The interested reader is referred to the extensive section of Morgan and Meier (1988) that includes eight articles representing some of the most contemporary expositions and critical statements by such authors as Best, Kupfer, Roberts, Wertz, and others (see Appendix II, section 7 for a listing of titles). An additional and altogether different collection of literary and philosophic perusals of the area may be found in Vanderwerken and Wertz (1985, 488–526).
2. *Sport and Social-Political Philosophy* analyzes sport from a macrocultural perspective and—to employ an admittedly simplistic dichotomy—largely condemns it as a jejune spectacle, repressive social indoctrination and reinforcement, and covert exploitation; or, conversely, vigorously defends it from these and other similar charges. Some of the most contemporary and informative philosophical position papers are to be found in a section of Morgan and Meier (1988) that incorporates essays by Adorno, Horkheimer, Lasch, Lenk, Morgan, and Perry (see Appendix II, section 6 for a listing of titles).
3. Additional philosophical topics include the following: (1) philosophical perspectives on drugs and sport; (2) women and sport; (3) gambling and sport; and (4) sport, religion, and altered states of consciousness. Once again, the interested reader is directed to Appendix II for a representative listing of the titles of applicable and helpful essays.

8

With the preceding discussion of content, order, and reading intensity in hand, it is now necessary to discuss other pedagogical matters; more specifically, the most appropriate means of conveying the information and nurturing student development.

As mentioned earlier, philosophy starts in wonder and culminates, ideally, in insight and understanding. Courses in the philosophy of sport, thus, should address themselves to the task of clarifying, in the sense of "root reflection"—that is, systematically working one's way to a well-formulated and substantiated set of contentions, not blindly accepting unexamined assertions or beliefs—the nature, role, meaning, and potential of sport, play, and games as significant human enterprises.

But, how does one best teach the philosophy of sport, that is, which of a wide variety of pedagogical commitments and diverse teaching techniques should be utilized to meet this end? Some insights helpful to answering this question may be obtained from a brief preliminary consideration of the purposes of teaching philosophy in general. Surely one of the primary objectives of such an enterprise is to teach the skill of philosophy, that is, to teach students how to develop abilities and competencies sufficient to undertake the proper and fruitful conduct of philosophic inquiry. The discipline, by its very nature, presents unique requirements; since it is essentially a "do-it-yourself enterprise," the instructor must ensure that the teaching methods and learning devices utilized in the classroom directly achieve the desired goals.

In philosophy it is less important to accumulate and transmit vast data banks, or a body of knowledge, than it is to think effectively. Philosophy is a method, a skill, something one learns to do. It involves learning how to ask questions until meaningful answers begin to appear; how to relate ideas, concepts, and materials; how to adjudicate differences, to check fact claims, to determine truth, and to reject fallacious assertions and arguments (Christian 1973, xvi); and, finally, it entails the creative exploration of new directions.

If this delineation of philosophy is correct, and I find it to be so, it is, at the very least, questionable whether the ubiquitous and traditional "forty-five minute lecture–five minutes of questions, if any–exam" method of teaching is the most conducive to the furthering of philosophic ideals. In such endeavors, the instructor imparts, speaks, or casts forth information that the student, only remotely attached to the pedagogical process, passively files in an appropriate receptacle in an unenthusiastic and uninformed manner to be resurrected solely in preparation for tests.

However, it may be ventured that teaching philosophy is rather empty if reduced to a memorization of "who said what, and when" or "how one philosophical view compares with another" as ends in themselves. It takes on significance only when students begin to manifest the capacity to think for themselves and to figure out their own answers to significant problems (Lipman 1977, 61).

The teaching of the philosophy of sport does not have to be a dreary, monotonous, authoritative affair, focusing upon a very delimited class of acceptable issues of one discursive line. It is helpful to remember here that "the word 'educate' is closely related to the word 'educe'" (Postman and Weingartner 1969, 62). In the oldest pedagogic sense of the term, this means helping to draw out insights and latent potentials from students. Surely it is possible to involve the students more and to generate sufficient interest and excitement from within to make them become active pursuers, not simply spectators, of wisdom and knowledge. Philosophic insight is best achieved through participatory and individually relevant modes (Postman and Weingartner 1969, 19).

Thus, it would appear that a class based upon active student involvement through discussion, questioning, dialogue, and personal inquiry would be a most appropriate procedure for the attainment of philosophic ends. However, it must be noted at this point that a philosophic discussion, if properly conducted, is not a random conversation and aimless bull session, but rather an attempt by the instructor to foster thoughtful, rational, and creative insights. Commencing with an appropriately limited problem or topic, the discussion, if properly guided, is a sequential, developing, and cumulatively enlarging enterprise, at best opening new vistas and eliciting new perceptions and ideas.

9

All teachers of philosophy are, or should be, conversant with the rudimentary elements necessary for productive discussion to occur so that space need not be allocated here to this facet. These include clarification of the issue at hand, preliminary discourse on whether or not the question can be answered philosophically, unearthing presuppositions as well as examining expressed or latent assumptions, analyzing the reasoning process and supportive material presented by the author, evaluating proposed solutions, and considering ensuing implications or consequences. Nonetheless, it is necessary to stress that during these sessions, the instructor should properly act as a motivator, facilitator, or inquisitive guide assisting in the cooperative pursuit of genuine philosophic inquiry by encouraging; stimulating; challenging; and, if need be, provoking students to engage in careful analysis and reflection, to exhibit resourcefulness and intellectual flexibility in seeking understanding, and to pursue new sensibilities and imaginative directions. In sum, the instructor is a fellow participant in the philosophical venture.

In my experience in teaching the philosophy of sport, I have found it to be particularly helpful to induce playfulness, temporarily tolerating disorder or even chaos, to produce a liberating educational occurrence. That is, to promote the sharing of ideas and insights, at times I deliberately seek to generate a *creative disturbance* within the classroom. To achieve this end, I utilize the technique of "improvised drama" or "role playing" to portray a character or represent a position that I anticipate will both excite and disturb my students, since it is chosen deliberately to challenge or refute what I expect they wish to, or indeed do, believe. The consequent emotional arousal elicited by playing the "devil's advocate" stimulates their intellectual curiosity and certainly facilitates discussion, even if it is limited at first to a desperate pursuit of attempted rational justifications of previously cherished positions.

Several components of the described course of study lend themselves to this particular technique. Some representative, but by no means exhaustive, examples are as follows:

1. Appropriating the mantle of a convinced and ardent dualist (say, Plato), to forward a doctrine acknowledging the clear superiority of the mind over the body and, consequently, advocating the subservience of "physical" education to "regular" education, or even the elimination of the entire program from secondary and tertiary institutions of learning, due to its lack of contribution to the development of the intellect. (Needless to say, physical education students' own clear awareness of the negative, anti-intellectual stereotypes attached to, and charges directed against, their chosen degree program, already marks this as a sensitive issue.)
2. Advocating that play is at heart a useless enterprise and, therefore, while it might be acceptable behavior for young children, its manifestations should not be tolerated among adults; consequently, every effort should be made to stamp it out in all of its insidious forms.
3. Championing the position, as a high school or university coach, that "winning is everything" or, conversely, that "winning is nothing," and acting on that principle.
4. Supporting the position that the philosophic case *against* banning the utilization of performance-enhancing drugs in preparation for athletic competition is so strong, that any such ban is unjustified and, consequently, should be discarded. After extensive, and at times heated, discussion over several class periods, students usually end up begrudgingly acknowledging that the ten or so reasons most often forwarded as rationales supporting a ban on drugs are all philosophically faulty and, therefore, that there is no sound justification for this restriction. (Since this is a position which I personally support, it makes it both easy and enjoyable to act out.)

In summary, I find that the "creative disturbance" resulting from the adroit utilization of this procedure is usually very productive as a starting, not culminating, venture that demonstrates the strengths and weaknesses of specific positions, points out challenging questions yet to be addressed, and suggests paths which must be traveled for resolutions to be manifested.

10

An important qualifying note must be introduced at this point. Despite the obvious importance of, and the positive benefits accruing from, in-class dialogue in its various forms—after all, questioning and discussion are at the heart of the philosophic venture, since these processes convert students from passive recipients of previously packaged information into active participants on the journey to enlightenment and understanding—there are serious limitations to relying solely on this technique. Three particular deficiencies warrant mention here: (1) the difficulty of finding time sufficient to handle all of the pertinent issues and ramifications, given the typical fifty-minute class; (2) the "dampening" effect of sheer student numbers that, of necessity, limit opportunities for all students to participate or to reply to queries raised; and (3) the potential negative aspect of the lack of willingness or ability of some students to venture forth in public discourse, much less to receive criticism from their classmates. All of these factors may truncate the effectiveness of this process.

On a somewhat related matter, I wish to discuss briefly and, concurrently, to advocate the abandonment of a device that is not infrequently employed in sport study classes—in physical education courses far more so than those offered in philosophy departments—namely, in-class, more or less formal, debates. Although I did on early occasions utilize this approach, I have become almost totally disenchanted with it for at least three substantial reasons. First, the imposition of truncated time limits (usually five to eight minutes for first affirmative, first negative, second affirmative, and rebuttal) often seriously damages, rather than facilitates, the careful development of an issue, the forwarding of meaningful counterarguments, or the presentation of supported premises culminating in well-developed conclusions. Second, the ability to provide rapid rather than telling retorts, facility in the utilization of inflammatory language, and gifts of audience persuasion, are all rhetorical skills highly rewarded in debates; unfortunately, these factors are often irrelevant to the meaningful investigation of a particular topic or the philosophical pursuit of truth. Third, the adversarial approach—if oriented toward attacking and discrediting the character or sincerity of the classmate-opponent rather than the substance of the issue, with the ultimate aim of producing passionate support among the spectators, is often counterproductive to competent philosophical analysis.

Thus, while I find the utilization of the "role-playing" approach to be an interesting and vibrant introductory means of demonstrating the questions that will have to be resolved, I do not support the employment of student debates. Frequently in such occurrences the impression is erroneously conveyed that something of substance has transpired and that a well-substantiated position, if not the final word on the issue, has been forwarded and duly anointed by means of a vote at the end of class. Unfortunately, this is seldom the case. In summary, debates are of limited value indeed (beyond reducing the instructor's class preparation time or providing relief from a normally dull course) and possess few meritorious pedagogical assets.

In my opinion, the solution to some of the difficulties previously alluded to is to provide students with an opportunity for serious and concerted reflection on the issues and assigned readings outside of the classroom. This can be handled in a beneficial manner in at least three ways. The first procedure is to assign a *reaction paper* at appropriate junctures in the course proceedings. This is a three- to five-page written report designed specifically to permit students the opportunity to organize and synthesize materials as they progress or, conversely, to explore and critically evaluate specific readings or postulated conclusions. The assignment demonstrates students' insight into and comprehension of the pertinent topics, without potentially usurping, or being unduly influenced by others' comments. (For several examples of potential reaction papers, see Appendix IV.) The second option is the standard *philosophical research paper* on a topic directly related to the course content. Many of the readings assigned during the semester provide ready examples of the appropriate procedures to be employed herein, so no further comment is required. The third and final option is the undertaking of a *philosophical project, creation, or production* different from that described in the previous two tasks. This exercise is usually chosen by students who feel that the other choices are, for whatever reasons, too limiting. Further details on this project are provided in the evaluation procedure section listed in Appendix II.

Of course, there are most assuredly additional teaching techniques that may be profitably employed in the philosophy of sport—including the use of motion pictures, philosophical diaries, group discussion papers; not to mention the devices and options described by the other authors in this volume in relation to their own specific subdisciplines—but, perhaps, enough has been said to provide some guidance to those who currently toil in these vineyards or wish to in the future.

11

It is my hope that this chapter has demonstrated that the philosophy of sport is an enticing and stimulating, applied venture; a philosophical journey to be experienced and cultivated, not merely professed. Courses in this area of intellectual inquiry, thus, if conducted in an appropriate manner, can be most meritorious and satisfying experiences for both students and instructors alike. In addition, it should now be apparent that serious philosophical research, particularly from a phenomenological perspective, has much to contribute to the continuing investigation, and expanded understanding of, the structure, inherent possibilities, and significance of sport, play, and games.

I wish to conclude, therefore, by asserting that such endeavors should be encouraged most vigorously, received very positively, and savored at considerable length; in such happy circumstances, all concerned will surely benefit.

NOTE

Some portions of this chapter are extended revisions of segments of a paper presented at a workshop on the teaching of philosophy entitled "The Phenomenon of Sport: Innovative Ways to Teach Philosophy," conducted as a component of the XVII World Congress of Philosophy held in Montreal, Canada, 21–27 August 1983.

APPENDIX I: COMPETITION, SPORTSMANSHIP, AND CHEATING

Somewhat surprisingly, there are few philosophical studies addressing themselves to the topic of competition; although economic and political theory takes the issue to heart, philosophy in general has not. However, an increasing body of literature is developing within the philosophy of sport that provides some amelioration of this rather obvious deficiency.

I usually begin this section of the course with a perusal of Alan Sillitoe's short story "The Loneliness of the Long Distance Runner" (1959). It should be noted that the prose version is preferred over the derivative motion picture, which inadequately presents or alters, for present purposes at least, certain important components of the original work. In addition to providing a good description of the exceptional possibilities for self-understanding available through participation in such activities as cross-country running, this piece graphically introduces negative assessments of the importance of winning in sport contests. The protagonist, an unrepentant petty thief sent to a British correctional institution for character reformation, deliberately loses a championship race that he could easily have won to present his own personal statement against manipulation, objectification, and exploitation in sport. This act, and the story as a whole, focus attention on the fact that there are difficulties in assuming a unitary structure or purpose to either sport or competition therein; conflicting orientations, value structures, and expectations potentially present major difficulties in sport participation.

To pursue this issue further, several analyses and position papers extolling or condemning competition are perused, including an exploration of certain myths concerned with its outcome. Sadler's argument that contemporary competition, including that evidenced in sport, has outstepped its proper boundaries (1973); Tutko's psychological analysis of the negative symptoms of the winning craze (1976); Ringer's exuberant extolling of "winning through intimidation" and "looking out for number one" (1976); Lasch's condemnation of the corruption of sport in the contemporary culture of narcissism (Morgan and Meier); and numerous other analyses all provide arguments worthy of philosophical investigation and discussion.

In an attempt to adjudicate the readily apparent divergence of arguments concerned with the importance and priority of winning and losing in sport, it is helpful to utilize the distinction between the playful and nonplayful sport repeatedly forwarded by Keating in several philosophical articles (e.g., Morgan and Meier 1988). The differentiation of nature, purpose and orientation presented here, although it does present difficulties of its own, assists in the resolution of some problems. For early critical reactions to Keating's position, see Sadler (1973) and Osterhoudt (1973); Feezell's essay (Morgan and Meier 1988) presents a more contemporary rebuttal. This entire unit conveniently draws the discussion back to the insights derived in the first section of the course, namely, the nature and interrelationships among sport, play, and games.

Obviously, this question is only one issue in a much larger axiological tapestry. There are numerous ethical situations that may be highlighted by the analysis of sport situations. At this point, I will do nothing more than list selected issues and questions worthy of consideration. Indeed, all have already been the object of various and extended analyses in the philosophy of sport literature. The interested reader is directed to the reading outline provided in Appendix II, particularly section 5, "Sport and Ethics," for a listing of the titles and publication sources for more than two dozen articles which directly address the concerns about to be delineated:

1. What are the requirements and forms of manifestation of "sportsmanship" in sport, play, and games?
2. Related to this, what moral imperatives are operational in sport; that is, what is "justice" or "fair play" in sport?
3. The question of obedience to the rules; namely, what types of agreements, contracts, promises or obligations, implicit or explicit, does a player have?
4. Further, do sanctions restore equilibrium and maintain the rules as well as the "integrity of the game"?
5. What is entailed in deception, deliberate cheating, and "the good foul"?
6. Issues concerned with surreptitious or blatant drug utilization; other aspects such as "blood doping"; and the more recent "urine transfusion" technique designed to avoid chemical detection.
7. The merits and demerits of permitting gambling in and on sports by spectators, coaches, and players.
8. The positive reinforcement of violent sports.
9. And finally, discrimination against women in sport, and the question of androgyny.

In summary, it is readily apparent that sport situations, either experienced first-hand through participation or as described every day in the various communications media, provide not only widespread "coins of exchange" among many university students, but also possibilities of careful reflection concerning problems of appropriate and inappropriate conduct in sports, and finally, useful avenues of entrance into the entire, broad realm of ethical discourse.

APPENDIX II: SYLLABUS PHYSICAL EDUCATION 390: PHILOSOPHY OF SPORT AND PHYSICAL ACTIVITY UNIVERSITY OF WESTERN ONTARIO

Dr. Klaus V. Meier
133 Somerville House
679-2111, Ext. 5479

INTRODUCTION

The purpose of this course is to provide the student with *introductory exposure* to the various techniques and fruits of philosophic research in the area of sport, exercise, games and play (hereafter referred to as SEGP). The readings, lectures, discussions, and presentations are designed to pursue carefully and vigorously the answers to questions and issues derived from the following *general course objectives:*

1. To propose that certain philosophic questions of a metaphysical, epistemological, and axiological nature are appropriate in studying and identifying the nature and meaning of SEGP.
2. To distinguish philosophic knowledge of SEGP from scientific knowledge.
3. To examine philosophic approaches of inquiry in the study of SEGP, including analysis of definable characteristics, similarities, and differences.
4. To determine whether participation in SEGP is necessary for understanding and comprehending these human activities.
5. To investigate participation in SEGP as a source of knowledge of the human condition and of personal identity.
6. To examine values of, and inherent within, SEGP; further, to identify postulated value demands (e.g., "fair play") of various forms of these activities.
7. To examine the relevance of the philosophic examination of SEGP for the study of physical education.

REQUIRED TEXT

Morgan, William J., and Klaus V. Meier, Eds. *Philosophic Inquiry in Sport*. Champaign, Ill.: Human Kinetics Publishers, 1988.

EVALUATION PROCEDURES

Preliminary Requirements:

1. The completion of all reading assignments.
2. Participation in discussion and critique sessions.

Reaction Papers:

One or two brief three- to five-page reaction papers, critical analysis and/or summary statements designed to provide opportunities to explore, to demonstrate comprehension of, and to evaluate specific readings or topics *may* be assigned.

CHOICE of term test, research paper, or philosophic project

Each student will select *one* of the following three options. The option selected should be the one that the student perceives to be the most appropriate vehicle to demonstrate insight into and competency with the subject matter under discussion.

1. A *term test* to be written at an appropriate time. The test will be composed of a combination of true and false, multiple choice, short-answer, and short essay questions. The specific format and materials included, as well as the specific test date, will be announced sufficiently in advance to minimize apprehension.

OR

2. A *philosophical research paper* on a topic directly related to the course content may be substituted for the term test with the prior permission of the instructor. A brief outline delineating the topic to be investigated, the sources of information, and a selected bibliography *must* be approved in writing by the instructor one week prior to the date of the term test. *Two* copies of this outline must be submitted; one will be retained. The final

paper should demonstrate appropriate form and style (use the *Journal of the Philosophy of Sport* as a guide), and range between twelve and twenty-five typed, double-spaced pages. *Two* copies of the completed paper must be submitted; one will be retained.

OR

3. A *philosophical project, creation, or production*, approved in advance by the instructor as satisfying the course requirements. This option is to be exercised if the student feels that the previously delineated options are too limited and a suitable critical, reasonably structured, alternative relevant to the philosophical analysis of sport, in accord with the course focus, is suggested as a project. To insure equity, the time commitment for such a project, in terms of preparation, execution, or presentation, should approximate that required for the satisfaction of the previous options.

Final examination:

The class will decide, as a whole, which *one* of the following three options it cares to exercise:

1. Traditional, sight unseen, two- or three-hour comprehensive examination, the format to be decided by the class and the instructor, to be written during the scheduled final examination period.
2. Exam questions to be distributed one week before the scheduled test period, but the exam to be written in that period without notes, texts, or any other physical or interpersonal supportive material.
3. Take-home examination to be distributed during the last week of classes and due before, or within, the scheduled examination period.

Additional Information

It should be noted that students will be expected to possess and demonstrate the following characteristics and competencies: (1) the ability to respond to oral and written questions and to write grammatically intelligible examinations: (2) the ability to think critically about written materials of some difficulty; (3) to be aware of the differences between opinions and philosophic arguments; and (4) to have commitment to rational inquiry. Thus, class attendance and an ability to memorize facts and lecture notes, although surely individually beneficial, will not suffice in total. Other competencies should be cultivated.

TOPIC AND READING OUTLINE

The following list should be utilized as a *guide* to selections to be read and discussed, not an inflexible schedule. *All of the following articles will not be assigned* during the semester. Class presentations, extended exploration of aspects perceived to be particularly significant by the class, and other similar occurrences will, of necessity require modification and alteration in the schedule.

Guide to Symbols:

(M&M): *Morgan and Meier* required text.
(LR): Library Reserve holdings.

The full bibliographical reference for Library Reserve holdings may be readily obtained from the "1987 PSSS Bibliography on the Philosophy of Sport" to be found in Volume 14 (1987), *Journal of the Philosophy of Sport* (containing more than 1,100 entries). For the sake of brevity, they are not repeated here. References for essays not listed therein will be provided when the individual topics are addressed.

1. Introduction to the Philosophy of Sport:

Introduction to Philosophy
The Nature of the Philosophy of Sport
Philosophic Modes of Inquiry
Philosophic and Scientific Knowledge
Physical Education as an Academic Discipline

Harper, "The Philosopher in Us." (LR).
Lyons, "You Asked About Philosophy?" (LR).
Fraleigh, "Toward a Conceptual Model of the Academic Subject of Physical Education as a Discipline." (LR).

2. The Nature of Sport, Play and Games

Huizinga, "The Nature of Play." (M&M).
Caillois, "The Structure and Classification of Games." (M&M).
Schmitz, "Sport and Play: Suspension of the Ordinary." (M&M).
Suits, "Words on Play." (M&M).
McBride, "Toward a Non-Definition of Sport." (LR).
Suits, "The Elements of Sport." (M&M).
McBride, "A Critique of Mr. Suits's Definition of Game Playing." (LR).
Suits, "On McBride on the Definition of Games." (M&M).
Osterhoudt, "The Term 'Sport': Some Thoughts on a Proper Name." (LR).
Meier, "On the Inadequacies of Sociological Definitions of Sport." (LR).

3. Sport and the Body

Plato, "The Separation of Body and Soul." (M&M).
Descartes, "The Real Distinction Between Mind and Body." (M&M).
Weiss, "The Challenge of the Body." (M&M).
Meier, "Embodiment, Sport and Meaning." (M&M).
Sartre, "The Body." (M&M).
Marcel, "If I Am My Body." (M&M).
Schrag, "The Lived Body as Phenomenological Datum." (M&M).
Zaner, "The Radical Reality of the Human Body." (LR).
Herman, "Mechanism and the Athlete." (LR).
Ravizza, "The Body Unaware." (LR).
Fahey, "The Passionate Body." (LR).
Keen, "The Importance of Being Carnal: Notes for a Visceral Theology." (LR).
DeWachter, "The Symbolism of the Healthy Body." (M&M).
Lingis, "Orchids and Muscles." (M&M).

4. Sport and Metaphysics

a. Sport as Meaningful Experience
Progen, "Man, Nature and Sport." (LR).
Harper, "Man Alone." (LR).
Slusher, "To Test the Wave is to Test Life." (LR).
Coutts, "Freedom in Sport." (LR).
Zaner, "Sport and the Moral Order." (LR).

b. Risk, Death and Sport
Tolstoy, "The Death of Ivan Ilyitch." (LR).
Gorer, "The Pornography of Death." (LR).
Koestenbaum, "The Vitality of Death." (LR).
Keen, "On Dying (and Living) with Dignity." (LR).
Herzog, *Annapurna*. (LR).
Alvarez, "I Like to Risk My Life." (LR).
Sayre, "Why Men Climb." (LR).
Petersen, "Because it's Nowhere." (LR).
Wyschogrod, "Sport, Death and the Elemental." (LR).

c. The World of Play
Fink, "The Ontology of Play." (M&M).
Burke, "Taking Play Seriously." (M&M).
Sartre, "Play and Sport." (M&M).
Esposito, "Play and Possibility." (M&M).
Sadler, "Play: A Basic Human Structure Involving Love and Freedom." (LR).
Algozin, "Man and Sport." (M&M).
Hyland, "The Stance of Play." (LR).
Meier, "An Affair of Flutes: An Appreciation of Play." (M&M).

5. Sport and Ethics
a. Competition, Sportsmanship, Cheating, and Failure
Sillitoe, *Loneliness of the Long Distance Runner*. (LR).
Sadler, "Competition Out of Bounds: Sport in American Life." (LR).
Kretchmar, "From Test to Contest: An Analysis of Two Kinds of Counterpoint in Sport." (M&M).
Keating, "Sportsmanship as a Moral Category." (M&M).
Osterhoudt, "On Keating on the Competitive Motif in Athletics and Playful Activities." (LR).
Feezell, "Sportsmanship." (M&M).
Keenan, "Justice and Sport." (LR).
Delattre, "Some Reflections on Success and Failure in Competitive Athletics." (M&M).
Hyland, "Competition and Friendship." (M&M).
Pearson, "Deception, Sportsmanship, and Ethics." (M&M).
Lehman, "Can Cheaters Play the Game?" (M&M).
Wertz, "The Varieties of Cheating." (LR).
Leaman, "Cheating and Fair Play in Sport." (M&M).

A. Drugs and Sport: Philosophical Issues
Simon, "Good Competition and Drug Enhanced Performance." (M&M).
Fraleigh, "Performance-Enhancing Drugs in Sport: The Ethical Issue." (LR).
Brown, "Paternalism, Drugs and the Nature of Sport." (M&M).
Perry, "Blood Doping and Athletic Competition." (M&M).
Thompson, "Privacy and the Urinalysis Testing of Athletes." (M&M).
Hoberman, "Sport and the Technological Image of Man." (M&M).

B. Women and Sport: Philosophical Issues
MacGuigan, "Is Woman a Question?" (LR).
English, "Sex Equality in Sports." (M&M).
Young, "The Exclusion of Women from Sport: Conceptual and Existential Dimensions." (M&M).

Belliotti, "Women, Sex and Sports." (M&M).
Wenz, "Human Equality in Sport." (M&M).
Pastow, "Women and Masculine Sport." (M&M).

C. Gambling and Sport
Thomas, "Do You 'Wanna' Bet: An Examination of Player Betting and the Integrity of the Sporting Event." (LR).
Keating, "The Philosophy of Gambling." (LR).

6. Sport and Social-Political Philosophy
Gasset, "The Sportive Origin of the State." (M&M).
Adorno, "Leisure." (M&M).
Horkheimer, "New Patterns of Social Relations." (M&M).
Lenk, "Towards a Social Philosophy of Achievement and Athletics." (M&M).
Lasch, "The Degradation of Sport." (M&M).
Morgan, "Play, Utopia, and Dystopia;: Prologue to a Ludic Theory of the State." (M&M).
Parry, "Hegemony and Sport." (M&M).

7. Sport and Aesthetics
Schiller, "Play and Beauty." (M&M).
Best, *Expression in Movement and the Arts.* (LR).
Cooper, "Do Sports Have an Aesthetic Content?" (LR).
Best, "The Aesthetic in Sport." (M&M).
Roberts, "Languages of Sport: Representation." (M&M).
Kupfer, "Sport: The Body Electric." (M&M).
Boxhill, "Beauty, Gender, and Sport." (M&M).
Kupfer, "A Commentary on 'Beauty, Gender, and Sport.'" (M&M).
Wertz, "Context and Intention in Sport and Art." (M&M).
Best, "Sport is not Art." (M&M).

APPENDIX III: SELECTIVE EXAMINATION QUESTION BANK

Over the course of more than a decade of teaching in the area of the philosophy of sport, I have found the following questions to be both appropriate and helpful in assessing students' understanding of some of the materials assigned and discussed extensively in class. Of course, not all questions are included in any one examination; however, some are included in all of the tests that students select to undertake. (A philosophical research paper may be substituted for a term test.) Although most of the questions allow the student to synthesize and expand upon the assigned readings in the area of phenomenology and existential philosophy, I have also included several items which address other pertinent areas of philosophical inquiry.

PHENOMENOLOGY AND EXISTENTIAL PHILOSOPHY

1. The class discussions and readings concerned with *embodiment* emphasized the problem of mind-body interaction inherent in *dualistic* conceptions of man. *Briefly describe*: (a) the history of the dualistic conception of man; (b) what the problems of mind-body interaction are in this dualistic conception; (c) how the contemporary phenomenological perspective of man resolves the mind-body problem; and (d)

some of the positive consequences of accepting the phenomenological perspective of man for physical education programs.

2. Answer Part A or B

A. Jean-Paul Sartre asserts that "man is not what he is, but is what he is not." What is the meaning of this statement?

OR

B. Kierkegaard asserts that "to venture causes anxiety, but not to venture is to lose one's self." What is the meaning of this statement?

3. In Beckett's *Waiting for Godot*, Estragon states that "we always find something, eh Didi, to give us the impression we exist." In relation to the proceedings of the play, what does Estragon mean by this statement?

4. Sport, Human Identity, and Authentic Existence. The following two questions allow the student to incorporate major segments of the course. *Only one of the two should be placed on any examination*, for reasons of obvious overlap. If Beckett, Heidegger, Sartre, and some of the other primary literature has been addressed (such as suggested for graduate courses) then question A is probably preferable; question B is more appropriate for undergraduate course experiences which concern themselves only to a limited extent with the original philosophic sources. Both questions should be allotted *forty-five to sixty minutes* for satisfactory responses. It is also possible to utilize either question as a *reaction paper assignment* to provide a conclusion for a particular course segment.

A. Beckett's *Waiting for Godot* graphically presents one view of the human condition in the present age and addresses itself, in part, to the question of authentic and inauthentic existence. Some of the essays discussed in class assert that sport may be viewed appropriately as "providing man with an opportunity to locate his own being." It is also contended in the literature that sport presents man with a potential forum for awareness and attainment of authentic existence. Describe how participation in sport, in your opinion, facilitates and contributes to the discovery, development, and fulfillment of authentic existence. In responding to this assignment you should also discuss the preliminary issue of just what is entailed in authentic and inauthentic existence before proceeding to an analysis of sport.

OR

B. A significant portion of the course concerned itself with sport as meaningful experience. Many of the readings strongly suggested and attempted to demonstrate that engagement in sport, play and games provides man with an opportunity to locate himself and presents him with a potential forum for the attainment of awareness of *personal human identity*. Delineate how participation in sport, *both alone and with others*, permits or facilitates the development of personal identity; that is, how does such engagement aid in developing a response to the question, "Who Am I?" Describe both the *importance* and the *process* of this occurrence, with sport examples when beneficial.

5. Zorba the Greek stated that "a man must have a little madness or else he will not be free." Explain the meaning of this statement utilizing insights derived from our extended discussions of man's participation in sports and physical activities.

6. *Death* is the question existence puts to everyone. Briefly discuss several significant and positive features resulting from the fact of death for man and relate these to participation in risk sports.

SPORT AND VALUE INQUIRY

7. Develop a philosophical argument in *support* of the following proposition: "Schools and/or programs of physical education should foster the *intrinsic* values of sport, games, and play in preference to the *instrumental* values of the same."

8. Kathleen Pearson ("Deception, Sportsmanship, and Ethics") condemns the deliberate or intentional foul as being an unethical act for two major reasons, namely: (1) such action is a "deliberate betrayal of the rules [that] destroys the vital frame of agreement which makes sport possible"; and (2) it is erroneous to suggest that due to the fact that penalties for fouling are contained within the rulebook for a particular sport, fouls are not outside the rules for the game, since this would be like asserting that since penalties for breaking the law in society are contained within the law books, all acts are within the law. Thus, it appears that according to Pearson, intentional acts are clearly instances of cheating. Do you agree or disagree with her position? Present reasons for your evaluation.

9. Clifton Perry ("Blood Doping and Athletic Performance") states that it is permissible to enhance athletic performance through supplementation *if* at least one of three specific functions is fulfilled. One of these three conditions is that "the enhanced performance may be seen as the reaction to an undesired inhibitor to better performance." Does blood doping not perform this function by enhancing the circulatory system's capacity to transport oxygen beyond its normally limited level? In other words, is blood doping not permissible under Perry's own condition? Present support for your decision.

10. In class we spent a considerable period of time discussing *ten specific reasons or arguments* often forwarded as moral justifications *for banning the utilization of drugs* to enhance athletic performance. In the end, *we dismissed them all* as lacking sufficient philosophical justification. *Answer either Part A or B below:*

A. It may be the case that not all possible supporting arguments for any one specific reason were raised in the class discussions. If you think that this is the case: (1) state which one of the ten reasons you wish to discuss further; (2) present the rationale leading to its dismissal in class; (3) discuss why you think that, upon further reflection, the rationale was not sufficient for dismissal; and (4) present any additional information, responses, or arguments supporting your case.

OR

B. Clearly describe and defend an *additional reason* that is different from the ten discussed in class.

11. Consider the following assertion:

> The imposition of a ban on the utilization of drugs to enhance athletic performance is of a similar nature to the imposition of other arbitrary rules and regulations in sport—for examples, permitting only four downs to move the ball ten yards in football; not permitting the use of the hands to move the ball in soccer by any player except the goalkeeper; permitting only three steps without dribbling the ball in basketball—and therefore the ban may be justified in a similar manner.

Do you agree or disagree with this assertion? Present philosophic support for your position.

OTHER ASPECTS OF THE PHILOSOPHY OF SPORT

12. How is *philosophic knowledge* of sport, games, and play distinct from *scientific knowledge*? Why are both relevant to the study and understanding of these three activities?

13. *Answer Part A or B:*

A. Huizinga, for one, expends considerable effort in discussing the "disinterestedness of play." Briefly explain this characterization.

OR

B. It is sometimes asserted, for example, by Huizinga, that the playworld is a "separate" world. Briefly explain this characterization.

14. The philosophical literature sometimes asserts that play, games, and sport may be placed on a continuum as follows

play games sport

in which increasing standardization and institutionalization determine the progressive changes from play to games to sport. According to the extensive discussions of the basic structures of these three human activities that transpired at the beginning of the course—including the three individual definitions finally accepted as being the most appropriate and accurate—is this continuum correct? Present reasons for your response, either positive or negative.

15. Utilize any concept or idea concerned with the philosophy of sport to which you assign significance (and which has *not* already been discussed extensively in the previous questions) arising from course orientation or focus, the readings, the lectures and discussions, or other appropriate sources *to formulate your own question* and to respond to it. State the question as clearly and precisely as possible. Demonstrate the significance of the problem. You will be evaluated both on the merit of the question and on the depth and insight of the answer.

APPENDIX IV: SELECTED REACTION PAPERS

THE QUESTION OF EMBODIMENT

Utilizing materials derived predominantly from the class discussions and readings concerned with embodiment, respond in some detail to the following *two* questions:

1. *Why* is physical education usually perceived to be at or near the nadir of the educational hierarchy or sometimes excluded totally from an educational program?
2. In your opinion, *what steps* should be taken to rectify this situation?

ANNAPURNA

1. Read *Annapurna* carefully; reflect on the insights, if any, gained from the book.
2. Write a short paper delineating your personal reactions to it. You may discuss any ideas, concepts, or portions of the book you deem significant, including the goals, actions, results, or merits of the expedition. You may also wish to describe how the book affected you, in one way or another, as an individual and/or physical education student.
3. NOTE: There are no right or wrong answers. The paper is designed to give you an opportunity to assess, positively or negatively, the significance of the venture and reflect upon any meanings and information about sport that you may find in Herzog's book.
4. The paper, preferably, should be typed and limited to five double-spaced pages. If it is written, please write clearly, double-spaced and on one side of the page only.

SPORT, HUMAN IDENTITY, AND AUTHENTIC EXISTENCE

See Appendix III, "Selective Examination Question Bank," question number 4, for two possible reaction paper assignments. The first deals with sport and authentic existence, the second with sport and the attainment of human identity; either may be utilized productively to provide a conclusion for a particular course segment.

WORKS CITED

Alvarez, A. 1976. "I Like to Risk My Life." *Saturday Evening Post*, 9 September, 10–12.

Beckett, Samuel. 1954. *Waiting for Godot*. New York: Grove Press.

Berman, Neil David. 1981. *Playful Fictions and Fictional Players*. Port Washington, N.Y.: Kennikat Press.

Caspar, Ruth. 1978. "Play Springs Eternal." *New Scholasticism* 52: 187–201.

Christian, James L. 1973. *Philosophy: An Introduction to the Art of Wondering*. San Francisco: Rinehart Press.

Coover, Robert. 1968. *The Universal Baseball Association, Inc., J. Henry Waugh, Prop*. New York: Plume Books.

Coutts, C. A. 1968. "Freedom and Sport." *Quest* 10: 68–71.

DeLillo, Don. 1973. *End Zone*. 1972. New York: Pocket Books.

Ehrmann, Jacques. 1968. "Homo Ludens Revisited." In *Game, Play, Literature*. Jacques Ehrmann, ed. Boston: Beacon Press.

Esposito, Joseph. 1974. "Play and Possibility." Reprinted in Morgan and Meier.

Feezell, Randolph. 1986. "Sportsmanship." In Morgan and Meier.

Fell, Joseph P. 1979. "The Ethics of Play and Freedom." In *Heidegger and Sartre: An Essay on Being and Place*. New York: Columbia University Press.

Fink, Eugen. 1960. "The Ontology of Play." Reprinted in Morgan and Meier.

Gardner, Leonard. 1969. *Fat City*. New York: Farrar, Straus and Giroux.

Gent, Peter. 1974. *North Dallas Forty*. 1973. New York: Signet.

Gerber, Ellen W., and William J. Morgan, eds. 1979. *Sport and the Body: A Philosophical Symposium*. 2d ed. Philadelphia: Lea and Febiger.

Gorer, Geoffrey. 1976. "The Pornography of Death." In *Death: Current Perspectives*. E. S. Shneidman, ed. Palo Alto, Calif.: Mayfield.

Harper, William. 1969. "Man Alone." *Quest* 12: 57–60.

Heidegger, Martin. 1962. *Being and Time*. Trans. J. Macquarrie and E. Robinson. New York: Harper and Row.

Herzog, Maurice. 1953. *Annapurna*. New York: Popular Library.

Hyland, Drew A. 1977. "'And That Is the Best Part of Us': Human Beings and Play." *Journal of the Philosophy of Sport* 4: 36–49.

Jaspers, Karl. 1970. *Philosophy 2*. Trans. E. B. Ashton. Chicago: University of Chicago Press.

Kaufman, Walter, ed. 1970. *Existentialism from Dostoevsky to Sartre*. Cleveland: Meridian Books.

Keating, James. 1964. "Sportsmanship as a Moral Category." Reprinted in Morgan and Meier.

Keen, Sam. 1970. *To a Dancing God*. New York: Harper and Row.

Koestenbaum, Peter. 1971. *The Vitality of Death*. Westport, Conn.: Greenwood Press.

Krell, David. 1972. "Towards and Ontology of Play." *Research in Phenomenology* 2: 63–93.

Lasch, Christopher. 1979. "The Degradation of Sport." Reprinted in Morgan and Meier.

Lipman, Matthew, Ann M. Sharp, and Frederick Oscanyon. 1977. *Philosophy in the Classroom.* West Caldwell, N.J.: Universal Diversified Services.

Macquarrie, John. 1973. *Existentialism*. Harmondsworth, England: Pelican.

Meier, Klaus V. 1979. "Embodiment, Sport and Meaning." In *Sport and the Body: A Philosophical Symposium*. 2d ed. E. W. Gerber and W. J. Morgan, eds. Philadelphia: Lea and Febiger. Reprinted in Morgan and Meier.

———. 1981. "On the Inadequacies of Sociological Definitions of Sport." *International Review of Sport Sociology* 16, 2 no.2: 79–102.

———. "Restless Sport." *Journal of the Philosophy of Sport* 12 (1985): 64–77.

———. 1980. "An Affair of Flutes: An Appreciation of Play." Reprinted in Morgan and Meier.

Miller, Jason. 1983. *That Championship Season*. 1972. New York: Penguin.

Morgan, William J., and Klaus V. Meier, eds. 1988. *Philosophic Inquiry in Sport*. Champaign, Ill.: Human Kinetics.

Netzky, Ralph. "Playful Freedom: Sartre's Ontology Re-Appraised." *Philosophy Today* 18: 125–36.

Novak, Michael. 1976. *The Joy of Sports*. New York: Basic Books.

Osterhoudt, R. G. 1973. "On Keating on the Competitive Motif in Athletics and Playful Activity." In *The Philosophy of Sport: A Collection of Original Essays*. R. G. Osterhoudt, ed. Springfield, Ill.: Charles C. Thomas.

Postman, Neil, and Charles Weingartner. 1969. *Teaching as a Subversive Activity*. New York: Delta Books.

Progen, Jan. 1979. "Man, Nature, and Sport." In Gerber and Morgan.

Ringer, Robert J. 1976. *Winning through Intimidation*. Greenwich, Conn: Fawcett.

Sadler, William A., Jr. 1973. "Competition Out of Bounds: Sport in American Life." *Quest* 19: 124–32.

———. 1973. "A Contextual Approach to an Understanding of Competition: A Response to Keating's Philosophy of Competition." In Osterhoudt.

Sartre, Jean-Paul. 1956. *Being and Nothingness: An Essay on Phenomenological Ontology*. Trans. Hazel Barnes. New York: Washington Square.

———. 1956. "Play and Sport." Reprinted in Morgan and Meier.

Sayre, Woodrow. 1964. *Four Against Everest*. Englewood Cliffs, N.J.: Prentice-Hall.

Schrader, George A., ed. 1967. *Existential Philosophers: Kierkegaard to Merleau-Ponty*. New York: McGraw-Hill.

Sillitoe, Alan. 1959. *The Loneliness of the Long-Distance Runner*. New York: Signet.

Slusher, Howard. 1969. "To Test the Wave Is to Test Life." *JOHPERD* 40: 32–33.

Storey, David. 1962. *This Sporting Life*. Harmondsworth, England: Penguin.

———. *The Changing Room*. 1972. Harmondsworth, England: Penguin.

Tolstoy, Leo. 1960. *The Death of Ivan Ilyitch and Other Stories*. Trans. J. D. Duff and A. Maude. New York: Signet.

Tutko, Thomas. 1976. *Winning Is Everything and Other American Myths*. New York: Macmillan.

Vanderwerken, David L., and Spencer K. Wertz, eds. 1985. *Sport Inside Out: Readings in Literature and Philosophy*. Fort Worth: Texas Christian University Press.

Wyschogrod, Edith. 1973. "Sport, Death, and the Elemental." In *The Phenomenon of Death: Faces of Mortality*. Edith Wyschogrod, ed. New York: Harper and Row.

PART 4
Religion of Sport

7
Teaching "Religion and Sport: The Meeting of Sacred and Profane"

CHARLES S. PREBISH

It should be stated at the outset that my professional, scholarly training in the study of sport is unlike that of any other contributor to this study. In fact, I have no formal background in the study of sport at all. With a Ph.D. in Buddhist Studies (University of Wisconsin, 1971), I was until 1978 pursuing a teaching career in the Religious Studies Department at Pennsylvania State University. My involvement in sport consisted of a daily perusal of the sports section of the local newspaper, a cursory glance at *Sports Illustrated* while occupying my dentist's waiting room and a heavy dose of whatever ESPN offered. In other words, I was the classic prototype for Hans Lenk's now famous remark: "He who only knows the sport pages does not know very much about sport."

In the early winter of 1978, I returned to running after almost a decade and a half of bodily neglect, dietary excesses, and a not so modest investment in the tobacco industry. Needless to say, the attempt to reverse the results of fifteen years of self-abuse was neither simple nor painless. There was agony from countless blisters and aching Achilles tendons. My stomach quaked regularly, protesting the meager intake that was part of my reform regimen. Compared to the physical and emotional energy expended running five miles per day and losing forty pounds, stopping smoking was easy. I was simply too tired to bother with withdrawal symptoms. Within no time, my no-nonsense approach produced results: several visits to a sports podiatrist and dismaying suspicion that I was lcarning more than any other runners about blisters. As fate would have it, in May 1978 I was confronted with the greatest potential stumbling block in the life of the "born-again" runner—the race! The gurus in the running scene extol the virtues of racing. They call it "the payoff" or "the ruuner's reward." Little did I know that this preliminary involvement in racing was going to lead to my first professional teaching experience with a course on sport and religion.

Several months after my first road race, I began a sabbatical year in the San Francisco Bay Area, splitting my time between the University of California at Berkeley and the Graduate Theological Union. I was doing follow-up research on my book *American Buddhism* (1979), and no geographical area in the United States was more Buddhologically alive than San Francisco. It was also a thriving runners' community, and as I continued indulging my growing addiction to racing, I was also inadvertently gathering fieldwork data for my as yet unplanned course on sport and religion. Early in my sabbatical year, I began to notice marked similarities in the language and vocabulary used by athletes and religious aspirants. In addition, I observed other correspondences between the two groups. They both had clearly defined ritual practices, parallel communal institutions, heavy reliance on various rituals, and a shared theological perspective. I promised myself that upon my return to Penn State, I would pursue the matter of the relationship between sport and religion more carefully and professionally.

From September 1979 until June 1980 I read everything I could find on the relationship between religion and sport. To my surprise, the corpus of scholarly literature was far less formidable than I had imagined. Needless to say, there was a fair volume of material on the philosophy of sport, but only a few important references to the issues that I was exploring. To make matters worse, I was rapidly becoming convinced that for many Americans, sport *was* religion in the full, sacred sense of that word, and I could simply not find any references supporting that thesis. By the time my first experimental course was offered in Spring Quarter 1981 (Religious Studies 198: Religion and Sport—The Meeting of Sacred and Profane), I was still groping in the dark, and, to some degree, the classroom atmosphere mirrored my dilemma. The course was repeated the following year, and I was much more in control of the subject matter during that second offering; so much so that I immediately proposed the course for a permanent slot in the Religious Studies curriculum. As is now well known, the course was rejected by the Curricular Affairs Committee of the Liberal Arts College. Although I never received a formal statement of rejection outlining the reasons for the course's rejection, I was informally told that the committee felt both the course and my topic titles were rather "frivolous." Nonetheless, I was encouraged to revise my syllabus and resubmit the proposal. I was delighted to try again, and followed the committee chairman's suggestions carefully. What followed was amply covered and accurately portrayed in a 16 May 1984 article in *The Chronicle of Higher Education*. The only item missing in *The Chronicle* article was the final resolution, which was still pending. Since that date, my proposed course on religion and sport has been finally rejected by the Administrative Affairs Committee. So, to some degree, what follows in this essay refers to a corpse of a course rather than a viable entity. To make matters more puzzling, concurrent with its rejection of my course on sport and religion, the university approved another of my course proposals for a Humanities offering entitled "Sport: A Humanistic Perspective."

When my course on Religion and Sport was announced for the Spring Quarter of 1981, I seriously questioned whether anyone at all would register for it. I was truly surprised to discover that fifty individuals were brave enough to enroll. The class roster for the course revealed that about 75 percent of the students were from the College of Liberal Arts. Further checking indicated that less than one-third were varsity athletes, despite the fact that most of the students engaged in sport activities of various sorts regularly. On the first day of class, I began by asking two basic questions: (1) what is religion? and (2) what is sport? I got lots of responses to the first question, with most of the definitions offered reflecting a simple, naive understanding of the term. To the second question, I received *not one single response*; not even a quiet giggle could be heard in the room. In addition, amid a mass of downcast eyes that I have come to recognize as a sign of the "don't call on me" syndrome, even the professor was rendered speechless by this overwhelming, if disappointing display. Undaunted, I returned for the next class armed with more than a suspicion that a lot of preliminary lecturing would be prerequisite to the serious, complicated issues I hoped to explore. By the following year, when the class was offered again, the general class background had changed considerably. In 1982, more than 75 percent of the class members were varsity athletes; and while half were Liberal Arts students, the other half was comprised of primarily Business students. It was obvious that "word had gotten around," but I was not quite sure just what that "word" was. Nonetheless, I tried my two questions again. In response to queries about religion, the result was the same: lots of basic, modest, elementary answers. In response to my question about sport, I was overwhelmed by a flurry of raised hands. Perhaps 50 percent of the students in the class were just itching to offer some definition. Excited by such a display, I concluded that these students' serious involvement in sport had to account for the abrupt change in response from one year to the next. Obviously these varsity athletes knew their subject. One-by-one I called on each raised hand, and one-by-one each student volunteered some outlandish, startling, even silly (and always incorrect) bit of nonsense. I was crushed! How could these students, most of whom were being supported financially in the university by their facility in sport, not know something (or anything) about the driving force in their lives? As an aside, I can report that not too long ago I was invited to give the opening two lectures in a graduate seminar on the philosophy of sport. The professor, a world renowned sport historian, asked me to provide a basic introduction to the study of philosophy. He wanted his class to know something about the history of philosophy, its structure, major components, and the like. I was relieved that I did not have to relive the experience of my own recently concluded classes. By the end of the second class in the graduate seminar, things had gone so well that I could feel myself beginning to lose my head. Almost as if possessed, I began to head toward asking this array of sophisticated Physical Education graduate students just what the term "sport" meant to them. And when I finally lost all vestiges of restraint, asking my question with feverish anticipation, I was met with an immediate return to the "don't call on me" syndrome. Not one single answer, good or otherwise, was offered.

The basic structure that I have come to adopt for my course on religion and sport centers around four basic units:

1. Introductory Materials: Religion
2. Introductory Materials: Sport
3. The Relationship Between Religion and Sport
4. Sport as Religion in America.

Units 1 and 2 are essentially a structural mirror image of one another. These two units occupy roughly 50 percent of the semester, and I try to utilize them to provide sufficiently comprehensive background material in each discipline to enable each student to fully understand the unusual thesis that will be developed in units 3 and 4. I will be more explicit about the specifics of each unit shortly. An examination follows each of the four units. In addition, each student is required to submit a formal term paper of no less than fifteen pages. The term paper must address a significant issue in the study of religion and sport, with the topic being approved by the instructor. I have frequently encouraged the more creative of my students to submit nontraditional term papers—short stories, short plays, poetry samplers, for example. Some students have chosen to attend a specific Penn State sport (very often cross-country, football, or wrestling) throughout its season, reflecting on it as a religious rather than sporting event. They have included with their findings the results of surveys consisting of interviews with fans, players, and coaches, often providing less than supportive comments. Nonetheless, the term papers, traditional or otherwise, have generally provided the most significant learning experience of the semester in affording each student a personal, intimate axis of interaction with the course material.

To date, there is really no satisfactory textbook that can be utilized to present a balanced, comprehensive study of the relationship between religion and sport. Although the list of scholarly articles available has grown exponentially in the last decade, I have had better results in suggesting these studies as ancillary reading rather than primary source material. It has been my traditional practice, in this and all my academic courses, to assign a reading list heavy in both length and content. This does not mean to say that I assign only turgid volumes, overlooking anything that might be simply enjoyable. Rather, I want it clearly emphasized to my students, from the outset, that I expect them to read seriously, regularly, and reflectively. *Saturday Night Live, MTV*, and *Wrestlemania* must necessarily occupy recreation hours, VCRs and videotape notwithstanding. Several years ago I assigned a small book entitled *Zen Comics* (1974) as one of the texts in an "Introduction to Buddhism" course amid snickers and giggles. The laughter *began* to diminish as the students tried to understand the hidden meanings in the seemingly unsophisticated and rustic cartoons, and *absolutely* evaporated when they were asked to interpret one of them on the final exam.

For unit 1, I require my students to read Frederick Streng's *Understanding Religious Life* ([1969] 3d ed., 1985) and Mircea Eliade's *The Sacred and the Profane* ([1957] 1959). Streng's volume is among the most historically and methodologically precise introductions to the study of religion available. As the lead volume in The Religious Life of Man Series (Wadsworth), it is insightful, extremely well organized, and highly readable, while also affording extensive reference materials. Eliade's work, on the other hand, focuses on myth, symbol, and ritual; emphasizing what has come to be known as the "history of religion methodology." In *The Sacred and the Profane*, Eliade provides the reader with an opportunity to contextually place man's life experiences in the religious domain. He shows how symbol, ritual, and myth empower ordinary reality, cosmicizing it in the processs. Unit 2 relies on two further studies: *Sociology of American Sport* (1978) by D. Stanley Eitzen and George H. Sage and Howard Slusher's *Man, Sport and Existence: A Critical Analysis* (1967). I rely heavily on Eitzen and Sage primarily because I feel they do an extremely good job of helping beginning students make clear definitional distinctions between the terms play, game, and sport. These distinctions are absolutely critical in establishing a foundation for what is to come later in the course. In addition, two other freatures of the volume are especially helpful, First, the book presents a fair overview of sport study in general, making it quite easy for the student to see how the disciplines of the history of sport, sociology of sport, psychology of sport, and philosophy of sport parallel their counterpart in religious studies. Second, the book offers a highly readable chapter on sport and religion. To be sure, the chapter on sport and religion is especially introductory, but it does provide a flavor of what is going to be presented, albeit in more sophisticated terms, later. Slusher's volume, I suppose, is one of those books that has both strong critics and powerful advocates. To my mind, it is among the most lucid introductions to the philosophy of sport, written in a style that is more engaging than Weiss's *Sport: A Philosophic Inquiry* (1969), and more to the point than the vast majority of other attempts. It is also probably true that when Slusher says, "Like religion, sport offers its 'followers' a grouping of myths, symbols and rituals that facilitate the total experience" (127), he comes close to approximating my own position. Again, in suggesting "the arenas and coliseums are little more than shrines for *spiritual* activity" (127), or "Sport, as religion, is a form of *symbolic* representation of meaningful realities" (129), Slusher is clearly on my wavelength.

As I move into unit 3, I begin to introduce the students to Michael Novak's *The Joy of Sports* (1976). There is little doubt that I have been somewhat critical of Novak's work in my own essays and articles. Nevertheless, despite my feeling that Novak simply stops short of what appears painfully obvious from his supportive, preliminary work, there are portions of this book that are just brilliant, mapping out in print much that had not been expressed previously. I also utilize in this unit materials from other required course readings that emphasize the historical context of sport in America. In unit 4, I will want to focus on modern America, and on some general themes, each of which presupposes some historical spadework. Unit 4 introduces the final two books: Eugen Herrigel's classic *Zen in the Art of Archery* (1964) and George Leonard's eclectic *The Ultimate Athlete* (1975). No doubt I am fond of Herrigel's work due to my training as an Orientalist. The mystical dimension in sport, as a means of providing personal transcendence, is something I want my students to be aware of early in this unit. Herrigel does this far better than the more modern and artificial attempts of his successors. George Leonard's book is important too, not only because he indirectly suggests much of my major thesis in this unit, but rather because he teaches his readers how to think and experience reality in a new way. Most of my students have never read anything like *The Ultimate Athlete* before, and it shocks them perhaps in the same way that novice anthropologist Carlos Castañeda must have been shocked by some of don Juan Matus's antics in *The Teachings of don Juan* ([1969] 1971).

Although the reading material assigned for this course is roughly one-fourth greater than what I generally require for more traditional undergraduate courses, rarely have any students arrived for class unprepared to discuss the material at hand. Primarily because, in additional to being substantial and often complicated, it is also *highly engaging*; it almost always gets read—and thoroughly. The one desideratum for a course such as this, I think, would be a textbook devoted solely to religion and sport. Of course a book such as this would likely not be highly marketable, and given my own novel approach and thesis, could not be authored by me. Perhaps an edited anthology of the best articles that have appeared in the past decade might well do the job, providing a spectrum of opinions on the topic.

With regard to the course material itself, the most obvious and logical starting point for unit 1 is a reasonable, working definition of the basic term religion. Such a task proves quite formidable, though, because there are as many definitions of religion as there are researchers in the field, and each is likely to be idiosyncratic. The definition of religion that I find most valuable is Streng's. He says, "Religion is a means of ultimate transformation" (1985, 2). On the surface this seems almost too simple. Yet it's not. Streng goes on to explain that religion is a *means* of ultimate transformation in two ways (23–24):

> First, it expresses a practical process for achieving the most comprehensive transformation of life. The process is both the model and the effective action for transforming the individual, society, and all existence from the problematic state to the ideal. It eliminates or reforms the problematic character of life so that the ultimate reality is evident. Second, the process is not just a means to some end external to it but the consummation as well. This is because, from the religious advocate's perspective, the activity of salvation, enlightenment, and harmonious living has its deepest resource in, and thus expresses, the ultimate reality.

In other words, man experiences *ultimate* reality, be it God or some other, less specific symbol, and is radically *changed* by the experience. This radical change is also manifested in two ways. The first Streng calls the *personal expression*, reflecting the internal experience of the individual as freedom replaces the initial problematic state. The second way is referred to as the *social expression*, portraying the individual's transformation with regard to groups, communities, and social institutions. Thus, religion is the raft that ferries us from profane reality to the realm of the sacred, that enables us to transcend ordinary reality and directly apprehend ultimate reality. Once students are able to integrate this definition and application as a common starting point, achieved by some only after screaming and protesting as they are forced to cast off simplistic, home-inspired variations, we are ready to advance.

The next problem facing beginning students of religion is just *how* they should approach such study. Catherine Albanese, in *America: Religion and Religions* (1981), suggests four primary components in each religious system, and in describing them, she provides a start in determining just how one might study this complex phenomenon called religion. She refers to these components as the four *Cs*: creed, code, cultus, and community (8). A *creed* is an authoritative statement of beliefs and principles. It expresses a viewpoint shared by a given group. Religion is also expressed in *codes*, or statements of rules that govern the behavior of the group. The *cultus* (not to be confused with cult) is an aggregate of the ritual forms in a religious tradition. It is the acting out of ceremonies. These first three components bind together groups of individuals who share these notions into *communities*, the fourth component of religious systems. Taken collectively, Albanese's four *Cs* provide concrete data about the way in which religion is practiced. Once a means is found to integrate the data collected under these headings, students will have a functional tool with which to extend their pursuit. Streng provides the key. He argues (3–9) that religious life has three essential dimensions: personal, cultural, and ultimate. The first two dimensions are quite straightforward. The personal dimension involves each individual's perspective not only about his own religiosity, but also about his relationship to other individuals with possibly differing viewpoints. The cultural dimension provides a context that goes beyond simple individuality. It provides breadth, scope, and a panoramic outlook. Further, it brings the larger picture into clear concise focus. Although expressed through the personal and cultural dimensions, the ultimate dimension, "is the sensitivity for that to which one gives one's loyalty as the true character of life" (7). More succinctly, it is that beyond which it is impossible to go. If one now takes each of the four *Cs*, and applies it in turn to each of Streng's three dimensions of religious life, we have a potent method that can be employed in the study of religion, both generally and specifically.

With this preliminary material under control, students are then ready to begin to examine the fashion in which religion has been studied as a scholarly discipline. In one lecture I try to present a guided tour of the early researchers in the field, highlighting such individuals as F. Max Müller, E. B. Tylor, Sir James G. Frazer, Friedrich Schleiermacher, Karl Marx, Ernst Troelstch, Karl Barth, Rudolf Otto, Paul Tillich, R. C. Zaehner, and others. We discuss briefly their major works, approach to the field, and significant coutributions. Students generally tend to dislike this material. Perhaps it seems too much like cataloging the past, and if they are to engage in such endeavors at all, they would rather record Grete Waitz's times for the marathon or Billy Martin's tours of duty with the Yankees.

As we begin to move into the modern, disciplinary approaches to the study of religion, interest picks up a bit, possibly because my students embark on an exercise that has some real application to their own lives, and of course that is precisely why I commence the discussion of disciplines with psychology of religion. I suggest they browse through William James's *The Varieties of Religious Experience* ([1902] 1929) since it represents the starting point for the field. From there, we proceed through the two basic approaches: (1) the clinical approach, primarily of Freud, and (2) the humanistic-transpersonal approach of Gordon Allport, Carl Jung, Abraham Maslow, and others. The more mystically oriented students love to digress into Jung's musings on Tibetan Buddhism, while psychology majors are more comfortable with Maslow's work on peak experience (which they wrongly *equate* with religious experience). And there is always a fringe group that wants to do term papers on Charles Tart's *Altered States of Consciounsness* (1969). Having established a pattern, though, each of the remaining disciplines in the study of religion is considered in this fashion.

Following some straightforward work on rituals, I try to conclude the unit on religion with a lecture each on theology and religious experience. These are fun exercises. In the former, I try to get my students to reveal their own notions of God and/or ultimate reality. It is curious to see how many students still perceive God to be an old man with a long white beard sitting on a throne in the sky. It is also curious to see how many individuals now perceive God as female. Class generally gets rowdy with the God-as-male camp arguing with the God-as-female group, while both of these resist the God-as-beyond-gender approach. Equally, the theists assault the nontheists. The net result, generally, is that everyone begins some personal new theological investigation as well as cultivating a new appreciation of tolerance.

Some polls indicate that as many as seventy percent of the American population have had religious experiences. In my final lecture of unit 1, I ask my students to describe their own religious experiences, and use that sense of sharing to try to establish some basic guidelines for verifying and validating the genuine from the false. At the end, I offer Joachim Wach's method for determining the validity of religious experience. In *The Comparative Study of Religions* (1958, 30–36), he outlines four criteria that must be present in religious experiences. First, "religious experience is a response to what is experienced as Ultimate Reality." Second, the experience must be, "a total response of the total being." Third, the experience must be, "the most powerful, comprehensive, shattering, and profound experience of which man is capable." Finally, the experience "involves an imperative; it is the most powerful source of motivation and action." Needless to say, there are other yardsticks that might be used here. I simply think Wach's is best, and my students relate to it well too.

Based on their experience in unit 1, students generally seem to assume that unit 2 will be significantly less difficult. After all, sport is much more familiar to them than religion. Nonetheless, they are no more adept at defining, and distinguishing between, play, game, and sport than they were at defining religion. Although it may initially seem a bit tedious, I have found that starting from Huizinga's two definitions of play in *Homo Ludens* works well. First, Huizinga argues (1955, 13) that play is

> a free activity standing quite consciously outside "ordinary" life as being "not serious," but at the same time absorbing the player intensely and utterly. It is an activity connected with no material interest, and no profit can be gained by it. It proceeds within its own proper boundaries of time and space according to fixed rules and in an orderly manner. It promotes the formation of social groupings which tend to surround themseleves with secrecy and to stress their difference from the common world by disguise or other means.

Second (28),

> play is a voluntary action or occupation executed within certain fixed limits of time and place, according to rules freely accepted but absolutely binding, having its aim in itself and accompanied by a feeling of tension, joy and the consciousness that it is "different" from ordinary life.

Following this preliminary investigation of play, I discuss Roger Caillois's (1962) six basic requirements for play: (1) that it is *free*, voluntary; (2) that it is *separate*, limited in time and space; (3) that it is *uncertain*, the unexpected may result; (4) that it is *unproductive*, it yields no good; (5) that it is *governed by rules*, certain standard procedures prevail; (6) that it *utilizes make-believe*, stands outside reality.

From here, I try to help my students understand games as, in Allen Guttmann's terms, "organized play" (1978). I introduce them to Caillois's distinction between *agon*, *alea*, *mimicry*, and *ilinx*, with which they struggle, and to the delineation between physical skill games, strategy games, and games of chance (as noted by John W. Roberts and Brian Sutton-Smith 1962; 1968), which they understand very well and find helpful.

Defining sport, however, remains the most ambitious task. At the outset, with a little cajoling and encouragement, I try to coax about half a dozen attempts out of the class. With the help of the class, as critics, I try to point out what is strongest, and weakest, in each definitional attempt. I then survey the conclusions of a wide variety of writers, including individuals such as Howard Slusher (1967), James Michener (1976), James Keating (1964), Allen Guttmann (1978), Harry Edwards (1973), and so forth, utilizing the same strength-and-weakness approach. Only then do I offer my own definition, attempting to integrate the best of what we have examined:

> Sport is a recreational activity, specifically involving a game, competition, or the like that requires bodily and often mental exertion, abides by fixed rules, aims at fun and/or play, and may be divided into (a) informal sport, (b) organized sport, and (c) corporate sport.

The relationship between play, game, and sport is then presented by introducing Guttmann's chart in *From Ritual to Record* (1978, 9):

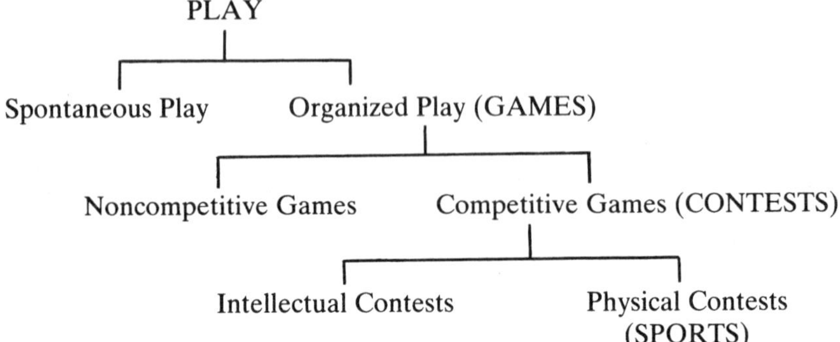

Having established a firm foundation from which to proceed, it now becomes possible to complete unit 2 in similar fashion to unit 1. Since we have been blessed with an immensely successful physical education department at Penn State, one cannot only develop the various disciplines in the study of sport by description, but also by inviting famous scholars from the faculty to visit class and lecture about their work. From time to time, I have been able to offer my class lectures from John Lucas, Ronald Smith, Dorothy Harris, Steven Danish, and others. The unit concludes with an attempt to get my students to talk about their personal experiences in sport, particularly those that fall under Maslow's definition of *peak experience*. I contrast my students' experiences with those recorded in popular literature, such as George Sheehan's (1978) musings about running, and results of my fieldwork in talking to a variety of amateur athletes.

Before advancing to unit 4, which for me is the most joyous part of the semester's work, I offer one further unit, focusing on the history of sport in America with particular emphasis on the relationship between religion and sport. I suggest that my students refer to a reasonable survey, such as *Saga of American Sport* (Lucas and Smith 1978) and I try to summarize and integrate the material in a fashion that makes students aware of the intimate relationship that has existed between religion and sport in America. Not only do I want my class to understand early American history, but I want the students to be familiar with groups such as the Fellowship of Christian Athletes, Athletes in Action, and Pro Athletes Outreach. I want my class to see how the relationship between religion and sport has been handled in the mass media. And I want them to see how the effects of a pluralistic, rapidly changing society that has spawned the death of god theology, an almost tacit acceptance of oriental religions in America, and the human-potential movement has emphasized and glorified sport, sometimes at the expense of all else. Once this awareness is established, my students are ready to move ahead to the unusual, controversial part of the course.

Unit 4 begins with the often forgotten (or overlooked) point that the ancient Olympic Games, the precursor of our modern *summum bonum* of sport, was a sacred festival. Allen Guttmann, in *From Ritual to Record* (1978, 21) quotes Ludwig Deubner on this point:

> The Olympic games were sacred games, staged in a sacred place and at a sacred festival; they were a religious act in honor of the deity. Those who took part did so in order to serve the god and the prizes they won came from the god. . . . The Olympic games had their roots in religion.

Following this beginning, I try to review the conclusions of those writers most aware of the similarities between religion and sport. I devote considerable space to Harry Edwards and his thirteen points of commonality between religion and sport. Equally, I work hard on the first forty-nine pages of Novak's *The Joy of Sports*, examining Novak's many statements about the parallels between religion and sport. However, when Edwards says, "In sum, sport is essentially a secular, quasi-religious institution. It does not, however, constitute an alternative to or substitute for formal sacred religious involvement" (*Sociology of Sport* [1973], 90), we part company. When Novak says, on page eighteen of *The Joy of Sports* (1976): "A sport is not a religion in the same way that Methodism, Presbyterianism, or Catholicism is a religion," but immediately follows by calling sport "secular religions, civil religions," he strains my patience. Only thirteen pages later he says,

> Sports are not Christianity, or Judaism, or Islam, or Buddhism, or any other of the world's religions. Sports are not the civil religion of the United States of America, or Great Britain, or Germany, or the Union of Soviet Socialist Republics, or Ghana, or any other nation.

Then, on the next *line*, he opines, "But sports are a form of religion." Well is it or isn't it, Mr. Novak? That's what I ask, and that's what my students ask. So I tell them: For me, it is not just a parallel that is emerging between sport and religion, but rather a complete identity. *Sport is religion* for growing numbers of Americans, and for many, sport religion has become a more appropriate expression of personal religiosity than Christianity, Judaism, or any of the traditional religions. This is what I tell my class, and I spend half a dozen lectures trying to prove this blasphemy. . . or at least to persuade them that it's not so outrageous as they might think.

How do I do it? In the first lecture on the topic, I examine the identity in language and terminology between religion and sport. I scrutinize expressions like *ultimate*, *dedicated*, *sacrifice*, *peace*, *commitment*, *spirit*, *suffering*, *worship*, *prayer*, *festival*, *holiday*, and others. Unlike most authors who presume a slightly altered meaning for the terms in each tradition's usage, I argue for their identity. I maintain, for example, that the marathoner who doggedly puts in one-hundred miles or more of training each week, irrespective of weather conditions, illness, or other obligations; the words dedication, sacrifice, and commitment mean precisely the same thing as they do to the pious, daily churchgoer who also compromises many worldly goals for the sake of that which is a higher reality. In the second lecture, I focus on sacred space in sport. For traditional religion, there are many sacred centers: churches, synagogues, temples, mosques, and so forth. Here I try to show that sacred centers in sport represent all the stadia, arenas, gymnasiums, and other sport structures that dot the cities and countrysides. The fact that there is a multiplicity of sacred centers rather than one single center is no problem at all, for it is existential and not geometric space that is being considered. The interior of each sacred center is a symbolic universe, and as such, it represents the boundary between chaos and cosmos. Consequently, churches and stadia alike are places of renewal, recreation, and sanctity. The third lecture on this topic considers sacred time in sport. For both religion and sport, there are two kinds of time: (1) ordinary, profane time, measured by the clock, and (2) sacred, festival time, that cannot be measured and has essentially no duration at all. Thus, the apparent timelessness of hours spent in church, synagogue, or mosque, or in long periods of private prayer and worship is identical to the suspension of ordinary time in sport, irrespective of whether this is reflected by the final two minutes of a professional football game or simply a long bicycle ride.

The fourth lecture on sport as religion considers the sacraments of sport religion. The point of ritual in religion is to approach purity through our actions so that our attained purity brings us closer to the attainment of specific religious goals. These rituals may be public or private also. Yet they must be properly done, for in the proper manifestation of the sacraments of religious life, these singular, curious-looking acts brings forth the sacred. Further, taken together, the sacraments are welded into festivals, providing a seasonal life to religious endeavor. Here, sport rituals are examined in the above perspective. The fifth lecture answers what by now has become an obvious question for almost all students: *is all* sport religion? *Absolutely not*! In the fifth lecture on the topic, we examine ultimate reality in sport, recalling that in Streng's original definition of religion, it was necessary to experience that which is genuinely ultimate to establish religion. The whole issue of sport as religion turns on the premise that sport is a religion only insofar as it brings its adherents to an experience of ultimate reality, radically alters their lives as a result of the experience of ultimacy, and then channels their positive gains back into society in a generally viable and useful fashion. This is not so simple as it sounds. In traditional religion, not everyone gets religious experience. That is to say, not everyone experiences God (or some other symbol for the ultimate), irrespective of how pious they might be or devout in their worship. Nor is the experience of ultimacy an occasion that repeats itself each time the worshipper attends church or synagogue. Yet it does happen for athletes. My work with althetes convinces me completely that this ultimate experience occurs regularly in sport. This is what I tell my students, and this is what we discuss—with much passion. In the final lecture devoted to sport as religion in America, we consider such issues as who can get religious experience in sport, how it manifests itself, how the sport clergy compares to the traditional religious clergy, and so forth. Essentially, I argue that religious experience avails itself to those who participate, even if this participation does not involve competitive activity. No special athletic talent is required in the quest for salvation in sport. Religious experience in sport is open to anyone, at any time, anywhere—just as it is in traditional religion. Religious experience in sport is no more confined to the participants on the playing field than is traditional experience confined to the priest, rabbi, or minister.

Do my students buy all this? Obviously not, but many more do than one might suspect, confirming my suspicion that many athletes who do feel as I do simply do not have the equipment to speak comfortably and intelligently about religion or sport. I am hopeful that as people actively involved in sport gain some real measure of intellectual facility in these areas, they will be able to recount numerous occasions in which the case for religious experience in sport is made thoroughly and believably. In other words, I am trying to provide those engaged in all aspects of sports with a new vocabulary and a new way of looking at themselves and their religious world. I also hope that athletes who find religious experience in sport will cease being afraid to speak out for fear of being held up to public ridicule.

At the conclusion of my last course on religion and sport, a young (and profoundly committed Christian) runner came up to me and said, "You know, this was all very interesting, but you really don't expect us to believe all that stuff, do you?" Before I could answer, he said goodbye and zipped out of the classroom. On my way back to my office, I ran into another class member who said, "I think there's a lot of promise in what you're suggesting, but I'm afraid that I'll never be able to just plain enjoy sports any more!" Needless to say, I was more than a bit depressed, and decided to take a quiet, solitary walk to ponder the term's work and its results. Heading out towards the football stadium and beyond, I ran into still another young student from class. She walked up to me, tried very hard to say something that apparently wasn't going to find verbal expression, and then just smiled and gave me an affectionate kiss on the cheek. Then she continued walking on her way.

APPENDIX: SYLLABUS

Religion and Sport: The Meeting of Sacred and Profane

COURSE DESCRIPTION

In the nearly century and a half that religion has been the focus of sophisticated, scholarly inquiries, the field has grown incredibly in perspective as well as depth. As a result, a continually expanding number of approaches and disciplines has emerged by which studies are enhanced. Scholars are now able to apply these approaches and disciplines in a manner that opens many new doors in our understanding of the religious situation in general and the modern circumstance in particular. Insofar as this course explores some of this new territory in the field of religion, at least the precedent for the religious impact of sport has already been well documented. John Lucas and Ronald Smith, for example, in *Saga of American Sport*, have amply demonstrated the profound influence sport has had on American culture since colonial times. Further, they indicate clearly that a deeply religious background underlies a significant portion of this enterprise. In other words, for nearly our entire history in America, religion and sport have been mutually influencing. This course, then, explores the relationships between religion and sport, focusing on the issues of myth, symbol, ritual, theology, and experience.

REQUIRED TEXTS:
Mircea Eliade, *The Sacred and the Profane.*
D. Stanley Eitzen and George H. Sage, *Sociology of American Sport.*
Eugen Herrigel, *Zen in the Art of Archery.*
George Leonard, *The Ultimate Athlete.*
Michael Novak, *The Joy of Sports.*
Howard Slusher, *Man, Sport and Existence: A Critical Analysis.*
Frederick Streng, *Understanding Religious Life.*

COURSE REQUIREMENTS:
There will be four formal examinations, essay in nature, and given at the end of the fourth, eighth, twelfth, and fifteenth weeks of the semester. Each examination will count 20 percent of the final course grade. A formal term paper will be required, typed (double-spaced), and not less than fifteen pages in length. The topic must be approved in advance by the professor and reflect significant attention to an issue in the study of religion and sport. The term paper will be due on the last day of class and will count 20 percent of the final course grade. Participation in class discussions is expected throughout the semester.

UNIT 1: INTRODUCTORY MATERIALS—RELIGION
1. A Definitional Attempt.
2. How We Study Religion.
3. Initial Approaches to Religious Investigation.
4. The Disciplines of Religious Studies: Psychology of Religion.
5. The Disciplines of Religious Studies: Sociology of Religion.
6. The Disciplines of Religious Studies: Philosophy of Religion.
7. The Disciplines of Religious Studies: Comparative Religion (History of Religion and Phenomenology).
8. The Role of Myth and Symbol.
9. The Varieties of Religious Rituals.
10. Theology and Ultimate Reality.
11. The Varieties of Religious Experience.
12. EXAMINATION

UNIT 2: INTRODUCTORY MATERIALS—SPORT
13. A Definitional Attempt.
14. Relationship of Sport to Play and Game Theology.
15. How We Study Sport.
16. The Disciplines of Sport: History of Sport.
17. The Disciplines of Sport: Sociology of Sport.

18. The Disciplines of Sport: Psychology of Sport.
19. The Disciplines of Sport: Philosophy of Sport.
20. The Disciplines of Sport: Economics and Politics of Sport.
21. The Role of Myth and Symbol.
22. The Varieties of Sport Rituals.
23. Total Experience in Sport.
24. EXAMINATION

UNIT 3: THE RELATIONSHIP BETWEEN RELIGION AND SPORT

25. The Traditional Role of Religion in Sport.
26. Religion Uses Sport: The Puritan Heritage.
27. Religion Uses Sport: The Industrial Age.
28. Modern Evangelism and Sport.
29. Sport Uses Religion.
30. The Jock Evangelists.
31. The Christian Athlete: Fellowship of Christian Athletes, Athletes in Action, Pro Athletes Outreach.
32. Sport and the Missionary Enterprise.
33. Religion, Sport, and the Mass Media.
34. The New Literature on Religion and Sport.
35. Civil Religion and Sport.
36. EXAMINATION

UNIT 4: SPORT AS RELIGION IN AMERICA

37. The Olympics: An Ancient Precedent.
38. Indentity in Language and Terminology.
39. Sacred Space in Sport.
40. Sacred Time in Sport.
41. The Sacraments of Sport Religion.
42. God, Ultimate Reality, and Revelation in Sport.
43. Sport as Religion in America.
44. Summary, Conclusions, and a Look at the Future.
45. EXAMINATION and SUBMISSION OF TERM PAPERS

SAMPLE EXAMINATION QUESTIONS

Unit 1: Define religion according to one of the people we have studied, or according to your own construction, including with your response some rationale for why the definition is viable. Discuss any two traditional ways of studying religion. Finally, briefly discuss each of the four traditional ways of being religious according to Streng.

Unit 2: Define sport according to one of the people we have studied, or according to your own construction, including with your response some rationale for why the definition is viable. Distinguish clearly between play, game, and sport. Which sport discipline, in your opinion, offers the most substantial input for understanding the complex issues that confront sport in America today (and explain why)?

Unit 3: Utilizing materials from the assigned reading, class lectures, and discussions, describe the ways in which sport and religion have used each other's main focus in order to promote the growth and development of each respective tradition.

In a preliminary sense, do you think sport can qualify as religion in America? Why or why not?

Unit 4: Discuss the manner in which religion and sport relate and interpenetrate. You *may* use the following issues as a potential guideline for your response:

1. A consideration of the degree to which sport facilitates an experience of the ultimate and thus produces what Streng refers to as "ultimate transformation."
2. The degree to which sport can be approached in terms of sacred space, sacred time, and sacred ritual.
3. The degree to which both sport and religion pursue freedom and perfection as the highest goals of humanity.

You may use an alternative framework if you choose.

WORKS CITED

Albanese, Catherine L. 1981. *America: Religion and Religions*. Belmont, Calif.: Wadsworth.

Caillois, Roger. 1962. *Man, Play, and Games*. Translated by Meyer Barash. London: Thames and Hudson.

Castañeda, Carlos. 1971. *The Teachings of don Juan: A Yaqui Way of Knowledge*. 1969. New York: Ballantine.

Edwards, Harry. 1973. *Sociology of Sport*. Homewood, Ill.: Dorsey Press.

Eitzen, D. Stanley, and George H. Sage. 1978. *Sociology of American Sport*. Dubuque, Iowa: Wm. C. Brown.

Eliade, Mircea. 1959. *The Sacred and the Profane*. Translated by Willard R. Trask. 1957. New York: Harcourt Brace.

Guttmann, Allen. 1978. *From Ritual to Record: The Nature of Modern Sports*. New York: Columbia University Press.

Herrigal, Eugen, 1964. *Zen in the Art of Archery*. Translated by R. G. C. Hull. New York: McGraw-Hill.

Huizinga, Johan. 1955. *Homo Ludens: A Study of the Play Element in Culture*. Boston: Beacon Press.

James, William. 1929. *The Varieties of Religious Experience*. 1902. New York: Modern Library.

Keating, James W. 1964. "Sportsmanship as a Moral Category." *Ethics* 75: 25–35. Reprinted in *Competition and Playful Activities*. Washington, D.C.: University Press of America, 1978, 39–53.

Leonard, George. 1975. *The Ultimate Athlete*. New York: Viking Press.

Lucas, John L., and Ronald A. Smith. 1978. *Saga of American Sport*. Philadelphia: Lea and Febiger.

Michener, James. 1976. *Sports in America*. Greenwich, Conn.: Fawcett.

Novak, Michael. 1976. *The Joy of Sports: End Zones, Bases, Baskets, Balls and the Consecration of the American Spirit*. New York: Basic Books.

Prebish, Charles S. 1979. *American Buddhism*. North Scituate, Mass.: Duxbury Press.

Salajan, Ioanna. *Zen Comics*. 1974. Rutland, Vt: Charles E. Tuttle.

Sutton-Smith, Brian. 1968. "Games-Play-Daydreams." *Quest* 10: 49–50.

Sutton-Smith, Brian, and John M. Roberts. 1962. "Child Training and Game Involvement." *Ethnology* 1, no. 2: 166–85.

Sheehan, George. 1978. *Running and Being: The Total Experience*. New York: Warner Books.

Slusher, Howard S. 1967. *Man, Sport and Existence: A Critical Analysis*. Philadelphia: Lea and Febiger.

Streng, Frederick J. 1985. *Understanding Religious Life*. 1969. 3d ed. Belmont, Calif.: Wadsworth.

Tart, Charles T., ed. 1969. *Altered States of Consciousness*. New York: John Wiley.

Vance, N. Scott. 1984. "Sport Is a Religion in America, Controversial Professor Argues." *The Chronicle of Higher Education*, 16 May, 25–27.

Wach, Joachim. 1958. *The Comparative Study of Religions*. Edited and introduced by Joseph Kitagawa. New York: Columbia University Press.

Weiss, Paul. 1969. *Sport: A Philosophic Inquiry*. Carbondale, Ill.: Southern Illinois University Press.

ADDITIONAL WORKS

Allen, Dorothy J., and Brian W. Fahey, eds. *Being Human in Sport*. Philadelphia: Lea and Febiger, 1977.

Beisser, Arnold. *The Madness in Sport*. New York: Appleton-Century-Crofts, 1967.

Calhoun, Don. *Sports Culture and Personality*. West Point, N.Y.: Leisure Press, 1981.

Deford, Frank. "Religion in Sport." *Sports Illustrated*, 19 April 1976, 88–102.

———. "The Word According to Tom." *Sports Illustrated*, 26 April 1976, 54–69.

———. "Reaching for the Stars." *Sports Illustrated*, 3 May 1976, 42–60.

Desmonde, W. "The Bullfight as a Religious Festival." *American Imago* 9 (1952): 173–95.

Dirkson, Jay. "The Place of Athletics in the Life of the Christian." *Sport Sociology Bulletin* 4 (1975): 48–55.

Fagin, Ralph, and Paul Brynteson. "The Cohesive Function of Religion and Sport at a Sectarian University." *Sport Sociology Bulletin* 4 (1975): 33–47.

Gallway, W. Timothy. *The Inner Game of Tennis*. New York: Random House, 1974.

Lipsky, Richard. *How We Play the Game*. Boston: Beacon Press, 1981.

Lipsyte, Robert. *SportsWorld: An American Dreamland*. New York: Quadrangle, 1976.

Miller, David L. *Gods and Games: Towards a Theology of Play*. New York: World, 1970.

Morgan, William J. "An Existential Phenomenological Analysis of Sport as a Religious Experience." In Robert C. Osterhoudt, ed. *The Philosophy of Sport: A Collection of Original Essays*. Springfield, Ill.: Charles C. Thomas, 1973.

Redmond, Gerald. "A Plethora of Shrines: Sport in the Museum and Hall of Fame." *Quest* 19 (January 1973): 41–48.

Rogers, Cornish. "Sports, Religion and Politics: The Renewal of the Alliance." *Christian Century* 89 (1972): 392–94.

Rudin, A. James. "America's New Religion," *Christian Century* 89 (1972): 384.

Sadler, W. A., Jr. "Competition Out Bounds: Sport in American Life." *Quest* 19 (January 1973): 124–32.

Scott, Jack. *The Athletic Revolution*. New York: Free Press, 1971.

Umphlett, Wiley. *The Sporting Myth and the American Experience*. Lewisburg, Pa.: Bucknell University Press, 1975.

PART 5
Anthropology of Sport

8
Buzkashi, *Toli*, and Football: Teaching an Anthropology Course on Sports

ANDREW W. MIRACLE
and
KENDALL A. BLANCHARD

In the Afghan game *buzkashi,* men on horseback struggle to capture the carcass of a goat or calf; in Choctaw *toli*, competitors with rackets of hickory and sinew move a small deerskin ball up and down a large playing field; in American football, two teams dressed in bulky protective uniforms clash in timed sequences to gain possession of territory and move an inflated pigskin. These physically combative games are more than grunts and sweat, more than interesting ways to spend an afternoon, more than the release of some instinctive aggression. These, like all sports, are patterned rituals, statements about their respective cultural contexts, and comments on the universal will to sport. From a pedagogical perspective they are windows on the complexities of human behavior and avenues that can lead to a better understanding and appreciation of human diversity. In short, they are teaching tools for the instructor, and for the student, an effective entrée into that elusive reality called the "anthropological experience." This is the rationale underlying the teaching of sport in the anthropology classroom.

The study of sport in anthropology is a relatively recent phenomenon. A few scholars have, over the years, given some attention to the ethnography of games (e.g., Culin 1907). In such contexts, the sports of non-Western, tribal, and preliterate societies received some treatment, but until the past two decades, anthropologists devoted little attention to "sport" as a distinctive category of human activity (see Blanchard 1985). Thus, it is to be expected that throughout much of anthropology's history, sport rarely found its way into the discipline's college and university curricula.

Currently, the study of sport by anthropologists is an emerging field of inquiry. Consequently, the focused study of sport is gradually appcaring in the curricula of an increasing number of North American colleges and universities. The first course on anthropology and sport was probably that offered by Allan Tindall at the University of California at Berkeley in the early 1970s.

The Association for the Anthropological Study of Play (TAASP) was formed in 1974. Several anthropologists interested in sport, including the authors, have been actively involved in that organization since its inception. A few anthropologists also have been participants in the North American Society for the Sociology of Sport, which held its first conference in 1980.

The number of publications on sport by anthropologists has increased, largely as a result of the annual TAASP proceedings. However, it should be noted that the first comprehensive volume on sport written by an anthropologist (Blanchard) did not appear until 1981 and the first textbook (Blanchard and Cheska) was not published until 1985. Recently, though, a few general anthropology textbooks have begun to devote space to the discussion of sport (e.g., Cohen and Eames 1982), and occasionally some anthropology readers include an article about sport (e.g., Spradley and McCurdy 1984; Cole 1982).

Given the obvious importance of sport, especially in Western Cultures and industrialized societies, this slow acceptance of sport as a legitimate topic of anthropological scholarship is difficult to explain. Perhaps it owes to the innate conservatism of academic disciplines and their resistance to changing their self-image. It also has been suggested that there is a reluctance to give serious attention to play (in this case including sport) since play traditionally has neither been regarded as serious nor productive. Such a position, however, is difficult to defend. Arguably, sport in America is culturally as important as religion. That is, Americans may spend more time, money, and energy in their involvement with sports than they do with religion.

PEDAGOGICAL GOALS

Teaching a topical undergraduate elective course, especially one that attracts many non majors, always presents a combination of challenges and opportunities. This is especially true for a course on sport, which may offer a superficial popular allure to students. There are no prerequisites for either of our courses, thus we can assume no prior knowledge about anthropology. This situation is best viewed as an opportunity to expose some students to the discipline who otherwise might never have taken an anthropology course. Thus, a primary goal of our courses is to teach basic anthropological concepts and encourage students to confront social theory from several perspectives. Experience has shown that this can be more palatable and more rewarding in a course on sport than in either an introductory anthropology course or one that pretends to focus on theoretical issues.

The second goal of a course on anthropology and sport is to promote students' understanding of this important cultural phenomenon. Any social institution that receives as much cultural attention as contemporary sport deserves serious academic consideration. In North America, for example, it is as important that individuals understand sport as it is that they understand science, religion, or the humanities. It matters not whether one enjoys sport or participates in sports; the well-educated individual needs to recognize the meaning of sport as a modern social institution and to realize its cultural power. To understand sport is useful in any attempt to understand one's place in society and to attempt to gain some measure of control of the forces that buffet one's life.

The basic concepts in anthropology include holism, the comparative method, and cultural relativity. Each of these can be illustrated in sport settings.

The traditional notion of holism in anthropology holds that the human condition is best understood through the synergistic integration of multiple perspectives. Broadly speaking, this has been taken to mean that each of the four subfields of anthropology—biological or physical anthropology, archaeology and ethnohistory, linguistic anthropology, and sociocultural anthropology—can make an important contribution to understanding humanity. However, to understand fully what it means to be human requires knowledge from all of these areas of specialization.

In the study of sport a commitment to holism means examining sport as physical activity and in terms of its biological consequences. It also means considering the available historical and archaeological data on sport, as well as looking for linguistic clues on the meaning of sport. Primarily, of course, it means relating these other sources of information to the study of social and cultural data on sport.

The comparative method is the utilization of cross-cultural analysis. It is easy to demonstrate this to students either by examining the same sport as it has been adapted culturally by different peoples, or by examining how similar functions are performed by sport in different societies. Cultural relativism can be addressed by getting students to appreciate the variety of sport practices and attitudes in cross-cultural settings that have value for the participants.

COURSE OBJECTIVES

Goals, such as those described above, may be realized in a course when they give rise to specific objectives. The following list for teaching a course on anthropology and sport is not comprehensive. Neither is it expected that one might achieve all fifteen in any single one-semester course. These objectives are derived from Blanchard (1985, 293–95):

1. Students will be able to define sport and describe it from a cross-

cultural perspective. This includes the analysis of sport-related concepts that can be applied across cultural lines and the testing of propositions about the general role of sport in human society.

2. Students will be able to identify and to describe sport and sporting activites in prehistoric, preliterate, band, and tribal societies; and in non-Western, Third World, and developing countries.

3. Students will be able to report on the analysis of sport as a factor in acculturation, enculturation, and cultural maintenance.

4. Students will be able to describe the relationships of sport with other institutions such as economics, politics, religion, and kinship.

5. Students will be able to describe sport as ritual and how it thus reflects the fundamental tenets of the social setting within which it is played.

6. Students will be able to describe the use of ritual in sport as an effort to control performance and outcomes.

7. Students will be able to apply symbolic interpretation to sport to derive an approximation of cultural meaning.

8. Students will be able to demonstrate an informed understanding of sport and sporting behaviors in prehistory. Although archaeology has provided little evidence for games and sports in prehistoric times, there is some indication of interest in this important arena (e.g., Fox 1977; Ventur 1980).

9. Students will be able to demonstrate an appreciation of the physical effects of sport participation, especially as they relate to social interaction and cultural meaning. Understanding the psychophysiological parameters of sport may yield clues about body-mind-culture relationships, as well as evolution.

10. Students will be able to report on analyses of sport language in non-Western and Western societies since sport jargons are important to understanding the mechanics of sport behavior.

11. Students will be able to cite studies concerning the role of sport in multicultural education as a facilitator of communication and learning.

12. Students, especially those with applied interests, will have an opportunity to learn about the development and administration of sport/recreation programs for special populations (e.g., handicapped, aged). This objective requires the expertise of physical anthropologists sensitive to both the physical and cultural dimensions of the sport experience.

13. Students will be able to demonstrate that they have an appreciation of the application of anthropological methods to the solution of practical human problems, the development of special programs, and the administration of these programs in physical education, recreation, intramurals, and the life sports. This is especially critical in multicultural, multi-ethnic, and multiracial situations.

14. Students will be able to explain the anthropological role in the creation of attitudes conducive to cross-cultural understanding. For as Cozens and Stumpf (1951) have noted, "If cultural anthropology teaches us anything, it teaches us to look beneath the surface of what we see and develop our tolerance of the other fellow's pleasures."

15. Students will be able to use data about sport from other times and places to further their understanding of contemporary sport behavior, as related to such issues as the role of women in sport, sport and international understanding, sport and the aging process, youth sport, and sport violence.

ANTHROPOLOGY AND SPORT AT TCU

"Anthropology and Sports" was first taught at Texas Christian University in Spring, 1977 as a special-topics course. The following year it was organized as ANTH 3633 and since that time has been taught as a regular course within the anthropology curriculum. Usually offered once each year, the course typically enrolls twenty to thirty-five undergraduates. Most of the students are social science majors or kinesiology/physical education majors, for whom the course is a requirement. The course may be used to fill the university's core curriculum requirement for social science (12 semester hours, up to six of which may be in anthropology).

There are usually a few university athletes enrolled in the course—for example, swimming, golf, tennis, and track team members. Through the years, there have been more female than male varsity athletes in the course. Rarely do scholarship athletes from the football, basketball, or baseball teams enroll in any anthropology courses. Having athletes from a variety of backgrounds and skill/experience levels (e.g., university varsity, club, intramural, and high school, as well as runners of all types) ensures a wide range of opinions and knowledge for class discussions.

The course is organized to move from definitions to social theories to the evolution of modern sport to the role of sport in culture to contemporary issues in sport, especially U.S. sport (see Appendix I). I view sports and games as categories of play; therefore, I find it useful to devote the initial weeks of the course to a discussion of the relationships of these three.

After the class has grasped the nature of sport, some time is spent on the anthropological perspective, with an overview of basic theoretical and methodological approaches. This is necessary since usually no more than 30 to 50 percent of the students will have had a previous anthropology course (e.g., Introductory Cultural Anthropology).

The course next examines the history of sport and looks at sport and sporting activities in a cross-section of cultures, including hunting-and-gathering and horticultural societies. This provides an opportunity to expose students to a variety of ethnographic examples, as well as to examine such major themes as culture change and ritual in some depth.

The last half of the course focuses on sport in contemporary North America, with most examples drawn from sport in the U.S. This part of the course begins with an examination of the structure and function of modern sport and then proceeds to investigate specific issues and areas of participation. This part of the course tends to change from semester to semester. This flexibility, of course, is important to the discussion of issues that may be receiving media coverage at the time (e.g., violence), issues that may affect some members of the class personally (e.g., women's collegiate sports), and issues relevant to my own current research (e.g., high school sports).

The course works well. Student attention seldom lags. In the past, weekly quizzes were used to encourage students to do the reading assignments before class discussions. However, I have found that these are not necessary. Students seem to find the readings sufficiently interesting so that the threat of sanctions is not required. There is never a problem stimulating class discussions. The only parameters that I have had to enforce relate to notions that in a social science course personal anecdotes do not constitute data, and a single occurrence does not substantiate a claim or prove a proposition.

Even those students not personally interested in sports often demonstrate at the end of the semester that they have learned quite a bit of anthropology. Such students may not have learned the same things that they would have acquired in an introductory anthropology class, but they probably have learned the same amount of anthropology.

The only real difficulty experienced with this course has been finding suitable textbooks. There have been a variety of anthropological anthologies on play, some of which contain a few articles on sport. Stevens (1977) and Schwartzman (1980) are two I have used in "Anthropology and Sports." Both are from the TAASP annual series. There also is *Play, Games and Sports in Cultural Contexts* edited by Harris and Park (1983). An ethnography on sport that works well is Blanchard's *The Mississippi Choctaws at Play* (1981), though there are now others that also would be appropriate. The real problem until 1985 was the lack of a textbook. Since then, Blanchard and Cheska (1985) has been available and it seems to work quite well. I especially appreciate it as a medium for teaching anthropological theories.

ANTHROPOLOGY AND SPORT AT MTSU

Sport's role in the anthropology curriculum at Middle Tennessee State University is quite similar to its role at TCU. The course, "Sport and Society," is cross-listed in anthropology, sociology, and physical education so that students have options regarding the nature of the credit received for the course. The course is broad in its coverage, but because I normally teach the course, it tends to maintain an anthropological focus consistent with that described for the TCU course, "Anthropology and Sports."

"Sport and Society" was initially proposed as a Sociology/Anthropology course in 1980. However, the course met resistance at the university curriculum committee level. The Health, Physical Education, Recreation, and Sport (HPERS) staff felt that the proposal violated its curriculum turf. Subsequent negotiations led to its cross-listing. As a result, HPERS staff members occasionally teach the course, though to date the majority of the 25 to 35 students who have taken "Sport and Society" each year have taken it under the tutelage of an anthropologist. The course meets no general education requirement and is generally taken as part of an anthropology, sociology, or recreation major.

The resulting mix of students creates some problems, just as it does at TCU. Some of the sociology and anthropology majors have had extensive course work in the social sciences; some of the recreation majors have had little, if any. As a result, I find it necessary to spend time in the early sessions of the course trying to give some of the students a social scientific perspective and to keep from boring the more enlightened. Also, I am forced on occasion to defend the unexpected rigor of the course. One of the common myths about a course on sport is that it is "easy," indeed, recreational. Every effort is made to ensure that "Sport and Society" belies the myth.

Similar to the situation at TCU, the "Sport and Society" course at MTSU attracts many scholarship athletes. Their personal/emotional ties to the athletic program provide a counterbalance to the more skeptical attitudes of the nonathletes in the class. The clash of opinions is frequently the basis for lively discussion.

The course format is quite like TCU's "Anthropology and Sports." An effort is made to cover prehistory, history, theory, method, ethnography, and contemporary issues (see Appendix II). From the student's perspective, perhaps the most valuable part of the course is the final presentation. Here the student is required to research a sport-related problem (e.g., academics and athletics), analyze the problem from a theoretical perspective, and defend a particular point of view relative to that problem in a formal oral presentation to the class.

The reading materials required each semester vary, but they are similar to those used at TCU. Unfortunately, because of the breadth of the course, it is impossible to find a single textbook that covers all the issues. However, with the ever increasing volume of literature relative to the anthropology and sociology of sport, the instructor now has a greater range of options.

CONCLUSIONS

Courses in the curriculum that bring together the subject matter of sport and the anthropological perspective are still limited to a handful of colleges and universities (e.g., MTSU, TCU, University of Illinois, and University of Pittsburgh). However, the requests for information and materials that we have received from various colleagues across the country in the past few years indicate that the interest is growing. This interest appears to be tied to more than the effort to increase student enrollment. Now, more than ever, the approach has real pedagogical merit. With the new emphases in higher education on the core curriculum, interdisciplinary courses, and cross-cultural experiences, the anthropology and sport offering could well become an important and highly demanded curricular option in the academy of the 1990s. Indeed, *buzkashi*, *toli*, and football may well become as lively in the classroom as they are on the playing field.

APPENDIX I: SYLLABUS

Anthropology 3633—Anthropology and Sports
Texas Christian University
Spring 1987
TR 11:00 a.m.
SWR 258
Dr. Miracle

Books: Blanchard and Cheska (1985), *The Anthropology of Sport*, Dunleavy, Miracle, and Rees (1982), *Sociology of Sport*
Readings: Additional readings have been placed on library reserve.

CLASS SCHEDULE AND REQUIRED READINGS

13 January. Sport and anthropology. Blanchard and Cheska: ix–29.
15 January. The meaning of sport. Blanchard and Cheska: 29–61.
20 January. The nature of play. Reserve: Stevens (1977); Sutton-Smith (1977); Csikszentmihalyi (1981). Optional (on reserve): MacAloon and Csikszentmihalyi (1977).
22 January. The work/play dichotomy. Reserve: Sack (1977); Stevens (1980); Lancy (1980).
27 January. Anthropological theory and method. Blanchard and Cheska: 63–89.
29 January. Studying play crossculturally. Reserve: Heider (1977); Olofson (1977); Fox, S. J. (1977).
3 February. History of sport. Blanchard and Cheska: 91–122. Reserve: Mergen (1977).
5 February. Sport in culture I. Blanchard and Cheska: 125–65.
10 February. Sport in culture II. Blanchard and Cheska: 167–97.
12 February. Sport, Culture and Society. Dunleavy: 1–49 (Brandmeyer and Alexander; Donnelly; Cheska).

17 February. Children's play and socialization: The case of the Aymara. Reserve: Miracle(1977); Duncan (1977).
19 February. Sport and culture change. Blanchard and Cheska: 199–231. Reserve: Ventur (1980).
24 February. Play and communication. Reserve: Salter (1977); Scotch (1961); Fox, J. R. (1961); Gmelch (1971).
26 February. Ritual and sport. Reserve: Beran (1981); Dunleavy and Miracle (1981).
3 March. Potpourri and review.
5 March. MIDTERM EXAM.
17 March. Film: Trobriand Cricket. (Class meets in library basement, Room B-17).
19 March. Guest lecturer: Professor Jerry Landwer, "High school and college wrestling." Dunleavy: 51–118 (Frisby: Yerles; Kjeldsen; Colwell).
24 March. Guest Lecturer: Professor Michael Katovich, "Drugs and sport." Dunleavy: 181–202 (Vanreusel and Renson)
26 March. Youth sport. Reserve: Coakley (1986).
31 March. Films: Play and games of the Yanamamo: !Kung and Pomo. (Class meets in library basement, Room B-17.) Dunleavy: 283–360 (Theberge; Curtis and Brown; Berlage; Podlichak; Dubois).
2 April. High school sport. Reserve: Burnett (1969); Miracle (1978); Howell, Miracle and Rees (1984).
4 April. Women and sport. Dunleavy: 119–65 (Brown; Hasbrook; Allison); 203–19 (Woodford and Scott).
9 April. Media and sport. Blanchard and Cheska: 233–76.
14 April. University sport. Dunleavy: 237–79 (Nixon; Messner and Grossier). Reserve: Coakley and Pacey (1984); Miracle (1980).
16 April. Professional sport. Dunleavy: 221–35 (Lerch).
21 April. Race and sport. Dunleavy: 271–282 (Chu and Griffey); Reserve: Miracle (1981); Rees and Miracle (1984) "participation."
23 April. Conflict and sport. Reserve: Rees and Miracle (1984) "conflict"; Pearton (1986).
28 April. Potpourri and review. Blanchard and Cheska: 277–80.
30 April. Study day—no class.
Tuesday, May 5, 3:00–5:00 PM: FINAL EXAM.

COURSE REQUIREMENTS

Grades
Grades will be determined in the following manner: midterm 35 percent; final 40 percent; project 25 percent.

Exams
You must take the exams at the scheduled time. Makeup exams, if allowed, are always more difficult. Exams will cover all readings, lectures, discussions, films, and other assignments.

Readings
The assigned readings should be done before class on the indicated date. Additional readings may be assigned during the course of the semester and placed on reserve at the library.

Project

Each student will undertake individual study on American sport. The subject is to be examined from an anthropological or sociological perspective. Individual approval must be secured for the chosen topic. It is expected that most investigations will result in a paper summarizing the project's findings. Projects are due April 28.

Remarks

Any necessary changes to this syllabus will be announced in class as early as possible. Absence from class does not relieve you of the responsibility to meet course requirements as scheduled or adjusted.

SELECTED ESSAY QUESTIONS

1. Discuss the following statement. "Sport is a subcategory of play."
2. Define play, game, and sport; then consider whether mountain climbing is or is not a sport.
3. Discuss culture change and sport through the examination of Trobriand cricket and the kula ring.
4. Discuss the following theories of play: preparatory, prophylactic, and adaptive potentiation.
5. It has been suggested that professional sports are not play. Provide a theoretically-based argument confirming or contradicting the statement.
6. "Play and games socialize children and prepare them for appropriate adult roles." Discuss this statement.
7. Are play, games, and sports found in all societies? Is the universal distribution of various play forms, games, and sports approximately equal? Provide examples from readings and lectures to illustrate your argument.
8. "Sport reflects culture." Discuss this relationship and provide illustrations from class and/or readings.
9. What are rites of passage and rites of intensification? How may these be applied to studies of sport?
10. "Work/play is a false dichotomy." Discuss this statement.
11. How might ethnocentrism affect our perceptions and definitions of play, games, and sport?
12. Discuss the manifest and latent functions of a specific form of play, a game, or a sport.
13. Discuss the notion that games are pre-adaptive.
14. Discuss the concept of ritual as a means of understanding sport behavior.
15. Describe the ballgames of pre-Columbian North and Central America. Analyze the ballgame of one culture through the perspective of a structural-functionalist or a cultural materialist.
16. Define sport. Cite the work of specific authors. Then discuss whether or not Olympic ice dancing and Trobriand cricket are really sports or not.
17. It might be suggested that the inequalities that characterize female sport participation historically paralleled those characteristic of society in general. Using the theoretical model of your choice, analyze the role of the female athlete in American society as a reflection of the American female role in general.
18. Describe the functions of high school sport at the individual, institutional, and community levels.
19. Write an essay on youth sport. Include a discussion of values, socialization, health, and athletic potential.

20. How might a structural-functionalist explain the physical aggression characteristic of American sport? Contrast this with a cultural materialist explanation.
21. Analyze some of the issues regarding race and sport. Review and critique the theoretical models of hypotheses that might help explain the situations described.
22. Define play; cite references from the readings and lectures if possible. Then discuss why play is seemingly a universal form of human behavior. (E.g., what are some of the possible theories that might explain the universality of this phenomenon?)
23. Define games; refer to the work of Caillois, Loy, and others if possible. Discuss the cross-cultural variations in structure and preference of games, giving specific examples from readings and class discussions.
24. Discuss the relationships between religion and sport. Refer to the works of specific authors and cite illustrative cases if possible.
25. What is the role of athletics in the university? Should a good athlete be admitted to a university regardless of the individual's past academic performance or skills?
26. How does the work of anthropologists and sociologists help us understand the current status of women's athletics in U.S. colleges and universities?
27. What is the role of the professional athlete? Are professional athletes entertainers or gladiators? Defend your answer on as many counts as possible.
28. Discuss the economics of Choctaw Sport—past and present—as well as the implications for the future.
29. Discuss the relationships between Choctaw values and sport.
30. Discuss the use of magic in Choctaw sport.
31. Define play, game and sport; then consider whether video games in which two players compete against one another constitute a sport. Explain your answer.
32. "Play and games socialize children and prepare them for appropriate adult roles, but the function of sports may be different." Discuss this statement.
33. Discuss the importance of cultural variation in basketball.
34. Compare the social functions of Trobriand cricket and Choctaw stickball.
35. Discuss the impact of television on sports in the U.S.
36. Discuss the social functions of sport in the U.S.
37. Discuss one of the following: sports in the Soviet Union; the differences between American and Japanese baseball; soccer in Brazil; play among the Aymara.
38. Discuss the following quote: "Sport teaches discipline and builds character."
39. Discuss the functions of spring football practice.
40. How do athletes differ from nonathletes?

APPENDIX II: SYLLABUS

SOC/HPERS 479/579: Sport and Society
Middle Tennessee State University
Spring 1986
Blanchard

OBJECTIVES

A. To underscore the importance of sport as a vital component in the sociocultural process.

B. To develop an appreciation for the social scientific analysis of sport behavior.

C. To treat the fundamental conceptual problems underlying the study of sport.

D. To look at the major contemporary sport issues from both sociological and anthropological perspectives.

E. To consider the various patterns of sport behavior as these are manifested in societies around the world.

REQUIREMENTS

A. Reading:
1. Blanchard and Cheska. *The Anthropology of Sport.*
2. Calhoun. *Sports, Culture and Personality.*

B. Quizzes (4).

C. Miscellaneous assignments/lab reports/essay questions.

D. Debate/presentation (relative to basic issues in contemporary sport sociology).

E. Attendance and participation.

EVALUATION

A. Quizzes	36 percent
B. Miscellaneous assignments	17 percent
C. Debate/presentation	12 percent
D. Final examination	25 percent
E. Attendance/participation	10 percent
Total	100 percent

ATTENDANCE POLICY

Class attendance is mandatory. Any student with more than three unexcused absences will automatically lose 10 percent of his or her total class grade. Makeup tests/quizzes are not given unless previous arrangements have been made.

QUIZ POLICY

There will be a total of four quizzes during the semester. It is recommended that a student make every effort to take all four. However, each student is allowed to drop his or her lowest quiz grade.

EXTRA CREDIT

Students concerned about about their grades can write a paper on their assigned debate topic and receive extra credit, the amount to be determined by the quality of the paper. The extra credit received from this special paper will be added to students' total grade for the course. This extra credit can lead to a significant raising of total semester grades. However, in no case, will this extra credit be used to raise a grade of "B" to "A."

COURSE TOPICS

A. Introduction: sport and the social sciences . . .
1. Sociology and anthropology.
2. History of sport and the social sciences.
3. General definitions and conceptual problems.

(Reading: Blanchard and Cheska, 1–27: 227–80).
(Reading: Calhoun, 1–17).

B. Theoretical approaches to the study of sport.
   1. Sport, theory, and methodology.
   2. A cultural approach to sport.
   3. Theoretical models and the study of sport.
   4. The anthropological study of sport: sport as paradigm.
   (Reading: Blanchard and Cheska, 28–78).
C. Methods in sport research.
   1. Research design.
   2. Data collection.
   3. Data analysis.
   (Reading: Blanchard and Cheska, 79–88).
D. The prehistory and history of sport.
   1. The question of sport origins.
   2. The evolution of sport.
   3. Sport in the history of Western society.
   (Reading: Blanchard and Cheska, 91–121).
   (Reading: Calhoun, 61–109).
E. Sport as an institution in human cultures around the world.
   1. The function of sport in human society.
   2. Sport in band and tribal societies.
   3. Sport, the state, and urban civilization.
   (Reading: Blanchard and Cheska, 125–96).
   (Reading: Calhoun, 112–52).
F. Sport and change
   1. Sport as a factor in change
   2. Sport as a result of change
   (Reading: Blanchard and Cheska, 202–15).
G. The issues in contemporary sport sociology.
   (Reading: Calhoun, 28–42).
   1. Sport and socialization.
   (Reading: Calhoun, 179–258).
   2. Sport and religion.
   3. Sport and social stratification.
   (Reading: Calhoun, 154–78).
   4. Sport and violence and war.
   (Reading: Blanchard and Cheska, 216–21: 225–63).
   (Reading: Calhoun, 259).
   5. Sport and the media.
   6. Sport and women.
   (Reading: Blanchard and Cheska, 233–274).
   7. Sport and youth education.
   8. Sport and higher education.
   9. Sport and the black athlete.
   10. Sport and the professional athlete.
   11. Sport as big business—the role of spectator.
   (Reading: Blanchard and Cheska, 274).
   (Reading: Calhoun, 300–314).
   12. Sport and international relations.
   (Reading: Blanchard and Cheska, 264–274).

13. Sport and the aging process.
(Reading: Balanchard and Cheska, 248–54).

H. Sport sociology/anthropology and the development of sport programs.
(Reading: Blanchard and Cheska, 222–30).

I. The future of sport.

DEBATE/PRESENTATION ISSUES

1. Youth Sports (e.g., Little League). Pro: Little League builds character and teaches children how to survive in a competitive society. Con: Little League forces children into harmful competitive situations, exposes them to the foibles of their parents, and has negative psychological effects.

2. Sport (as an institution). Pro: (A functionalist perspective). Con: (A conflict perspective).

3. Women's sports. Pro: Clear lines should be maintained between sports appropriate for men and those appropriate for women. Con: All gender lines between sports should be abolished.

4. Sport and the media. Pro: The media have distorted and corrupted the sport institution, focusing on and reinforcing its worst images. Con: The media have made sport a prominent social institution and helped curb corruption and excesses in sport.

5. College athletics. Pro: College athletics are important to college life in particular and education in general. Con: College athletics as we know them should be abolished, athletic scholarships outlawed, and more extensive intramural programs developed in their place.

6. High school athletics. Pro: The importance of a "no pass, no play" rule. Con: The dangers of removing marginal students from participation in extracurricular activities.

7. Sport and mobility. Pro: Sport is a means to success in life, a "way out" for poor and disadvantaged students. Con: Sport is a trap, an institution that misdirects student energies and creates delusions and leads in most cases to failure.

8. Professional athletics. Pro: Professional sports are important to American society and players should be paid whatever the market can stand. Con: Professional sports are not sports, but big business and a sad commentary on American values; and, player salaries and other income should be regulated by municipalities that support them.

WORKS CITED

Blanchard, Kendall. 1981. *The Mississippi Choctaws at Play: The Serious Side of Leisure.* Urbana: University of Illinois Press.

———. 1985. "Sport Studies and the Anthropology Curriculum." In *American Sport Culture: The Humanistic Dimensions.* Edited by Wiley Lee Umphlett. Lewisburg, Pa: Bucknell University Press, 284–97.

Blanchard, Kendall, and Alyce Taylor Cheska. 1985. *The Anthropology of Sport: An Introduction.* South Hadley, Mass.: Bergin and Garvey.

Cohen, Eugene N., and Edwin Eames. 1982. *Cultural Anthropology.* Boston: Little, Brown.

Cole, Johnnetta B., ed. 1982. *Anthropology for the Eighties: Introductory Readings.* New York: Free Press.

Cozens, Frederick W., and Florence Stumpf. 1951. *Implications of Cultural Anthropology for Physical Education.* American Academy of Physical Education. Professional Contributions, No. 1. Washington, D.C.

Culin, Stewart. 1907. *Games of the North American Indians*. Twenty-fourth Annual Report of the Bureau of American Ethnology. Washington, D.C.: Government Printing Office.

Fox, Steven J. 1977. "A Paleoanthropological Approach to Recreation and Sporting Behaviors. In *Studies in the Anthropology of Play*. Edited by Phillips Stevens, Jr. West Point, N.Y.: Leisure Press, 65–70.

Harris, Janet C., and Roberta J. Park, eds. 1983. *Play, Games, and Sports in Cultural Contexts*. Champaign, Ill.: Human Kinetics.

Spradley, James P., and David W. McCurdy, eds. 1984. *Conformity and Conflict: Readings in Cultural Anthropology*. Boston: Little, Brown.

Schwartzman, Helen B., ed. 1980. *Play and Culture*. West Point, N.Y.: Leisure Press.

Stevens, Phillips, Jr., ed. 1977. *Studies in the Anthropology of Play: Papers in Memory of B. Allan Tindall*. West Point, N.Y.: Leisure Press.

Ventur, Pierre. 1980. "Mopan Maya Games from the Southern Peten." In *Play and Culture*. *242–62*.

ADDITIONAL WORKS

Blanchard, Kendall A. "Basketball and the Culture-Change Process: The Rimrock Navajo Case." *Council on Anthropology and Education Quarterly* 5, no.4 (1974): 8–13.

Burnett, Jacquetta Hill. "Ceremony, Rites and Economy in the Student System of an American High School." *Human Organization* 28 (1969): 1–10.

Calhoun, Don. *Sports, Culture and Personality*. West Point, N.Y.: Leisure Press, 1981.

Chalip, Laurence, Mihaly Csikszentmihalyi, Douglas Kleiber, and Reed Larson. "Variations of Experience in Formal and Informal Sports." *Research Quarterly* 55 (1984): 109–16.

Cheska, Alyce Taylor, ed. *Play As Context*. West Point, N.Y.: Leisure Press, 1981.

Csikszentmihalyi, Mihaly, and Stith Bennett. "An Exploratory Model of Play." *American Anthropologist* 73 (1971): 45–58.

Culin, Stewart. "Street Games of Boys in Brooklyn, N.Y." *Journal of American Folklore* 4 (1981): 221–37.

Dunleavy, Aidan O., Andrew W. Miracle, and C. Roger Rees, eds. *Studies in the Sociology of Sport*. Fort Worth: Texas Christian University Press, 1982.

Fox, J. Robin. "Pueblo Baseball: A New Use for Old Witchcraft." *Journal of American Folklore* 74 (1961): 9–16.

Geertz, Clifford. "Deep Play: Notes on the Balinese Cockfight." *Daedalus* 101 (1972): 1–37.

Gmelch, George. "Baseball Magic." *Trans-Action* 8 (1971): 39–41, 54.

Howell, Frank M., Andrew W. Miracle, and C. Roger Rees. "Do High School Athletics Pay? The Effects of Varsity Participation on Socioeconomic Attainment." *Sociology of Sport Journal* 1 (1984): 15–25.

Laughlin, Charles D., and John McManus. "The Biopsychological Determinants of Play and Games." In *Social Approaches to Sport*. Edited by Robert M. Pankin. Cranbury, N.J.: Associated University Presses, 1982, 42–79.

Lever, Janet. "Sex Differences in the Complexity of Children's Play." *American Sociological Review* 43 (1978): 471–83.

Loy, John W. "The Nature of Sport: A Definitional Effort." *Quest* 10 (1968): 1–15.

———. "The Cultural System of Sport." *Quest Monograph* 29 (1978): 73–102.

MacAloon, John, and Mihaly Csikszentmihalyi. "Deep Play and the Flow Experience in Rock Climbing." In *Play, Games and Sports in Cultural Contexts*. Edited by Janet C. Harris and Roberta Park. Champaign, Ill.: Human Kinetics, 1983, 361–84.

Manning, Frank. "Celebrating Cricket: The Symbolic Construction of Caribbean Politics." *American Ethnologist* 83 (1981): 616–32.

Miller, Stephen. "Ends, Means, and Galumphing: Some Leitmotifs of Play." *American Anthropologist* 75 (1973): 87–98.

Miracle, Andrew W. "Factors Affecting Interracial Cooperation: A Case Study of a High School Football Team." *Human Organization* 40 (1981): 150–54.

Norbeck, Edward, ed. *The Anthropological Study of Human Play.* Rice University Studies, vol. 60, no. 3. Houston: Rice University Press, 1974.

———. "The Biological and Cultural Significance of Human Play: An Anthropological View." *Journal of Physical Education and Recreation* 50, Leisure Today Insert (1979): 33–6.

Poirier, Frank E., and E. O. Smith. "Socializing Functions of Primate Play." *American Zoologist* 14 (1976): 275–87.

Polgar, Sylvia K. "The Social Context of Games: Or When Is Play Not Play?" *Sociology of Education* 49 (1976): 256–71.

Rees, C. Roger, and Andrew W. Miracle. "Conflict Resolution in Games and Sports." *International Review of Sport Sociology* 19 (1984): 145–56.

Rees, C. Roger, and Andrew W. Miracle, eds. *Sport and Social Theory.* Champaign, Ill.: Human Kinetics, 1986.

Roberts, John M., Malcolm J. Arth, and Robert R. Rush. "Games in Culture." *American Anthropologist* 61 (1959): 597–605.

Roberts, John M., and Brian Sutton-Smith. "Child Training and Game Involvement." *Ethnology* 1 (1962): 166–85.

Salter, Michael A., ed. *Play: Anthropological Perspectives.* West Point, N.Y.: Leisure Press, 1978.

Schwartzman, Helen B. *Transformations: The Anthropology of Children's Play.* New York: Plenum Press, 1978.

Scotch, N. A. "Magic, Sorcery, and Football Among Urban Zulu: A Case of Reinterpretation Under Acculturation." *Journal of Conflict Resolution* 5 (1961): 70–74.

Sipes, Richard G. "War, Sports and Aggression: An Empirical Test of Two Rival Theories." *American Anthropologist* 75 (1973): 64–86.

Theberge, Nancy, and Peter Donnelly, eds. *Sport and the Sociological Imagination.* Fort Worth: Texas Christian University Press, 1984.

Tindall, B. Allan. "The Cultural Transmissive Function of Physical Education." *Council on Anthropology and Education Quarterly* 6, no. 2 (1975): 10–12.

PART 6

Sociology of Sport

9

Teaching the Sociology of Sport: It's More Than a Reflection of Society

JAY J. COAKLEY

IN THE BEGINNING . . .

After a late-night conversation about how sport had escaped the critical attention of sociologists through the 1960s, a colleague and I worked up a proposal for a new course on the sociology of sport. It was 1970 and we were both young enough and naive enough to assume that the curriculum committee members would share our excitement about using the "sociological imagination" to take a look at sport in society. They didn't, and they rejected our proposal. Their short letter of explanation indicated that courses about sport, if they were offered at all, belonged in the Physical Education Department. We were disappointed but other options remained. As in any bureaucracy, rules in the university can be sidestepped if one is determined and subtle. So we quietly planned to do our course under the title of "Seminar on Special Topics in Sociology." Our department chairperson was more understanding than the members of the curriculum committee.

Word of mouth information about the course spread quickly, and two weeks before the start of the term we had nearly one hundred applicants. Selecting sixteen for the seminar was a challenge. We decided that diversity among students should be the major criterion guiding our selection. We chose eight men and eight women. Six were members of intercollegiate sport teams, a few were members of fraternities and sororities, a few belonged to radical student organizations, five were blacks and two were hispanics. Over half were sociology majors, and there were two business majors, two philosophy majors, and two physical education majors. All but two were twenty- to twenty-two-year-old upper division students, but we were pleased with the overall diversity on other characteristics.

Since my colleague and I felt unsure about organizing a complete syllabus for the course, our first two class sessions were spent discussing and debating what we would cover during the term. We finally arrived at a dozen questions and controversial issues related to sport in society. We set things up so three people would be responsible for finding readings and leading the discussions on each of the questions or issues. We met once a week at my home and our sessions usually went long into the night. We discussed, we argued, we developed research designs for studies that might be done if we ever had the time, we read Jack Scott's book on *The Athletic Revolution* (1971), Harry Edwards's book on *The Revolt of the Black Athlete* (1969), Loy's and Kenyon's anthology on *Sport, Culture and Society* (1969), and articles from local newspapers and national magazines. We examined popular beliefs about the social dimensions of sport, and we discovered how useful sociological concepts and theories could be in our analyses.

That first course was so successful that I've stayed with an "issues and controversies" approach ever since. Each of my sociology of sport courses has been organized around a set of questions and controversial issues related to sport and society. The questions have been modified and extended over the past seventeen years, but class materials have focused on issues related to sport as a social phenomenon and sport's relationship to the social world in which it exists. (See Appendix I for a list of the major issues currently discussed in the course.)

When I moved to the University of Colorado at Colorado Springs in 1972, my sociology of sport course proposal was accepted by the curriculum committee on my first try. I had learned how to write better proposals and there was no physical education or athletic department to object to what I did in the course. Student interest was widespread and I immediately lost the luxury of offering seminars. My students were and still are undergraduate "urban commuters" ranging in age from nineteen to seventy-five years old. Few of them have ever participated in sports apart from high school or local community teams and leagues, and many have never participated in any organized sports. Less than 25 percent are sociology majors, and many come from the colleges of business and education. Some are parents with children in organized youth programs. Some are committed sport fans; others dislike sports and have bad memories about past experiences in sport during their childhoods. There are always a few who think the course will simply be an extension of past locker room conversations they've had about sport. This diversity has created constant challenges, but it has also served as the basis for stimulating class discussions and considerable learning experiences for students and instructor alike.

THE CURRENT COURSE

The purpose of my course is to provide a sound introduction to the sociology of sport through the stimulation of systematic, issue-related thinking.

Through the sixteen-week semester, I want the students to expand their understanding of society, social organization, and social change; and of the ways sports are linked to the structure and dynamics of social life in the U.S. as well as in other countries. I also want them to understand the extent to which theoretical approaches influence analyses of sport in society, and the extent to which it is necessary to think critically about social issues if they want to contribute to the creation of a more humane world. There will be more information on course content later in this chapter.

READING MATERIALS

The required reading for the course has usually included my text, *Sport in Society: Issues and Controversies* (1986), although I have also used Eitzen's and Sage's text, *Sociology of North American Sport* (1986). Both these books are in their third editions and offer good reading material for undergraduate students. Along with a main text I have used a variety of supplemental anthologies including Eitzen's *Sport in Contemporary Society* (1984); Tomlinson's and Whannel's *Five Ring Circus: Money, Power and Politics at the Olympic Games* (1984); Hart's and Birrell's *Sport in the Sociocultural Process* (1981); and Yiannakis, et al., *Sport Sociology: Contemporary Themes* (1986). However, there are a few other texts that might be considered, and numerous supplemental books to fit a variety of instructor preferences and student interests.

It should be remembered that my students are all undergraduates coming from backgrounds that may not include any sociology. If I were teaching a course made up of graduate students or upper division sociology majors, I would consider other reading materials, including Richard Gruneau's *Class, Sports, and Social Development* (1983); Allen Guttmannn's *From Ritual to Record* (1978); Elias's and Dunning's *The Quest For Excitement* (1986); Rees's and Miracle's anthology, *Sport and Social Theory* (1986); Loy's, McPherson's, and Kenyon's *Sport and Social Systems* (1978); Loy's, Kenyon's, and McPherson's anthology, *Sport, Culture and Society* (1981); and Hargreaves's anthology, *Sport, Culture and Ideology* (1982). Each of these books provide representations or overviews of major theoretical approaches and issues in the sociology of sport.

CLASS SESSIONS

After reading over 20 sets of student evaluations for my sociology of sport course, I can say with confidence that the students appreciate two things in particular during class sessions: (1) lively class discussions in which they have opportunities to contribute to the development of ideas going beyond the readings or leading to a critique of the readings, and (2) presentations made by speakers and panels of people from outside the class. Films and other audiovisual materials are often appreciated if they are not too long, and if they are directly related to course materials so they evoke good discussions. The students also enjoy group projects that take them into sport settings as observers as long as they don't have to do group assignments for which they are given "group grades."

Lively class discussions are best based on questions and issues directly related to the lives of the students, but it is also possible to facilitate good discussions on more general topics and issues. Some of the essay questions in the Instructor's Manual accompanying *Sport in Society: Issues and Controversies* serve as good discussion generators. (See Appendix II for sample essay questions.) The same is true of many of the sixteen projects described in the manual. (See Appendix III for sample projects.) Since students are often interested in how things might be changed or improved, many good discussions are related to applied issues.

Presentations by outside speakers have usually generated considerable student interest. But I have taken care in selecting people who are especially knowledgeable about the topics we are discussing in class or people who have unique ways of viewing sport and sport experiences. Some of the best received presentations have included the following:

1. A panel discussion with five nine- to twelve-year-old children who have participated in a variety of organized youth sport programs. Through the years I have used about fifteen different panels of children. Each has been comprised of both boys and girls selected because of their active involvement in sports and because they would not be overwhelmed by the prospect of talking to a relatively large group of college students. I talk to the children's parents to get their permissions, and then I brief the children before the class session. I serve as the panel moderator by asking the initial questions and making sure all the panel members have opportunities to speak their minds in response. Class members are invited to ask questions, but sometimes I rephrase what is asked or I direct the question to a particular panel member. We ask questions about their favorite coaches, their unfavorite coaches, their favorite sports, the things they like and dislike, their informal games, and the differences between informal games and games in organized leagues. We discuss gender issues, training issues, family issues, things related to school, to their friendships, and to their futures. I have never had a problem in getting the panel to talk for at least an hour, and my students have never been less than amazed at how much they've learned simply by listening to children.

2. A presentation by one of the local high school coaches. The presentation focuses on the definition of the coaching role as well as how the actual behavior of coaches is influenced by factors grounded in social relationships and the organizational structure of the school. I have selected many different coaches to make this presentation, and I have always sent them copies of the chapters or articles the class is reading on the topics in

question. Furthermore, I send them a list of questions they may be asked by students and a list of issues I'd like them to discuss during their presentations.

3. A presentation on the media and sport made by one of the local news sportscasters or sports journalists. Again, I send them a copy of the class reading materials on the topic and a list of questions and issues that the class would like to hear addressed. Among those issues are things related to the profession of sports journalism or sportscasting, and related to how they as individuals became involved in their field.

4. A panel of three women who have been actively involved in sports—one who is over sixty years old, one about forty, and the third under 24. The purpose of this panel is to highlight historical differences in access to opportunities for participation in sport, and the changes occasioned by Title IX legislation. Each of the panelists is asked to give brief biographical accounts of her involvement and her impressions of how sport was defined by and for girls and women as she was growing up. This is done informally, and class members are invited to ask questions at any point in the presentations. We have had a few occasions where the older women have captivated the young students with stories about how things were years ago. My students have also been asked to make lists of changes while they are listening to the presenters. These lists are then discussed during the following class.

5. A panel of intercollegiate hockey players talking about physical contact and aggression in their sport. I've only done this a few times, but it has been successful on each occasion. The panel is held during the first class session after the entire class has attended an intercollegiate hockey game. For most of the students, this is a first-time experience, and a number of them abhor the intensity of the physical contact during the game. The panel members are asked to give their impressions of the events in the last game, and then the students ask them questions about aggression, violence, cheating, "cheap shots," fear, risk, and other things related to the experience of involvement. The purpose of the discussion is to not only discover how the hockey players think and feel about these things, but why they think and feel the way they do, and the consequences of these thoughts and feelings.

The success of any panel or presentation partly rests in the discussions during the subsequent class session. I usually ask the students to summarize the most significant thing they've learned during the presentation, and then we discuss those points further during class. A similar approach is used when the students are shown a film. I don't use many films although their availability in video shops makes it feasible to show feature length movies if they fit into the subject matter of the class. But care must be taken to select films that have enough substantive content to provide the basis for discussion. And it is often necessary to provide students with lists of "things to look for" in the film if the viewing experience is to be worthwhile.

TESTS

Class size, ranging from twenty-five to 160 students for my course, usually determines the type of testing used. Our department does not have resources for teaching assistants, so when there are more than fifty students, the tests consist of multiple choice questions. When there are fewer than fifty students, essay tests are used in combination with a written project based on field observations of some sort.

I have ambivalent feelings about so-called objective tests. A series of distinct questions on separate issues does not facilitate the kind of studying and learning most of us would like to see among our students. However, I think it is possible to encourage integrated, issue-related thinking when these tests are constructed carefully and when students are given opportunities to know what will be covered on the test and opportunities to discuss the tests after they are graded. Over the past fifteen years, I have tried to develop multiple choice questions that focus on ideas rather than single facts. (See Appendix IV for sample questions.) Of course, this is difficult, and my success rate is far from perfect. Therefore, these tests are discussed thoroughly when they are returned to the students, and I have a method of determining ambiguous and misleading questions during the grading process. These questions are eliminated from the exam before the grades are determined. Out of every fifty new questions I make up, about three to five of them are lousy; they are ambiguous, misleading, or unrelated to what has been happening in the course in terms of the students' perspectives.

Essay tests are not necessarily any better than the multiple choice format, but the potential for such tests to be facilitators and indicators of learning is great. One of the most successful but challenging essay test formats involves getting the students to write their own personal essay questions—one on each topic covered in the period prior to the test. This means that students have the opportunity to make up their own tests, to study at their own pace, and to ask themselves questions on topics related to their own interests. Since we cover about fifteen major issues during a semester, this means we have three tests with five questions based specifically on each student's interests. For each test the students are asked to make up their questions and turn them in at least one week prior to the exam. I take a look at them to see if they are appropriate. If, for some reason, they are not appropriate, I ask for new questions. During the actual test period, I return these personalized questions to each student with two of them circled. They must prepare responses to all five questions because they don't know which two I might choose. But I only have to read answers to two of them. This means that they know their questions in advance, and I get to read different essays for every student in the class. (I was always bored reading fifty of the same answers to the same question and trying to keep from making unfair comparisons of the essays and their authors; this method forces me to deal with each student as an individual). Students inevitably complain about this testing method because they have never learned to ask themselves good questions. Their experiences in U.S. schools have been answer-oriented, rather than question-oriented. But we practice making up questions in class, and after they've made up a couple of tests, the majority appreciate the autonomy and freedom this method affords. In fact, after the first test, many of the students begin to feel comfortable with the challenge of asking themselves good, interesting questions. For this reason I've used this method for years. When students continue to have difficulty making up their own questions I may refer them to selected essay questions from the Instructor's Manual for *Sport in Society: Issues and Controversies.* Many of the questions in the manual represent revised versions of questions made up by students over the past fifteen years. (See Appendix II for sample questions.)

There are other forms of testing in addition to the two I've used and discussed. It may be that neither of these approaches is appropriate for courses other than mine. It is important to remember that the evaluation of student work is a crucial part of the classroom experience and that the method of evaluation should grow out of the nature and organization of the class itself. In fact, in some cases, tests of any type may be inappropriate; projects, papers, and the organization of seminar discussions may be better indicators of learning in certain courses.

GETTING INTO THE FIELD

Most of my students have also appreciated opportunities to go out into the community to make observations and gather data related to sport. We have observed student and adult spectators at high school football and basketball games, parents at youth league games, coaches working with youth teams, and children engaged in a variety of physical-activity settings including spontaneous play, informal games, and adult-organized competitive youth sports.

The most successful project has consistently been the one in which children have been observed. It has been organized in a variety of different ways over the years, but it has usually involved observations and/or informal interviews with children who are participating in physical activities of some sort. The purpose is to provide students opportunities to collect data on an interesting topic and bring them back to the classroom for analysis and discussion. The classroom discussions have then focused on the differences between spontaneous play, informal games, and organized competitive sports. These differences have then been discussed in terms of social development issues and in terms of their policy implications for adults involved in planning, organizing, and administering competitive youth sports. Furthermore, I was able to use the data collected during a succession of three semesters for my own research on children in sport. (See my paper in Harris and Park 1983.)

CHANGES THROUGH THE YEARS: FROM EXPOSÉ TO ANALYSIS

From 1970 through 1980, an important part of my sociology of sport course consisted of exposing the injustice, inequality, violence, racism, sexism, nationalism, exploitation, drug-taking, cheating, and the overemphasis on winning that existed in sports at all levels of competition, but especially on the highest levels. In other words, we spent considerable time destroying myths. Through the mid-1970s my students were shocked and dismayed when they discovered that sports were not like they had been told while growing up. From the mid-1970s to the early 1980s, the students were still dismayed to hear such things, but they were no longer shocked. The popular press had opened their eyes prior to registering for my course. Many myths had already been destroyed. Now, in the mid-1980s, my students are less likely to be shocked or dismayed when these things are introduced and discussed. They have already heard them numerous times. The foundations for many past myths have been eroded by novelists, journalists, and former athletes turning their collective attention to telling everyone about the "darker side of sport." This means that to keep students interested and thinking I have to deal more with their cynicism than their lack of awareness.

As the students have changed in this respect, so has my course content. I now depend less on exposé and more on analysis in my class materials. We spend more time on issues such as sport and social development, sport as a form of leisure, and the relationship between sport and the dynamics of change in society as a whole. We talk more about societies other than the U.S. We now ask many more "why?" questions than "what?" or "how?" questions. Theory has become more important; understanding society as a whole and its history has become more important. The discussions of change and reform have become more detailed, and our suggestions developed during class have become more carefully constructed.

In general, we talk less about how sport is a reflection of society and more about how people themselves do or might define and create sport in various ways. Of course, we do not ignore the powerful influence exerted by social conditions on the structure and dynamics of sport and sport activities. But we call into question the deterministic and self-defeating idea that sport is a mirror of the social order and that, as a mirror, it simply reflects the social order in which it exists. In line with this we have gradually moved away from the ideas that athletes and spectators are simply victims in a series of processes over which they have no control, and that changes will not occur in sport until they have occurred in society at large. The idea that humane sports cannot exist until we have a humane society is one that has stopped many energetic and reform-oriented students in their tracks. They have become justifiably discouraged when they thought sports could not be changed in any meaningful ways until they changed all of society. Therefore, we emphasize the dialectical relationship between sport and society and the possibility of merging an interest in changing sport with an interest in changing society as a whole.

THINGS THAT HAVEN'T CHANGED THROUGH THE YEARS

One of the challenges faced at the beginning of every semester is to get students to use sociological rather than psychological explanations for what goes on in the world. For example, many of them come into class ready to explain violence in sport by focusing on the characteristics of those who engage in violent behavior rather than on the ways various sports have been organized and linked to what is going on in the rest of society. Similarly, they are ready to explain the low sport participation rates among low-income married women with children by referring to individual motivation and individual experiences rather than to social stratification and the unequal distribution of resources and access to participation opportunities and facilities. This means that they often begin the course with the idea that changes in sports simply involve changes in the individuals who make up sports. However, it doesn't take long to show them there is a need to go beyond the individuals in sport and to consider how issues are related to social organization and social relationships. They are also quick to understand that while motivation and perception may be important in explaining individual performances in sport, it is necessary to understand the implications of power and inequality when dealing with issues related to change in the organization of sport.

Other things that have not changed much through the years include (1) the need to integrate material on women into the course, (2) the need to focus attention on issues going beyond professional and top-level intercollegiate sports, and (3) the need to include information on countries other than the United States. The media coverage of sport as well as the literature in the sociology of sport in the U.S. tends to be about American males participating in highly competitive sport settings. This provides a very limited view of what sport is as a social phenomenon. Women are often ignored or given only passing attention. The issue of mass participation is seldom discussed despite the fact that it is a more significant social phenomenon than professional sports. And the existence of sport in other countries is hardly acknowledged even though the U.S. accounts for only 5 percent of the world's population.

In an effort to provide students with a more realistic view of sport as a social phenomenon, it has always been necessary to facilitate additional class discussions of issues related to gender, mass participation, and countries other than the U.S. My record in responding to this challenge has not been perfect, but it has been getting better with each new semester. Through the years I've tried to organize course content in ways that acknowledge the changing reality of my students' experiences, but I've also tried to make sure the course is not simply a reflection of the society in which it exists.

APPENDIX I: MAJOR ISSUES DISCUSSED IN CURRENT COURSE

1. The sociology of sport: what is it and why study it?
2. Sport in society: an inspiration or an opiate?
3. A look at the past: how have sports changed through history?
4. Sport and the economy: what are the effects of commercialization?
5. Sport and the mass media: could they survive without one another?
6. Females in sport: are the barriers gone?
7. Blacks in sport: is sport a model of equal opportunity?
8. Violent behavior: is sport a cause or a cure?
9. Sport and politics: do games create unity and peace?
10. Competition in sport: does it prepare people for life?
11. Organized sport programs for children: are they worth the effort?
12. Sport in high school and college: do interscholastic programs contribute to education?
13. Sport and social mobility: is participation a path to success?
14. Coaches: are they teachers or tyrants?
15. Sport and religion: is it a promising combination?
16. Sport in the future: what can we expect?

APPENDIX II: SAMPLE ESSAY QUESTIONS

1. In a conversation with your parents, you mention that you are taking a sociology of sport class at college. Your father accuses you of wasting his money and your time on a worthless course. It is up to you to explain to him that his money and your time is not being wasted. What would you say in your explanation?

2. You have just been appointed to a committee that has been asked to develop a set of policy recommendations for changing the organized youth sport programs in your town. There are three other people on the committee: a functionalist, a conflict theorist, and a critical theorist. Explain the recommendations you would expect from each of them and then say whom you would agree with when it came to writing your final report for the committee.

3. The instructor in your introductory sociology class says that there is more sexism in sport during the 1980s than at any other point in human history. You disagree with him and he asks you to back up your case with some good examples from history. What would you say in making your case?

4. In one of your business classes, one of the students argues that American professional football is an inspiration to all those who believe that competition is at the basis of progress and development in American society. The instructor knows you are a sport studies major and calls on you to respond to the student's remark. What would you say in your response? Would you agree or disagree? Why?

5. You are a new editor at *Sports Illustrated.* At your first editorial meeting the major item on the agenda is a debate on the pros and cons of the February swimsuit issue. As the discussion goes on, it is decided that it would be economically unwise to drop the swimsuit issue. But it is also decided that if the swimsuit issue is continued, there must be other changes in the magazine to present a fair image of women in sport. As a new editor, you are called on to make some suggestions for changes. How would you respond?

6. Your fourteen-year-old sister has always been one of the best ice hockey players in your town. Ever since she was seven, she has outskated boys her own age. All of a sudden she decides to quit hockey even though there are programs she could play in all the way through college. All of her male teammates decide to continue their involvement. How could you explain why she dropped out and why her male friends stayed in? Why would male adolescents be more likely to continue their participation in such a sport while female adolescents would usually drop out?

7. During your Christmas break you are watching a professional basketball game with your father. During the game he mentions that the majority of players on both teams are black. In commenting on this, he says that blacks have always gotten a fair shake in American sports despite discrimination in other areas. How would you tell your father that this is not the case? What historical data would you use to back up your argument?

8. You are a staff worker in a juvenile treatment center. Your boss says that he would like to develop a boxing program for the boys in the program so they will have a chance to "work out their violent feelings and become well-adjusted human beings." He then gives you an opportunity to respond to his idea. What would you say?

9. You are watching the 1988 Olympics with a group of your friends. During the telecast a number of your friends make comments expressing their dislike of the Soviet Union and East Germany. This is surprising in light of the fact that you have always been told that sport creates international friendship and understanding. How would you explain your friends' behavior in this situation?

10. A coach of a high school all-star basketball team tells you that after working with the players on her team she thinks that sport competition definitely builds character. You tell her she should be careful when making such a conclusion. She tells you that you are crazy, that she has personal experience to back up her conclusion. Explain why the coach clings to her belief that competition builds character?

11. You are a member of the city council in a large city in the East. Many of the children in your district play street ball during the warm months. One of the council members suggests that there should be a rule banning street ball because it is a dangerous, worthless activity that interferes with traffic in the city. You are interested in the safety of the young people in your district, but you also want to come to their defense and show that street ball is not a useless activity. What would you say to the council about street ball, and what kinds of policy suggestions might you make in this situation?

12. You are a member of a local school board. The board has just been presented with data showing that varsity athletes in the ten high schools in your district receive higher grades than nonathletes. The data are being used by a parent group who want more funds for interscholastic sports in the district. What are the questions you would ask the parents about the data, and why would you ask them?

13. You are in a group of white adults. In their conversation about sports one of them says that if it weren't for sports, blacks in this country would be in much worse shape (socioeconomically) than they are now. He continues by saying that being a good athlete is still the best way out of the ghetto for a young black. How would you respond to these comments? Would you agree or disagree, and what would you say to back up your position?

14. Your English composition teacher is talking to you and a couple of other students after one of your classes. As the conversation gets around to the intercollegiate sport program on your campus, your teacher complains about the coaches. He asks why the coaches can't be more like the faculty, why can't they deal with students in the same manner that faculty members deal with students? Since you are taking a sociology of sport class, he looks to you for an answer. What would you say to explain the differences between the role of coach and the role of a classroom teacher at the university?

15. Imagine that you are a Christian boxer. How can you combine your religious beliefs and your participation in sport? What kinds of problems would you have in making this combination?

16. You are working as an administrator in a local parks and recreation department. As more and more people participate in sports in your city, a serious shortage of spaces and facilities develops. You realize that unless you do something, this scarcity of spaces and facilities will lead to more and more regulations. You also realize that with the regulations will come more bureaucratization, more specialization, and more commercialization in sports. You do not want to see this happen. How could you prevent these things from happening?

APPENDIX III: SAMPLE PROJECTS

FOR A DISCUSSION ON RACE AND SPORT:
Depending on the size and nature of your student body, your class members could do a "racial history" of sport at your school. Have each student take a different men's or women's sport and find out when the first black, hispanic, or other minority student participated as a team member. What proportions of various teams have been made up by minority athletes through the years? Do the patterns fit what might be expected after reading the chapter in Coakley (1986)? If not, why not? Did the first players who broke "color lines" on various teams have performance statistics that were better than the statistics for the whites on the teams?

For the football, basketball, and baseball teams, see if your students can get data on the positions played by different minority athletes. Do the patterns match the stacking patterns described in the chapter in Coakley (1986)? Have patterns changed over the past twenty years? Use yearbooks or information guides put out by the athletic department as data sources.

If you are at a large university, you might be able to do a project to call into question racist beliefs about sport abilities. You would have to be careful with this one, but you could get the coaches from the men's and women's volleyball and basketball teams to give you the vertical jump data for both their white athletes and their black athletes. I would bet that the vertical jumps of the white volleyball players would be as high as the vertical jumps of the black basketball players, especially if both teams recruited at the same level in their sports. (For example, the comparison would be useless if your men's basketball team was ranked 15th in the nation and your men's volleyball team was 0–20 last year.) This project might be a good way to make the point that jumping ability is not distributed unequally by race. However, be careful to qualify your data in light of the characteristics of the samples used. The samples will not be representative for either race!

FOR A DISCUSSION ON INTERSCHOLASTIC SPORT:
Use your own campus as a laboratory. An in-depth analysis of an intercollegiate sport program can be a very interesting project for students. If groups of class members are given different tasks, a wide range of information can be gathered. Some of the relevant areas of investigation would include:

- Budgets for each of the sports, major and minor.
- Sources of funding (student fees, outside contributions, gate receipts by sport, state support, foundation support, etc.).
- The "hourly wages" of athletes with different types of scholarships in different sports.
- The revenues generated by athletes in different sports.
- The use of sport facilities by intercollegiate teams relative to the usage by the student body as a whole.
- The academic life of student athletes in different sports (e.g., course schedules, number of hours taken per semester, per year, in summer school).
- The graduation rates of athletes by sport.
- The economic impact of different sports on the local community.

APPENDIX IV: SAMPLE LIST OF MULTIPLE CHOICE QUESTIONS

1. When applied to physical activities, the term "institutionalization" implied the existence of
   *a. a formalized and patterned structure.
   b. at least two teams of individuals.
   c. an indoor competitive game.
   d. games controlled by players and coaches.
2. If a functionalist was making policy recommendations for sport, the recommendations would probably call for
   a. the development of players' unions.
   *b. more organized programs and more supervision for athletes.
   c. increased choices for the participants in sport.
   d. less structured sport experiences.
3. Those who organized sport programs for young males around the turn of the century were interested in
   a. turning lower-class boys into competitive leaders.
   b. teaching lower-class boys how to fit into upper class activities.
   *c. turning overfeminized middle-class boys into assertive leaders.
   d. teaching boys from all backgrounds the importance of leisure in their lives.
4. Television has had a positive impact on the growth of commercial sports because it has

a. decreased interests in nonsport forms of entertainment.
b. created more competition for revenues between sport teams.
c. increased the rivalries between players on various teams.
*d. served as a tool for creating new spectators and fans.

5. Being a sportswriter is in some ways like being a sport sociologist. However, there are some important differences. Compared to sport sociologists, sportswriters have
a. more limited budgets.
b. more time to do detailed stories.
*c. more deadlines to meet.
d. more opportunities to gather systematic data.

6. Young girls in North America are less likely than their brothers to be involved in informal competitive games because
a. their parents generally discourage them from participating in any physical activities.
*b. their parents often give them only "conditional permission" to participate in leisure activities.
c. girls have a more difficult time making good friends than boys do.
d. fathers take less interest in their daughters than in their sons.

7. The desegregation of sport is related to the development of sport skills among blacks. Blacks have developed high-level skills in certain sports, especially those which
a. open up opportunities for them to interact with whites in informal social settings.
b. require the use of highly technical equipment.
*c. can be learned without the use of expensive equipment and facilities.
d. lead to contacts with people in the business community.

8. The idea that violence may be connected to the structure of certain sport teams is grounded in the notion that people are likely to use violence as a means of responding to
a. competitive challenges.
*b. rigidly organized social groups and authoritarian leaders.
c. heavy physical training schedules.
d. pressures from spectators who influence the organization of sports.

9. Research on race relations has shown that contact between the races is most likely to lead to favorable changes in attitudes when blacks and whites
a. behave in conformity with stereotypes.
*b. depend on one another's cooperation to achieve their goals.
c. pursue different goals in different activities.
d. have unequal status.

10. The ideas that many people have about the benefits of competition for character building are often biased because they focus their attention on athletes who
a. drop out at an early age.
b. are involved in recreational programs.
*c. are successful at the highest levels of competition.
d. have become coaches in high schools and colleges.

11. After reading chapter 11 in Coakley (1986), which of the following would you expect to observe if you attended both an organized Little League baseball game and a pickup game in a vacant lot?
a. There would be fewer strikeouts in the Little League game.
*b. The combined scores of the two teams in the pickup game would be higher.

c. Unique playing styles would be more frequently seen in the Little League game.
d. The rules would be applied to all players equally in the pickup game.

12. Role conflict among college athletes is most likely for those who are in schools with
    a. good academic reputations.
    b. small-time athletic programs.
    *c. big-time athletic programs.
    d. athletic programs administered by the physical education department.
13. Information on women's intercollegiate teams shows that as the number of teams has increased
    a. the proportion of women in coaching and administration has increased.
    *b. the proportion of female head coaches and assistant coaches has declined.
    c. the number of male head coaches has declined and the number of male assistant coaches has increased.
    d. the number of women coaches has declined.
14. Coaches are most likely to become "significant others" in the lives of athletes when they
    a. treat their athletes in an impersonal but firm manner.
    *b. develop close, personal relationships with their athletes.
    c. deal with athletes who have numerous other adult role models.
    d. experience a high degree of pressure to have winning records.
15. In recent years there has been a growth in religious-sport organizations. In general, these organizations tend to be
    a. concerned with social issues and social change.
    b. tied directly to major religious denominations.
    c. grounded in non-Christian belief systems.
    *d. based on conservative, fundamentalist orientations.
16. Technosport involves the combination of technology and sport competition. It is ultimately based on the notion that humans reach their potential when they
    *a. become machine-like.
    b. face unpredictable challenges.
    c. work as members of teams.
    d. engage in risky and dangerous activities.

WORKS CITED

Coakley, Jay J. 1986. *Sport in Society: Issues and Controversies.* 3d ed. St. Louis, Mo.: C. V. Mosby.

Edwards, Harry. 1969. *The Revolt of the Black Athlete.* New York: Free Press.

Eitzen, D. Stanley, ed. 1984. *Sport in Contemporary Society.* New York: St. Martin's Press.

Eitzen, D. Stanley, and George H. Sage. 1986. *Sociology of North American Sport.* 3d ed. Dubuque, Iowa: Wm. C. Brown.

Elias, Norbert, and Eric Dunning. 1986. *The Quest for Excitement.* Oxford: Basil Blackwell.

Gruneau, Richard. 1983. *Class, Sports, and Social Development.* Amherst: University of Massachusetts Press.

Guttmann, Allen. 1978. *From Ritual to Record: The Nature of Modern Sports.* New York: Columbia University Press.

Hargreaves, Jennifer, ed. 1982. *Sport, Culture and Ideology.* London: Routledge and Kegan Paul.

Harris, Janet C., and Roberta J. Park, eds. 1983. *Play, Games and Sports in Cultural Contexts*. Champaign, Ill.: Human Kinetics.

Hart, M. Marie., and Susan Birrell, eds. 1981. *Sport in the Sociocultural Process*. 3d ed. Dubuque, Iowa: Wm. C. Brown.

Loy, John W., and Gerald S. Kenyon, eds. 1969. *Sport, Culture and Society*. New York: Macmillan.

Loy, John W., Gerald S. Kenyon, and Barry D. McPherson, eds. 1981. *Sport, Culture and Society*. Philadelphia: Lea and Febiger.

Loy, John W., Barry D. McPherson, and Gerald S. Kenyon, eds. 1978. *Sport and Social Systems*. Reading, Mass.: Addison-Wesley.

Rees, C. Roger, and Andrew W. Miracle, eds. 1986. *Sport and Social Theory*. Champaign, Ill.: Human Kinetics.

Scott, Jack. 1971. *The Athletic Revolution*. New York: Free Press.

Tomlinson, A., and G. Whannel, eds. 1984. *Five Ring Circus: Money, Power and Politics at the Olympic Games*. London: Pluto Press.

Yiannakis, A. et al., eds. 1986. *Sport Sociology: Contemporary Themes*. 3d ed. Dubuque, Iowa: Kendall/Hunt.

10
The Dynamics of Sport in American Society: Some Thoughts on Experiencing Sociology of Sport in the Classroom

MARY McELROY

The contemporary sport world is filled with anomalies, contradictions, and ironies. For example, as the financial climate at colleges and universities worsens, the expenditures by their sport teams skyrocket. And even though women have experienced increased opportunities in some areas of sport, the doors to the "profession" of sport (playing careers, coaching) remain virtually shut. Educators, church officials, and parents find fault with the erosion of the American work ethic, but at the same time, all are witnessing an explosion of sport academies, youth camps, and other forms of highly organized children's sport programs—indicators of a willingness to invest in the time, energy, and financial resources necessary for serious pursuit of a sport career.

These examples of contemporary sport in American society illustrate the complex interaction of our society with its sports. While Robert Redford's portrayal of Roy Hobbs in the screen version of *The Natural* insisted upon a dramatic game winning home run, in its original literary form, Hobbs can offer too little too late, and the slugger strikes out. Roy Hobbs's failure, however, does more than suggest that sport mirrors the harshness of American life. For such a microscopic view of American society only reduces sport to the role of an "innocent bystander," able to reflect social ills, yet somehow, in its passivity, not responsible for the current condition of any of them.

A passive conception of sport has also infiltrated some of our traditional approaches to the teaching of sociology of sport. Students study elite athletes very unlike themselves, listen to professors lecture on the social dynamics between sport and traditional American social institutions (family, education, mass media, politics), and spend an enormous amount of time objectively sifting through the facts. By course's end, they have amassed numerous statistics, dates, and studies. Students enter sport courses with diverse backgrounds, but despite these differences they share a common denominator, that of experience at some level in sport. These personal experiences should not be taken lightly and can also be used to make students feel and live sporting roles of which they are less familar. While the sociology of sport class provides a forum to bring to life the dynamic interrelationship between sport participation and society, these courses often fall short of their potential. The purpose of this essay is to share some of the strategies I have considered and put into practice during the past ten years in an effort to make the study of sport in society more relevant to the students and to make them active participants in the classroom.

CHANGING COMPOSITION OF THE SOCIOLOGY OF SPORT CLASS

When I first started teaching "Sport in American Society" as a physical education graduate student at the University of Maryland, the class was largely comprised of enthusiastic sport fans. They could list the starting lineups of most sports teams, comment on recent big trades, and many could recite yesterday's box scores. Curiosity likely attracted many of them to my class. What could an academic class tell them about that which they lived and experienced during their leisure time? Examples from the world of professional sport often helped me to clarify otherwise elusive sociological concepts. Guest speakers from the sports world (easier to find in the Washington, D. C., area) drew near perfect student attendance.

Upon moving to Kansas in 1978, I became familiar with the regional sports. Big Eight football dominated early fall. The Kansas City Chiefs and the Kansas City Royals, the professional teams, captured the television market. But before too long, students in my sociology of sport classes seemed to change. Many of them had never attended a professional sporting event or played on a varsity sports team, and some were not able to recite the starting lineup of the Kansas City Royals. I even caught myself wondering how many of them knew of George Brett. What was happening to the sociology of sport student? Was there something occurring in the world of sport that I did not know about? After all, interest in sport was not waning. In fact, indicators suggested quite the opposite. I looked for changes in the university to help explain the disappearance of my sport fans. First, there was the increase in the number of sport-related classes taught in other departments. In addition to the Sociology Department; History, English, and Psychology also regularly offered sport courses. Perhaps my sports fans enrolled in these courses instead of mine. But I also wondered about the effects of the increased specialization within the field of physical education (the department in which I teach). Physical education students no longer were restricted to only teacher-training programs. They specialized in areas such as sports medicine, fitness programs, dance, leisure studies, and coaching. I wondered if students could still see themselves in certain sporting roles. If they could not, would they be able to appreciate the complexities of these sporting roles in contemporary society? It became evident that my initial emphasis on only the most formal organized sport setting was no longer personally meaningful to a large number of students. My job was still the same, to make the connections between sport and society; however, my strategy had to change: I needed to expand the definition of sport to include other forms of physical activity, and I needed to encourage students to consider forms of sport heretofore unfamilar to them.

INTRODUCING THE SOCIOLOGY OF SPORT

The first day of class brings together a wide assortment of university students. They come skeptical as to whether insights can be gained through applying the "sociological imagination" to sport and physical activity. First, they are introduced to some of the underlying assumptions of sociological inquiry. We discuss that "groups" can be identified by their common characteristics; and group roles, not the names of individuals, are important. Furthermore, we discuss how groups are influenced by their social environments. Then, as early as the first session, the students are introduced to the ambiguities and contradictions present in the sports world. I refer to this as a *hierarchichal value system* and it is depicted in Diagram 1. Society has created a regulatory system based on a set of consequences. As depicted in Diagram 1, certain violations (rape, murder,

Diagram 1
Hierarchical Value System

Societal Infractions	Sport Infractions
murder/rape drunken driving cocaine abuse family violence	hitting someone with a baseball bat touching an umpire undercut in basketball "fixing" games
driving over 55 mph	sliding spikes up
Infraction in Society But Not in Sport	**Infraction in Sport But Not in Society**
sport celebration riots taking erogenic aids (some) aggressive (harmful) acts fighting "special treatment" for college student-athletes	curfew violations missing classes dress code violations being a left-handed catcher player draft system association with "legal" gambling

etc.) are clear infractions, while others are more ambiguous (driving over 55 mph).

Within the social system of sport the same distinctions are evident. The bottom half of diagram 1 highlights the ambiguity between the sport order and that of society, and depicts instances where behaviors are *violations in sport but not in society* (breaking training rules or curfews) or *violations in society but not in sport* (sport celebration riots).

By the end of the first class session, many students think differently about sport; some begin to acknowledge the importance of examining specific social contexts, others may be frustrated by this disarray present in our society. In all cases, students begin to develop a new appreciation for sport. They see that despite its straightforward simplicity, sport can also be complex. That which appears on the surface is not all what it seems; sport is often more than a simple lens to the larger society.

CONTROVERSIAL ISSUES AND ROLE-PLAYING

I have found one of the best ways to make students "live" sociology of sport is to make them defend cetain controversial positions through structured role-playing. Nothing seems to arouse a lively class quite like a well-structured debate. The keyword is "well-structured" as over the years I have learned that students initially opt for the passive roles of listeners; they reluctantly voice their convictions or will back down from a position because someone else presents contrary evidence. They avoid the devil's advocate role that brings forth a less-than-popular side to particular issues. Structured debates also allow for students to freely engage in all three. I have continually modified the interactive debate structures and, with increasing success, have transformed my audience from passive students to confident role-playing debaters. Significant controversial issues are formally scrutinized, merits and demerits of each side are supported by specific examples (from newspapers, television, readings), and each issue is subject to formal rebuttal and a subsequent comeback. Potential topics are listed in Appendix I.

Unless the class is very small, entire-group debates usually do not work well since large groups create a false sense of security. Students seem to count on someone else to defend the positions. Debate teams best consist of four members, two on each side. A fifth student may act as the moderator. Each student should be given at least two opportunities to debate. For most of them, role-playing is a new experience; anxiety is associated with the first experience but generally disappears by the second run.

Although it is important that students select the specific topics and issues to be debated, it is worthwhile to devote a full class session to choosing the debate topics. In so doing, I stress the following: the importance of the two opposing sides working together as one team to select issues that can be argued from two positions; making sure each team is arguing the same issue; including all the critical arguments for each issue. Once the debate issues and arguments have been determined, students need to support their respective positions with convincing examples. Support evidence usually ranges from newspapers articles to research studies. The debate format allows for each team to make opening arguments and rebuttal statements. Evaluation is based on the ability to articulate the major positions and demonstrate conviction. Evaluation of the rebuttal stresses the team's ability to listen to the other team's position and systematically refute their argument. Students not directly involved in the debate are asked to evaluate the performance of their peers, although only my evaluation is used for grading purposes. A point system is used to evaluate the strengths and weaknesses of the presented arguments, and the final grade is based on the overall group performance. A collective score encourages students to choose the "less popular" positions and fosters a cooperative rather than competitive spirit between the teams. Students are more likely to share information and prepare stronger cases, all which contribute to a more satisfying debate.

POTENTIAL PITFALLS IN DEBATE TOPICS

Although in the example in Table 1 both teams identified several relevant arguments, the evidence was not set up in a way in which Team A and Team B could directly argue opposing views. With such a setup, there is no way to evaluate the merits of one position relative to the other. Concepts remain cloudy and the students become confused. While both teams have presented some interesting points, the debate is likely to come to an abrupt halt, leaving the instructor to wonder where to go from there.

Alternatively, the issues must be structured so that each team can argue

Table 1
Impact of Sport in the High School Setting

Team A	Team B
a. sport stimulates interest in physical activites among all students.	a. sport distracts attention from academic pursuits.
b. sport generates school spirit.	b. sport relegates most to a role of spectator.
c. sport evokes school spirit from teachers, peers, parents, alumni, and community.	c. Sport deprives educational programs of resources, facilities, personnel, and community awareness and support.
d. sport serves as an advertising vehicle.	d. sport creates an anti-intellectual spirit among students that has little to do with the educational goals of the school.

(Adapted from Coakley 1982, 113)

Table 2
Issues in Intercollegiate Sports Programs and their Consequences

	student/athlete	university academicians	university athletic department
recruiting practices	–	–	+
scholarships	+ –	–	+
athletic dorms	–	–	+
transfer rules	–	–	+
post-season tournaments	+ –	+	+
two season tournaments	–	–	+
length of season	–	–	+
Title IX legislation	+	+	+ –
alumni involvement	–	+	+
wages for athletes	+ –	–	–

\+ may be argued from a beneficial position
– may be argued from a detrimental position
\+ – may be argued from both positions

opposing viewpoints on the same issue. One way to accomplish this is to defend positions based on special interest groups. For example, the traditional issues surrounding intercollegiate sport are presented in Table 2. Clearly, the benefits of each issue vary markedly according to each group: student-athletes, university academicians, and athletic department personnel. Other forms of role playing may include such face-offs as team owners versus team fans, female athletes versus male athletes, and perhaps when considering gambling in sport, even organized crime versus ordinary citizens.

INCLUSION OF EXPERIMENTAL TOPICS

While over the years I have standardized much of the course's content, I make it a regular policy to include at least one topic that is *not* covered in standard sociology of sport textbooks. Such topics include superstition and sport, sport fanaticism, compulsive exercise, or sport as popular culture. The selection of these topics is endless. I choose topics that force students to gather information from nontraditional sources. Recently, a class considered whether sport met the criteria of an art from. We considered whether sport exercised imaginative and intellectual faculties (usually associated with an art form), or rather, did sport exercise only those of the physical. The class questioned the relationship between high culture and sport culture, and hypothesized whether sport was viewed by some as only amusement for crude people. Students were asked to attend theatrical events at the local playhouses and to interview actors, producers, and theater-goers.

Good topics may also surface from current events. For example, when the Soviet Union boycotted the Los Angeles Olympic Games, I asked students to assume roles of Soviet athletes, Soviet officials, and the Olympic Committee as well as their American counterparts. Other topics, such as the use of instant replays in the NFL, the Goodwill Games in Moscow, or the highly publicized deaths of young athletes, should create good discussions and encourage students to keep on the lookout for other potential topics. They also force me to consider new material each semester.

SPORT FICTION AS SPORT EXPERIENCE

Finally, one more strategy that seems to have successfully brought concepts of sociology of sport to life in the classroom has been the inclusion of one sports novel each semester. The twentieth-century novelist has discovered America's love of sport. Popular fiction features athletes past and present, and some novels focused wholly on sport have now achieved the distinction of contemporary classics. But what benefit can sport fiction have specifically to the study of sport in society? While many cultural historians have turned freely to American fiction for clues to what Russell Nye calls the "feel of society" (1966, 140), sport sociologists have been resistant, noticeable more for their neglect of sport fiction than their observance of it. Perhaps they question the use of imaginative sources in reconstructing the social order. After all, the sociologist and the novelist begin quite differently. The sociologist seeks to first know what happened. Literary facts, on the other hand, exist only in the imagination to the extent that they have any existence at all. In fiction, moreover, the object is not to accumulate more and more details. Rather, it is to feel and appreciate, and what counts is not the number of facts but the degree to which we may have been made to live with them. Literature explores the meaning and value attached to a given set of circumstances. Imaginative literature can help the student recognize the critical connections and significances. We cannot fully understand and appreciate the ambiance of a time period, even our own, and the coherent shape of its events with numerical facts alone; for such a sensibility, we need the kind of information fiction may provide. While novels, for example, may not be held to historical accountability, they still stand in recognizable relation to life. Indeed, it is literature that allows the student to feel and live with the facts. Curiously enough, the very absence of strict verisimilitude in fiction forges a powerful bond between the author and the student (reader). We love stories, according to Marjorie Bolton for two reasons: our readiness to comfort and entertain ourselves with fantasy and our curiosity and desire for insight about reality (1975, 4). Though these two seem like opposites, it is not always easy to separate them completely. We should not underestimate the need to separate fact from fiction, but the real challenge given to the student of American sport rests in considering the significance of their interdependence.

And it is just here that literature allows the student to understand the relationship between sport and society. Concepts are best initially introduced using the traditional theoretical frameworks and then applying sport examples to make the case.

"Retirement from sport roles" or, more appropriately termed, "desocialization" may be presented using theories of mid-career change and forced retirement. The difficulties involved in leaving sport and resocializing into a second career are presented, and although students respectfully listen, many have difficulty relating to the plight of such financially successful and highly publicized athletes. I then introduce them to Henry Wiggen, a fictitious baseball pitching star and central character in four novels by Mark Harris: *The Southpaw* (1952), *Bang the Drum Slowly* (1956), *Ticket for a Seamstitch* (1957), *It Looked Like Forever* (1979). In the most recent, *It Looked Like Forever,* Henry Wiggen, now 40, is released suddenly from his ball club, and we learn to live with his day-to-day agony of adjustment. Eventually, he is given a chance to pitch again, but this time it is only at an old-timer's game. Henry Wiggen painstakingly takes us through his return to the mound. He strikes out the side of old men on nine pitches and proudly runs into the showers as he used to do. Students then begin to appreciate the difficulty Henry has in giving up his baseball career. The comical scene abruptly turns tragic as we witness his failure to cling to his youth as he faces the reality of his own mortality. While certainly not all professional athletes live Henry's existence, the despair in all of us seems to know Henry's agony.

The universal acceptance of sport in America makes it a ripe metaphor for such central cultural and human experiences as loss, control, failure, and conquest. The versatility of the athletic figure as an American symbol is also enhanced by the innocence traditionally attached to him, "a child existing in the idealized world of game," a condition of innocence that is heightened by the athlete's dream of immortality, his desire to remain forever young or at least for as long as the body can meet the demands of the competition. The fictional athlete, then, is a kind of tabula rasa upon which the novelist can exercise an enormous range of encounters, turning them comic, tragic, or satirical as one chooses, and developing meanings relevant both in and out of the sporting arena.

Although students may approach such reading assignments with initial skepticism, by semester's end they generally agree they have experienced sport in a way they had not done before and seem to appreciate the opportunity to step into the roles of the literary athletes. Examples of some appropriate sporting novels are suggested in Appendix II as well as elsewhere in this collection. In general, sport novels that I consider for inclusion in my class must meet the following criteria:

Works must be of literary quality: The abundance of novels about sport include shallow treatments about stereotypical athletes. It is important to choose novels where plot and characters are fully developed. Stay away from adolescent sport fiction.

Central characters must be cast in sporting roles: Because of the importance of sport in everyday life, we find mention of sport in a great number of novels or the development of sporting characters in secondary roles. For example, we find Tom Buchanan in F. Scott Fitzgerald's *The Great Gatsby* (1925) and sport scenes in Raymond Chandler's detective fiction. While these small passages and characterizations are likely critical to the development of the novel, they tend not to make a major statement concerning sport and society sufficient for inclusion in a sociology of sport class.

The interplay of the novel must comment on both the qualities of sport and those of society: If nonsporting characters can be substituted without radically changing the novel it is likely not commenting on the unique interplay between sport and social order.

Students can choose their sport novel, or the entire class may be assigned the same piece of fiction. Generally, the latter provides for a more fruitful class discussion, but if used as a written assignment alone, choice allows for a greater variety in topics. In either case, the instructor should make sure that the books are available (in the bookstore or library) and should be able to provide students with guidance in their selections.

As British novelist Virginia Woolf has observed, sport solves one of the American writer's most difficult artistic problems: "It has given him a clue, a centre, a meeting place for the diverse activities of people whom a vast continent isolates" (1963, 4). Sport offer the novelist a metaphor powerful enough both to explore the ambiguities of present life and to reveal the enduring structure of the American experience. Sport captures what Michael Oriard describes as "the shared dreams of a culture" (1982, 8), those collectively held that are fundamentally important to the way people think and live. It is through this power of sport that the sociologist can take full advantage of the importance of sport and physical activity in everyday life and help students consider its relevance within the highly structured society in which they live.

APPENDIX I: SYLLABUS

Sociology of Sport
PE 745/Soc 745
Dr. Mary McElroy
Office, Ahearn 12C
Telephone, 532-6765

REQUIRED TEXTS
Sport in Society: Issues and controversies by Jay Coakley, 3d ed.
A Separate Peace by John Knowles.

COURSE OBJECTIVES

To create a greater awareness of the social significance of contemporary sport.

To foster an appreciation of the utility of social scientific methodology for understanding sport.

To analyze contemporary sport problems.

COURSE REQUIREMENTS:

Required Readings	
Mid-term examination	25 points
Final examination	35 points
Book critique	10 points
Debate participation	20 points
Class participation	10 points

TOPICS TO BE COVERED

Week 1. Introduction.
2. Nature of sport: play, games, and sport.
3. Sport and American culture.
4. Sport and socialization.
5. Sport and education: interscholastic.
6. Sport and education: intercollegiate.
7. Sport and social mobility.
8. Examination.
9. Sport and physical activity: commercialism and big business.
10. Violence and sport.
11. Social issues in sport (drugs, gambling).
12. Racial and sex discrimination in sport.
13. Sport and the mass media.
14. Appeal of sport: "fanaticism."
15. Sociological considerations of the physical education environment.
16. Social issues in contemporary exercise. exercise dependence. eating disorders. fat versus fad.
17. Sport and the American dream—past, present, and future.

ISSUES IN AMERICAN SPORTS

The following includes some of the controversial issues present in the sport scene today that will be covered in this class. As you read each statement consider both the positive and negative aspects. Consider under what conditions these statements are true.

1. Sport is merely a reflection of American Society, and abuses in sport cannot be eliminated.
2. Competitive, highly organized athletics for children do not build strong character.
3. Adults conducting children's programs place too much emphasis on winning.
4. The popular contention that sports are an escape for ghetto youth is overstated.
5. Those who do attain a professional sports career enjoy a short-lived success and upon retirement encounter numerous problems.
6. Interscholastic and intercollegiate sport participation provide positive influences such as increasing achievement motivation, aspirations to attend college, and better grades.
7. Those athletes that dedicate all their time and energy to sport have few alternatives when their sport careers end.
8. Although many black athletes are participating, discrimination still exists at all levels of sport.
9. Girls and women are unjustly deprived of an adequate share of the sports budget.
10. Professional sport is a business and should be treated accordingly with respect to (1) paying taxes, (2) treatment of player (employee) contracts, (3) labor unions, and (4) other economic considerations.
11. Throughout sports programs, there is an undue emphasis on violence.
12. The media—television, radio, and newspapers—should report the sporting news, not create it.
13. Violence on the sports field serves as an acceptable release of aggression.
14. The escalation of players' salaries is unfair to spectators who must deal with higher ticket prices.
15. Players should not have to tolerate fan abuse such as booing and cursing. On the other hand, high ticket prices should allow the spectator more privileges.
16. Gambling is a prevalent part of sport and should be legalized because it really does not influence the outcome of the game.
17. The U.S. should provide for more national sporting programs so we can better compete in international events such as the Olympic Games.
18. Sport participation is really hazardous to one's health, leading to drug abuse, serious injuries, overexertion.

CLASS DEBATES

The class will participate in weekly debates concerning controversial issues in the world of sport and physical activity. Each student will have at least two opportunities to defend a particular issue. These discussions often become quite lively and therefore, your instructor will serve as referee.

DEBATE PROJECTS

Intercollegiate Athletics

1. Are athletic scholarships beneficial to student athletes?
2. Are postseason tournaments in the best interest of student athletes?
3. Should college athletes be paid a wage for their athletic services?

4. Should universities continue two-season sports?

Women's Equity in Intercollegiate Athletics
1. Should women be allocated an equal number of scholarships as men?
2. Should males be allowed to coach female teams?
3. Should females' sporting events be scheduled with the men's (double-headers)?
4. Should women compete in postseason play?

Professional Sports
1. Does the college draft equalize sports teams?
2. Does free agency work?
3. Should sport franchises be able to relocate freely?
4. Should sport teams be allowed to strike?

Drugs in Sport
1. Do athletes use drugs more often than their nonathletic counterparts?
2. Should athletes receive severe penalties for drug infractions?
3. Does mandatory drug testing of athletes represent the public good?
4. Should athletes be allowed to use steroids under medical supervision?

Violence in Sport
1. Do fans really want violence?
2. Does sport serve as a cathartic release of aggression?
3. Should sport franchises be accountable for fan violence?
4. Does the media encourage violence in sport?

Gambling in Sport
1. Will cities benefit financially from legalized gambling?
2. Will legalized gambling increase fan interest in sport?
3. Will legalized gambling encourage fixing of games by athletes?

Technology
1. Should video replay be used in officiating sporting events?
2. Has television made positive changes in professional sport?
3. Has technology taken out the uncertainty in sport performance?

Exercise in Contemporary Society
1. Is the physical fitness boom detrimental to one's physical health?
2. Is exercise a cure or cause of psychological disorders such an anorexia-nervosa, depression, and obsessions and compulsions?

OFFICIAL DEBATE RULES
1. Four or Five Rounds.
2. Each team must alternate leadoff.
3. Lead off will be judged on the following:
   a. use of examples (people, places, studies).
   b. articulation of the whole argument.
   c. conviction (academy award performance).
4. Rebuttal will be judged on the following:

a. ability to speak to points mentioned.
b. ability to speak to points not mentioned.
c. conviction.
5. Comebacks judged on the following:
a. ability to stay on point.
b. examples used to make case.

CRITIQUE OF JOHN KNOWLES'S *A SEPARATE PEACE*

Length: Approximately five type-written pages.

Requirements: (1) Read the book, (2) read one article of criticism on the book, and (3) answer the following questions:

1. Phineas and Gene are characters in contrast. In terms of their athletic prowess, describe how the two young men differ.
2. Identify five ways in which sport and/or physical activity is used in the novel.
3. The sporting character in the novel fails (as is customary in serious adult fiction). For what purpose does Knowles create a failed sports hero?
4. In your opinion, is Knowles differentiating sport from war, or does he feel the two are very similar? Support your position.

DUE: LAST DAY OF CLASS.

APPENDIX II: LIST OF SPORT NOVELS USED IN SOCIOLOGY OF SPORT CLASSES

Nelson Algren, *Never Come Morning*, 1942. Through boxing roles, examines the relationship between sport and urban society.

Barry Beckham, *Runner Mack*, 1972. Features a black baseball player and explores his perceptions concerning the futility of striving for success in white America.

Rita Mae Brown, *Sudden Death*, 1983. Explores life on the women's professional tennis tour: examines traditional and nontraditional sex roles within sport and social relationships.

Gary Cartwright, *The Hundred Yard War*, 1968. Examines the seedy side of professional football. While using extreme examples, examines the world of pain and loneliness among pampered professional athletes.

Robert Coover, *The Universal Baseball Association, Inc., J. Henry Waugh, Prop.*, 1968. Explores the unique world of sports fan, J. Henry Waugh, who has devised a baseball game that ultimately becomes an obsession and consumes him.

Edwin Fadiman, *The Professional*, 1973. Necessary pursuit of perfection among tennis players; consequences of meteoric rise to fame.

Peter Gent, *North Dallas Forty*, 1973. Focuses on the brutality of football and its association with war; players' inability to turn it off at the end of the game.

Sandra Hochman, *Jogging*, 1979. Examines the compulsion of a middle class jogger for his activity. This new exercise lifestyle becomes a symbol of man's quest to adjust to changes in contemporary society.

John Hough, *The Conduct of the Game*, 1986. Insight into socialization of a baseball umpire; sport and family relations and small-town lifestyles.

W. P. Kinsella, *Shoeless Joe*, 1982. Explores the mythical and ritualistic dimensions of the national game and how baseball captures the imagination of Americans.

John Knowles, *A Separate Peace*, 1960. Sport plays an important role in defining Phineas and his relationship with his best friend, Gene; attitudes toward growing up, school, and war.

Bernard Malamud, *The Natural*, 1952. Deals with mythology of baseball; gambling, player versus management, and sex roles.
Jay Neugeboren, *Big Man*, 1966. Classic case of superstar basketball player and how his sport role contributes to his inability to exist off the court; includes consequences of fixing games and a rapid descent back to the ghetto.
Philip J. O'Conner, *Stealing Home*, 1979. Youth sport setting in which player/coach relationships are explored; also subordinating goals for the good of the team. Adult values in youth sport.
Philip Roth, *The Great American Novel*, 1973. A parodic history of baseball; uses sport to comment on life in the twentieth century; sport and politics; sport and religion.
Lawrence Shainberg, *One on One*, 1970. Explores basketball player as an artist.
Sylvia Tennenbaum, *Rachel, The Rabbi's Wife*, 1978. Uses baseball, a traditional male preserve, to comment on how a woman comes to understand her family and herself; comments on sport spectatorship; a fine example of a feminist analysis of sport.

APPENDIX III: SYLLABUS

PE 340—Social & Psychological Dimensions of Physical Activity
Dr. Mary EcElroy
Office: Room 12C Ahearn
Phone: 532-6765 (office); 776-3723 (residence)
Office Hours: to be arranged

COURSE DESCRIPTION

Theories and research on the social and psychological significance of physical activity including implications for physical education and athletic programs.

COURSE OBJECTIVES

To provide the prospective teacher, exercise leader, and/or coach with an opportunity to gain knowledge and understanding of the operating principles in the areas of the sociology of sport and the psychology of sport and physical activity. Upon the completion of this course the student should be able to (orally or in writing):

1. Demonstrate an understanding of the fundamental findings and principles operating in the areas of sociology and psychology of sport and physical activity.
2. Discuss the influence that various social and psychological factors have in sport and physical activity settings.
3. Demonstrate the skills and and knowledge needed to apply principles of sociology and psychology to practical sport and physical activity settings.

COURSE REQUIREMENTS:

1. Readings: There is no textbook for this course. Specially selected readings will be used. A set of these readings will be on reserve at Farrell Library and will also be available in the Physical Education Library. Arrangements can be made with the instructor to copy the articles. (Copyright laws prohibit the distribution of these by the instructor.)
2. Attendance: Unless there are extenuating circumstances (a legal excuse) you are expected to be in class.

3. Class Procedures: Class time will be spent in lecture and discussion-interaction sessions.
4. Class Preparation and Participation: All students are expected to be prepared for each class. In essence, this means that all assigned readings should be read and outlined and that lecture notes from the previous class should be reviewed. Additionally, students are expected to contribute to class discussions. Quizzes will be given over the required reading.
5. Examinations: Three examinations will be scheduled during the semester, with the final exam being given during the final exam period. All exams will be composed of objective (i.e., multiple choice, true-false, matching) and essay questions. It should also be noted that the first two exams will be independent, but the final will be comprehensive.

TOPIC OUTLINE

Part I. Introduction and Background
1. Why study sport and physical activity?
2. Defining sport and physical activity.
3. Defining sociology and sport sociology.
4. Defining psychology and sport psychology.
5. Nature of sport/physical activity (involvement, degree, type).

Part II. Social Dimensions of Sport
1. Socialization via sport.
2. Socialization into sport.
3. Social stratification, social mobility (discrimination) and desocialization.
4. High school and college sport.
5. Sport and big business.
6. Sport and social issues (delinquency, gambling, drugs).
7. Sport and American culture.
8. Future trends in American sport.

Part III. Psychological Dimensions of Sport
1. Social reinforcement and sport performance.
2. Motivation and sport performance.
3. Aggression and sport.
4. Anxiety and sport performance—mental preparation.
5. Self-esteem and sport.
6. Coaching behaviors—attitudes and behavioral change mechanisms.

Part IV. Social Psychological Issues of Exercise
1. Exercise adherence.
2. Compulsive exercisers.
3. Exercise and eating disorders—incessant dieting.
4. Exercise for the aged.

COURSE REQUIREMENTS
First examination .... 20 percent
Second examination .... 20 percent
Comprehensive final examination .... 30 percent

Quizzes .... 20 percent
Class attendance/participation .... 10 percent

NOTE: Failure to complete any of the above will result in a failing grade!

WORKS CITED

Bolton, Marjorie. 1975. *The Anatomy of the Novel.* London: Routledge & Kegan Paul.

Coakley, Jay J. 1986. *Sport in Society: Issues and Controversies.* 3d ed. St. Louis: C. V. Mosby.

Fitzgerald, F. Scott. 1925. *The Great Gatsby.* New York: Scribner's.

Harris, Mark. 1979. *It Looked Like Forever.* New York: McGraw-Hill.

Nye, Russell. 1966. "History and Literature: Branches of the Same Tree." In *Essays on History and Literature*, ed. Robert Bremmer. Columbus: Ohio State University Press.

Oriard, Michael. 1982. *Dreaming of Heroes: American Sports Fiction, 1868–1980.* Chicago: Nelson Hall.

Woolf, Virginia. 1963. *The Moment and Other Essays.* Boston: Little, Brown.

PART 7
Psychology of Sport

11
Teaching Sport Psychology from a Humanist Perspective

JEFFREY H. GOLDSTEIN

INTRODUCTION

Sport psychology is a one-semester course I have offered at both the undergraduate level and as a graduate seminar. In the former case, it meets four hours per week, and in the latter instance three hours. Each time I have taught the course, its content has changed, partly because sport psychology is a young and dynamic field with a new and rapidly growing literature. Therefore, the texts and required readings have also changed. Just as I sometimes edit books to learn more about a field of study, so teaching sport psychology affords me an opportunity to examine the latest literature in the area, gives me a chance to discuss with others issues that I find of interest, and helps crystallize my own thinking on some of these issues. What follows is more or less typical of the way the course is structured and is based on my most recently offered sport psychology course, which was for undergraduate students.

GOALS FOR THE COURSE

My primary purpose in the course is to distance students sufficiently from their personal involvement in sports, whether as participants or as fans, to examine sport as an interesting, complex, and informative psychological and social phenomenon. The goals of the course are:

1. To show that sport is amenable to study using the same theories and methods as are applied by social scientists to the analysis of other social groups and institutions, such as the family or the university.

The possibility of a science of sport is discussed, with brief mention of the field of biomechanics, physics of sport, and the social and psychological study of sport. Some basic research terms and methods are introduced, since a good portion of the course, both readings and lectures, focuses sometimes critically on empirical research.

Social scientists have the unenviable task of studying through empirical and more or less objective methods the very experiences that are the phenomenological substance of people's lives. Looking at life from the outside perspective of the social scientist does not always produce imagery that one looking from the inside would find acceptable. Nor is it easy to deal empirically with the abstract and philosophical issues that surround sports. The social scientist is caught between mundane experience with sport and sport as a cultural abstraction. Yet a case can be made that attempts at empirically verifiable theory may be a good way for answering questions all along this continuum. While I attempt to present the virtues of an attempt at scientific objectivity in the study of sport, I acknowledge the inherent weaknesses in a scientific approach and note that science is simply one kind of knowing among others.

The role of theory in science is discussed mainly from the position of Karl Popper, and varieties of psychological theory are summarized. These range from psychoanalytic and sociobiological theories of sport to social learning and humanistic theories. At this early point of the semester, this discussion is simply a brief overview of theoretical perspectives. Specific theories about specific sport-related behaviors are discussed at appropriate points in the course.

2. To provide an overview of the history of sport psychology. This is a critical and not merely a chronological summary of sport studies. That is, the purpose is not merely to present who has studied sport and how, but also to examine why certain questions are asked by sport psychologists while other issues are not examined at all. I have found Allen Guttmann's *From Ritual to Record* (1978) particularly useful in this regard.

The history of sport psychology can be compared to that of industrial/organizational psychology (Goldstein, in Umphlett 1985). In its initial phase, it was an adjunct of management, used to increase productivity among workers. Among the first appearances by an academician on the sports scene was in 1938, when Coleman Griffith of the University of Illinois was hired by Philip K. Wrigley to study the Chicago Cubs baseball club (see Wiggins, in Silva and Weinberg 1984). The attention of early sport psychologists (and of many still) was focused on the professional or elite athlete in an attempt to enhance performance. When in the employment of team owners, managers,or coaches; it is not necessarily the athlete on whose behalf the sport psychologist labors. In its intermediate stage, just as industrial psychologists began to focus on the well-being of employees, so did sport psychologists recognize that "athletes are people, too," and began to consider their psychological and social needs. Even so, the focus here has almost invariably been on the "elite athlete," the potential All-American, Olympian, or professional athlete, rather than on the average or occasional athlete, the intramural or weekend athlete whose enjoyment of and benefits from sports are often overlooked or taken for granted. In the final stage, there have appeared critics of traditional sport psychology, beginning perhaps with Harry Edwards (1969) and Jack Scott (1971), eventuating in the development of a set of ethical principles for sport psychologists (Nideffer 1981), discussion of accreditation, and the beginnings of a "humanistic sport psychology" (Umphlett 1986).

3. To explore the mythology of modern sports and the social functions of this set of beliefs.

This is perhaps the most social psychological part of the course. The origins and functions of people's beliefs about sports are explored. These include the belief that sports build character (Ogilvie and Tutko 1971); that they permit athletes and sports fans the opportunity to "get rid" of their aggression (Goldstein 1983); that sports are in some way "pure," untainted by the "real" world; that sports are an egalitarian pursuit, free of racial prejudice; and the social Darwinian position that sports are a microcosm of society (Balbus, in Yiannakis et al. 1979). Many of the popular myths of sport are presented in Lipsyte's (1976) *SportsWorld* and Tutko's and Bruns's (1976) *Winning Is Everything and Other American Myths.* The main focus of this discussion is the purposes that may be served by such an "ideology." I ask them why they think sports make such a ubiquitous topic of conversation, particularly among men. It is pointed out that for two people to discuss sports they must share a common frame of reference, some common experiences and assumptions, and these reflect cultural values and mores.

Sports talk is itself compared to a game in which one may adopt a variety of roles, from the expert/intellectual (which may be played passively or aggressively) to the loyal defender of the home team. Even refusal to engage in sports talk is an acceptable cultural role, one that helps to define the nonparticipant, just as participation helps to define the "players." It is sociocultural issues such as these that often form the basis for classroom discussions.

4. Finally, I hope to demonstrate to students the important role that sports can play in their personal lives, regardless of their prior experiences with sports.

Many, perhaps the majority of students, have at some time in their young lives had the experience of being "cut" from a school team, of being chosen last in a pickup baseball game, or of being made to feel generally unathletic. Many have been told by coaches, teachers, and even their own parents that they are not athletes. These are the individuals who, as adults, stand to benefit most from involvement in sports. We discuss the medical/physical and psychosocial benefits of participation in sports, the increased sense of self-control, greater coordination and stamina, a stronger sense of self, and the heightened consciousness that accompanies (or is) what Csikszentmihalyi (1975) has called the "flow experience." The benefits of a lifetime of participation in sports are emphasized.

COURSE STRUCTURE

The course is designed to begin with abstract and more general aspects of sports. This broad historical and theoretical background serves as a framework for discussing the more specific topics that follow. A further reason for structuring the course this way is to establish sport psychology as a legitimate academic discipline by disillusioning those students who erroneously believe that the level of discourse will be the same informal street talk about sports with which they are familiar. In fact, the functions of informal talk about sports is one of the topics included in the course (under the heading of "The Functions of Sports for Fans"). An attempt is made to separate the roles of student/scholar and sports fan so that sports can be discussed dispassionately and analytically. The increasing specificity of topics also allows the class to evaluate contemporary sports events (such as the Olympic Games, the Super Bowl, the World Series) that may occur while the course is in progress. Toward the end of the course, the class discusses such events in terms of the theories and perspectives covered at the beginning of the term (see Appendix I). This is a form of "rehearsal," affording students practice in applying these novel ideas to the day-to-day world of sports, and also a way of reviewing for the last quiz of the term.

TEXTS AND READINGS

Classic and current writings in sport psychology are presented to students in the form of a Sport Psychology Bibliography (see Appendix I), which includes books, chapters, and journal articles. Because students typically write a term paper for the course, the bibliography can direct them to basic sources. This allows them to examine a few publications to get a feel for a particular area before deciding upon a topic for their term papers. In many cases, students are struck by particular titles that become the themes of their papers. If a student is interested in independently exploring a particular topic further (as has happened with such topics as women and sports, gambling in sports, play therapy, and cross-cultural studies of play), the bibliography can direct them to some of the pertinent literature. Finally, there are occasional required readings in addition to the textbooks used in the course. References may be found in the bibliography. The purpose of the nontextbook readings is to increase the flexibility of the course and to respond to the interests of a particular class. One or two readings may be assigned to provide background information on questions of interest or that relate to specific concurrent events in sports. Different texts are required depending on whether the course is taught at the graduate or undergraduate level. For example, the Eitzen (1989) and Guttmann (1978) books, below, are more accessible to undergraduate students than the Goldstein (1979) and Silva and Weinberg (1984) books, which have been used in graduate seminars. Here are books I have used to date:

D. S. Eitzen, ed. 1989. *Sport in Contemporary Society: An Anthology.* 3d ed. New York: St. Martin's Press.

J. H. Goldstein, ed. 1979. *Sports, Games, and Play.* Hillsdale, N. J.: Lawrence Erlbaum Associates.

A. Guttmann. 1978. *From Ritual to Record: The Nature of Modern Sports.* New York: Columbia University Press.

J. M. Silva and R. S. Weinberg, eds. 1984. *Psychological Foundations of Sport.* Champaign, Ill: Human Kinetics.

Because my own research in sports focuses primarily on violence, I spend what is probably a disproportionate amount of time on the subject. It is a topic in which students are interested and one that invariably generates lively discussion. It is also a topic that permits me to reintroduce several theories and concepts—such as psychoanalytic theory and attribution processes—that were discussed during the initial lectures of the course. Coming as it does near the middle of the semester, the topic of violence in sports allows me to stress that theories and abstract concepts introduced at the beginning of the course are useful, indeed they are indispensible, in understanding and coming to grips with the very real problems surrounding violence.

EVALUATION OF STUDENT PERFORMANCE

Requirements for the course vary with the size and level of the class. If the class is a small undergraduate course (fewer than twenty students), there are two exams and one term paper. If the class has twenty or more students, then there are three exams, though the student is given the option of writing a paper in lieu of taking the second exam. All graduate courses require at least one paper. In all cases, exams consist of combinations of short answer (multiple-choice and identification) and essay questions (see Appendix I). Each type of question is designed for a different purpose. Short-answer questions are best for assessing how much of the basic material and vocabulary the student has mastered. Because ambiguous multiple-choice questions are inevitable, students are permitted to write a sentence explaining or justifying their answers to any questions they wish. Essay questions are designed to indicate how well the student can use, criticize, or extend this material. But they also have a pedagogical purpose, which I owe to a story related by James McConnell (1978) of the University of Michigan. He wrote of a psychology professor who gave a ride to a hitchhiker, a young man who had taken his introductory psychology course several years earlier. The young man could recall only that a ringing bell will cause a dog to salivate. How could a person read a five or six hundred page textbook, listen to forty or so hours of lecture, participate in several experiments, see films and lab demonstrations of psychological principles, and remember virtually nothing of the experience? I interpret this incident to mean that the student found nothing in the course connected to whatever abiding passions he held. Perhaps by encouraging students to make these connections themselves, the material will remain anchored to their own concerns and be retained at least as long as these interests persist. As often as possible I design essay questions that require the students to relate course material to some enduring interest of theirs. The purpose is to establish cognitive connections between course material and interests of the student in the hope that the course matter will be better retained and used.

The graded exams are returned at the beginning of the next class and are gone over question by question in class in an effort to enhance their pedagogical value. To forestall the occasional complaint about grades, and to have an opportunity to discuss the reliability of tests, I offer to regrade any student's entire exam. The second grade, which may be the same as, lower or higher than the first, will be the one recorded for the student. This offer is rarely accepted.

EVALUATION OF MY PERFORMANCE.

For each undergraduate course at Temple Univerity, there is usually a questionnaire distributed to students in class. When this is not done, I distribute for my own information a brief course evaluation form (see Appendix II).

WHO TAKES SPORT PSYCHOLOGY COURSES?

There are few subjects besides sports (sex being one of them) about which undergraduate students are so intrinsically motivated to learn and to which they bring such a high degree of enthusiasm. While I have been offering a sport psychology course for only a few years, it has been my experience that students may be interested in sport studies for several different, and sometimes complementary, reasons. First, there are athletes and former athletes whose first-hand experience with sports they wish to supplement. These students are particularly valuable in class discussions, where their sports experiences are often used by them to illustrate an abstract point made in class or in the readings. Second is the contingent of sports fans who, among all the groups of students enrolled in a sport studies course, may be the most problematic. They are often less interested in analyses of sport as a social and psychological phenomenon than in the analysis of a particular athlete or Super Bowl game. Such students frequently have a difficult time standing back from sports to examine them historically and critically. I have found a third group of students to be especially interesting to have in class. These are the nonathletes and nonfans, those who don't know what all the fuss over sports is about and who are curious to learn what others find of interest or value in sportsfandom. Whereas the first two groups of students—athletes and sports fans—are involved with sports, the last group is characterized by a lack of involvement. Perhaps because of this they seem best able to grasp difficult critical views of sports, such as the theoretical papers to be found in Luschen's and Sage's *Handbook of Social Science of Sport* (1981).

Since teaching is a dynamic, interactive process, it is inevitable that it changes not only the student but the teacher. I have learned to appreciate more the importance of sports in the lives of my nonathlete students. Sports for them serve important social functions. They provide a relatively nonthreatening, noncontroversial topic of conversation. They enable the shy to excel in conversation and, as with gossip, to play the role of opinion leader, having the latest information on players, managers, and strategy. The fans of a given team, who may have little else in common, share among themselves a sense of comraderie and esprit. In the large urban areas where professional sports franchises reside, and on large university campuses where major college teams thrive, this sense of community is otherwise difficult to achieve. Sports also provide drama, excitement, and entertainment. Teaching a sport psychology course also reinforces my own commitment to participation in sports, which these days consists mostly of racquetball.

APPENDIX I: SYLLABUS

Psychology 546
Fall 1984
Sport Psychology
Jeffrey H. Goldstein

TEXTS

D. Stanley Eitzen, ed. *Sport in Contemporary Society: An Anthology*. 2d ed. New York: St. Martin's Press, 1984.
Jeffrey H. Goldstein, ed. *Sports, Games, and Play*. Hillsdale, N.J.: Lawrence Erlbaum, 1979.
Other readings to be assigned.

COURSE OUTLINE:

What is Sport Psychology?

A. The Development of Sport Psychology.

B. The Roles of the Sport Psychologist: Theory, Research, and Counseling in Sport.

Readings in Eitzen: "Sportsworld," Lipsyte. "Sport in American Society," Sage. "Sport in Society," Coakley.

The Nature of Play, Games, and Sport

A. The Relation Between Leisure and Work.
B. The Rise of Competitive Sport in Western Society.
C. Culture and Sport.

Readings in Eitzen: "Baseball in Japan," Snyder and Spreitzer. "Sport and American Society," Sage.

Readings in Goldstein: Chap. 11, Zillmann, Sapolsky, and Bryant.

Socialization, Personality, and Play

A. Children's Play.
B. Personality and Sport.
C. Gender, Race, and Sport.
D. Peak Experience in Sport.
E. The Functions of Sport for Fans.

Readings in Eitzen: "Myths of Early Competition," Tutko and Bruns. "What's Best for Kids?" Orlick and Botterill. "Sports Don't Build Character," Tutko and Bruns. "Mass Media, Sport and Socialization," Goldstein. "Race in Contemporary American Sport," Edwards. "Opening Doors for Women," Coakley and Westkott.

Readings in Goldstein: Chap. 1, Sherrod and Singer. Chap. 4, Tutko. Chap. 7, Jones and Williamson. Chap. 8, Winer. Chap. 9, Sloan.

Quiz 1

Violence in Sports

A. History of Sports-Related Violence.
B. Theories of Research on Sports Violence.
C. International Sports Competition and International Relations.
D. The Control and Reduction of Sports Violence.

Readings in Eitzen: "Sports As a Control. . . ," Sipes. "Sports Violence," Goldstein. "Sociological Perspective," Coakley. "Violence: Out of Hand. . . ," Gilbert and Twyman.

Readings in Goldstein: Chap. 10, Gaskell and Pearton. Chap. 12, Mann. Others to be assigned.

The Psychology of Team Sports

A. Social Facilitation and the Home Field Advantage.
B. Attributions for Success and Failure.
C. Team Structure and Performance.
D. Situational Factors and Team Performance.

Readings in Goldstein: Chap. 5, King and Chi. Chap. 15, Edwards. Others to be assigned.

Therapeutic Recreation

A. Sport as Therapy.
B. Emotional Uses of Sport.
C. Sport through Life Span.

Readings: To be assigned

Future Trends and Prospects

Quiz 2

GRADES:
There will be two quizzes during the course. Each will include essay, short answer, and multiple-choice questions, and each will be worth 30 percent of the final grade. The student will write a paper on some aspect of sport psychology, the topic to be mutually agreed upon. The paper will be worth 30 percent of the final grade and will be due one week before the second quiz. Late papers will lose one point per day. Ten percent of the grade will be determined by general class participation and the fulfillment of such other requirements as are announced in class.

SUGGESTED TERM PAPER TOPICS
While you are free to select for your term paper any topic within the broad field of sport psychology, you may find the following list of some assistance in choosing a theme for your paper. Classic and current references on any topic(s) of interest will be provided during consultation with me.

Achievement motivation
"Addiction" to exercise
Aggression
Aging and sports
Anxiety and performance
Arousal and performance
Attitudes toward sports
Attribution for performance
Catharsis
Children's sports
Coaching children, adults, and/or elite athletes
Cohesiveness of teams
Collective behavior and sports fans
Cross-cultural studies of sports, games, play
Competition
Conflict (social, political)
Cooperation in sports
Drug use by athletes
Endorphins, their role in performance
Entertainment, sport as
Exercise and health
Exercise as therapy
Fans, their functions and characteristics
Fear of failure
Functions of sports for athletes, fans, society
Gambling
Games of chance
History of sport psychology
Home team effect
Hunting, aggression, and ecology

Industrialization and sport
Intrinsic motivation of athletes
Leadership in team sports
Level of aspiration
Moral development and sports
Motivation
Noncompetitive games
Olympic Games and international relations
Peak performance
Performance outcome, determinants
Personality and performance
Personality measurement in sport psychology
Politics and sports
Race and racism in sports
Relaxation and performance
Risk-taking in sports
Self-efficacy
Sex roles
Social class differences in sports participation
Social control functions of sports
Social facilitation
Socialization
"Special Olympics"
Sports metaphors
Sports talk
Stress
Team morale
Team structure and performance
Television and its effects on sports
Therapeutic recreation
Violence
Women and sport

SPORTS PSYCHOLOGY BIBLIOGRAPHY

(Note: The following is a selection of items from a more complete bibliography that is distributed to students in class. For the sake of brevity, only a sample of books, chapters, and journal articles is included here.)

Books

Beisser, Arnold. *The Madness in Sports.* New York: Appleton-Century-Crofts, 1967.

Butt, Dorcas Susan. *Psychology of Sport.* New York: Van Nostrand Reinhold, 1976.

Caillois, Roger. *Man, Play and Games.* Translated by Meyer Barash. Glencoe, Ill.: Free Press, 1980.

Carron, Albert V. *Social Psychology of Sport.* Ithaca, N.Y.: Mouvement, 1980.

Cherfas, Jeremy, and Roger Lewin, eds. *Not Work Alone: A Cross-Cultural View of Activities Superfluous to Survival.* London: Temple Smith, 1980.

Chu, Donald, ed. *Dimensions of Sport Studies.* New York: Wiley, 1982.

Coakley, Jay J. *Sport in Society: Issues and Controversies.* 3d ed. St. Louis, Mo.: Mosby, 1986.

Cox, Richard H. *Sport Psychology.* Dubuque, Iowa: W. C. Brown, 1986.

Dickinson, John. *A Behavioral Analysis of Sport.* Princeton: Princeton Book Co., 1977.

Eitzen, D. Stanley, and George H. Sage, eds. *Sociology of American Sport.* 2d ed. Dubuque, Iowa: W. C. Brown, 1982.

Elias, Norbert, and Eric Dunning. *Quest for Excitement.* Oxford: Basil Blackwell, 1986.

Fisher, A. Craig, ed. *Psychology of Sport.* Palo Alto, Calif.: Mayfield, 1976.

Garvey, Catherine. *Play.* Cambridge: Harvard University Press, 1977.

Griffith, Coleman Roberts. *Psychology of Athletics.* New York: Scribner's, 1928.

Guttmann, Allen. *Sports Spectators.* New York: Columbia University Press, 1986.

Hart, Marie, and Susan Birrell, eds. *Sport in the Sociocultural Process.* 3d ed. Dubuque, Iowa: W. C. Brown, 1981.

Hoberman, John M. *Sport and Political Ideology.* Austin: University of Texas Press, 1984.

Huizinga, Johan. *Homo Ludens: A Study of the Play Element in Culture.* Boston: Beacon Press, 1955.

Iso-Ahola, Seppo E. *The Social Psychology of Leisure and Recreation.* Dubuque, Iowa: W. C. Brown, 1980.

Jerome, John. *The Sweet Spot in Time.* New York: Simon & Schuster, 1980.

Lever, Janet. *Soccer Madness.* Chicago: University of Chicago Press, 1983.

Loy, John W., and Gerald S. Kenyon. *Sport, Culture and Society.* New York: Macmillan, 1969.

Mandell, Richard D. *The First Modern Olympics.* Berkeley: University of California Press, 1976.

Marsh, Peter, Elizabeth Rosser, and Rom Harre. *The Rules of Disorder.* London: Routledge & Kegan Paul, 1978.

Martens, Rainer. *Joy and Sadness in Children's Sports.* Champaign, Ill.: Human Kinetics, 1978.

Michener, James A. *Sports in America.* New York: Random House, 1976.

Murphy, Mirchael, and Rhea A. White. *The Psychic Side of Sports.* Reading, Mass.: Addison-Wesley, 1978.

Oglesby, Carole A., ed. *Women and Sport: From Myth to Reality.* Philadelphia: Lea and Febiger, 1978.

Oxendine, Joseph B. *Psychology of Motor Learning.* New York: Appleton-Century-Crofts, 1967.

Rooney, John. *Geography of American Sport.* Reading, Mass.: Addison-Wesley, 1974.

Sachs, M. H., and M. L. Sachs, eds. *Psychology of Running.* Champaign, Ill.: Human Kinetics, 1981.

Sachs, M. L., and G. W. Buffone, eds. *Running as Therapy.* Lincoln: University of Nebraska Press, 1984.

Sage, George H., ed. *Sport and American Society.* Reading, Mass.: Addison-Wesley, 1970.

Smoll, Frank L., and Ronald E. Smith, eds. *Psychological Perspectives in Youth Sports.* Washington, D.C.: Hemisphere (Wiley), 1978.

Spears, Betty, and Richard A. Swanson. *History of Sport and Physical Activity in the United States.* Dubuque, Iowa: W. C. Brown, 1978.

Voigt, David Q. *America Through Baseball.* Chicago: Nelson-Hall, 1976.

Weiss, P. *Sport: A Philosophic Inquiry.* Carbondale: Southern Illinois University Press, 1969.

Widmeyer, W. Neil, ed. *Physical Activity and the Social Sciences.* 2d ed. Waterloo, Ontario: University of Waterloo Press, 1976.

Yeager, Robert C. *Seasons of Shame: The New Violence in Sports.* New York: McGraw-Hill, 1979.

Yiannakis, A., et al., eds. *Sport Sociology.* 2d ed. Dubuque, Iowa: Kendall/Hunt, 1979.

Chapters and Articles

Adler, P., and P. A. Adler. "The Role of Momentum in Sport." *Urban Life* 7, no. 2 (1978): 153–76.

Allison, Maria. "Sport, Culture and Socialization." *International Review of Sport Sociology* 4 (1982): 11–37.

Allison, M. T., and G. Luschen. "A Comparative Analysis of Navaho Indian and Anglo Basketball Sport Systems." *International Review of Sport Sociology* 3/4 (1978): 75–86.

Ball, D. W. "Olympic Games Competition: Structural Correlates of National Success." *International Journal of Comparative Sociology* 13 (1972): 186–200.

Berkowitz, L., and J. T. Alioto. "The Meaning of an Observed Event as a Determinant of its Aggressive Consequences." *Journal of Personality and Social Psychology* 28 (1973): 206–17.

Biggs, J. "A Nomographic Paradigm for Applied Behavioral Research: An Example from Sports Psychology." *Human Learning* 2 (1983): 251–58.

Brickman, P. "Crime and Punishment in Sports and Society." *Journal of Social Issues* 33 (1977): 140–64.

Browne, M. A., and M. J. Mahoney. "Sport Psychology." *Annual Review of Psychology* 35 (1984): 605–25.

Cialdini, R. B., R. J. Borden, A. Thorne, M. R. Walker, S. Freeman, and L. R. Sloan. "Basking in Reflected Glory: Three (Football) Field Studies." *Journal of Personality and Social Psychology* 34 (1976): 366–75.

Danish, S. J., and B. D. Hale. "Toward an Understanding of the Practice of Sport Psychology." *Journal of Sport Psychology* 3 (1981): 90–99.

Devereux, E. C. "Backyard Versus Little League Baseball: The Impoverishment of Children's Games." In *Social Problems in Athletics*. D. M. Landers, ed. Urbana: University of Illinois Press, 1976.

Dishman, R. K., W. Ickes, and W. P. Morgan. "Self-Motivation and Adherence to Habitual Physical Activity." *Journal of Applied Psychology* 10 (1980): 115–32.

Dundes, A. "Into the Endzone for a Touchdown: A Psychoanalytic Consideration of American Football." *Western Folklore* 37 (1978): 75–88.

Eitzen, D. S. "The Effect of Group Structure on the Success of Athletic Teams." *International Review of Sport Sociology* 1 (1978): 7–17.

Felson, R. B. "Self- and Reflected Appraisal among Football Players: A Test of the Meadian Hypothesis." *Social Psychology Quarterly* 44 (1981): 116–26.

Fisher, K. "Sport Psychology Comes of Age in the '80s." *APA Monitor* (September 1982): lff.

Folkins, C. H., and W. E. Sime. "Physical Fitness and Mental Health." *American Psychologist* 36 (1981): 373–89.

Gamson, W. A., and N. A. Scotch. "Scapegoating in Baseball." *American Journal of Sociology* 70 (1964): 69–72.

Gelber, S. M., "Working at Playing: The Culture of the Workplace and the Rise of Baseball." *Journal of Social History* 16, no. 4 (1982): 3–22.

Greer. D. L. "Spectator Booing and the Home Advantage: A Study of Social Influence in the Basketball Arena." *Social Psychology Quarterly* 46 (1983): 252–61.

Grusky, O. "Managerial Succession and Organizational Effectiveness." *American Journal of Sociology* 69 (1963): 21–31.

Guttmann, A. "On the Alleged Dehumanization of the Sports Spectator." *Journal of Popular Culture* 12, no. 2 (1980): 275–82.

Harrell, W. A. "Verbal Aggressiveness in Spectators at Professional Hockey Games: The Effects of Tolerance of Violence and Amount of Exposure to Hockey." *Human Relations* 34 (1981): 643–55.

Harville, D. "Predictions for National Football League Games via Linear-Model Methodology." *Journal of the American Statistical Association.* 75 (1980): 516–24.

Hastorf, A., and H. Cantril. "They Saw a Game: A Case Study." *Journal of Abnormal and Social Psychology* 49 (1954): 129–34.

Iso-Ahola, S. "Effects of Team Outcome on Children's Self-Perception: Little League Baseball." *Scandinavian Journal of Psychology* 18 (1977): 38–42.

Iso-Aloha, S., and G. C. Roberts. "Causal Attributions following Success and Failure at an Achievement Motor Task." *Research Quarterly* 48 (1977): 541–49.

Jones, J. M., and A. R. Hochner. "Racial Differences in Sports Activities: A Look at the Self-Paced versus Reactive Hypothesis." *Journal of Personality and Social Psychology* 27 (1973): 83–95.

Kaplan, Robert M. "How Do Fans and Oddsmakers Differ in their Judgments of Football Teams?" *Personality and Social Psychology Bulletin* 6 (1980): 287–92.

Kirkcaldy, B. D. "Catastrophic Performance." *Sportwissenschaft* 13 (1983): 46–53.

Kirschenbaum, D. S. "Self-Regulation and Sport Psychology." *Journal of Sport Psychology* 6 (1984): 159–83.

Kraus, J. F., and C. Conroy. "Mortality and Morbidity from Injuries in Sports and Recreation." *Annual Review of Public Health* 5 (1984): 163–92.

Lever, J. "Soccer: Opium of the Brazilian people." *Transaction* 7, no. 2 (1969): 36–43.

Lord, R. G., and J. A. Hohenfeld. "Longitudinal Field Assessment of Equity Effects on the Performance of Major League Baseball Players." *Journal of Applied Psychology* 64 (1980): 19–26.

Luschen, G. "Sociology of Sport: Development, Past State, and Prospects." *Annual Review of Sociology* 6 (1980): 315–47.

Mahoney, M. J., and M. Avener. "Psychology of the Elite Athlete: An Exploratory Study." *Cognitive Therapy and Research* 1 (1977): 135–41.

Mann, L. "On Being a Sore Loser: How Fans React to their Team's Failure." *Australian Journal of Psychology* 26 (1974): 37–47.

Mark, M. M., N. Mutrie, D. R. Brooks, and D. V. Harris. "Causal Attributions of Winners and Losers in Individual Competitive Sports: Toward a Reformulation of the Self-Serving Bias." *Journal of Sport Psychology* 6 (1984): 11–15.

Markoff, R. A., P. Ryan, and T. Young. "Endorphins and Mood Changes in Long-Distance Running." *Medicine and Science in Sports and Exercise* 14 (1982): 11–15.

Murphy, M. "Sport as Yoga." *Journal of Humanistic Psychology* 17, no. 4 (1977): 21–33.

Ogilvie, B. C., and T. Tutko. "Sport: If you Want to Build Character, Try Something Else." *Psychology Today* 5 (1971): 60–63.

Phillips, D. P. "The Impact of Mass Media Violence on U.S. Homicides." *American Sociological Review* 48 (1983): 560–68.

Prisuta, R. H. "Televised Sports and Political Values." *Journal of Communication* 29, no. 1 (1979): 94–102.

Privette, G. "Peak Experience, Peak Performance, and Flow." *Journal of Personality and Social Psychology* 45 (1977): 35–40.

Rainville, R. E., and E. McCormick. "Extent of Covert Racial Prejudice in Pro Football Announcers' Speech." *Journalism Quarterly* 54 (1977): 20–26.

Ravizza, K. "Peak Experiences in Sport." *Journal of Humanistic Psychology* 17, no. 4 (1977): 35–40.

Rieder, H. "Sport Psychology for the Handicapped." *International Journal of Sport Psychology* 10, no. 3 (1979): 184–89.

Roberts, G. C. "Children in Competition: A Theoretical Perspective and Recommendation for Practice." *Motor Skills: Theory into Practice* 4 (1980): 37–50.

Ruder, M. K., and D. L. Gill. "Immediate Effects of Win-Loss on Perceptions of Cohesion in Intramural and Intercollegiate Volleyball Teams." *Journal of Sport Psychology* 4 (1982): 227–34.

Rushall, B. S. "Three Studies Relating Personality Variables to Football Performance." *International Journal of Sport Psychology* 9 (1972): 723–77.

Russell, G. W., and B. R. Drewry. "Crowd Size and Competitive Aspects of Aggression in Ice Hockey: An Archival Study." *Human Relations* 29 (1976): 723–27.

Sage, G. H. "An Assessment of Personality Profiles Between and Within Intercollegiate Athletes from 8 Different Sports." *Sportswissenschaft* 2 (1972): 409–18.

Sapolsky, B. S., and D. Zillmann. "Enjoyment of a Televised Sport Contest under Different Social Conditions of Viewing." *Perceptual and Motor Skills* 46 (1978): 29–30.

Schwartz, B., and S. Barsky. "The Home Advantage." *Social Forces* 55 (1977): 641–61.

Sheedy, J. "Attribution Theory: Sport and Female Athletes." *Australian Journal of Sport Sciences* 3 (1983): 29–31.

Silva, John M., III. "The Perceived Legitimacy of Rule Violating Behavior in Sport." *Journal of Sport Psychology* 5 (1983): 438–48.

Singer, R. N., and J. E. Kane. "Research in Sport Psychology." *International Journal of Sport Psychology* 10, no. 3 (1979): 190–96.

Sipes, R. G. "War, Sports and Aggression: An Empirical Test of Two Rival Theories." *American Anthropologist* 75 (1973): 64–86.

Straub, W. F. "Sensation Seeking among High and Low-Risk Male Athletes." *Journal of Sport Psychology* 4 (1982) 246–53.

Suinn, R. M., "Body Thinking: Psychology for Olympic Champions." *Psychology Today* 10 (1976): 38–44.

Triplett, N. "The Dynamogenic Factors in Pacemaking and Competition." *American Journal of Psychology* 9 (1987): 507–33.

Vamplew, W. "Sports Crowd Disorder in Britain, 1870–1914: Causes and Controls." *Journal of Sport History* 7 (1980): 5–20.

Varca, P. E. "An Analysis of Home and Away Game Performance of Male College Basketball Teams." *Journal of Sport Psychology* 2 (1980): 245–57.

Weinberg, R. S., and A. Jackson. "Competition of Extrinsic Rewards: Effect of Intrinsic Motivation and Attribution." *Research Quarterly* 50 (1979): 494–502.

Weiss, Maureen R., and Brenda L. Bredemeier. "Developmental Sport Psychology: A Theoretical Perspective for Studying Children in Sport." *Journal of Sport Psychology* 5 (1983): 216–30.

Whitman, R. M. "Psychoanalytic Speculations about Play: Tennis—The Duel." *Psychoanalytic Review* 56, no. 2 (1969): 197–214.

Worringham, C. J., and D. M. Messick. "Social Facilitation of Running: An Unobtrusive Study." *Journal of Social Issues* 121 (1983): 23–29.

Zillmann, D., R. C. Johnson, and K. D. Day. "Provoked and Uprovoked Aggressiveness in Athletes." *Journal of Research in Personality* 8 (1974): 139–52.

QUIZ I

Multiple Choice:

Worth 1 point each. For each item, select the letter corresponding to the most correct answer. Place your answers in your examination booklet. You may write sentences explaining any of your answers.

1. C. R. Griffith in the 1920s identified three key areas of sport psychology. Which of the following is NOT among them? (A) learning, (B) personality and its relation to sports, (C) psychotherapy, (D) psychomotor skills.

2. The first experiment in social psychology considered whether bicycle racers would do better alone or in competition. This issue is referred to as (A) social facilitation, (B) the energetic effect, (C) diffusion of responsibility, (D) the Redfield effect.

3. Which of the following goes from the most general category to the most specific? (A) sport, play, game, contest, (B) play, game, contest, sport, (C) game, contest, play, sport, (D) contest, sport, play, game.

4. Sherrod and Singer (in "Sports, Games and Play") note that the benefits of play include (A) coping with overstimulation, (B) controlling emotion, (C) reality-testing, (D) all of the above, (E) none of the above.

5. Jones and Williamson (in "Sports, Games and Play") note that sport provides a rich area of study for social psychologists because (A) individuals are integrated into a social unit, the team, (B) the social structure of a team or league is clear, (C) the issue of sex roles is increasingly important, (D) all of the above, (E) none of the above.

6. Japanese play baseball (A) in the same way as Americans do, (B) like Americans, but limit players' salaries, (C) but have made the game more compatible with Japanese culture, (D) because they industrialized after World War II.

7. Which of the following is NOT an explanation for the rise of modern sport? (A) the Industrial Revolution, (B) the spread of Protestantism, (C) the need for cardiovascular exercise, (D) the adoption of a scientific view of the world.

8. Orlick and Botterill (in Eitzen) list suggestions that children themselves have offered for youth sports. These include all but which of the following? (A) Make games easier, for example, by lowering basketball nets. (B) Add more referees and umpires. (C) Cut down on rough play. (D) Have fewer practice sessions.

9. George Sage (in Eitzen book) notes that (A) sports reflect American values, (B) sports influence American values, (C) adults teach values to children by the way they organize and coach youth sports programs, (D) all of the above, (E) none of the above.

10. According to research by Sloan and others, sports fans identify more with their team after it wins than after it loses. This is best explained as (A) a response to an unfulfilled unconscious desire, (B) a response acquired through positive reinforcement (winning), (C) an attempt to enhance their own esteem and prestige, (D) none of the above.

Essay:
Answer ANY TWO of the following: Each is worth 10 points.

16A. Since losing in sports is at least as common as winning, the winner cannot be the only one to profit from a contest. Why do teams and individual athletes persist in the face of losing? What social or cultural values might be learned from losing?

16B. Why do you think football has replaced baseball as the most popular American sport? Refer to course readings in your answer where relevant.

16C. What changes have been called for by sport psychologists in youth sports? What effects would these changes have on children? What effects might they have on the society as a whole?

16D. What factors have traditionally been said to limit women's participation in sport? What evidence is there bearing on these factors?

APPENDIX II: COURSE EVALUATION

Psychology 115
Summer 1984
Sports Psychology

1. Compared to all other courses I have had, this course was:
——1 worse than
——2 average
——3
——4 about average
——5
——6 better than
——7 average

2. Compared to other psychology courses I have had, this course was:
——1 worse than
——2 average
——3
——4 about average
——5
——5 better than
——7 average

3. Compared to other professors I have had, this professor was:
——1 worse than
——2 average
——3
——4 about average
——5
——6 better than
——7 average

4. The lectures in this course were:
(check all that apply):
——informative
——repetitive
——interesting
——boring
——funny
——dull
——same as the readings
——different from the readings
——other (specify)

5. The readings for this course were
(check all that apply):
——informative
——repetitive
——interesting
——boring
——funny
——dull
——things I already knew
——well written
——other (specify)

6. If I could change any one thing in this course, it would be:

7. The three best things about this course were:

8. The three worst things about this course were:
9. Other comments about this course or suggestions for improving it.

WORKS CITED

Csikszentmihalyi, M. 1975. *A Behavioral Analysis of Sport.* San Francisco: Jossey-Bass.

Edwards, Harry. 1969. *The Revolt of the Black Athlete.* New York: Free Press.

Eitzen, D. Stanley, ed. 1989. *Sport in Contemporary Society* 3d ed. New York: St. Martin's Press.

Goldstein, Jeffrey H., ed. 1979. *Sports, Games, and Play.* Hillsdale, N.J.: Lawrence Erlbaum (Wiley). 2d ed. in preparation.

———. 1983. *Sports Violence.* New York: Springer-Verlag.

———. 1985. "Athletic Performance and Spectator Behavior: The Humanistic Concerns of Sport Psychology." In *American Sport Culture: The Humanistic Dimensions.* Wiley Lee Umphlett, ed. Lewisburg, P.A.: Bucknell University Press, 159–79.

Guttmann, Allen. 1978. *From Ritual to Record: The Nature of Modern Sports.* New York: Columbia University Press.

Lipsyte, Robert. 1975. *SportsWorld.* New York: Quadrangle.

Luschen, Gunther, and George H. Sage, eds. 1981. *Handbook of Social Science of Sport.* Champaign, Ill.: Stipes.

McConnell, J. V. 1978. "Confessions of a Textbook Writer." *American Psychologist* 33: 159–69.

Nideffer, R. M. 1981. *The Ethics and Practice of Applied Sport Psychology.* Ithaca, N.Y.: Mouvement.

Ogilvie, Bruce C., and Thomas T. Tutko. 1966. *Problem Athletes and How to Handle Them.* London: Pelham Books.

Scott, Jack. 1971. *The Athletic Revolution.* New York: Collier.

Silva, John M., and Robert S. Weinberg, eds. 1984. *Psychological Foundations of Sport.* Champaign, Ill.: Human Kinetics.

Tutko, Thomas, and William Bruns. 1976. *Winning is Everything and Other American Myths.* New York: Macmillan.

Umphlett, Wiley Lee, ed. 1985. *American Sport Culture: The Humanistic Dimensions.* Lewisburg, P.A.: Bucknell University Press.

Yiannakis, A., et al., eds. 1979. *Sport Sociology.* 2d ed. Dubuque, Iowa: Kendall/Hunt.

12
Sport Psychology: An Applied Approach

WAYNE A. BURROUGHS

INTRODUCTION

The purpose of any scientific endeavor is to gather information that will enhance the understanding, prediction, and control of events. Sport situations provide excellent opportunities for us to observe and document events that would be extremely difficult to study in everyday settings.

Since its beginning, the field of sport psychology and its practitioners have been heavily involved in the pursuit of higher levels of performance by athletes of all ages and descriptions. Through this pursuit of excellence, as Orlick calls it (1980), we can strive to understand how excellence occurs, make predictions about the variables that affect it, and actually control (to varying degrees) its occurrence. Thus athletes who seek to improve their performances have been and will continue to be an important influence on the direction of sport psychology.

In the preceding chapter, Goldstein drew an analogy between the beginnings of industrial/organizational psychology and sport psychology. We can also compare the two fields today in terms of their goals. Industrial/organizational psychology is concerned with enhancing the productivity and satisfaction of people at work. So, too, sport psychologists seek to enhance the performance and enjoyment of people at play, whether they play professionally or for other reasons.

The application of psychological principles toward enhancing athletic performance is therefore an important goal in my course in sport psychology at the University of Central Florida. In addition, we emphasize the importance of using psychological principles to create healthy, well adjusted, positive, and supportive environments in which althletes of all ages and types may pursue their individual goals.

A CASE FOR THOUGHT

A few years ago during baseball's Fall Instructional League in Florida, I was doing a workshop for professional baseball players designed to enhance their visual skills at the plate. Following a two-hour session with six players in the batting cage, we summarized the day's activities and called it quits. One of the players was nice enough to help me gather the equipment and we began talking about his ability as a hitter. I complimented him on his visual skills since he had demonstrated some effective information processing during the afternoon. (He was consistent in his recognition of breaking pitches and accurately noted the location of pitches even after seeing only the first part of the ball's flight.) The following conversation ensued:

Player: Thanks, I usually see the ball pretty early, I think.
Me: That's really important because it gives you more information.
Player: That's not what bothers me though.
Me: Oh? What does bother you?
Player: The first time at bat—I don't do well early in the game.
Me: What do you mean?
Player: Well, last year my batting average for the first time at the plate was only .150. Since my overall average was .280 you can see that first at-bats ruined my chances of a .300 year. How can I get better early in the game?

This is the gist of applying sport psychology to enhance the performance of athletes. As it turned out, the problem was not physical—after all, he could hit well after his first at-bat in the game. And pitchers are not that much stronger in early innings. His problem was both cognitive and behavioral. He tended to be highly anxious when the game began. His anxiety interfered with both his physical performance and his ability to focus his concentration on relevant tasks. Then his poor performance early in the game led him to expect to be anxious and perform poorly early in the next game. Why didn't he do poorly the second, third, and fourth time at the plate? He knew he had ability, and he believed he could hit. Anxiety was too highly elevated early but not later in the game. Our approach to helping him out of this cycle of poor early performance involved relaxation training and breathing techniques that be began to use in the dugout, the on-deck circle, and between pitches at the plate.

Here, the role of the sport psychologist was to draw on his knowledge of psychological principles and relate the most appropriate ones to this particular athlete's problem. This is a skill we strive to develop in our students of sport psychology.

SPORT PSYCHOLOGY AT THE UNIVERSITY OF CENTRAL FLORIDA

Sport Psychology is a three-hour undergraduate course offered each Spring semester and tends to be a course that fills on the first day of registration.

This means that the class enrollment of forty to fifty students is comprised mainly of juniors and seniors. Approximately one-third of the students are physical education majors, one-third are psychology majors, and the remaining third come from all other colleges and majors on the campus. Of the total number of students, roughly one-fourth are collegiate level competitors on varsity teams. Over ninety percent of the students are actively involved in athletics in some way. The course is typically recommended for those physical education majors who are actively pursuing coaching careers or other avenues that include work with youngsters. The course meets three times per week for fifty minutes.

COURSE OBJECTIVES

Objectives for the course have been conceptualized in three categories. First there are "cognitive" objectives, which relate to the learning of principles, theory, and research in sport psychology. Second, there are "cognitive/behavioral" objectives, which involve the application of principles and techniques to actual or hypothetical situations. Third, there are "behavioral" objectives, which require students to improve actual skills relating to sport performance or to the observation, documentation, and measurement of various conceptual and/or performance dimensions of sport behavior.

Table 1 shows examples of the various types of objectives and how they are measured in the course.

Table 1
Course Objectives

Type of objective	Example	How it is measured
Cognitive*	To develop a thorough understanding of the research findings in the textbook.	Examination
Cognitive*	To learn the contents of major theoretical approaches to sport behavior.	Examination
Cognitive/ Behavioral*	To apply relevant theoretical concepts to sport settings.	Case-study, homework
Cognitive/ Behavioral	To develop a relaxation training program for use by high divers and implement it.	Project

Type of objective	Example	How it is measured
Behavioral	To develop an overt behavioral measure of baseball batters' performance on every pitch.	Project
Behavioral	To develop a behavioral measure of the degree of positive encouragement used by coaches.	Project
Behavioral	To observe and document aggressive behavior during a hockey game.	Project
Behavioral	To lower the arousal levels of golfers during competitive play.	Project

*Major course objective

These are examples of goals that are actually used in the course and some goals that students might develop for themselves in their project and case-study work. In all cases, the measurement process must focus on specific evidence of goal accomplishment. It seems important that beyond the "major course objective," there should be great flexibility regarding which specific goals each student decides to focus on in his/her project. This is insured by encouraging all students to select a project based on their own interests and goals for taking the course.

COURSE SYLLABUS

The most recent example of the course syllabus is shown in Table 2.

Table 2
Course Syllabus—Spring 1986

PET 3210—Sport Psychology
Class meets M, W, F from 9:00–9:50 AM.
Professor: Dr. Wayne Burroughs
Office: PH 313
Phone: 275–2216

Text 1: Bird, A. M. and Cripe, B. K. *Psychology and Sport Behavior*, 1986.
Text 2: Orlick, T. *In Pursuit of Excellence*, 1980.

Week of	Topic	Assignment Text 1	Assignment Text 2
Jan. 6	I. Section I: Scientific Basis of Sport Psychology		
	a. Scientific dimensions		
	b. Understanding sport behavior	chap. 1 chap. 2	chaps. 1–2
Jan. 13	II. Arousal, anxiety, and intervention in sport		chaps. 3–9
	a. Arousal and sport behavior	chap. 3	
Jan. 20	b. Anxiety and sport	chap. 4	
Jan. 27	c. Intervention strategies	chap. 5	
Feb. 3	Review: TEST 1		
Feb. 10	III. Cognitive processes and sport behavior		chap. 10 and chaps. 12–17
	a. Attentional style	chap. 6	
Feb. 17	b. Observational learning	chap. 7	
Feb. 24	c. Imagery	chap. 8	
March 3	d. Cognitive basis of motivation	chap. 9	
March 10	Review: TEST 2		
March 24	IV. Aggression, group performance, and coaching		
	a. Aggression	chap. 10	chaps. 18–24
March 31	b. Group productivity	chap. 11	
April 7	c. Leadership and Coaching	chap. 12	
April 14	Project presentations	Review	
April 21	Review: TEST 3		

Important Dates:

TEST 1: February 5
TEST 2: March 12
TEST 3: April 23

Project or paper due: April 14

What the course's syllabus does not clearly show is that each topic area is first addressed in terms of theoretical concepts and research findings. Then, one or more classes are devoted to discussions and exercises relating to the application of the concepts to help improve or solve problems in particular settings. The course has not always been structured in this manner. In earlier versions, I spent the first eight weeks of the semester covering theory and research. Then the second half of the course dealt with applying the concepts to cases, problems, and project areas. It has been my experience that it is best to address the application of material very quickly after it is learned. Therefore we currently structure the course by topic (concepts then application) as opposed to covering all topics on a theoretical level and then revisiting all topic areas in an application mode. Also, the students seem to enjoy the course more this way.

TESTS

Tests are used in the course as direct measures of the students' mastery of the cognitive and cognitive/behavioral objectives set out in the course (see Appendix). Cognitive/behavioral objectives typically involve application problems such as, "List in chronological order the steps you might take to increase a collegiate wrestler's control over his prematch anxiety (arousal)." This type of problem requires that the student know about arousal and its characteristics as well as practical ways to use what we know to control it. These "what would you do?" type of questions are usually asked in a traditional essay format. Answers are graded in terms of their content (accuracy and thoroughness) and also in terms of their creativity and practicality.

Two other types of items are used to assess mastery of cognitive course objectives. Class size usually dictates that we include multiple choice items for ease of scoring. Of course, carefully written multiple choice items can be excellent measures of the student's knowledge of specific or detailed research findings, theoretical concepts, and principles of applying this knowledge. I never ask questions that absolutely require students to associate authors' names with research findings or theories. Instead I encourage the students to read and study for findings, concepts, and principles. Knowing the names of authors may help the student place a certain study in perspective, but it will not be absolutely necessary for the student to choose the "correct" or "best" answer to a multiple choice question.

The third type of test item that is used is one we call an "association" item. This type of item resembles an identification item but differs in three main respects. First, answers to association items need not include complete sentences or paragraphs; words and phrases with necessary content are sufficient. Second, association items may appear more than once on the same test (up to four times). Third, because the same association items can occur several times, a measure of the students' breadth and depth of knowledge may be obtained. Let's look at an example. Suppose a class had been discussing the various issues involved in passing federal legislation to curb violence or aggressive behavior in professional sports. In addition, several readings might have dealt with these issues. It is now time for us to create the test. We might decide to ask about the concepts by means of association items since these types of items can cover a lot of ground without requiring the student to write lengthy answers during the test.

Part of the test page would look like this:

1. Legislation and Violence:
2. Legislation and Violence:
3. Legislation and Violence:

Block 1 says to the student, "Tell me something you know about "Legislation and Violence." The student must write something inside the block that convinces the professor that he/she knows something about this topic—or something "associated with" this topic. The student could choose several different things to write. For example, possible answers might include problems with passage of such legislation, issues involved with the definition of "violence" (e.g., intent, consent of the victim, part of the game, etc.), survey findings about such legislation and current status of legislation. In Block 2 the student must write an answer to convince the professor that he/she knows something else (not mentioned in Block 1) about "Legislation and Violence" and so on.

Answers are scored as +2 for a clearly convincing answer, +1 for a partially correct or general answer, and 0 for an incorrect or irrelevant answer. Students tend to learn to like these items after the initial "break in" time.

Three tests are given each semester. I allow the students to decide as a class whether they want a two-part (over two class days) test or a one-part (day) test. Most classes choose two-day tests so that time is not as much of an influencing factor on their test scores. Each test counts one-fourth of the course grade with the last fourth coming from the project/paper assignment.

PROJECT OR PAPER ASSIGNMENT

Each student must complete either a traditional library research paper on a topic of his/her choice or carry out an applied project. Students are allowed to work on applied projects individually, in pairs, or in three-person teams with approval of the professor. Students must choose their own topics of interest for applied projects or papers. Approximately five weeks into the semester students are required to turn in outlines of their selected paper or project topics. The professor then provides individual feedback to them regarding ideas for expansion, relevant literature, suggested methods, and problems they might encounter. This process continues until both students and professor are satisfied with the proposed project or library paper.

Students then carry out the necessary steps and submit a paper of ten pages or less that clearly communicates the results of their endeavors. Students who decide to do projects are encouraged to structure their reports in a journal article format including an introduction or problem statement, method section, results, and discussion or interpretation.

Near the end of the semester each student or team makes a six- to ten-minute presentation of findings to the class in a relatively informal round-table atmosphere. Recent examples of topic areas chosen by students include:

—Behavior modification training and youth sports coaches.
—The effect of expectancy on Nautilus strength training gains.
—Imagery and free-throw shooting.
—Arousal levels of collegiate pitchers.
—Goal setting for divers and swimmers.
—Locus of control and athletic performance.
—Sources of motivation in triathletes.
—Use of associative strategies by distance runners.
—Motion analysis and hurdling.

In many of these applied projects, students have designed a training technique and actually implemented it with athletic teams. We feel that the hands on learning experience of an applied project is perhaps the strongest part of our course in sport psychology.

TEXTBOOKS

Since the inception of the course in 1981, I have used three different textbooks. The first book I used was Suinn's *Psychology in Sports: Methods and Applications* (1980). This book contains a collection of articles and essays by many different sport psychologists on a variety of topics including motivation, emotional states, mental states, behavioral strategies, and issues in sport psychology. In conjunction with Suinn's book, I began during 1982 to use Terry Orlick's *In Pursuit of Excellence* (1980). This is a very straightforward, applied book that students enjoy and from which they derive great benefit. The book does a very good job of encouraging athletes to analyze their personal behavior and design ways to enhance their "pursuit of excellence." I still use this book although I currently use Bird's and Cripe's *Psychology and Sport Behavior* (1986) as our main textbook. This book does a good job of covering traditional sport psychology topic areas and includes a number of pedagogical design features. These features include a "unifying model" in eight of the twelve chapters, case studies, review questions, chapter summaries, sections on "implications for sport," glossaries, annotated readings, and thorough reference lists.

In addition to these books, I have considered several recent publications for use in our course. A brief description of these books follows:

Williams, Jean M., ed. 1986. *Applied Sport Psychology: Personal Growth to Peak Performance.* Palo Alto, Calif.: Mayfield. This book presents an excellent series of well-chosen applied topics, each discussed by a leading sport psychologist. Thorough reference lists follow each chapter. Topics include motor skill learning, goal setting for peak performance, relaxation and energizing techniques for regulation of arousal, imagery training, and eighteen other topics. Many exercises, questionnaires and training techniques are included.

Cox, Richard H. 1985. *Sport Psychology: Concepts and Applications.* Dubuque, Iowa: W. C. Brown. This book is organized in a manner similar to traditional approaches to sport psychology. Its ten chapters cover topics such as personality, attention, anxiety and arousal, motivation, attribution theory, social psychology, audience effects, team cohesion, leadership, and intervention strategies. At the conclusion of each chapter, Cox lists the major principles to be derived from the chapter and ways these principles can be applied. This is a highly useful feature of the book.

Iso-Ahola, Seppo E., and Brad Hatfield. 1986. *Psychology of Sports: A Social Psychological Approach.* Dubuque, Iowa: W. C. Brown. This book emphasizes the social psychology perspective on sport. It includes chapters on topics such as the social psychology of youth sports, socialization into sport, the effects of spectators on athletes and vice versa, the psychology of coaching and the social psychology of team performance.

Sandweiss, Jack H., and Steven L. Wolf, eds. 1985. *Biofeedback and Sports Science.* New York: Plenum Press. Although this book is certainly not a textbook in sport psychology, the editors have done a very creditable job of gathering current information on biofeedback as it relates to sport. Topics include physiological perception, biofeedback, and biomechanics in athletic training; biofeedback and sports medicine, and biofeedback applications in rehabilitation medicine. These are topics highly related to sport psychology, and this book seems to be a good summary and integration of biofeedback concepts, theory, and application.

CLASS EXERCISES

Since one of the major goals of the course is to apply sport psychology and its concepts to actual sport situations, various practical exercises are done in class to encourage such application. For example, after discussing relaxation and reading about it, the class takes two periods to practice various relaxation techniques. There are several different approaches to relaxation. We typically demonstrate two approaches—deep breathing and muscle tensing and relaxing. Various audio tapes are available for purchase and many of these provide an entire session that can be used in class. On these exercise days, students are encouraged to wear comfortable clothing and to bring towels or exercise pads so they can sit on the floor.

Other types of exercises include filling out a motivational questionnaire; trait/state anxiety measures; a goal-setting workshop in which students analyze their own goals and learn to write them in measureable ways; and imagery analysis in small groups. In this latter exercise I ask athletes who have learned to use imagery techniques successfully to share their experiences with other students. Students generally enjoy these workshop days and often learn a great deal from one another.

USE OF CONSULTING EXPERIENCE

One thing seems very clear about student interest in applying the principles of sport psychology. If the professor has actually used these techniques or practices while employed by athletic teams or players, his/her credibility is tremendously enhanced. Therefore, if possible, the professor needs to draw from personal consulting experience. My work with professional baseball players has served as an entry point for many conversations with students who are beginning to see the variety of possibilities for the field of sport psychology. Similarly, on-going research programs enhance the quality of the course and encourage student involvement in the empirical process.

APPENDIX: EXCERPTS FROM TYPICAL EXAMS

Sport Psychology
Test 2: Suinn chaps. 7–10. Orlick chaps. 1–24.

PART I: MULTIPLE CHOICE (3 POINTS EACH)

1. According to Barbara Zaremski's article, which of the following is a critical question the coach must ask himself prior to preparing an athlete psychologically for competition?
   A. How do I handle myself with regard to the athlete's perception of me?
   B. Do I help athletes grow with competitive situations?

C. What can I do to improve and add that extra something to bring an athlete to the top?
D. All of the above.

2. In an athletic competition between *world class* athletes, which of the following is least likely to make the difference between winning and losing?
A. Being in the best physical condition possible.
B. Being able to concentrate totally on the athletic event.
C. Having a coach that stresses the psychological fitness of the athlete.
D. Having the ability to cope with the stress of the athletic event.

3. The coach knows that preparation of an athlete is complete when:
A. The athlete's physical conditioning has been maximized.
B. The athlete's personal growth and development has been maximized.
C. The athlete is psychologically ready for the event.
D. The athlete no longer needs the coach.

4. As an individual approaches the theoretical limit of an athletic event:
A. The easier it is to improve performance.
B. The harder it is to improve performance.
C. Other things being equal, his rate of improvement will not change.
D. None of the above.

5. According to Robert M. Nideffer's chapter, "Attentional Focus-Self Assessment," if a person has a Broad External (BET) psychological make-up, then the individual:
A. Is distracted by his own thought and ideas.
B. Will make mistakes in games because he watches one person and forgets about the others.
C. Can analyze complex situations such as how a play develops in a rugby game.
D. Can develop a lot of ideas with only a little information.

PART II: ESSAYS

1. Choose one of the motivational models discussed in class and/or the textbook and discuss how it might be used to explain why some people run in marathons. (Choices of models include those of Lawler, Singer, Atkinson, or Butt.)

2. The study of the relationship between personalities and sport performance and interest has provided some insight into differences in interest and performance. However, most would agree that the study of personality variables has been only moderately helpful. Discuss reasons for this situation. Please *cite specific examples*.

3. What is simulation training and what are its advantages and disadvantages?

WORKS CITED

Bird, Anne Marie, and Bernette K. Cripe. 1986. *Psychology and Sport Behavior*. St. Louis: Times Mirror/C. V. Mosby College Publishing.

Cox, Richard. 1985. *Sport Psychology: Concepts and Applications*. Dubuque, Iowa: W. C. Brown.

Iso-Ahola, Seppo E., and Brad Hatfield. 1986. *Psychology of Sports: A Social Psychological Approach.* Dubuque, Iowa: W. C. Brown.

Orlick, Terry. 1980. *In Pursuit of Excellence.* Champaign, Ill.: Human Kinetics.

Sandweiss, Jack H., and Steven L. Wolf, eds. 1985. *Biofeedback and Sports Science.* New York: Plenum Press.

Suinn, Richard M. 1980. *Psychology in Sports: Methods and Applications.* Minneapolis: Burgess.

Williams, Jean M., ed. 1986. *Applied Sport Psychology: Personal Growth to Peak Performance.* Palo Alto, Calif.: Mayfield.

PART 8
Interdisciplinary Approaches to Sport

13

Teaching "Sport and Society"

ALLEN GUTTMANN

On the possibly immodest assumption that anyone interested in my interdisciplinary course, "Sport and Society," might also be curious about the academic path I trod prior to the appearance of the course in Amherst College's sociology listings, a word of "prehistory" seems in order. Torn between the intellectual attractions of the social sciences and the humanities, I opted to obtain a Ph.D. in American Studies, an interdisciplinary field. After a dozen years of teaching, after the publication of several books on American history and literature, I began to work, naively, on a book comparing American to European sports. Since I happened to be teaching in Germany when I began serious research on the project, I dove into the vast sea of *Sportwissenschaft* produced by three generations of German scholars. By the time I surfaced, I was hooked on sport history and sport sociology. All thoughts of a contemporary comparative focus vanished and my first book in my new field of research, *From Ritual to Record* (1978), argued that the most significant cultural differences are those between modern and premodern sports rather than those between American and European sports. My methods included literary analysis and elementary statistical techniques as well as historical examples drawn from primitive, ancient, medieval, and modern sports. Having published the book, having been encouraged by its reception to continue in the field, I decided to offer a course on the social significance of sport. Since I did not want to limit myself to the American scene, I decided to knock on the doors of my sociological colleagues. I asked impertinently if I might offer "Sport and Society" in their department. My colleagues in sociology are admirably liberal (some might say recklessly permissive) and the result was Sociology 22.

In the ten years since I first offered the course, it has gone through many revisions. My description is based principally on the Spring 1985 and Spring 1987 versions. Perhaps, as a kind of preface, I should say that Amherst College is a typical liberal-arts institution and that it has no physical education majors for whom "Sport and Society" might be a preprofessional course. The students of Sociology 22 are majoring in Greek, biology, economics, and so forth. In other words, the interdisciplinary approach more or less matches the mix of interests represented in the classroom. Very few of the students find sport-related careers, but I am proud to say that Jane Bachman Wulf, then a student at nearby Mount Holyoke College, registered for the course, took her term paper to New York, found employment at *Sports Illustrated*, and is now that magazine's chief of reporters. During my time at Amherst, two students have gone on to play in the National Football League, but neither took my course.

The closest thing to a textbook for the course is presently Eldon E. Snyder and Elmer Spreitzer, *Social Aspects of Sport* (1983), a text chosen for its clarity, brevity, and unity of focus. (I have used various other excellent texts and am ready to concede that my present choice is somewhat arbitrary.) Since I want students to read monographs and essays as well as textbook syntheses, I usually ask them to buy my own *From Ritual to Record* (1978) and the anthologies edited by Marie Hart and Susan Birrell (*Sport and the Sociocultural Process* 1981) and by Roger G. Noll (*Government and the Sports Business* 1974). I also use one important work of fiction, Ernest Hemingway's *The Sun Also Rises* (1926). Although placing books on reserve in the library is not the best way to insure that they are actually read by the students, there is a limit to what one can ask students to spend. For Richard Mandell's *Sport: A Cultural History* (1984), for Bero Rigauer's *Sport and Work* ([1969] 1981), and for my own *The Games Must Go On* (1984), I sent the students to the library. I usually supplement the texts with four or five multilithed essays. Unlike some curricular ventures into sports studies, this course does not feature celebrity appearances by famous athletes who "tell it like it is."

Normally, I begin with "Philosophical Approaches," that is, with the definitional efforts found in the first chapter of Johan Huizinga's *Homo Ludens* (1955), in Snyder's and Spreitzer's text (1983), and in *From Ritual to Record* (1978). A paradigm that distinguishes clearly among the categories play, games, contests, and sports seems to me absolutely essential if one is not to end up with chess, sunbathing, and walking to work as instances of sports participation. There is usually some puzzlement when I argue that training for a football game is merely preparation for a sports event rather than sport per se, but students are usually ready to accept a working definition of sports that describes them as autotelic, that is, nonutilitarian, physical contests. Perhaps I should add that when I first began to ask students to read *From Ritual to Record* (1978), I felt awkward when I *lectured* on the topic. Most of my students are good readers and I asked myself, "Do I really need to repeat all this?" In the meantime, however, positive and negative criticisms of the book by various scholars have given me more than enough to talk about.

The next step is historical. Using *From Ritual to Record* (1978) plus sections from Mandell's *Sport: A Cultural History* (1984), the class discusses the extraordinary historical differences between primitive, ancient, medieval, and modern sports. That the sports festivals of the ancient Greeks took place without significant quantification and without the modern obsession with the sport record is, for most students, a great surprise. The "otherness" of primitive sport becomes obvious from my examples, from Mandell's, and from Clifford Geertz's brilliant account of the cultural significance of the Balinese cockfight (from Hart and Birrell 1981). If Patricia Cuyler's splendid 1979 study of Japanese sumo is available in an American paperback, I may further revise the course and ask the students to read the book, which traces the evolution of sumo from religious ritual to a more-or-less-modern sport. This philosophical-anthropological section is always one of the most successful parts of the course simply because students assume, despite their relative sophistication, that the way we do sports is the way people have always done sports. Most students are ready to abandon this assumption, but they still want to believe that the way we do sports is the way sports *should* be done.

This theoretical section, which takes us through the second week, concludes with Hemingway's *The Sun Also Rises* (1926), which I use to dramatize the theoretical distinctions discussed in the first classes. I begin with the conventional literary approach that interprets the novel as a T. S. Eliot–inspired story of the "lost generation," with Jake Barnes and Lady Brett as estranged wanderers in the modern wasteland and Pedro Romero and the Spanish peasants as symbols of primitive community. I try to demonstrate that sports are crucial metaphors for the modern and the premodern. French professional cycling and Spanish festival-related bullfighting are two of Hemingway's major symbols for corrupt modernity and threatened community. The focus on sports is something new for the students, most of whom had read the book in high school or in some previous course. They have often told me that the book now appears in a wholly different light. I have, incidently, never encountered a student at Amherst who resisted the notion that works of fiction have a place in a sociology course.

The next phase is more strictly sociological and begins with the question of socialization into sport, with readings from Snyder and Spreitzer (1983) and Hart and Birrell (1981). The weighting of factors predisposing one to do sports is one of the main themes. The relationship between sports participation and academic achievement is another. I also discuss the value of adult-organized sports leagues for small children and the phenomenon of adolescent "burn out." At this point, some students have trouble reading the statistical tables, and it is necessary to explain some elementary correlational techniques. Hard going for those who dreamed of a thrice-weekly "bull session" in which the class speculates on the Red Sox and their pennant chances.

I usually spend one day on the question of intercollegiate athletics. In addition to the chapter in Snyder and Spreitzer, I ask students to read an essay of mine that originally appeared in James Frey's collection, *The Governance of Intercollegiate Athletics* (1982). The essay maintains that the American tradition of school-sponsored sports is less socially satisfactory than the German system of club sports independent of the education system. German clubs, which enroll 25 percent of the whole population, allow sports participation from childhood to old age. There is no need to pretend that the best athletes, who represent the clubs at the professional level, are students. While students concede that big-time intercollegiate athletics in the United States have occasioned numerous ethical abuses by coaches and by athletes, they are usually unshaken in their conviction that colleges and universities ought to sponsor semiprofessional teams. There are always, however, a few who are distressed by the hypocrisy of the present system. The discussion is invariably lively.

The next section of the course is the most difficult. Using Noll's *Government and the Sports Business* (1974), I lecture on the economic theory of professional team sports, on the variables that contribute to attendance and price setting, and on the tax laws and how they made it possible, for years, to reap huge financial benefits from alleged losses incurred by the ownership of sports franchises. The magical depreciation of the players did the trick and Benjamin Okner's "Taxation and Sports Enterprises" (Noll 1974) is a real eye-opener. I make no effort to clarify the economists' mathematical appendixes (which I myself do not understand), but I consider it essential to explain to the students the theory behind a regression formula and to show them how to interpret such formulas. It seems to me irresponsible to shirk the explanatory effort, but, at this point, many of the humanities majors mutter the words of Huckleberry Finn as he tried vainly to read *Pilgrim's Progress*: "The statements was interesting but tough."

The statements become somewhat less tough when we turn to legal questions and to the ethical rights and wrongs of the various reserve and option clauses that, for a century, gave franchise owners almost complete control over the players' careers. Since the owners' principal argument was that strict control was necessary to secure equality of competition among the teams, one line of counterargument was that such control did *not* contribute to equality and one technique of the counterargument involved such statistical measures as standard deviation and rank-order correlation (both of which enable us to be precise about year-to-year changes in the teams' performance). The precision of the standard deviation in the number of games won, which neatly shows how nearly equal the teams were, contrasts beautifully with the owners' pompous rhetoric about "the good of the game." Following the Supreme Court's crazy-quilt pattern of answers to the question of whether or not sports leagues are really businesses in the sense meant by the Sherman Antitrust Act, I conclude by asking the students to ponder the confused lyricism of Justic Blackmun's famous decision in the Flood Case (Curtis C. Flood *v*. Bowie K. Kuhn 407 U.S. 258 1972), in which the baseball-flustered jurist recites "Casey at the Bat," names the sacred names of some eighty-five Hall-of-Famers, and defends the reserve clause as a "confirmed aberration." The real fun comes, however, when the students debate the rights and wrongs of the owners' claim. To my astonishment, students destined eventually to sell *their* professional legal and medical services to the highest bidder are usually persuaded that "overpaid" professional athletes should *not* share the same right. Beneath the infant scholar lurks the fan. Perhaps, since Justice Blackmun and his colleagues on the court reacted with the same illogic, one shouldn't be surprised by adolescent emotion.

In the past, I have devoted a single day to the question of "Sport and the Media," using the Snyder and Spreitzer chapter (1983), Ira Horowitz's contribution to the Noll collection (1974) and Susan Birrell and John Loy versus Marshall McLuhan (in Hart and Birrell 1981). Now that the money paid for TV rights has passed the $1 billion mark, now that TV networks can create as well as influence international sports events, I intend to expand this section, probably by assigning the relevant chapter from my *Sports Spectators* (1986). The interaction of television and sport is unquestionably a central theme for sport sociology in the 1980s.

A mere two days are devoted to "Race and Ethnicity in Sport." The text (Snyder and Spreitzer 1983) and the anthologies enable me to focus on the hypotheses of John Loy and Joseph McElvogue, centrality in baseball and football (Hart and Birrell 1981), and on Gerald W. Scully's use of statistics to show that black baseball players whose average salary is higher than that of white players suffer nonetheless from discrimination because they are *underpaid* in relation to their quantified achievements as measured by their statistics (Noll 1974). Here too, I try to show students how necessary it is to be able at least to interpret a chi-square test (used by Loy and McElvogue) and a regression formula (used by Scully). I hammer away at this point like a crazed carpenter because too many students with extraordinary verbal skills fall apart at the mere mention of statistics.

Predictably, a unit on race and ethnicity is followed by units on sport and social class and on sport and sex, with readings drawn, once again, from Snyder and Spreitzer (1983) and Hart and Birrell (1981). For the subtopic of sport and social mobility, I also assign a multilithed version of John Loy's study of social mobility through sports at UCLA. Peter Marsh's "The World of Football Hooligans" (Hart and Birrell 1981) has stimulated good discussions, but I will probably move it to the unit on spectators. The unit on "Sport and Sex" includes two films, *The Knute Rockne Story*, which illustrates certain still conventional attitudes towards masculinity and sports, and *Personal Best*, which has been the center of considerable controversy. Some critics have objected to the "crotch shots" and others have argued that the conclusion belittles lesbians (because the heroine turns from a female to a male lover) while still others, with whom I agree, have praised the authenticity of a track-and-field film most of whose actors are *athletes* rather than film stars. Since the readings raise important questions about body image, role conflict, and discrimination against female athletes within and without the educational process, a week is much too short a time to exhaust the topic. I am tempted to use a third film, *Pumping Iron: II*, to raise further questions about body image and gender roles, but I shall probably stay with *Personal Best* and add readings with photographs of female bodybuilders. Robert Mapplethorpe's *Lady Lisa Lyon* (1985) is a possibility.

On to the Olympic Games. Although I have at times used *The Modern Olympic Games* (1976), edited by Peter Graham and Horst Ueberhorst, I have had more success with my own *The Games Must Go On: Avery Brundage and the Olympic Movement* (1984). The main theme of this section is the politicization of the games. The "Nazi Olympics" of 1936 are still controversial. Since Brundage was a central figure in the fight over American participation, he provides a clear focus for the discussion. Thirty-six years later came "Black September," the massacre of Israeli athletes by Palestinian terrorists at the 1972 games in Munich. In Munich as well as in Berlin, Brundage was present to insist naively that politics not be allowed to intrude upon "amateur" sport. Indeed, the entire International Olympic Committee shared his conviction that "the games must go on." Should they have? The film *Visions of Eight*, in which eight directors from eight different countries interpret the 1972 games, raises the question with visceral intensity when viewers hear Ron Hill, the British runner, telling the interviewer that he just doesn't want to think about the massacre because he came to Munich to run a marathon. (The film, incidently, is an aesthetic marvel.) After Munich came the boycotts of Montreal and Moscow. In 1980, most of my students applauded the U.S. Olympic Committee for jumping through Jimmy Carter's hoop. In 1984, most condemned the Soviet Union for its retaliation.

I should probably add that I tried for several years to use Leni Riefenstahl's documentary film *Olympia* as a way to show the power of the 1936 games. The opening scenes of the film are a highly romantic evocation of the Greek heritage, with pastoral landscape, naked maidens in ritual dance, ancient statues that turn magically into modern athletes, with the torch lit at Olympia and carried, to impassioned Wagnerian music, to Berlin. But my students' response to these scenes was to giggle nervously and thus to destroy the film aesthetically. It was, as Henry David Thoreau remarked of his attempt to gnaw at uncooked corn, "an experiment that failed."

After five sessions on the Olympics come two on "Sport and National Character," one on baseball as America's national game and one on the attempted usurpation of that title by football. I ask students to read two chapters from *From Ritual to Record* as well as the cross-cultural observations in Snyder and Spreitzer (1983) on Japanese baseball and in Hart and Birrell (1981) on Mexican bullfighting versus American baseball. Since last teaching the course, I have spent a semester in Japan and look forward to more extensive discussion of Japanese baseball, for which Robert Whiting's book *The Chrysanthemum and the Bat* (1977) is an excellent resource.

The penultimate unit is devoted to the spectators. In the past, I used a pair of my essays in multilithed form, but I now plan to ask the students to read most of *Sports Spectators* (1986). The book is partly historical (from the Greeks to the present) and partly sociological and psychological (focus on the mid-twentieth century). Among the many subtopics is the question of the alleged catharsis which supposedly, in the course of the sports event, renders the fans calm and tranquil (Neo-Marxists say "apathetic, dehumanized"). Since a variety of psychological experiments by Leonard Berkowitz and Jeffrey Goldstein (1983) and their associates have shown what any observer already knew—that is, that the spectators are more aggressive *after* the game than before it—I raise the question of whether or not sports should be played without spectators (see Guttmann 1986, 212). Should society not, to avoid the inevitable increase in aggression that televised sports generate, eliminate TV sports? At the very least, shouldn't it eliminate violent sports that encourage the viewers to enact what they see? The question raises some of the same issues that are raised by proposals to ban pornography, and the discussion is often heated. My own "solution" is to allow freedom of expression, that is, TV sports, and to hope for the kind of internalization of restraint that Norbert Elias describes in *The Civilizing Process* (1978–82). The book ends with a discussion of spectator identification as an important factor in the demise of fair play and I expect my views, here too, to meet with some resistance from the students (as they already have from a number of American and European scholars).

The classs ends with the Marxist and the neo-Marxist critiques of Western sport, the first motivated by the alleged racism and chauvinism of American and European sport, the second driven by the rejection of *all* forms of sport as "the capitalistically deformed form of play." I use a chapter from *From Ritual to Record* to clarify for the students this important distinction between the Marxists condemning Western sports and the Neo-Marxists condemning sports per se whether done in the United States or the USSR. Although Bero Rigauer's book *Sport and Work* ([1969] 1981) is not easy to read, even for my highly literate Amherst students, I consider it the classic statement of the Neo-Marxist position and I have found that it provokes most students into passionate disagreement. Indeed, on one occasion, an older student, a former professional athlete, asked to be allowed to address the class with an oral presentation on the distortions of Herr Professor Rigauer. As long as Rigauer's little book can stir such emotions, I'll continue to assign it. It seems appropriate to end the course with fundamental questions about the *value* of this institution—modern sport—that the students now, presumably, understand.

Grades? They are based mostly but not entirely on written work. There are two hour-long short-essay-type examinations, that is, a mid-term and a final. The examinations are intended to coerce the students into keeping up with the course. I do not pretend that they are in themselves educational. The typical question? "What are the most significant Marxist and neo-Marxist criticisms of American sports?" The term paper, on the other hand, *is* meant to be educational. The topic I leave to the students with the proviso that I consult with them before they begin work. Papers have ranged widely and interestingly. I have had, for instance, an interpretation of the artist Thomas Rowlandson's eighteenth-century sporting scenes, a statistical analysis of sports participation at Amherst College, a test of the hypothesis that althletes are physically more attractive than nonathletes, a study of sports in Ernest Hemingway's fiction, a survey of attitudes towards female bodybuilders, to name a few. Needless to say, some of the term papers have been delights, some have been disappointments, but, on the whole, I find that I enjoy rather than dread reading them. This happy fact tells a great deal about the course. The quality of the term papers is one of the factors that motivate me to say to inquiries from scholars thinking about generating a course in sport studies, "Come on in, the water's fine."

APPENDIX: SYLLABUS SPORT AND SOCIETY

TEXTBOOKS

Allen Guttmann, *From Ritual to Record*.
Marie Hart and Susan Birrell, eds., *Sport and the Sociocultural Process*, 3d ed.
Ernest Hemingway, *The Sun Also Rises*.
Rogert G. Noll, ed., *Government and the Sports Business*.
Eldon E. Snyder and Elmer Spreitzer, *Social Aspects of Sport*, 2d ed.

In addition, the following books are on reserve in the Frost library:
Allen Guttmann, *The Games Must Go On*.
Allen Guttmann, *Sports Spectators*.
Richard Mandell, *Sport: A Cultural History*.
Bero Rigauer, *Sport and Work*.

ASSIGNMENTS

Play and Sport: Philosophical Approaches

Mon.: Introduction.
Wed.: Huizinga, *Homo Ludens* (multilith); Loy, "The Nature of Sport" (Hart and Birrell, 21–39).

Fri.: Snyder and Spreitzer, 12–28; Guttmann, *From Ritual to Record*, 1–14.

From Primitive to Modern Sports

Mon.: Geertz, "Deep Play" (Hart and Birrell, 624–53); Guttmann, *From Ritual to Record*, 15–55; Mandell, *Sport*, Chaps. 1, 3–5 (on reserve).
Wed.: Hemingway, 3–125.
Fri.: Hemingway, 126–247.

Socialization into Sport

Mon.: Snyder and Spreitzer, 65–81; Sherif, "The Social Context of Competition" (Hart and Birrell, 132–55; Fine, "Preadolescent Socialization" (Hart and Birrell, 164–91).

Participation, Achievement, Mobility

Wed.: Snyder and Spreitzer, 123–38; Jerome and Phillips, "The Relationship between Academic Achievement and Interscholastic Participation" (Hart and Birrell, 150–55).

Interscholastic and Intercollegiate Athletics

Wed.: Snyder and Spreitzer, 123–38; Jerome and Phillips, "The Relationship between Academic Achievement and Interscholastic Participation" (Hart and Birrell, 150–55).
Fri.: Snyder and Spreitzer, 105–22; Guttmann, "The Tiger Devours the Literary Magazine" (multilith).

Professional Sport: Economic Aspects

Mon.: Noll, "The U.S. Team Sports Industry" (Noll, 1–32); Quirk and El Hodiri, "The Economic Theory of a Sports League" (Noll, 33–58).
Wed.: Canes, "The Social Benefits of Restrictions on Team Quality" (Noll, 81–106).
Fri.: Noll, "Attendance and Price Setting" (Noll, 115–57).
Mon.: Okner, "Taxation and Sports Enterprises" (Noll, 159–83); Okner, "Subsidies of Stadiums and Arenas" (Noll, 325–47).

Professional Sport: Legal Aspects

Wed.: Staudchar, "Player Salary Issues. . ." (Hart and Birrell, 269–76); Davis, "Self-Regulation in Baseball" (Noll, 349–86).
Fri.: Rivkin, "Sports Leagues and the Federal Antitrust Laws" (Noll, 387–428).

VIII. Sport and the Media

Mon.: Snyder and Spreitzer, 211–28; Horowitz, "Sports Broadcasting" (Noll, 275–323); Birrell and Loy, "Media Sport" (Hart and Birrell, 314–28); Guttmann, *Sports Spectators*, chap. 6 (on reserve).

Race and Ethnicity in Sport

Wed.: Snyder and Spreitzer, 174–91; Loy and McElvogue, "Racial Segregation" (Hart and Birrell, 314–28); Ball, "Ascription and Position" (Hart and Birrell, 410–29).
Fri.: Scully, "Discrimination in Baseball" (Noll, 221–70).

Sport and Social Class

Mon.: Snyder and Spreitzer, 138–54; Loy, "The Study of Sport and Social Mobility" (multilith).

Wed.: Gruneau, "Class or Mass" (Hart and Birrell, 495–531); Listiak, "'Legitimate Deviance' and Social Class" (Hart and Birrell, 532–62).

Fri.: HOUR EXAM (Makeups will be given for illness or family crises but not for athletic trips.)

SPRING RECESS

Mon.: Marsh and Hare, "The World of Football Hooligans" (Hart and Birrell, 609–19).

Sport and Sex

Tues.: Film: *The Knute Rockne Story* (shown at 4 and 7:30).

Wed.: Snyder and Spreitzer, 155–73; Fiske, "Pigskin Review" (Hart and Birrell, 350–68);

Thurs.: Film: *Personal Best* (shown at 4 and 7:30).

Fri.: Hart, "On Being Female in Sport" (Hart and Birrell, 450–60); Sherif, "Females in the Competitive Process" (Hart and Birrell, 461–86);

Mon.: Felshin, "The Triple Option . . ." (Hart and Birrell, 487–92).

The Modern Olympics

Wed.: Leiper, "The International Olympic Committee . . ." (Hart and Birrell, 39–62).

Fri.: Guttmann, *The Games Must Go On*, 1–11, 23–50, 62–81 (on reserve); Guttmann, *The Games Must Go On*, 132–69; Guttmann, *The Games Must Go On*, 223–255.

Thurs.: Film: *Visions of Eight* (shown at 4 and 7:30).

Sport and National character

Fri.: Guttmann, *From Ritual to Record*, 91–116; Zurcher and Meadow, "On Bullfights and Baseball" (Hart and Birrell, 654–75); Snyder and Spreitzer, 53–56.

Mon.: Riesman and Denney, "Football in America" (Hart and Birrell, 678–93); Guttmann, *From Ritual to Record*, 117–36.

Spectators

Wed.: Guttmann, *Sports Spectators*, Chaps. 7–9 (on reserve).

Conservatism, Marxism, Neo-Marxism

Mon.: Huizinga, "The Play Element" (Hart and Birrell, 4–20);

Wed.: Brohm, "Theses . . ." (Hart and Birrell, 107–13); Guttmann, *From Ritual to Record*, 57–69.

Fri.: Rigauer, *Sport and Work*, 1–79 (on reserve).

Mon.: Rigauer, 83–111.

Wed.: Guttmann, *From Ritual to Record*, 69–89.

Fri.: Guttmann, *From Ritual to Record*, 157–61.

Mon.: HOUR EXAM (Makeups will be given for illness and for family crises but not for athletic trips.)

WORKS CITED

Cuyler, Patricia. 1979. *Sumo*. New York: Weatherhill.

Elias, Norbert. 1978–82. *The Civilizing Process*. 2 vols. Oxford: Basil Blackwell.

Frey, James, ed. 1982. *The Governance of Intercollegiate Athletics*. West Point, N.Y.: Leisure Press.

Goldstein, Jeffrey H. 1983. *Sports Violence*. New York: Springer Verlag.

Graham, Peter, and Horst Ueberhorst, eds. 1976. *The Modern Olympics*. Cornwall, N.Y.: Leisure Press.

Guttmann, Allen. 1978. *From Ritual to Record: The Nature of Modern Sports*. New York: Columbia University Press.

———. 1984. *The Games Must Go On: Avery Brundage and the Olympic Movement*. New York: Columbia University Press.

———. 1986. *Sports Spectators*. New York: Columbia University Press.

Hart, M. Marie, and Susan Birrell, eds. 1981. *Sport and the Sociocultural Process*. 3d ed. Dubuque, Iowa: W. C. Brown.

Hemingway, Ernest. 1926. *The Sun Also Rises*. New York: Scribner's.

Huizinga, Johan. 1955. *Homo Ludens: A Study of the Play Element in Culture*. Boston: Beacon Press.

Mandell, Richard. 1984. *Sport: A Cultural History*. New York: Columbia University Press.

Mapplethorpe, Robert. 1985. *Lady Lisa Lyon*. Munich: Schirmer Mosel Verlag.

Noll, Roger G., ed. 1974. *Government and the Sports Business*. Washington, D.C.: Brookings Institute.

Rigauer, Bero. *Sport and Work*. 1969. Translated by Allen Guttmann. New York: Columbia University Press, 1981.

Snyder, Eldon E., and Elmer Spreitzer, eds. 1983. *Social Aspects of Sports*. 2d ed. Englewood Cliffs, N.J.: Prentice-Hall.

Whiting, Robert. 1977. *The Chrysanthemum and the Bat*. New York: Dodd, Mead.

14

Teaching "Sport and U.S. Society"

JOAN. M. CHANDLER

This course was designed for undergraduates at the University of Texas at Dallas. All are commuters; aged 29 on average but ranging from 19–74, 71 percent of them hold full-time jobs, and 40 percent are married. They are all juniors and seniors; 56.5 percent come from the local community college system. All must take two university-wide interdisciplinary studies courses; these courses are authorized by a university committee that may refuse to accept a particular course or allow a course already in the catalog to be taught by a new instructor. This course, "Sport and U.S. Society," although it was specifically designed, could be adapted to fit the needs of any college because its structure and content are defined but flexible. I have taught a version of it in an interdisciplinary graduate program.

People in the Dallas area are fanatical about sport. In designing a sport course, I intended to attract some students who would regard English, history, anthropology, or sociology courses as boring or unrelated to their careers. I therefore framed the course in a way that I hoped would force students to examine their assumptions, and to come to grips with some of the relevant historical, sociological, and anthropological concepts and evidence.

Some students come into the course thinking that sport belongs in the toy department; it is a revelation to them to begin to comprehend the extent to which sport affects not only the formal educational system, but the economic and social life of this country. Some students take the course because, as concerned parents or amateur coaches, they are worried about the effects of school and club athletic programs on their children. Some students—particularly ex-professional players, ex-holders of athletic scholarships, or aspiring sportswriters—take sport seriously and have very strong opinions about it, but have derived almost all their knowledge from their own experience. Some students have no interest in sport; they take the course because it fits conveniently into their crowded schedules.

This heterogeneity of expertise and interest also extends to students' abilities; some can use English only as a blunt instrument, while others write quite beautifully. Some are well-trained and highly intelligent, others the reverse. I am dealing with a mixed bag; it seems to me therefore of prime importance that everyone should gain shared, substantive knowledge while being allowed to develop his/her own interests. I also believed it important for students to work together; in a commuter institution, intellectual discourse rarely continues over the snatched cup of coffee or the vending machine sandwich unless people already know each other and are sufficiently engaged in an argument to want to continue it.

In the first class session I go through the syllabus (Appendix I) so that students can see exactly what will be required of them. I explain that the authors of books on List A are writing about what they consider to be the corruption or misuse of sport; the authors of books on List B are interested primarily in the history and/or delight of sport. Students are instructed to look at several of the books, all of which are available in the college and surrounding public libraries, and to read a book that really interests them. A review, *not* the hoary high school book report, is to be written on the first book they choose, which can be taken from either list; I explain briefly what is required, but spend more time on precise details later. I stress at this point that I have read all the books, so I don't need a rerun; what I do need is some independent thinking on each student's part. Again, I make the point that if one finds a book interesting, one is more likely to find something to say about it; but anyone is free to bore himself/herself to inanition by reading the first book he/she happens to find.

Besides this individual reading, everyone in the class will read most of Eitzen's (1984) and Michener's (1976) books as a basis for class discussion. I point out that the authors of the readings in Eitzen's book usually focus on something that they feel is wrong with sport, while Michener believes he owes a great deal to sport, and writes accordingly. This reading will give the class, I say, a collective body of facts and ideas that will be supplemented by lectures, films, and discussions on that material.

Students will also be required to watch a sporting event and analyze it, or examine UTD's sports program, and to read an autobiography. The examination will be essay-type, because the questions will require development of a train of thought. But it will be open-book, so students may bring to it any books, notes, dictionaries, or whatever other materials they think might help.

By now, someone has done a bit of addition; others have thought of questions that reveal both their preoccupations and their past experience of formal education.

"We've got five books to read, right?"

"Yes."

"And we get to choose two?"

"No, three; there's the autobiography."

"Then there's two papers and an exam? Do we get graded on class participation?"

"Not as such, because there are too many of you for me to do it fairly. But you can't participate if you're not here, so one grade will be given for attendance. I may test you in class on your reading for that day—your predecessors suggested I do that, and it works. Those tests will count for a grade, too."

"All we have to do is here? You won't suddenly set a midterm or another paper?"

"No."

"You really don't care which books on these lists we choose? I mean, are there some here you'd really rather we read?"

"No. I've tried to put books on the list that in some way will make you think about the ways sport and U.S. society relate. I don't know what particular sports you're each interested in, so I've tried to give you a range. But there are some sports I know little about, so if you know of a really good book that isn't on the list, let me know about it. But I *must* see, beforehand, any book you want to substitute; it may be excellent, but so much trash has been published on sport that it's easy to waste one's time without realizing it."

The idea of choosing books to read instead of having texts thrust upon one is both novel and disturbing. Many students are visibly cheered by the thought; others are having second thoughts about the course. I deliberately take everyone a step further, by pointing out that we shall not be dealing with material in a linear fashion, as one must in statistics or accounting; but that we shall be dealing with subjects rather as if sport were the rim of a wheel and various topics were the spokes. We could start, for instance, with racism or sexism in U.S. sport, or with the history of college football; whereas, you can't multiply until you've learned to add. However, wherever we start, we shall find ourselves referring back; the history of college football does relate to racism and sexism, as well as being a subject in its own right. "Only connect," as E. M. Forster once said.

All this takes about thirty to forty-five minutes. As UTD class periods are 1:15 or 2:30 hours long, we then have time to settle on a definition of sport for class purposes. I ask students to write down their definitions of a sport, a game, and a hobby. A few volunteers then read their suggestions, which I put up on the board. Interest quickens, because areas of disagreement emerge at once. Most definitions of a sport contain ideas about competition, rules, physical exertion, practice, talent, coaching; most definitions of a hobby mention personal expression and fun. Games are more problematic, and specific examples are quickly brought up. But not everyone wants to accept car racing or hunting and fishing as sports, the former because the result is so dependent on equipment, the latter because many people hunt and fish for food.

"And what about chess?" asks one student.

"Or bridge?" asks another.

Before anyone has time to retreat into the "What-a-waste-of-time-all-this-is-I-know-what-I-think" state of mind, I point out that there is no agreed definition of sport among players, officials, or writers. But for purposes of this course, the class needs to agree on what it's talking about. It is already clear to the class that to try to decide whether or not fishing *per se* is a sport is not likely to be productive. Drawing on what is already on the board, I suggest that one solution to the dilemma is to consider the *purpose* of an activity. That is, when Tom Sawyer goes fishing, he's just having fun—so that's a hobby. But when someone competes for a fishing trophy, that's a sport—there are rules, competitors, a winner; it needs lots of practice and skill. We then draw up a definition that contains the elements the students want; what emerges are working definitions that run something as follows:

Sport: A competitive activity requiring physical prowess, skill, and longterm practice, with codified rules in which the object is to win, and which is often played for reasons other than the activity itself. Normally watched by spectators who pay admission charges; may be organized as a business.

Game: Competitive activity involving skill or chance, played according to rules recognized by the participants, and usually played for the enjoyment of the participants. May be watched by spectators who do not pay admission charges.

Hobby: Uncompetitive activity that may involve physical skill.

The same activity may fall into each of these categories, depending on its purpose. Swimming done by Tom Sawyer is a hobby. Swimming done competitively by friends is a game. Swimming done at a swim meet is a sport.

I point out that this definition of sport is idiosyncratic, as are all definitions of sport; that many writers would not agree with it, but that it will serve its purpose if it keeps our subsequent discussions on track.

To begin the class by devising a definition of sport could well be disastrous. The class definition has no "authority," yet students might think I had asked them for their ideas only to persuade them of the superiority of mine. To extract articulate, unselfconscious statements from students in a class of sixty[1] requires some skill in facilitating discussion. It would be a lot simpler to mandate the definition the class is to use; if one were to do that, the rest of the course would not necessarily change.

I do it this way because it serves my teaching purposes. First, the exercise draws students into the course immediately. It makes many of them realize that they've used the word "sport" all their lives without really knowing what they meant. Second, students quickly understand that we are dealing with a complex subject, on which equally sane, thoughtful, and studious people differ, and that unless students can be sure what others mean, discussion is not likely to be productive. Third, students begin to perceive that while the instructor intends to provide a clear framework for the course, there is no "party line" which students must first intuit and then adhere to, and that there is room for student contributions.

At the beginning of the second class session, there has been a shift of personnel. Some students have dropped; more have arrived, as UTD allows late registration. I distribute more handouts, but tell the late arrivals that they must ask someone else what I said. I then enquire whether anyone has had second thoughts about the definition we're going to use. A few students have; their ideas have invariably been useful, in that they have led to further emendations or clarifications. We look briefly at Michener's (1976) definition and compare it to our own. I then ask the class to divide into groups of not more than six students, and to decide in each group whether members perceive all or any of the "major accusations" Michener lists as having been made "against sports as now conducted" are still valid, and whether they would add other "accusations" to the list, as Michener does. I also ask them to group together those "accusations" that they perceive to be related; for instance, the alleged overspending on university football programs derives in part from the necessity to pursue high school stars.

There is some confusion as students group themselves; they are not used to such activity in a university class. I leave them to sort themselves out, unless groups are too big. The new students have not done the reading, but can rapidly scan Michener's list. Talk begins quietly, then rapidly becomes animated, at which point I walk among the groups listening to the comments to gauge their quality. Has everyone done the reading? (Usually not.) Can students talk coherently and listen to each other's arguments? (Some, but not all.) Does anyone care about these issues? (Most are passionate.) Are there problems? (Yes. "We're having trouble. When he says children are playing sports too young, how young does he mean?") However, no one has ever found the presence of other groups inhibiting or too noisy. After about fifteen minutes, I ask for groups to tell us which "accusations" they found still valid, tallying the results on the board. The first real divergence of opinion occurs over the question of whether girls and women have an adequate share of the sports budget; most females in the class believe that they do not, most males that they do. I enquire about the grounds of these opinions, and the answers turn on what one means by "adequate." Does it mean, "the same as that of males?" or, "sufficient to field equivalent teams?" or, "related to the number of females who want to participate?" or what?

"But the men make all the money," an irate male always explodes.

"That's not the point," snaps back an equally irate female. "We're talking equal rights here. What about golf?"

If no one else does, I stop the argument to make the point that we'd better agree on what we're actually discussing. Are we talking about the *sources* of an athletic budget and whether its distribution should be made in relation to those who provide it, or are we discussing an athletic budget *per se*, whatever amount it is and wherever it comes from, and the *principles* on which the money should be distributed? Students reflect; all passion is certainly not spent, but someone always clarifies matters, by beginning, "Are you saying . . . ?" I add that Michener takes up these very points in chapters 5 and 7 if anyone wants to look at them, but that we'll be discussing them in detail later.

I tally a few more "accusations," and then turn to the classification question. Not all groups have got this far; usually, one group has categorized the "accusations" into the government, the media, and "what we want," or American values. One group once said the "accusations" deal with the "exploiters and the exploited," another that everything was related, because if you tried to alter one thing, you'd affect all the rest.

All that I add is that we're now going to explore some of these topics in more depth and find out what research has been done and what has not. In the rest of the session, I begin a lecture on sport programs for children under twelve (for sources, see Appendix II). The points I want to establish are that children vary developmentally, so that too early specialization may exclude children from sport for life; that talented youngsters welcome competition and delight in using their talent in it, but that pressure to win may destroy interest, retard growth of game-related skills, and give them a false self-image; that the formal educational system has abandoned sport for young children; and that Americans have not yet solved the problem of providing for the potential Olympic champion and for the lifelong dabbler.

We then look at the film *Two Games* (see Appendix III) in which a pickup baseball game is intercut, without commentary, with a little league game. Students discuss, in groups, the questions:

1. What skills and values are the children in each of these games learning?
2. What incidents in the film illustrate Coakley's article, and in what ways?
3. If you had to choose, which of the two situations would you want your child to be in, and why?

Again, students form their own groups; I request them to sit with people they did not talk with before, so as to decide with whom they want to work (or avoid) for the rest of the course. I circulate among the groups, not to intervene, but to gauge the intellectual level of the proceedings. As soon as one group has completed the third question to its satisfaction, I halt the individual discussions (often with difficulty). One group then gives the class its answer to the first question and other groups add to it as necessary. If answers are inarticulate, thin, or in any other way unsatisfactory, I push and pull until we have made an intellectual point; but it is immediately clear that equally precise and pertinent answers can be different.

What always emerges from this class session is that parents want different things for their children, and that what they want is linked to their views on what constitutes "the good life" or "success" in the United States. Students very quickly perceive that there can be no "right" answer to the third question, and that so apparently simple a matter as volunteering to teach soccer to six-year olds after school is to act on (usually) unexamined assumptions about such matters as adult direction of children's leisure, socialization processes, and American values.

This integration of lectures, group discussions based on reading, films, the assignments as they become due and are returned (I often read the better ones to the class, which sets standards but induces deep gloom in the inept), and a very occasional outside speaker sets the pattern for the course. We move through topics such as the effects, anticipated and unexpected, of Title IX on school and college athletic programs, and the relationship between sexism in sport and in the larger society; the ways in which ethnic discrimination has been demonstrated in sport; the symbiotic relationship of media and sport, including the vexed question of whether TV is an ogre, sugar daddy, or neither; whether sport in a university contributes to or detracts from the proper function of the institution; the effects of violence on the part of players and spectators, including discussion of the verbal abuse of children and referees by parents; what core values of American society are reflected in or refracted by the structures and conduct of sports Americans play and watch; the model of athletes as commodities, role models, and/or human beings; how federal law and the federal government does/should control the sports industry and its feeder sources of schools and colleges.

En route, we make comparisons between what happens in the U.S. and what happens elsewhere, by considering such concepts as sponsored and contest mobility,[2] amateurism, and "fair play." Rules, for instance, are treated differently in societies that honor the spirit rather than the letter of the law; in the U.S. where every political question ultimately becomes a legal question, the letter must be paramount. Each topic is firmly tethered to the reading, but the line of discussion may reel out quite far. Each topic is also firmly located in its historical context, which I usually supply in lecture form.

My purpose throughout the course is to make students think. The class's task is to "consider," not to make pronouncements about, the relationship between sport and U.S. society. The students have to be engaged, but this is a risky business. Students have learned that they'd better find out what the professor wants, and when that professor announces that she wants *you* to think, what she really means is that she wants to be persuaded you came to the same conclusions she did, but by yourself. As a student said to me years ago, "It's all right to think independently around here, as long as you think independently along the right lines."

Given this mind-set and the rushed lives our students lead, precautions have to be taken to ensure that the course does not become simply idle chatter. Overall, for instance, the group discussions serve their purpose very well; as one student wrote,[3] "Discussions were easily participated in and made the class a pleasure"; another, "Lectures are well-prepared, class exercises promote active consideration of course topics." Ideas often emerge that we should not otherwise have had; "[the course] got you thinking with questions and group discussion." The discussions "gave everybody a chance to share in the class"; and, as many of the students had first-hand experience of some topics, their contributions brought the literature alive. One student, for instance, told us that she and her husband, both convinced of the necessity of equal opportunities for girls in sport, had pulled their nine-year old soccer star from her coed team. "The problem is that she's very good at soccer, but she's also very pretty—long blond hair, the whole bit. And the boys started treating her like a mascot; they were even boasting about her to other teams, and things like that. She got uncomfortable, and some of the boys got mad at each other, and we just decided she ought to play on a girls' team, at least for the present." The class has heard similarly thought-provoking remarks from a baseball pro, cut when he was injured; a basketball scholarship holder who quit "because I couldn't ever study"; team coaches; and others. All had something to say and were comfortable saying it because they did not have to "make an oral presentation" at a specific time, but had become used to the cut and thrust of the small groups.

But the groups are not easy to handle. Some groups always work faster and more effectively than others; a few students are frustrated because their groups rarely finish discussing all the questions. A more serious problem is that the abler and more diligent students quickly find each other; their group work is productive. The less able and the lazy often come to class unprepared; thus, as one student wrote, "Putting college students in groups to discuss material is a waste of time." To give tests on what should have been prepared material seemed to me demeaning; but several students in different classes wrote that discussions would have been more effective had the work been graded, tested, or quizzed. The first time I did this, some students were outraged, but the standard of preparation immediately went up. Two such exercises (unannounced) during the semester are sufficient to guarantee that all but the most irretrievable students have done their reading, while few of the serious students feel insulted.

I rarely lecture for more than half an hour, splitting a long lecture into a "to-be-continued" format. I use lectures either to give students access to out-of-print or otherwise unobtainable material, or to supplement assigned reading. The lectures hold the course together, in that I can show how topics relate, and set each in a larger context. I spend a good deal of time on sport history; inspired to choose Tygiel's book (1984) as one of his readings, a computer science major announced, "I never thought of history as being about people before—real ones, I mean."

The class texts are not wholly satisfactory. I use Michener (1976), although he is dated, because he writes in a positive, clear, and interesting fashion, and his voice speaks throughout the book. The Eitzen (1984) readings address problems more pitilessly and are more up-to-date.

What I should really like would be a book of readings that ran the gamut of anthropology, history, literature, psychology, and sociology; but then I should probably be the only instructor ever to use it. I could put together such a book using one of the firms that construct sport-specific anthologies, but am not willing now to invest the time. Moreover, most students enjoy the reading as it stands, and several have echoed the student who wrote, "Flexibility in reading material and their subjects is appreciated." Some want "up-to-date" material from sources like *Time*, and a number simply want less reading altogether. The films (I usually show five or six) are uniformly praised; a typical comment has been, "Very interesting and *pertinent* films were presented."

Early in the course I use *A False Spring* in a lecture. To discuss the autobiography, students divide into groups according to the book they have read. Each group is asked to decide:

1. What they believe they learned about sport and U.S. society from reading an autobiography;
2. Whether they believe participation in organized sport was beneficial or detrimental to the writer, and why;
3. What they believe prompted the writer to publish the book.

Members of the group rarely agree. Shaw and Rentzel are perceived equally clearly as victims of circumstances and "cry-babies"; Tatum is perceived as self-serving and as a man doing his appointed job; Staubach as a "goody-two-shoes" and a hero. By no means does everyone agree that athletes publish their life stories "just for the money." "Everybody writes about them—why can't they get to write their side of it?" "They want people to understand what pro sport is really about." Some students do not want to accept alternative readings of the evidence; their decoding of the text must be the right one. By this stage of the course, however, most students are prepared to believe that what one thnks about sport will be related not simply to sport itself, but to the assumptions that lie behind one's own worldview. "I think it's interesting," said one, "that we could see Rentzel so differently, when we all read the same book. It seems to depend on whether you think you control life or it controls you. Yet we all agreed he wouldn't have got in such a mess if he hadn't been protected all his life, just because he was an athlete."

I am now rethinking my insistence that students write the English language with a minimal degree of competence. On the principle that one learns by doing, I have allowed students to rewrite and resubmit their reviews; a number of students were grateful for the opportunity, others simply resented the notion that they should learn to use their own tongue. "This course should be renamed English 3332." I have never asked a teaching assistant to read all the books reviewed, so the grading becomes a burden that I am increasingly unwilling to take up. I get better work if I give very specific instructions and suggestions, because few students can believe I will take their ideas seriously. "I mean, how can I say what I think about this book? *I'm* not an expert." I therefore spend some time discussing the kinds of audiences a writer might address. Is a writer concerned with those who know very little and may not initially be interested? Is he/she writing for other scholars in the field? Is he/she writing for a well-informed but not professional audience? Or what? Does the author have an ax to grind? Given his/her purposes, are the sources used appropriate?

As a computer science major once said, "This course will be quite a challenge. I don't read books. I know I should, but I don't." To ask such a student to write a review is to push him to the limit of his intellectual skills and beyond. Nevertheless, the students whose previous education has made them literate write in so engaged and stimulating a fashion that I cannot conceive of changing the assignment. Nor could I achieve my aims for the course by asking for a research paper; many students are not up to it, and some would certainly pay someone else to do it.

Students always want to know what's going to be on the exam (see Appendix IV). They all realize that they will be asked to discuss the relationships between sport and society in the book chosen from List A or B. During the penultimate class, I ask them to consider what topics we have covered in class, and what—given their readings, discussion, films and lectures—they could reasonably be asked. In the last class, they tell me what they think the course has been about; most of their ideas demonstrate that the course material has been integrated, and that they are clear about what they know and what they don't. Far more goes up on the board than I could possibly ask about; I suggest they prepare several of the topics listed, as they will have a choice of questions on the paper; I also tell them to be sure to answer the actual question asked, not what they hoped or expected to be asked on any given topic.

The exam papers are normally better written than anything else in the course. By this time students know what they are about, have developed their own views, and have some confidence in expressing them. Most of them have learned how to use opinion and evidence appropriately. These papers and the evaluations of the course demonstrate that most students have understood and appreciated the intent of the course. "Topics were of interest and required both thinking and consideration of your opinion"; "This course certainly opened both eyes and mind to the subject matter of sports and its effect on U.S. society"; "This course has made me think of sports in a different perspective and I believe it will affect my views of sport in the future also." Husbands and wives I didn't know have stopped by my office to tell me about the arguments they've had with their spouses in the course; books and articles have been passed on to kin, including sons and daughters, to workmates, and to friends.

But for some students, the course has been frustrating and mystifying. One student could write, "The class dealt with *questions*, not answers. Therefore we were stimulated to respond"; but another wrote, "This course could've been much more interesting if occasionally we were allowed to tackle problems which were not total paradoxes." For a third, the course, "Placed to [*sic*] much emphasis on teaching idea's [*sic*] that don't have a reason for it [*sic*]." Whatever I say at the beginning of the course, a few students persist in believing that we shall end up in a bar mulling over the Mavericks. After all, "This is just an I/S course. In-class was fine. But all the papers, gee." I do not propose to alter the course to meet the demands of such folk, but I wish I could persuade them to drop it early.

As it stands, I thoroughly enjoy teaching the course. I have stressed the problems with it because unless the difficulties are properly perceived, the course could quickly become a "gut" disaster area. It is always risky to *depend* on student input rather than asking them for comments; but most students have brought so much to the class, I do not want to change it. Students have taught me a great deal about show-jumping, rodeo, hockey, and other sports I have never played; the city-wide network of children's and adults' soccer and softball leagues and their ramifications in social structure, economics, labor relations, and use of leisure time, has been a revelation. Students have been very perceptive. "It was not until I started to write up this assignment that I realized I have attended my son's football games since junior high only because he is a quarterback." "There's a real generation gap between me and my son. He plays soccer; I played football and it meant everything to me. He seemed to be spitting on all I cared about." "I've always tuned out the commercials in a game. I've just had to count them, and I'm *outraged*!" "Athletes know what they're in for when they sign a contract. But now I have to ask myself, would I like to be just an item of depreciation?"

One possible problem I have never encountered. No one, except a journalist interviewing me about the course, has ever asked why a woman would be teaching a course on sport. I suspect that is because I have an English accent, in Texas still a guarantee of acceptance and prestige. It's an advantage I do not hesitate to use . . .

NOTES

1. The smallest class has been sixteen (summer session), the largest over 100. UTD now allows I/S courses to be closed at 80.

2. Ralph H. Turner (1960) examines the "manner in which the *accepted mode of upward mobility* shapes the school system directly and indirectly through its effects on the values that implement social control." Turner suggests that the "organizing folk norm" in America is that of "contest," while in Britain it is "sponsorship." That is, "*Contest* mobility is a system in which elite status is the prize in an open contest and taken by the aspirants' own efforts." In contrast, "Under *sponsored* mobility, elite recruits are chosen by the established elite or their agents, and élite status is *given* on the basis of some criterion of supposed merit and cannot be *taken* by any amount of effort or strategy."

Turner does not apply these "ideal-types" to sport, but clearly they fit. Football, for instance, is regarded in the U.S. as a means of contest mobility because anyone can try out and has to beat out the competition to play. In fact, however, football is a case of sponsored mobility because it is the coach who decides who will play, for how long, and on what grounds. (A boy finds out in junior high that he had better have a "good attitude," or learn to warm the bench.) Turner's ideas can very usefully be extended further.

3. Remarks quoted are taken from the evaluation forms students fill out (UTD has used several different forms since I started to teach the course). Other quotations come from student papers; a few (obviously identified in the text) are reconstructed, but are true to the spirit of what was said.

APPENDIX I: SYLLABUS

IS 3332
SPORT AND U.S. SOCIETY
Spring, 1985

The purpose of this course is to enable students to consider some of the ways in which organized sport affects life in the United States. Much class work will involve discussion; class attendance is therefore an essential part of this course, which MAY NOT BE TAKEN PASS/FAIL.

WORK REQUIRED

1. During the semester, reading of two books, one taken from the attached List A and one from List B.
2. Written review of a book from List A or B, due on Feb. 12. The review should consist of two parts:
   - A. ". . . every review . . . should name, correctly and in detail, the work being reviewed. Then it should describe the contents, and indicate the purpose of the work. Next it should tell the reader how well or how badly the contents are presented, and how near the work comes to achieving its purpose." (Traeger, *IJAL* 1960, 23:168.)
   - B. Discussion of the relationships between sport and U.S. society the author of the book appears to have had in mind, and/or which the writer of the review discerned in reading the book.
3. Reading of two texts, Michener, *Sports in America*, and Eitzen, *Sport in Contemporary Society* (2d ed.) as follows:
   - Jan. 15: Michener 1, 2.
   - Jan. 18: Michener 4, Eitzen 4 (Coakley only).
   - Jan. 25: Eitzen 4 (all except Coakley).
   - Feb. 1: Michener 5.

Feb. 5: Eitzen 10.
Feb. 15: Michener 6, Eitzen 9.
Feb. 22: Michener 10.
Feb. 26: Eitzen 8.
March 5: Eitzen 5, 6.
March 8: Michener 7.
March 19: Eitzen 3, Michener 13.
March 26: Eitzen 2.
April 9: Eitzen 7.
April 12: Michener 12.
April 16: Michener 11.
April 19: Michener 9.
April 23: Eitzen 11.

4. Preparation for discussion so that it is more than "the mutual exchange of ignorance."
5. One piece of written work, due on March 22.

EITHER

Attend one live sporting event and analyze it (follow guidelines provided).

OR

Watch one televised game and analyze it (follow guidelines provided).

OR

Write on more than five pages in answer to the question: What sports program should UTD offer students? Why?

6. Reading of one book from attached List C, for discussion in class on April 2.
7. Open book examination: May 3, 2:00 PM–4:45PM. Will include one question on book chosen from Lists A and B but not previously written about.

LIST A: READ ONE OF THE FOLLOWING

Asinof, Eliot. *Eight Men Out: The Black Sox and the 1919 World Series*. Holt, Rinehart and Winston, 1963.

Durso, Joseph. *The All-American Dollar: The Big Business of Sports*. Houghton-Mifflin, 1971.

Halberstam, David. *The Breaks of the Game*. Knopf, 1981.

Jordan, Pat. *Chase the Game*. Dodd, Mead, 1979.

Koster, Rich. *The Tennis Bubble. Big Money Tennis: How it Grew and Where It's Going*. Quadrangle, 1976.

Lawrence, Paul. *Unsportsmanlike Conduct: The NCAA and the Business of College Football.* Greenwood Press, 1985.

Mandell, Arnold. *The Nightmare Season*. Random House, 1976.

Parrish, Bernie. *They Call It a Game*. Dial, 1971.

Ralbovsky, Martin. *Destiny's Darlings: A World Championship Little League Team Twenty Years Later*. Hawthorn, 1974.

Rosen, Charles. *The Scandals of '51: How the Gamblers Almost Killed College Basketball.* Holt, Rinehart, and Winston, 1978.

Underwood, John. *The Death of an American Game: The Crisis in Football.* Little, Brown, 1979.
Vare, Robert. *Buckeye, A Study of Coach Woody Hayes and the Ohio State Football Machine.* Harper's Magazine Press, 1974.
Wolf, David. *Foul! The Connie Hawkins Story.* Holt, Rinehart and Winston, 1972.
Woolf, Bob. *Behind Closed Doors.* New American Library, 1976.
Yeager, Robert. *Seasons of Shame: The New Violence in Sports.* McGraw-Hill, 1979.

LIST B: READ ONE OF THE FOLLOWING

Axthelm, Pete. *The City Game: Basketball From the Garden to the Playgrounds.* Harper's Magazine Press, 1970.
Baker, William J. *Jesse Owens: An American Life.* Free Press, 1986.
Betts, John. *America's Sporting Heritage, 1850–1950.* Addison-Wesley, 1974.
Cady, Edwin. *The Big Game: College Sports and American Life.* University of Tennessee Press, 1978.
Crepeau, Richard. *Baseball: America's Diamond Mind, 1919–1941.* University Presses of Florida, 1980.
Guttmann, Allen. *From Ritual to Record: The Nature of Modern Sports.* Columbia University Press, 1978.
Halberstam, David. *The Amateurs.* William Morrow, 1985.
Karrane, Kevin. *Dollar Sign on the Muscle: The World of Baseball Scouting,* Beaufort Books, 1984.
Mead, Chris. *Champion: Joe Louis, Black Hero in White America.* Scribner's, 1985.
Novak, Michael. *The Joy of Sports.* Basic Books, 1976.
Parkhouse, Bonnie, and Jackie Lapin. *Women Who Win: Exercising Your Rights in Sports.* Prentice-Hall, 1980.
Riess, Steven. *Touching Base: Professional Baseball and American Culture in the Progressive Era.* Greenwood Press, 1980.
Rooney, John. *The Recruiting Game: Toward a New System of Intercollegiate Sports.* University of Nebraska Press, 1980.
Seymour, Harold. *Baseball: The Early Years.* Oxford University Press, 1960. *Baseball: The Golden Years.* Oxford University Press, 1971.
Tygiel, Jules. *Baseball's Great Experiment: Jackie Robinson and His Legacy.* Vintage Press, 1983.
Twin, Stephanie. *Out of the Bleachers: Writings on Women and Sport.* Feminist Press, 1979.
Voigt, David Q. *American Baseball: From Gentleman's Sport to the Commissioner System.* University of Oklahoma Press, 1966.

If you have a book you want particularly to read that does not appear on either of these lists, please bring the book to class and ask me about it. *Prior* approval *must* be obtained for the book to be acceptable as part of the reading for this course.

LIST C

Ashe, Arthur. *Off the Court.* New American Library, 1981.
Evert-Lloyd, Chris. *Chrissie: My Own Story.* New York: Simon and Schuster, 1984.
Rentzel, Lance. *When All the Laughter Died in Sorrow.* Saturday Review Press, 1972.

Retton, Mary Lou, and Bela Korolyi, with John Powers. *Mary Lou: Creating an Olympic Champion*. McGraw-Hill, 1986.
Robinson, Jackie. *I Never Had It Made*. G. P. Putnam's Sons, 1972.
Shaw, Gary. *Meat on the Hoof*. St. Martin's Press, 1972.
Staubach, Roger. *First Down: Lifetime to Go*. Word Books, 1976.
Tatum, Jack. *They Call Me Assassin*. Everest House, 1979.

If you have an autobiography you want particularly to read that does not appear on this list, please bring it to class and ask me about it. *Prior* approval *must* be obtained for the book to be acceptable as part of the reading for this course.

APPENDIX II: CHIEF SOURCES USED FOR LECTURE ON YOUNG CHILDREN'S SPORT EXPERIENCES

Albinson, J., and G. Andrews, eds. *The Child in Sport and Physical Activity*. Baltimore: Park Press, 1976.
American Association for Health, Physical Education and Recreation. *Desirable Athletic Competition for Children of Elementary School Age*. Washington, D.C.: AAHPER, 1968.
Dewey, John. *Democracy and Education*. Various eds., original 1916.
———. *Experience and Education*. Various eds., original 1938.
Flavell, J. H. *The Developmental Psychology of Jean Piaget*. Princeton: Van Nostrand, 1968.
Gerber, Ellen. "The Controlled Development of Collegiate Sport for Women, 1923–1936. *Journal of Sport History* 2 (1975): 1–28.
Jordan, Pat. *A False Spring*. New York: Dodd, Mead, 1975.
Magill, Richard, Michael Ash, and Frank Smoll, eds. *Children in Sport: A Contemporary Anthology*. Champaign, Ill.: Human Kinetics Publishers, 1968.
Voigt, David. *A Little League Journal*. Ohio: Bowling Green University Popular Press, 1974.

APPENDIX III: FILMS

FREQUENTLY USED BECAUSE THEY WORK WELL IN THIS CLASS

Beauty Knows No Pain. 25 minutes. 1971. Benchmark.
Promotional documentary film of Kilgore Rangerettes, showing the two-week training and selection period. (A former Rangerette vouched for the accuracy of the film, wincing the whole while.) In 1986 it is hard to believe that any group could have allowed this film to be made, much less shown it with pride. Raises questions about changing attitudes (what will ours look like in fifteen years time?); sexuality in sport; role models; sport in college settings. Can lead into lecture material on institutional use of sport as an arm of public relations; sport as a reflection or refraction of societal values; consideration of cheerleaders as a uniquely American phenomenon.

Chariots of Fire. 124 minutes. 1981.
Commercial, Academy Award Winning docudrama of the track rivalry between a Jew and a budding Christian missionary, culminating in the 1924 Olympics. Really too long for this class and could be considered irrelevant because it has little directly to do with the U.S.; but raises questions about amateurism; the politics of the

Olympics; sport and status/class; media coverage of sport before TV; who pays for sport. Can lead into lecture material on fair play; the 1936 and 1984 Olympics; and national control and influence over sport.

Danger in Sports (two reels—each can be used separately). 56 minutes. 1974. Macmillan Films.
Documentary on the long- and short-term medical problems posed by specific sports, particularly football, and what can be done to make training and the games themselves safer. Graphic shots of quadriplegics who were injured while tackling; interviews with medical specialists, officials, and coaches; game films. Too long, but authoritative, enlightening. Raises questions about violence in sport; special interest groups; choice and chance; conditioning. Can lead into lectures on liability; changing attitudes towards care, use, and images of the human body, especially in relation to concepts of masculinity and femininity.

Rookie of the Year. 47 minutes. 1974. University of Michigan Media.
Commercial film (based on a book based on a true incident) about a young girl who wants to play baseball on a boys' team and is given her chance, but then runs into antagonism from her girlfriends, her younger brother, the parents of some of her teammates, and coaches of other teams. Unsentimental, although somewhat stereotypic. Raises questions not only about equal opportunity, but about the function of law in sport and society; what constitutes "fair play"; the place of supportive adults in children's sport; and the influence of coaches. Can lead into lecture material on sponsored and contest mobility; and the community constraints under which all school, college, and league coaches operate.

There Was Always Sun Shining Someplace. 58 minutes. 1984. Refocus Films.
Documentary of the Negro Leagues, including interviews with former players, contemporary film footage and stills, and narration. Too long, but brings to life an activity and period students know little about. Raises questions about sport and societal power structures; racism; entrepreneurial opportunities in sport. Can lead into lectures on blacks in sport; comparisons between racism and sexism in sport and society at large; persistence of, as well as, changes in, attitudes.

Two Ball Games. 29 minutes. 1976. Cornell University.
Documentary of a children's pick-up baseball game played without adult supervision on a village green intercut with a little league baseball game complete with coaches, officials, uniforms, and spectators. No narration; the juxtaposed scenes speak for themselves. Evenhanded, perceptive. Raises questions about the social and kinesthetic skills each set of children is learning; the place of adults in children's sport and parenting responsibilities. Can lead into lecture material on the function of a coach.

Trobriand Cricket: An Ingenious Response to Colonialism. 54 minutes. 1976. University of California Media.
Documentary showing how Trobriand islanders have adopted cricket for political purposes, incorporating ritual and magic previously associated with war. Extremely well constructed and narrated, colorful, and compelling. Raises questions about the function of sport in any society; community and personal values epitomized in sport; and comparable rituals in U.S. sport such as marching bands, mascots, halftime shows. Can lead into lecture material comparing the structures of baseball and cricket; consideration of the reasons why cricket did not become the American national game; and how American Indians have used basketball as a boundary marking mechanism.

Winning 16 mins. 1976. Time-Life Multimedia.
Documentary, broadcast on *60 Minutes*, that asks whether training young boys to win football games at all costs is worth it. Uses scenes from practice and games of a "professional" Miami boys' team, as well as interviews and narration. Typical and compelling *60 Minutes* hatchet job. Raises questions about the symbiotic relationship between media and sport character training and development; adult's use of children for their own gratification. Can lead into lecture material on sponsored and contest mobility; the psychic rewards and punishments of organized sport for young children.

TRIED AND DISCARDED BECAUSE IT DID NOT WORK WELL IN THIS CLASS

Women in Sports—An Informal History. 28 minutes. 1976. Atlanta.
Documents women's increasing participation in sports, using original footage, stills, and commentary. Students, female and male, complained that it was superficial, stereotypic, and boring. Looks at the past through the lens of the present.

FILMS I SHOULD LIKE TO SHOW IF I COULD FIND THEM

Rule Changes in Football.
A documentary history of rule changes, using stills and film, to show how the game has evolved. Students cannot envisage a game without "the long bomb," and have no idea of the visual effects that rule changes provide and allow.

Where Are They Now?
A documentary equivalent of *Destiny's Darlings*. Few students believe that outstanding athletic talent can lead to anything but fame, wealth, and living happily ever after.

Collegiate Athletics for Women.
A documentary history of the athletic programs in women's colleges, from the early twentieth century. It treats the past seriously and not merely as a backdrop for the present.

Biographical documentaries for adults on such sports figures as Babe Didrikson, Althea Gibson, Jack Kramer, Jesse Owens, Jackie Robinson, Babe Ruth, and Wilma Rudolph.

APPENDIX IV: SPECIMEN EXAMINATION PAPER

Answer Section A and *2* questions from section B. Do *not* repeat material in different answers. *Refer to your reading*; use your lecture and discussion notes as well as your own thinking and experience. (UTD allows a maximum of two hours and forty-five minutes.)

SECTION A

1. What relationships between sport and U.S. society did your chosen book suggest to you? (Give the book's title, author, publisher, and date of publication.)

SECTION B

2. How was the professional player whose autobiography you read affected by the

values attached to sport in the U.S. as a child, an adolescent, and a professional player? (Identify the book as in Section A.)
3. "College athletics in the United States can never be honest." Discuss.
4. What forms has discrimination in sport taken in the U.S., and what has been done to remedy such discrimination?
5. What out-of-school athletic program would you want your eleven-year-old son or daughter to participate in? Why?
6. You have a sufficient budget to make a thirty-minute film for this class. Explain what topic you would choose and why, what specifically you would include in the film and why, and what you would hope to achieve by showing the film.
7. How would you define "fair play"? Why?
8. "Violence among athletes has many causes." What do you think causes violence at sporting events, on and off the field? Why?

WORKS CITED

Eitzen, D. Stanley, ed. 1989. *Sport in Contemporary Society*. 3d ed. New York: St. Martin's Press.

Michener, James. 1976. *Sports in America*. Greenwich, Conn.: Fawcett.

Turner, Ralph H. 1960. "Sponsored and Contest Mobility and the School System." *American Sociological Review* 25, no. 5: Reprinted in A. H. Halsey, et al., eds. *Education, Economy, and Society*. New York: Free Press, 121–39.

Tygiel, Jules. 1984. *Baseball's Great Experiment: Jackie Robinson and His Legacy*. New York: Vintage.

15

Teaching an American Sports Culture Class: A Paradigmatic Approach

GREGORY S. SOJKA

"Unlike most other fields, American Studies is not so much a subject as an outlook . . . a broad, open minded perspective upon the American past and present," notes one university's recruiting brochure (Whitlow circa 1980). As a field of academic pursuit, American Studies operates upon two basic assumptions: (1) that the American experience, in its entirety, provides a suitable focus for detailed and extensive study, and (2) that both historical and contemporary dimensions of "the American experience" may be best understood *not* when students confine themselves within the boundaries of any one conventional discipline (history, literature, sociology, or others), but when they pursue it *across* those disciplines and gather insights from each of them.

With a commitment toward this methodology, I first taught a course entitled "Sports in America" in the fall of 1978, my first semester in the Department of American Studies at Wichita State University (see Appendix I). I had mentioned a sports course during a job interview as one which I was willing and able to teach and my colleagues encouraged me to offer the class as a "special topics" course. My academic training was in American literature and my dissertation on Ernest Hemingway dealt with the role of sports and competitive activities, particularly fishing, in his fiction. I had acquired a basic knowledge of "game theory" and "philosophy of play" from work such as Johan Huizinga's *Homo Ludens* (1955). But these concepts had been utilized to provide the background for and approach to discussing Hemingway's fiction: the main subject of my inquiry (rev. 1985). Now, I was challenged to utilize sports, not Hemingway, as the focus of an entire course taught in a Department of American Studies and *not* in a Department of English.

True to the spirit of American Studies—described by another critic as "an arena for disciplinary encounter and a staging ground for fresh topical pursuits" (Bailis 1974, 203)—my course needed to extend beyond the disciplinary boundaries of American literature to encompass the history of sports in America and other similar topics. Thus, my first syllabus included a chronological approach that I borrowed from one of the anthologies I utilized as a text (Talamini and Page 1973). My students that first semester consisted of five adults in search of a Monday night class who also had an interest in sports. For the most part, the class discussed the essays and related several personal or contemporary experiences to the material. The semester concluded with both students and teacher fairly pleased with the outcome. Our initial exploration of sports in America succeeded in that we each learned about aspects of sports hitherto unknown to us: Puritan "detestation of idleness" from Foster Rhea Dulles; the "rise of sport" by Frederic L. Paxson; and the "role of the school in the sports life" of America by Frederic Cozens and Florence Stumpf (Talamini and Page 1973).

The course also provided my initiation into higher education politics. Several colleagues in other departments either believed that the course was properly part of their academic "turf," or questioned whether such a class or subject could even be academically substantive enough for students to receive three hours of credit. Their comments prompted a revision of the course syllabus to encompass a number of issues, topics, and themes. I also added additional texts to the course. Selected films and guest speakers were incorporated into the course to supplement themes and ideas, not to replace lectures or reading material (see Appendix II). Supporting documents from colleagues in sociology who recognized the sociology of leisure and sport as a proper disciplinary specialty assisted in addressing concerns of historians and physical educators who believed the course properly belonged in *their* curricula. Most important, their questions crystallized my basic premise that I was *not* teaching a sports history or physical education class, but rather a truly multidisciplinary course with a focus on teaching American culture as it might be defined by an anthropologist: values, beliefs, and heritage that characterize and distinguish one society from another.

As a result, I adopted a key issue or topic approach that would allow me to discuss what Gene Wise called "paradigm dramas" (1979): a sequence of key representative acts or episodes that would dramatize and provide possibilities for integrating discussion of sports and American culture throughout stages of the twentieth century. Historical ideas or concepts concerning sports could be perceived as a sequence of dramatic acts that "play" on wider cultural scenes or historial stages to convey their significance. These acts would spotlight changing boundaries of what was possible for a person or group at a particular time, place, and milieu. The "transactual" interplay between the act and the actor and the scene around them produces a dialogue that both focuses the student's attention upon its significance and stimulates discussion of its role in American culture. For my course, I eventually decided upon five major developments in athletics that paralleled actual developments in the society in which they took place: (1) the involvement of children in organized, competitive athletics; (2) the commercialization of intercollegiate athletics; (3) the participation of both women and minorities in athletics; (4) the professionalism of sports; and (5) the influence of the media, especially television, upon athletics.

Within this rather encompassing scenario, I utilized one or more "paradigm dramas" to dramatize the close relationship between a historical occurrence in sport and its greater impact upon society. Thus, discussion of the All American Soap Box Derby scandal of 1973 focused upon the illegal efforts of a parent to enable his adopted child to win a series of races within the context of increased emphasis upon victory, even in activities presumed to be enjoyable and even instructive. Several dramatic moments provide focus upon whether increased participation in athletics by minority groups, particularly blacks, provided opportunities for upward mobility and equality or merely occasions for additional segregation and utility. Jack Johnson's victories over heavyweight champion Tommy Burns on 26 December 1908 and his title defense against the first of many "great white hopes," Jim Jeffries on 4 July 1910, dramatized these triumphs within a segregated society. Jesse Owens's four-gold-medal performance in Berlin during the 1936 Nazi Olympics would illustrate the concept of the black American athletic hero "defending" our democratic culture from the threat of Hitler's Aryan supremacy as well as the ideas of assimilation and upward mobility via athletic participation. The same would apply to Joe Louis's 22 June 1938 knockout of Max Schmeling. Jackie Robinson's debut with the National League Brooklyn Dodgers in 1947 provided another opportunity to study attempts to integrate sports and society. The protest by black runners at the 1968 Mexico City Olympics and the partial boycott of the competition led by Harry Edwards comprised another occasion to perceive athletics and the black militant movements occuring in the same milieu. Likewise Billie Jean King's triumph over Bobby Riggs in the heralded "Battle of the Sexes" provided a paradigmatic moment in the consideration of women as competitive athletes, specifically, and in the acceptance of women as equals in society in general (Sojka 1984).

The impact of mass media upon sports and society in general can be dramatized by consideration of the third Super Bowl football game played on 12 January 1969 between the Baltimore Colts and the New York Jets before a television audience of 60 million viewers. TV viewers not only viewed commerical advertisements that sold for $135,000 per minute, but also witnessed the evolution of a new type of sports hero in cocky, long-haired Joe Namath, the Jets quarterback who led his AFC team to a triumph over the more conservative, NFC Colts led by crewcut, veteran quarterback Earl Morrall. Television's impact upon athletics can be linked with the evolution of intercollegiate athletics as entertainment, profit-making auxiliary enterprises and public relations for many universities, and the concomitant growth of professional athletics that entertain millions, but exploit their own performers. St. Louis Cardinals star Curt Flood's challenge to the reserve clause in 1969 can be perceived as a paradigmatic act foreshadowing the eventual free agency of baseball players who can determine their own value and destinies in a competitive marketplace. My interest in the history of intercollegiate athletics led to research and writing of the "Evolution of the Student-Athlete in America: From the Divinity to the Divine," an article that demonstrates how the participant in intercollegiate athletics changed as the educational institutions themselves evolved to serve the needs of the varied constituencies over a period of 350 years (Sojka 1983).

This broadened approach also allowed the use of additional personal research in class discussions. Thus, a lecture on Plato's conception of the well-rounded athlete could be discussed in conjunction with the success and hard work ethics in America as documented in turn-of-the-century dime novels for boys such as the Lester Chadwick's "Baseball Joe Matson" series. I have concluded that Joe Matson, as well as Frank Merriwell and other sports fiction heroes, provided cultural ideals to both entertain and inspire young boys (Sojka, "Baseball Joe," 1981). True to my disciplinary training, I added additional literary content to the course with Peter Gent's novel, *North Dallas Forty* (1973) and the Higgs and Isaacs anthology, *The Sporting Spirit* (1977). Discussion of Gent's searing criticism of materialistic and violent professional football and American society provided possible theses for American studies courses I would teach later dealing with regional approaches to culture of the Southwest. An original draft of my essay surveying recent football fiction with a Texas setting began with the following verse (Sojka, "Texas Football," 1981):

Oh, give me a home
Where the millionaires roam
And three-hundred grand is just hay.
Where seldom is allowed
A discouraging crowd
And the Cotton Bowl is jammed every day.

Obviously, the verse was penned *before* Texas stadium was constructed and *before* oil prices dropped so steeply. But Gent's *North Dallas Forty* (1973) and *Texas Celebrity Turkey Trot.* (1978), Don DeLillo's *End Zone* (1972), Dan Jenkins's *Semi-Tough* (1972), and other novels reflect a regional locale where football enjoys a socio-economic-cultural status of immense importance. Sport biographies should not be overlooked as additional sources of documentation. Gary Shaw's *Meat on the Hoof* (1972) and Lance Rentzel's *When All The Laughter Died in Sorrow* (1972) provide personal testimonials to the negative impact of football upon its Texan participants.

When the class was scheduled to a prime slot—twice a week in the morning—enrollment increased rapidly, eventually growing to ninety students. Very large students in sweatsuits, shorts, and T-shirts (all males, of course) filled the back rows of the lecture hall as so many shocks of wheat piled against a Kansas hedge row. Since they participated in sports; logic dictated that a course in sports would not only be appropriate, but possibly provide an easy grade given their specializations in intercollegiate athletics. While the athletes' rationale for enrolling might be based upon a false assumption, my course did not follow the grading scale recounted in one class at an anonymous institution: A for athletes, B for boys, C for coeds—the effect upon those who did survive in the course was positive and most desirable. The course, now titled "American Sports Culture," included a unit on the "business of intercollegiate athletics" and thus provided great insights into the system that demanded that these student-athletes spend the majority of their time practicing and learning their own sport.

In addition, I incorporated several local guest speakers to share their experiences in athletics with the students. When a distinguished black alumnus and former Wichita State football player recounted his experiences traveling on segregated trains and eating in restaurant kitchens in the 1940s as well as his great desire to gain an education to accompany his bumps and bruises, the students, especially the black athletes, gained a historical perspective and understanding of the concepts of upward mobility in a manner not possible from a textbook or from a lecture. I discovered another local guest speaker and former alum who had participated in the 1936 Olympic games and stood alongside the long-jump pit where Jesse Owens had nearly lost the competition with Luz Long. His version of the events concerning Owens's victories and Adolph Hitler's snubbing of the black winner added an additional perspective for the students who were most amazed that Eleanor Holm could be expelled from the team for merely drinking a glass of champagne during the trans-Atlantic passage.

The guest's collection of Olympic and Nazi Olympic memorabilia stood as a chilling testimony toward the purpose of the games as the means to achieve political propoganda. Other local guest speakers contributed to the success of the class when I used them judiciously, shared class reading assignments with them *in advance of the period*, and asked them to direct their comments toward the topic of class discussion. One of the most persuasive and energetic speakers was an assistant women's athletic director who stimulated much fruitful debate concerning the abilities of female athletes. Later I discovered that her employment was contingent upon raising a certain amount of money from private sources.

Students, too can provide sources of information to encourage a debate or even conclude a discussion. On one occasion, a visiting summer school student, a varsity basketball player from the University of Kansas, concluded a debate on the physical ability of male and female basketball players by stating that Lynette Woodard, the Jayhawks' All-American women's player, would likely compete well enough to qualify for the men's squad. For another class, I invited a panel of former students who now played professional football to discuss the "professionalization of athletics." In response to a student question concerning the increasing use of drugs in professional sports, one athlete replied, "In college they warned us not to take drugs. In the NFL they warn us not to take *too many* drugs!"

An endless quest facing each instructor in an American Studies course involves the identification of a suitable textbook. As the general field of "Sports Culture Studies" evolved, available anthologies edited by sociologists, psychologists, and philosophers became even more specialized to their own disciplines and thus less readable for a class of students in a more general, multidisciplinary sports course. The solution came in the form of James Michener's *Sport in America* (1976), which brought together a readable, reasoned discussion of the topics in my class—children, women, and minorities in sports, intercollegiate athletics, media and sports, and others—accompanied by contemporary research on these areas. Michener claims no scholarly pretentions, but does present basic concepts in a colloquial style that encourages the average student to pursue further reading in academic journals or texts. In recent years I've supplemented *Sport in America* (1976) with other academic texts such as Jay Coakley's *Sport in Society* (1986), which takes an "issues and controversies" approach and Baker's and Carroll's *Sports in Modern America* (1981).

The use of films as "visual texts" in a class, with subject matter that lends itself to showing as well as telling, constitutes another successful technique in both generating interest and emphasizing certain ideas (Sojka, "Filmography," 1981). In the introduction to an annotated filmography, I have noted that "one picture is worth a thousand words" may rightfully be considered as a trite cliche, but the use of "visual texts" can be an effective educational tool to instruct today's media-oriented generation. Surely the visual media have contributed greatly toward the universal recognition of sports heroes. I never tire of stating that viewers of one television broadcast greatly outnumber the total number of baseball fans who were able to watch Babe Ruth during his entire career! Students must be taught how to interpret these visual texts and how to take meaningful notes during the screenings. Introductory comments and summary discussion of the films afterward are necessary to provide the proper academic environment and purpose for the film showings, which otherwise might provide entertainment and not education. Given proper class preparation, the John Hancock film adaptation of Gene Williams's *New Yorker* story, "Sticky My Fingers, Fleet My Feet" (1965), portraying a weekend touch-football player whose ego is crushed by a skinny schoolboy named Wesley, can provide an effective dramatization of the dangers of competing solely to win. Although somewhat dated, "Of Sports And Man," narrated by French philosopher and critic Roland Barthes, provides a distinctive European perspective to bullfighting, Gran Prix racing, Tour de France bicycling, soccer, and ice hockey. Barthes stresses the skill, courage, and sportsmanship of men who challenge nature, animal instinct, and time in contests that endow athletes with distinction and honor even in defeat: a direct contrast to the American emphasis on victory or dishonor.

The study of American minority participation in athletics can be greatly enhanced by several visual texts. "Jeffries-Johnson 1910" utilizes many original photographs and original silent action footage to dramatize another of American sports culture's "paradigm dramas": Jack Johnson's heavyweight championship defense against the original "Great White Hope," Jim Jeffries, in Reno. Commentary and cartoons effectively communicate the negative stereotyping of Johnson who antagonized racist Americans with his sports cars, spending habits, white wives, and girlfriends. Olympic documentary filmmaker Bud Greenspan's "Jessie Owens Returns to Berlin" utilizes the sprinter's 1951 visit to West Germany to flashback to the 1936 Nazi Olympic where the American's four gold medals punctured the myth of Aryan superiority and black inferiority. Finally, "Body and Soul: Part I, Body" has Harry Reasoner, on the eve of the black boycott and demonstrations at the 1968 Mexico City Olympics, consider several of the myths and stereotypes that accompany the increased participation of blacks in athletics. Interviews with Harry Edwards, Tommie Smith, Jim Hines, Ralph Boston, Lee Evans, and Charlie Greene indicate the complexity of the 1968 situation to today's students who may not even have been born at that time.

The issue of competition versus participation in athletics by children can be illuminated by several short films. "The Long Happy Race," originally produced by General Motors in 1962 to preach the virtues of sportsmanship, international goodwill, educational merits, and developmental processes all associated with the Soap Box Derby, can provide an effective context for discussing Richard Woodley's account (1974) of the cheating scandal that permanently damaged the Derby's credibility in 1973. Several years ago, I predicted that "It's All in The Game," another self-serving propaganda vehicle for interscholastic sports, would become to athletics what the farcical "Reefer Madness" is now to drug education. No evidence contrary to my prediction has yet appeared! "Youth Sports: Is Winning Everything?" provides a sane counterpoint by cautioning against the potential destructive effect of competitive youth sports programs.

"Seconds to Play" provides a behind-the-scenes look at an ABC-TV broadcast of a 1975 Ohio State-UCLA football game. The actions and statements by producer Chuck Howard and director Andy Sidaris demonstrate emphatically how they and the television production crew, *not* the coaches and teams, decide when the game will begin and just how it will be reproduced for viewer mass consumption.

The instructor of an American sports culture class should not overlook the many feature length commercial films that vary greatly in quality but that can visually reinforce themes discussed in such a course. I have obtained better results from such films depicting fictional sports heroes rather than biographies of actual athletes including Jim Thorpe, Babe Ruth, Lou Gehrig, and Brian Priccolo to name several. Currently I utilize Roy Hobbs in *The Natural* (1984) and Phil Elliott in *North Dallas Forty* (1979) to discuss both the triumphant hero versus the rebel or antihero as well as the different historical periods presented in the film: the nostalgia of baseball and the high technology of football. In addition, contemporary videotape technology allows the instructor to show *selected* scenes from full-length feature films, without the hazards and additional expenses that accompanied prints of these films and balky projectors with ever-flickering bulbs and noisy movement.

Today, a wide variety of improved texts in inexpensive paperback editions, scholarly journals focusing upon sport culture studies, and professional organizations either dealing with a traditional discipline and its focus upon sports—The Association for the Study of Play, for example—or dealing exclusively with sport studies—such as the *Journal of Sport History*—enable the teacher of such a course to gain additional insights into instructional methods, subject matter, and content issues. Moreover, the publications provide a validation of the instructor's scholarly research. For example, *Aethlon: The Journal of Sport Literature* provides publication of high quality scholarship dealing with sport literature. Each semester I select several "academic articles" on sport culture studies and distribute them to students as supplementary course reading.

"Interesting, but what use is it?" exclaimed one spectator of J. A. C. Charles's balloon launch on 24 August 1783. "What use is a newborn baby?" replied Benjamin Franklin, who could foresee the potential of such scientific innovation, even though the Philosophical Society (which he founded) would not (cited in Ward 1958). The increasing numbers and quality of American sports culture courses taught across the country attest to the validity of their content and the success of their methodology.

APPENDIX I: SYLLABUS

SPORTS IN AMERICA, AS315C
Spring, 1979
Dr. Gregory S. Sojka
406 Jardine
689-3149/688-0317
T, TH: 8–9:30, 3–4:30
and by appointment

READINGS
Talamini and Page, *Sport and Society*.
Higgs and Isaacs, *The Sporting Spirit*.
Gent, *North Dallas Forty*.

SCHEDULE
Jan. 25 H. Intro.
Feb. 1, H. Stone, "American Sports: Play and Display," from *Sport and Society*.
Feb. 6, T. Beisser, "Modern Man and Sports," from *Sport and Society*.
Feb. 8, H. Spino, "Running as Spiritual Experience," from *The Sporting Spirit*.
Feb. 13, T. Dr. Howard Mickel, WSU Religion Department, "The Athlete and Humanistic Psychology."
Feb. 15, H. Mishima, "Testament of a Samurai"; Nyad, "Mind Over Water," from *The Sporting Spirit*
Feb. 20, T. Mr. Neal Daugherty, The Handicapped and Sports: The United Blind Athletic Association; Mr. Dave Greer, Wichita Beep Baseball Team; Mr. Barney Hoss, Wichita Wings Wheelchair Basketball Team.
Feb. 22, H. Ogilvie and Tutko, "Success Phobia," from *Sport and Society*.
Feb. 27, T. Guest Coaches, WSU: Athletics and Higher Education
March 1, H. Elliott, "The Crisis of Athletics."
March 6, T. Gary Griffith, Assistant AD, WSU, and Mike Needleman, Executive Director, SAS): "The Business of Intercollegiate Sports."
March 8, H. Midterm Learning Experience.
March 13, T. Spring Break—No Class (yeah!).
March 20, T. Minorities of Sports: Edwards, "The Black Athlete on the College Campus" and "The Black Professional Athlete," from *Sport and Society*.
March 22, H. Film, "Jesse Owens Returns to Berlin" and discussion.
March 27, T. Film, "Jeffries-Johnson," discuss Edwards, "The Myth of the Racially Superior Athlete," from *The Sporting Spirit*.
March 29, H. Film, "Body & Soul: Part I: The 1968 Olympic Protest."
April 3, T. "Women and Sports," Jane Sojak, WSU ICAA Academic Coordinator and Associate Instructor of English.
April 5, H. Gent's *North Dallas Forty*.
April 10, T. Gent's *North Dallas Forty*.
April 12, H. Gent's *North Dallas Forty*.
April 17, T. Gent's *North Dallas Forty*.
April 19, H. Guest Lecturer, Peter Gent.
April 24, T. Media and Sports.
April 26, H. Film "Seconds to Play" and discussion.
May 1, T. Film, "Baseball the Now Career."
May 3, H. Film, "Baseball vs. Drugs."
May 8, T. Last Class—review.
May 10–16, FINALS.

APPENDIX II: SYLLABUS

American Studies 350
American Sports Culture
Summer, 1982
Dr. Gregory S. Sojka
Office: 406 Jardine, 689-3149
Hours: M-F 8:30–9:30, and by appointment

TEXTS

Baker and Carroll, *Sports in Modern America*; Jay J. Coakley, *Sport in Society*; James Michener, *Sport in America*; Peter Gent, *North Dallas Forty*.

Also, the films we see in the course are our "visual texts" for which you are responsible. In addition, guest speakers might occasionally lecture about their personal experience in sports.

FORMAT

Combination lecture, discussion: all material should be read for the date noted on the syllabus so that you can be actively engaged in the learning process during our scheduled classes. Attendance is expected as one absence during a four-week summer sesssion is equivalent to several during fall or spring.

EVALUATION

Three exams equally spaced during the semester will determine course grades. The examinations will test your knowledge of the assigned readings, lecture material, and film presentations. The examinations will contain both objective (multiple choice) and subjective (essay) evaluations.

EDUCATIONAL PHILOSOPHY

As an educator, I am here to help you learn; I am no mere dispenser of information. I need your cooperation as learning is a two-way process. Thus, I will challenge you by asking you questions that deal with the "whys," not just the "whats" of sports in America. Strive to understand the significance of the people, places, and ideas we discuss in the class, not merely the facts.

COURSE THEMES

Sports as businesses; evolution of minorities in American sports; the business of intercollegiate athletics; women in sports and the issue of equality; sports and character building; sports and the media; and more.

CALENDAR

June 1. Introduction: Film—*War Games*.
June 2. Readings: Michener, 15–32; Coakley, 1–35; Baker and Carroll, 101–13; Film: *Of Sport and Men*.
June 3. Readings: Gent, 1–180.
June 4. Readings: Gent, 183–294.
June 7. Film: *North Dallas Forty*.
June 8. FIRST EXAMINATION.
June 9. Minorities in Sport: Readings—Michener, 183–217; Coakley, 239–76; Baker and Carroll, 63–75; Film–*Jeffries vs. Johnson*.
June 10. Discussion: Films—*Jesse Owens Returns to Berlin* and *Body and Soul*.
June 11. Film: *Michener's Black Athletes*.
June 14. Women in Sport: Readings—Michener, 155–82; Coakley, 213–38; Baker and Carroll, 63–75; Film—*Sports Challenge*.
June 15. Film: *Michener's Women Athletes*.
June 16. SECOND EXAMINATION.
June 17. Media and Sports: Readings—Michener, 355–415; Baker and Carroll, 77–87.
June 18. The Athlete Hero in film, fiction, and TV trashsports: Film: *Seconds to Play*.

June 21. Film: *Breaking Away*.
June 22. Intercollegiate Athletics: Readings—Michener 219–80; Baker and Carroll, 63–75; Coakley, 136–61.
June 23. Evolution of Student Athlete and his/her "Mainstreaming"; Film: *Scandal in College Sport*.
June 24. THIRD EXAMINATION.

WORKS CITED

Bailis, Stanley. 1974. "The Social Sciences in American Studies: An Integrative Conception." *American Quarterly* 26:203.

Baker, William J., and John M. Carroll, eds. 1981. *Sports in Modern America*. St. Louis: River City Publishers.

Coakley, Jay J. 1986. *Sport in Society: Issues and Controversies*. 3d ed. St. Louis: C. V. Mosby.

DeLillo, Don. 1972. *End Zone*. New York: Pocket Books, 1973.

Gent, Peter. 1973. *North Dallas Forty*. New York: Signet, 1974. Film version released 1979.

———. 1978. *Texas Celebrity Turkey Trot: A Novel*. New York: Morrow.

Higgs, Robert J., and Neil D. Isaacs, eds. 1977. *The Sporting Spirit: Athletes in Literature and Life*. New York: Harcourt Brace.

Huizinga, Johan. 1955. *Homo Ludens: A Study of the Play Element in Culture*. Boston: Beacon Press.

Jenkins, Dan. 1972. *Semi-Tough*. New York: Signet, 1973.

Malamud, Bernard. 1952. *The Natural*. New York: Avon-Bard, 1982. Film version released 1984.

Michener, James. 1976. *Sport in America*. New York: Random House.

Rentzel, Lance. 1972. *When All the Laughter Died in Sorrow*. New York: Saturday Review Press.

Shaw, Gary. 1972. *Meat on the Hoof*. New York: St. Martin's Press.

Sojka, Gregory S. 1981a. "Going from Rags to Riches with Baseball Joe: or A Pitcher's Progress." In *Essays on the Self-Made Man in America*. Thomas Clark, ed. Bowling Green, Ohio: Bowling Green University Popular Press, 113–21.

———. 1981b. "Texas Football: Recent Literary Scouting Reports." *Journal of Regional Culture* 1:140–48.

———. 1981c. "An Annotated Sports Shorts Filmography: Visual Texts for Sports Culture Classes." *Midwest Popular Culture Association Newsletter* 5:3–6.

———. 1983. "The Evolution of the Student-Athlete in America: From the Divinity to the Divine." *Journal of Popular Culture* 16:54–67. Revised and reprinted in *Sport in Higher Education*. Donald Chu, ed. Champaign, Ill.: Human Kinetics, 1985. 17–33.

———. 1984. "TV Trashsports." Paper presented at the annual meeting of the Popular Culture Association, Toronto.

———. 1985. *Ernest Hemingway: The Angler as Artist*. Bern: Peter Lang.

Talamini, John T., and Charles H. Page, eds. *Sport and Society*. Boston: Little, Brown, 1973.

Ward, John W. 1958. "The Meaning of Lindbergh's Flight." *American Quarterly* 10:3–16.

Whitlow, Roger. Circa 1980. "A Survey of American Studies Undergraduate Curricula in the United States." California State College at Dominguez Hills.

Williams, Gene. 1965. "Sticky My Fingers, Fleet My Feet." *New Yorker*, 11 September. Reprinted in *The Roar of the Sneakers*. Robert S. Gold, ed. New York: Bantam Books, 1977. 28–34.

Wise, Gene. 1979. "'Paradigm Dramas' in American Studies: A Cultural and Institutional History of the Movement." *American Quarterly* 31:295.

Woodley, Richard. 1974. "How to Win the Soap Box Derby: in which craftsmanship abets the passion for success to produce a tale of moral confusion." *Harper's*, August: 62–69. Reprinted in *Sport in Contemporary Society: An Anthology*. D. Stanley Eitzen, ed. New York: St. Martin's Press, 1979. 136–48.

16
Teaching "Sports in Canadian Life"

FRANK COSENTINO

There are certain facets that must be taken into account in dealing with the topic of sports in Canadian life. First, it is a fact that, relatively speaking, Canada is a young country and that it is adjacent to the largest, most powerful free-enterprise nation in the world, with all the benefits and disadvantages which accrue from that. Within this milieu it is the task of this course to examine sport, its growth, development, and status.

During the teaching of the course, it soon becomes apparent that little is known of Canadian history, less of its social history, and least of all, Canada's sporting history. There are reasons for this. British institutions, influences, and ideas were prevalent from the fall of Quebec onwards. The British, through their garrisons, civil servants, and immigrants, brought their approach to sport and so clothed the activities of the *Canadiens.* As Canada grew and continued on its path to independent nationhood, British influences receded into the background, their place filled by the growing and glamorous nation to the south.

This latter point is significant when one considers how history is perceived. When scholars speak of prehistory, it simply means that changes have not been communicated usually by the written word. This is a significant point when the written word is expanded to include radio, television, magazines, movies, newspapers, and similar culture-shaping media. Moreover for the greater part of Canada, the "written" word is in the English language common to both Canada and the United States. As a result, Canada becomes an extension of the American market for periodicals, films, and similiar informational culture-shaping devices. It becomes mush easier for Canadian educational institutions to use American texts and film strips. After all, they are in English, they're less expensive, and they're well done. When one considers that Canadians are exposed to a variety of American culture-shaping products, it is no wonder that our youth have known more about Knute Rockne than Percy Page; more about Jim Thorpe than Lionel Conacher; more about Wilma Rudolph than Marilyn Bell.

This Americanization has left many Canadians with a form of cultural amnesia. One of the purposes of this course, therefore, is to fill in this void nts and personages that give form and substance to ... tant to point out that the Americans cannot be held ... state of affairs. Rather, Canadians have willingly fallen ... ierican style, sizzle, and packaging, preferring what has ... the "big time" as opposed to the "homebrew" approach. ... the Canadian Football League, the American players are referred to ... "imports" while the Canadian local is classified as a "non-import." Perhaps it is only coincidental that these terms are so similar to "important" and "nonimportant."

A secondary concern that must be addressed is the concern in the area of amateurism and professionalism in the sports world. In some ways, the popular media have preferred to dwell on professional sport, the implication being that people are interested in the "best" practitioners of a particular skill and that the "best" are rewarded with money; the more money one earns, the more publicity is generated. Conversely, the less money, the more amateur or less proficient to some, and therefore the less publicity. The situation is further compounded when one realizes that professional groups generate their own publicity through their public releases. What newspapers and news releases purport to be "news" really is more like unpaid advertising that loses any sense of objectivity because of how and why it is prepared.

That is the context of the course "Sports in Canadian Life." It is the overriding reality that must be addressed. As Prime Minister Trudeau put it: "Having the United States as a neighbour is like sleeping with an elephant. You become conscious of every movement being made." One of my concerns is to be nationalistic in the sense of exploring the essence of the Canadian experience while not being antagonistic towards the United States.

One of the advantages of being in a young country is that much of its history is available through primary source material. It is difficult for undergraduate students to delve too deeply into these materials especially when they consist of books and diaries. On the other hand, much of the information is available on microfilm and in personal interviews.

Many students are not familiar with the use of microfilm and therefore one of the first tasks is to familiarize them with it. Their first assignment, given usually during the first or second class, is to find the microfilm area, locate a newspaper that published the day the student was born, and hand in information that contains the name of the newspaper, the front page headline, and a summary of one story on the sports page.

Usually the student finds all of that information and in the process learns where the film is kept, what is available, and how the machine is loaded. There is also a sense of history about it as well. Students generally have the idea that anything that occurred before they were born is "ancient." With this exercise, they have a feeling for the immediate past, are able to identify with the events and stories current with their birth, and in general have a better feel for the milieu into which they arrived. Interestingly enough, many students continue to read the newspaper, especially if it is one from their home town, not only for that particular day but for days before and after.

The use of microfilm also solves another problem for the history student. Contemporary history is sometimes the most difficult to determine. It's too recent to have books written about it. In a course called "Sports in Canadian Life," microfilm plays a major role for the reason that much of what has happened in Canada is contemporary and therefore unwritten. If it does happen to be written, more than likely it will be by Americans for the American market. Certainly for student seminars (see Appendix I) and for student papers, microfilm plays a major role.

A second assignment that the student has is a seminar or tutorial presentation. When the topics are determined, an attempt is made to have a variety of historical eras among them. Some topics (e.g., aboriginal games and physical activities) lend themselves to research of books, periodicals, and first hand documents such as the *Jesuit Relations*. Developments will occur over a period of many years. Other topics (e.g., hockey gold medal in the 1982 Winter Olympics) focus on a specific period of time. They are of national and international importance drawing reporters from a number of countries, primarily the U.S. and Canada. The student becomes aware of any bias that might be present in the correspondent's account. The message comes through that eyewitness accounts of themselves do not guarantee impartiality. Indeed one of the lessons to be learned by the student is that bias is a part of each report and the student's task is to determine that slant in the reporter's story. Of course the emphasis given here on newspaper and periodical accounts or microfilm does not preclude that personal interviews and reminiscences by participants in the event are also important. By combining these with the microfilm report, one is able to also see that there are lapses in memory even among those who were directly involved in the event.

In this course students can earn 15 percent of their grades through the seminar. Twenty percent can be earned through an essay or equivalent. This means that research is a requirement of the course. That research may manifest itself in traditional essay form or in any creative way the student can conceive as long as it is approved beforehand.

First the paper. Because of reasons previously mentioned, students are encouraged to look at a specific event that took place over a short period of time. There might be a boat race, a hockey series, a Grey Cup, a boxing match, an Olympic event or game, and similar such possibilities. By restricting the paper to such as the above, the student can read, through microfilm, a number of correspondents' views, learn of the greater setting, and pre- and post-competition information.

A term paper can also be a team effort or group project. The assignment can be divided into equal parts to be assigned to each member of the group. For example, if the topic were the Grey Cup game of 1962, four students might be assigned to work on the project, one to look at each participant and how they each won the right to appear in the national championship game, one to look at the pregame buildup and Saturday's development, one to look at the decision to halt the game and Sunday's continuation, and one to look at postgame discussion. In such an approach, the students work as a team in that they must collaborate to diminish any overlap, but yet they can be marked individually since each section is a unit in itself.

Research has always been part of history courses, and in most cases the research has been expressed in a "major essay." From time to time I have experimented with the concept of having the research manifested in other ways, some written, some not. With respect to other written ways, students have been given the option of presenting their research in the form of play, short story, or a poem. A bibliography and footnotes are still essential and the material used in the creative milieu must reflect the research done.

With respect to the nonwritten project, the possibilities are as numerous as the students in the course. Photographs, films, slides, mosaics, bronzes, weaving, rugs, and paintings are only some of the creative areas that can be pursued. These may deal with a moment in Canadian sport. It is also necessary to submit a written explanation of the event depicted, how the project was done and a bibliography of further reading about the event. Students are usually eager to try one of these approaches, perhaps because it is a change from the normal writing assignment. They soon become aware that as much, if not more, work is needed.

As far as grading these assignments, I have tried two basic ways. I have been sole judge and graded the work as best as I could. I have had displays in trophy cases and in corridors to allow students and other faculty to examine the work. I would try to be around to hear comments about the appropriateness and expertise. I have also had a mass presentation before the total class where each project was presented and explained to the class as a whole. The class was then invited to submit a grade to me and I would use it as a guideline in arriving at the student's mark.

With respect to other student course requirements, there are the conventional term test and final exam (see Appendix II). The course outline will identify the weighting for all of the above (see appendix I).

With a term course such as "Sports in Canadian Life," there is only so much that can be covered. Two times per week are set aside for lecture material and one hour for seminars. In concrete terms, this translates into thirteen seminars and twenty-six lecture classes, one of which is used for a term test. Seven areas have been identified as those that comprise the lecture material supplemented by film, slides, personal reminiscences.

One of my favorite lectures deals with Marilyn Bell's swim across Lake Ontario in 1954. The Canadian National Exhibition had invited American swim star Florence Chadwick to give an exhibition of distance swimming across the lake in return for $10,000. It was a controversial gesture since no Canadian had been asked in spite of some notable local distance swimmers. Amid much publicity a sixteen-year-old Toronto girl, Marilyn Bell, offered to swim across Lake Ontario. She made it clear that she wasn't trying to upstage Chadwick; she was trying to show that a Canadian could do it. She wanted to swim for the "honour of Canada."

The lecture is presented in the form of a letter to Arthur Hailey trying to interest him in a book called *Exhibition.* In an attempt to boost sagging attendance in the exhibition city located on the shore of Lake Ontario, it's decided by the board of directors to have a cross-the-lake swim. In keeping with the novelty, however, it is decided to have a woman do it; in order to delve into American/Canadian concerns, an American woman. Into this area of female liberation enters a Canadian woman, and to identify with the teeny-bopper crowd, she is a young sixteen-year-old Canadian girl. Another woman, a "super woman," also enters the field as does a "token male." All seek to be the first to cross Lake Ontario; all except Marilyn drop out at various stages of the swim. She alone perseveres overcoming a variety of obstacles and being given a hero's welcome. Yet another subplot is the competition among the media: radio, the newly arrived television, and the various major metro newspapers vying with one another for news of the city's newest darling. It's always an enjoyable class because, as relatively recent as it is, it has been shrouded in the cultural amnesia previously mentioned. The students are always surprised to find out that the characters and story are real and cannot understand why they have been unfamiliar with it.

Poetry is yet another way to convey information as well as emotions and feelings. After all, an event of great proportions such as the Team Canada-Soviet series of 1972 remains imbedded in people's hearts and minds because of the emotional roller coaster the whole nation moved through. Because it occurred within the students' lifetimes, they can associate with that event. Songs, poems, editorial page cartoons, films, documentaries, and books all attest to the fact that it was the most followed event in Canadian sporting history, perhaps in Canadian history.

While this feeling occurred on a national level, it is pointed out that similar emotional involvement took place in other regions of Canada at other times. Intranational east-west competition, intercity contests, and international events have all gripped people with the drama of the moment. In many cases poems have been written to commemorate an event.

Usually they are not great poems by the standards of iambic pentameter blank verse; but, nonetheless, they do express classical feelings of sadness, joy, despair, hope, love, and loss.

Audio tapes, films, and film strips are also used for a variety of purposes. An audio tape might be of a central figure reminiscing or being interviewed on radio. Similarly, film might give a visual portrayal of an event central to a lecture. "A picture is worth a thousand words" is a cliche, but nonetheless it is meaningful since it involves more of the students' senses than a straight lecture. A few years ago, I felt that there was a lack of these materials available that could provide an overview of the area and yet highlight important components. To that end I decided to make an audio filmstrip in three sections: pre-Confederation, Confederation to the end of World War I, and post–World War I. It's a useful filmstrip in that it provides either a good lead-in or summary of a period of time.

One of the major areas of the course has to do with government involvement. Canada has an interventionist approach in fields deemed to be important to promote a national and cultural identity. Especially since 1968, the Federal Government has taken an active role in sport: Canada has a Sports Minister. The Federal approach has been duplicated in every province. Indeed it plays such a major role in Canadian sporting life that a course in government involvement in Canadian sport could easily be constructed. In many ways, it is a reaction to the reality of Canada previously referred to above.

Perhaps one of the nicest feelings a teacher can have is when a student wonders aloud why he had to come to university to learn material that should be part of every Canadian's early life or to overhear a student excitedly telling another over coffee of the morning's lecture or seminar. Perhaps the veil of cultural amnesia is beginning to lift.

APPENDIX I: SYLLABUS

York University
Faculty of Arts
Faculty of Science
Department of Physical Education and Athletics
As/PE 3403W Sports in Canadian Life
222 SC
Frank Cosentino
358 Stong College
667-3478

PURPOSE OF THE COURSE

1. To acquaint the student with the sporting history of Canada by the use of books, theses, periodicals, newspapers, personal contact and similar approaches of history.

2. To acquaint the student with various and varying research techniques using the study of sport as the instrument.
3. To view the events of today in a better perspective by the examination of those of the past.

TOPICS TO BE INVESTIGATED

1. Growth of sport from spontaneous and casual affairs to highly organized and structured activities.
2. Sport heroes and their effect on the local and national scene.
3. Women and sport.
4. Developments and manifestations of amateur and professional concepts in Canadian sport.
5. Government involvement in Canadian sport.
6. Hockey in Canada—origins, growth and direction.
7. Canada at the international and intranational levels of sporting competition.

ASSIGNMENTS

1. Term Paper Due March 7 (details to be provided)—20 percent.
2. Term Test—February 28—15 percent.
3. Exam during the scheduled exam period—50 percent.
4. Seminar presentation—15 percent.

COURSE TEXTS

Wise, S. F., and Douglas Fisher. *Canada's Sporting Heroes.* Toronto: General Publishing Company, 1974.

Cosentino, F. *Ned Hanlan.* The Canadians Series. Toronto: Fitzhenry and Whiteside, 1977.

Cosentino, F., and Don Morrow. *Lionel Conacher.* The Canadians Series. Toronto: Fitzhenry and Whiteside, 1981.

SUPPLEMENTARY READING LIST

Books

Batten, Jack. *Champions.* Toronto: New Press, 1971.

Barnes, Laverne. *The Plastic Orgasm.* Toronto: McClelland and Stewart, 1971.

Bolt, Carol. *Cyclone Jack.* Toronto: Great North Agency Limited, 1974.

Boucher, Frank, with Trent Frayne. *When The Rangers Were Young.* New York: Dodd, Mead and Company, 1973.

Cahill, Leo, and Scott Young. *Goodbye Argos.* Toronto: Simon and Schuster of Canada Ltd., 1972.

Carroll, Jock. *The Summer Olympic Games.* Toronto: Simon and Schuster of Canada, Ltd., 1972.

Conacher, Brian. *Hockey in Canada—The Way It Is.* Toronto: Gateway Press Ltd., 1970.

Cochrane, Jean, Abby Hoffman, and Pat Kincaid. *Women in Canadian Life—Sports.* Toronto: Fitzhenry and Whiteside, 1977.

Cosentino, Frank, and Glynn Leyshon. *Olympic Gold.* Toronto: Holt, Rinehart and Winston, 1975.

Cosentino, Frank. *Canadian Football: The Grey Cup Years.* Toronto: Musson Book Company, 1969.

Currie, Gordon. *One Hundred Years of Canadian Football.* Toronto: Pagurian Press, 1968.
Dryden, Ken, and Mark Mulvoy. *Face-Off at the Summit.* Toronto: Little, Brown and Co., 1973.
Fillmore, Stanley. *The Pleasure of the Game: The Story of The Toronto Cricket, Skating and Curling Club, 1827–1977.* Toronto: Toronto Cricket, Skating and Curling Club, 1977.
Fitness and Amateur Sport Department. *Report of the Task Force on Sports for Canadians.* Ottowa: Queen's Printer, 1969.
Goodhart, Philip, and Christopher Chataway. *War Without Weapons.* London: W. H. Allen, 1968.
Greene, Nancy. *Nancy Greene, An Autobiography.* Toronto: Pagurian Press, 1968.
Gross, George. *Donald Jackson.* Toronto: Queen City Publishing, 1977.
Gzowski, Peter, and Trent Frayne. *Great Canadian Sports Stories.* Toronto: Weekend Magazine/McClelland and Stewart Ltd., 1965.
Hockey Canada. *Twenty Seven Days in September.* Toronto: Hockey Canada and Prosport Productions, 1973.
Howell, M. L., and Nancy Howell. *Sports and Games in Canadian Life.* Toronto: Macmillan and Company, 1969.
Jowett, George F. *The Strongest Man That Ever Lived.* Philadelphia: Milo Publishing Company, 1927.
Kavanaugh, L. V. *History of Golf in Canada.* Toronto: Fitzhenry and Whiteside, Ltd., 1973.
Kidd, Bruce, and John McFarlane. *The Death of Hockey.* Toronto: New Press, 1972.
———. *Tom Longboat.* The Canadians Series. Toronto: Fitzhenry and Whiteside, 1980.
Leveridge, Bill. *Fair Sport: A History of Sports At the Canadian National Exhibition Since 1879.* Toronto: C. N. E., 1978.
Ludwig, Jack. *Hockey Night in Moscow.* Toronto: McClelland and Stewart, 1972.
Magnussen, Karen, and Jeff Cross. *Karen.* Toronto: Collier-Macmillan Canada Ltd., 1973.
Michel, Doug, and Bob Mellor. *Left Wing and a Prayer.* Ottowa: Excalibur Sports Publications, Inc., 1974.
Morrow, Don. *A Sporting Revolution.* Montreal: M.A.A.A., 1981.
The Olympians. Montreal: Publinova, 1974.
Ondaatje, Christopher, and Gordon Currie. *Olympic Victory.* Toronto: Pagurian Press, 1967.
Profit, Mel. *For Love, Money and Future Considerations.* Toronto: D. C. Heath Canada Ltd., 1972.
Reed, T. A., *The Blue and White.* Toronto: The University of Toronto Press, 1944.
Roxborough, H. H. *Great Days in Canadian Sport.* Toronto: The Ryerson Press, 1957.
———. *One Hundred Not Out.* Toronto: The Ryerson Press, 1966.
———. *The Stanley Cup Story.* Toronto: McGraw-Hill, Ryerson, Revised, 1971.
———. *Canada at the Olympics.* Toronto: McGraw-Hill, Ryerson, 1975.
Sullivan, Jack. *The Grey Cup Story.* Toronto: Greywood Publishing, 1971.
Van Vliet, M. *Physical Education in Canada.* Toronto: Prentice-Hall, 1965.
Whitehead, Eric. *Cyclone Taylor.* Toronto: Doubleday Canada Ltd., 1977.
Wilson, J. Donald, Robert Stamp, and Louis-Philippe Audet. *Canadian Education: A History.* Toronto: Prentice-Hall, 1970.
Weider, Ben. *Les Hommes forts du Quebec.* Montreal: Editions du Jour, 1973.

Theses and Dissertations

Agbogun, Jacob. "A History of the British Commonwealth Games, 1930–1966." M.A. thesis, University of Alberta, 1970.

Cosentino, Frank. "A History of Canadian Football, 1909 to 1968." M.A. thesis, University of Alberta, 1969.

Cox, Allan. "A History of Sports in Canada, 1868 to 1900." Ph.D. diss., University of Alberta, 1969.

Danielson, Karen F. "Development in Eskimo Play." M.A. thesis, University of Alberta, 1971.

Dinning, Michael. "The Role of the Government of Canada and the Province of Ontario In the Implementation of the F. and A. S. Act 1961–74." M.A. thesis, University of Alberta, 1968.

Hall, Margaret Ann. "A History of Women's Sport in Canada: Prior to World War I." M.A. thesis, University of Western Ontario, 1974.

Jobling, Ian F. "Sport in Nineteenth Century Canada: The Effects of Technological Changes on its Development." Ph.D. diss., University of Alberta, 1970.

Jones, Kevin. "Sport in Canada, 1900–1920." Ph.D. diss., University of Alberta, 1970.

Lansley, Keith. "The Amateur Athletic Union of Canada and Changing Concepts of Amateurism." Ph.D. diss., University of Alberta, 1971.

Lindsay, Peter. "A History of Sport in Canada, 1807 to 1867." Ph.D. diss., University of Alberta, 1969.

Louw, Johan. "Canada's Participation At the Olympic Games." M.A. thesis, University of Alberta, 1971.

Lund, Rolf. "A History of Skiing in Canada Prior to 1940." M.A. thesis, University of Alberta, 1970.

Mitchelson, Edward Barry. "The Evolution of Men's Basketball in Canada, 1892–1936." M.A. thesis, University of Alberta, 1968.

Nurmberg, Reet. "A History of Competitive Gymnastics in Canada." M.A. thesis, University of Alberta, 1970.

Pendleton, Brian. "Sport in Sculpture in Canada and the United States since 1920." M.A. thesis, University of Alberta, 1970.

Reid, John. "Sports and Games in Alberta before 1900." M.A. thesis, University of Alberta, 1969.

Redmond, Gerald. "The Scots and Sport in Nineteenth Century Canada." Ph.D. diss., University of Alberta, 1972.

Semotiuk, Darwin. "The Development of Theoretical Framework for Analyzing the Role of National Government Involvement in Sport and Physical Education and its Application to Canada." Ph.D. diss., Ohio State University, 1970.

Salter, Michael. "Games in Ritual: A Study of Selected North American Indian Tribes." Ph.D. diss., University of Alberta, 1972.

Sturrock, Douglas. "A History of Rugby Football in Canada." M.A. thesis, University of Alberta, 1971.

Vellathottam, T. George. "A History of Lacrosse in Canada prior to 1914." M.A. thesis, University of Alberta, 1968.

Watkins, Glenn G. "Professional Team Sports and Competition Policy: A Case Study of the Canadian Football League." Ph.D. diss., University of Alberta, 1972.

Watson, Geoffrey. "Sports and Games in Ontario Private Schools: 1830–1930." M.A. thesis, University of Alberta, 1970.

Wilkie, David. "Fitness and Amateur Sport Act in Alberta." M.A. thesis, University of Alberta, 1968.

TUTORIALS

Group 1—SC219 Fl
Group 2—SC220 Fl

Jan. 7. A. Sports and games of aboriginal people. B. Pioneer pastimes, sports, bees.
Jan. 14. A. Beginnings of sport—hockey. B. Beginnings of sport—football.
Jan. 21. A. Beginnings of sport—baseball. B. Beginnings of sport—lacrosse.
Jan. 28. A. Transportation and sport—nineteenth century. B. Communications and sport—nineteenth century.
Feb. 4. A. Radio and sport. B. Television and sport.
Feb. 11. A. Governors general and sport. B. Religion and influences on sport.
Feb. 25. A. Gold medal in hockey, 1920 Olympics. B. Gold medal in hockey, 1924 Olympics.
March 4. A. Gold medal in hockey, 1928 Olympics. B. Gold medal in hockey, 1932 Olympics.
March 11. A. Gold medal in hockey, 1948 Olympics. B. Gold medal in hockey, 1952 Olympics.
March 18. A. Gold medal and career in figure skating, Barbara Ann Scott, 1948. B. Gold medal and career in figure skating, Barbara Wagner and Robert Paul, 1960.
March 25. A. Gold medal and career, A. Heggtveit, 1960. B. Gold medal and career, bob sled team, 1964.
April 8. A. Gold medal and career, Nancy Greene, 1968. B. Gold medal and career, Kathy Kreiner, 1976.

TUTORIAL INSTRUCTIONS

Presentation—20–25 minutes, typewritten material complete with bibliography and footnotes to be submitted by 10 days after tutorial.

APPENDIX II: FINAL EXAM

Read all instructions and questions carefully. Please write legibly and in good, complete sentences. All students do Part A (10 Marks). In the space provided in Column 1, please put the appropriate number from Column 2.

1.	2.
——Ethological	1. Nancy Greene
——Eskimo	2. Saint John
——L'Ordre de bontemps	3. Matchless Six
——Winnipeg Falcons	4. Arthur Pelkey
——Eton	5. George Brown
——Rugby	6. Man of Kintail
——Barbarian	7. Percy Page
——Time	8. Bloomers
——Henley	9. Soviet Win
——Neptune	10. 1908 Olympics
——Halifax	11. High Kick
——Technological Advantage	12. Lord Strathcona
——Hop Bitter's Race	13. Sakatoon Lily
——R. Tait McKenzie	14. The Big Train
——Bobbie Rosenfeld	15. Basketball
——Marilyn Bell	16. Wonder goalie

——Task Force
——Lyndhursts
——Hockey Canada
——Father David Bauer
——St. Pat's
——Ethel Catherwood
——James Naismith
——Hamilton Tigers
——Seth Martin
——Tommy Burns
——Lionel Conacher
——Tom Longboat
——Florence Bell
——Underwood Torphy

17. Lake Ontario
18. Gentleman Amateur
19. 1920 Olympics
20. New York Americans
21. Battle of Waterloo
22. Pierre de Coubertin
23. Chaplain
24. Maple Leafs
25. Tom Brown's School Days
26. Sliding Seat
27. Female Athlete of first fifty years
28. Territory
29. International Hockey Withdrawal
30. Manual Labor
31. National Amateur
32. John Courtney
33. Excellence

All students do Part B (10 Marks).

Assuming that you control the funds which sports will need to prepare themselves for the 1988 Calgary Winter Olympic Games, you have consultant's reports which deal with the past gold medal winners. Based on these reports (the seminars) which sports would you be inclined to fund more? less? Give a thoughtful analysis of the rationale to your decision.

Part C (80 Marks). Answer four questions

1. It was said after the Team Canada-Soviet Series of 1972: "We won the Games. We lost a legend." (Hoppener 1972). Comment fully on the "legend" and how it developed.

2. "These are Canadian episodes; (we have been) denied knowledge of a good deal of excitement; we are denied, as well, a good deal of ourselves. We need to be reminded regularly of the miracles wrought by Canadians."—P. E. Trudeau, 1972. Select a topic studied this year in this course (one that has not been addressed in any other question on this exam) about which Canadians should know and that answers the criteria in the above quotation. Explain your choice fully.

3. "It has seemed quite clear that it has become a matter of national interest for the Federal Government to involve itself in the field of sports in Canada to a much greater extent than ever before."—Task Force Report. Give specific examples of past Federal Government involvement in sport (in the widest sense of the word) in Canada. Why did the government become involved? Should it have been involved? Should it be involved? Why?

4. The "class" concept of Amateurism in England manifested itself as one based on "race" in Canada. Discuss the above statement using specific examples from the lectures and/or texts to support your answer.

5. In 1984, a women's Marathon was held at the Olympics for the first time. Based on material covered in this course this year use this information to make a good case for the statement: "Sport mirrors society."

17

Teaching "Women in Sport" from a Feminist Perspective

SUSAN BIRRELL

Courses in women in sport are necessary as a corrective to the impression left in many of our sport studies courses that women's position in the sport world is marginal or insignificant. I suspect that many of the courses described in this self-conscious book on what counts as important information in sport studies courses include only mimimal mention of either gender or race as significant categories for understanding the American sport experience. To overcome such oversights a course that places women at the center of the analysis of their own lives is essential.

A more compelling reason for offering a course specifically focused on women is to offer to sport the fresh insight of feminist analysis. Women's relatively small numbers in sport is hardly a reason to exclude them from scholarly consideration: it is the whole point. Exploring and understanding the historical exclusion of half the population from a cultural form as visible and popular as sport should be a central project of sport studies. In understanding the exclusion of women—and blacks and the working class—we understand much about the nature and meaning of sport in society. This theme underlies my course on Women in Sport.

The course I teach is entitled "Sociology of Women and Sport" because it is a companion course at Iowa to courses in "History of Women in Sport" and "Physiological Research on Women in Sport." When I first developed the course, I relied on information, research, and analyses generated by sport sociologists, but as I have become more influenced by the theoretical power of interdisciplinary approaches of women's studies and cultural studies, the class has become more interdisciplinary. I intend to continue to move in that direction.

The course is open to undergraduate and graduate students, and enrollments have been evenly split. It is crosslisted with Women's Studies and draws about a third of its students from fields outside of physical education and sports studies. Enrollment ranges from ten to fifteen students, an optimal size for a course that uses class discussion as the major pedagogical strategy. Most, sometimes all, of the students are women, a situation that greatly influences my approach to the class.

I was asked to develop a course on women in sport when I arrived at the University of Iowa in 1980. I did not then view the assignment with the excitement and delight I now take in teaching the course that has evolved. Despite initial disinterest, I was better prepared to teach that new course than most would have been. As a graduate student at the University of Massachusetts in 1972, I had taken Ellen Gerber's course, "The American Woman in Sport," surely one of the earliest such courses. Eight years after taking Gerber's course, I found there was still not much material available. Few research studies included women; fewer still focused on them. But some early pioneers—like Gerber, Jan Felshin, Marie Hart, and Carol Oglesby—had begun to reflect on and analyze women's relationship to sport (see course readings in Appendix I).

Those of us who teach women in sport courses today have more resources available and, even more important, theoretically informed feminist analyses of sport provide us with a powerful theoretical context within which to understand women's relationship to sport.

My course is taught from a feminist perspective, which means I accept as given the fact that women have been severely disadvantaged by patriarchal value systems and structures, and I take seriously the central aim of feminist teaching and research, to make clear the extent and nature of those disadvantages. A feminist approach provides a context for understanding women's position in sport in relationship to women's position in other social settings: the business world, the family, the political arena, the media. Thus the salient comparison is not only between women in sport and men in sport, but between women in sport and women in society.

Courses on women in sport can be taught without a feminist approach. In my opinion, however, courses that do not take advantage of the insight furnished by such a comprehensive approach are intellectually suspect. I fear that in the false pursuit of objectivity or value-neutrality, they shortchange the students, depriving them of exposure to an exciting and provocative analysis of sport. I state on the first day of class that the course will be taught from a feminist perspective, because I believe a primary responsibility teachers share in the classroom is to make clear our assumptions or biases and let them work constructively for us. In that way we may avoid the particularly rampant bias that our biases can be kept from intruding into the classroom and that we can be totally objective presenters of neutral facts.

A course on women in sport works best when it is not only informed by a feminist perspective, but is sensitive to issues of race and class. This lesson became painfully clear to me a few years ago when a black woman asked politely after class if she could present some information she had gathered on the history of black women in sport, since my presentation on the history of women in sport had almost entirely overlooked the black experience. As that student's complaint makes clear, courses on women in sport are too often courses on white, middle-class women in sport. To overcome that problem, we have to work hard to find material on *all* women and to insure that theories of women's experiences reflect the experiences of *all* women. This is not an easy task.

Material on women of color in sport is particularly sparse. Very little historical material exists, research in the psychology and sociology of sport rarely includes women of color, and social analyses of sport pay no special attention to their perspectives and experiences. On my reading list I include virtually everything I can find on women athletes of color. I continue to search for more material and to encourage my students to turn their research energy in that direction as well.

FEMINISM IN THE CLASSROOM

The new scholarship on women is gradually excavating lost or forgotten stories of women's lives, and by so doing, transforming the academy in profound ways. Thus feminist research works to remove the male bias in education, which has resulted in ignoring women and women's issues and generalizing about "human" experience from data or perceptions compiled on half the population (guess which half). Feminist pedagogy joins that process not only by incorporating the latest information unearthed by feminist scholars, but also by seeking a parallel transformation in the classroom.

In the classroom, feminist consciousness works to deconstruct the traditional hierarchy that revolves around unequal access to preferred information and to replace it with an atmosphere that recognizes and rewards the different contributions teachers and students bring to class. While concern with these matters is part of a heritage of educational criticism by such revisionists as Paulo Friere, John Holt, A. S. Neill, Neil Postman, and Charles Weingartner; these issues take on particular importance in classes in which most of the students are women and/or in which women's experiences comprise the subject matter.

A good teacher is able to synthesize, condense, and make accessible large bodies of often complex knowledge, but while this synthetic process is efficient, there is a danger that, in the interests of arriving at a homogenous package of dominant mainstream knowledge, the rich diversity of variant perspectives will be lost. Moreover, when dominant forms of knowledge are processed and distributed by an intellectual authority figure (usually male), the student becomes a silent partner in his or her education and is reduced to a passive recipient of socially preferred knowledge that may or may not have any relevance to his or her life experiences.

To me, teaching women in sport from a feminist perspective means not only uncovering missing data on women in sport and presenting it within a sensible theoretical framework, but also acknowledging that I must keep my role as "an authority" in proper perspective. The sheer length of time that I have been engaged in analyzing the status of women in sport privileges me. I have immediate access to a greater store of preferred information than they do, and thus I appear to know more than they do. But in reality, I merely know different things. I possess a different sort of information: data sets, research reports, theoretical analyses, rhetorical tracts. My responsibility is to make that information accessible to them so that the class can use it as a resource to provide a broader context within which to locate and understand our own experiences of sport. As a white, middle-class, baby-boomer; I can never know some things in quite the same way they do. I can never really know what a scholarship means to a black, working-class, urban high school athlete, but I have access to a broader context than she might, and the combination of our knowledge enriches us both. My responsibility as a teacher is to provide that broader context, to help students move beyond their own personal experiences and see these experiences as part of a larger pattern of social relations surrounding sport.

I did not always see things this way. Students in my first women in sport class still enjoy reminding me of the gradual evolution I underwent during that semester. I began the semester lecturing from a lectern to six amused students; we ended the semester around a small table, absorbed in our discussions of the readings and our own experiences as women in sport. From them I learned that teaching and learning are inseparable processes, and those processes can engage us both intellectually and personally.

COURSE MATERIALS AND REQUIREMENTS

Since my course is taught from a feminist perspective, the materials I find most enlightening are often informed with that perspective. Like many teachers, I am greatly influenced by particular traditions and writers. My canon includes Jaggar and Rothenberg (1984), Boutilier and SanGiovanni (1983), Ritzer (1975), and the work of Nancy Theberge (University of Waterloo), Ann Hall (University of Alberta), and my Iowa colleagues Bonnie Slatton, Christine Grant, and Cheryl Cole.

Since much of the most recent material on gender relations and sport is difficult to obtain, I assemble it for the students and make it available to them at our local Xerox outlet. For their convenience, I include more than the required material. In addition to the packet, the class reads most of Helen Lenskyj's *Out of Bounds* (1986).

Course requirements include contributions to class discussions, two exams, and a course project. Since the course relies a great deal on class discussion, one quarter of the students' grade is assessed by their contributions. The exams are in a format I call modified take home. I prepare four questions that I hand out a week before the exam. On exam day I select two of the questions for them to answer. They cannot bring notes nor write out the answers in advance, and I require that they prepare for the exam on their own. The procedure works well and appears to minimize test anxiety for those students affected by it. The quality of answers is higher than when I spring unexpected questions, and the format allows students to bring their full analytical powers to bear on the subject matter. Examples of test questions can be found in Appendix II.

The student project usually is research-based—a review of literature, a research proposal, a small-scale study, an analysis of some aspect of women's involvement in sport. Students may also design their own projects. I have had several wonderful short stories that capture the essence of women's sport worlds or that fantasize about women's sport utopias. One woman wrote a modern-day *You Know Me Al*, a delightful and insightful analysis of American women's sporting practices in the guise of letters home to England from a new assistant field hockey coach. Two other students analyzed the television coverage of women in the 1988 Winter Olympics and provided a video tape to illustrate their points.

THE ORGANIZATION OF THE COURSE

The course is organized not only to provide the latest research and analysis on women in sport, but also to provide a scholarly context for understanding women's place in sport as it relates to women's position in society.

The first two sections of the course introduce important theories and concepts and set the stage for the third section, which contains much of the substantive information in the course. These early sections comprise a fairly lengthy amount of stage setting. This seems essential for a course that attempts not only to supply students with useful information about the dimensions of women's sport experience but also to introduce them to a different perspective on the social world.

Since the course revolves around the relationship between sport and gender, early classes explore those key concepts. The section on sex/gender examines the distinction between sex (a biological category) and gender (a social construct), thus introducing a theme that will continue throughout the semester: the tension between biological and social differences and the political implications of favoring either of those distinctions or explanations over the other. If some of the students have an incomplete background on the status of women in North America, I prepare a lecture to cover that information, drawing from diverse sources to give an overview of women's status in major institutions: the business world, the educational system, the legal system, the family, the military, the media. The picture that emerges is of a society in which gender stratification is a central feature and in which women are excluded, underrepresented, or devalued.

We explore traditional gender role prescriptions through personal accounts and observations, matching these accounts with the research in the area. Popular attitudes toward women in sport are then examined and related to attitudes toward strong, assertive, or nontraditional women.

To establish the nature and extent of women's sport involvement, I present baseline figures from whatever sources I can cultivate: the NCAA, the Sporting Goods Dealers of America, the Neilsen reports, the National Federation of State High School Athletic Associations, Gallup Polls, and research reports such as the Miller Lite Survey. The purpose is to provide an overview of women's involvement at many levels including active participation, coaching, officiating, entrepreneurial, and managerial involvement, and spectatorship. Racial and class differences in these patterns are explored.

Having documented that men usually outnumber women in sport, I challenge a basic assumption: that students know what "sport" is. The class makes its way quickly through the classic statements of Huizinga, Caillois, and Loy, and eventually focuses its discussion not on *what sport is* but on the cultural forces that determine *what counts as sport* in particular cultures and how certain activities (in the United States, namely baseball, football, and basketball) are canonized while others are pushed to marginal status or not acknowledged as sport. We read Edwards's (1973) ideas on the "dominant American sports creed" and Eitzen's and Sage's (1986) ideas on the dominant qualities of North American sport. The class discusses the ways in which dominant cultural forms, such as big time sport, influence and control related forms such as Little League, intramurals, and recreational sport. And the class begins to explore the effect on women of the dominant notion of sport as an activity that features aggressiveness, strength, and power.

Having established some frames of reference in terms of gender and sports, I provide a broader theoretical context by introducing a variety of feminist approaches to understanding the social world. Again we build from personal experience as we discuss common sense understandings of concepts such as equality, discrimination, oppression, opportunity, sexism, racism, patriarchy, and feminism. To provide safe space for those who are unfamiliar or uncomfortable with such political terms, I report a study done by a student in the class several years ago. Seeking common sense understandings of feminism, she stopped fifty people outside the student union and asked them "Are you a feminist?" and then "How do you know?" To her surprise, fully one third of this highly educated, relatively liberal sample had no idea what feminism was, confusing it with "femininity" and in some cases with feminine hygiene. When students realize feminism isn't *one* monolithic theory, *one* strategy for change, when they are convinced that feminism includes many varied approaches; they feel freer to express their own discomfort, confusion, distrust, dislike, or despair.

The class moves to a more academic approach by examining the distinctions Allison Jaggar and Paula Rothenberg (1984) make between feminist frameworks. Modifying their scheme, we discuss three general approaches to women's proper place in society: conservatism, liberal feminism, and radical feminism, which includes cultural feminism, Marxist feminism, and socialist feminism. Conservatism and/or antifeminism holds that men and women are by nature different and that the difference should be honored as the natural order of things. Conservatives advocate a return to traditional gender roles. Liberal feminism assumes that men and women are essentially alike (we are all *human*) and that whatever differences exist are the result of gender role socialization that can be reversed. Liberals put their faith in legislative remedies that they believe will provide equal access, equal opportunity, and equal rewards. Radical feminism views men and women as fundamentally different because they experience the world differently. Radicals challenge not the access to social structures, but the values and assumptions that underlie those structures. Radical approaches vary. Cultural feminists focus on gender as the primary and most fundamental oppression; they believe the world we live in, designed by men, could be improved if it moved toward women's values. Marxist feminists focus on class as the primary oppression and understand women's oppression as derivative of class oppression, while socialist feminists see class and gender as categories of experience so profoundly and complexly linked that separating them either theoretically or practically is both impossible and undesirable.

In my opinion, the most exciting work in feminist theory today follows from critiques of its inability to deal adequately with issues of difference and diversity. Women of color are particularly outspoken about this problem, and the class reads a selection from Angela Davis's excellent analysis (1983) of the intersections of gender, race, and class. Finally we discuss the rich possibilities of a feminist cultural studies. Cultural studies is a critical, interdisciplinary approach to the analysis of culture and cultural forms that provides a sophisticated theory of the relations of dominance and subordination structured along class lines. Feminist cultural studies seeks to further diversify that model by theorizing about the complex connections of relations of dominance and subordination structured along gender, racial, and class lines. The approach is just beginning to enlighten our analyses of gender relations and sport.

As the students become more adept at recognizing and applying these different perspectives, they begin to understand why people who "want what's best for women" don't always agree on what that is. At this point, based on their own background and understanding of the status of women's sport in the U.S. today, students begin to investigate sport from feminist perspectives. A key question of the course is voiced here: if women had designed sport, what would it look like? What would a sport utopia look like to the liberal feminist, the cultural feminist, the Marxist feminist, and the socialist feminist? Students never get very far from this question for the rest of the semester, and some variant of it is likely to show up on their final exam.

To provide a bridge between feminist theory and the research the class will be reading, it examines feminist critiques of scholarship, beginning with an examination of the underrepresentation of women in academia, moving to an exploration of the impact that low representation has had on the neglect of women's issues and the woman as subject, and concluding with samples of the recent critique and transformation of traditional methodologies and theory building.

The stage is now set for the main substantive part of the course: the analysis of the relationship between women and sport. We begin with three introductory topics. First Helen Lenskyj's perceptive book (1986) provides invaluable grounding for an understanding of the historical forces that have worked to exclude women from sport. Second, for a taste of more recent issues, we turn to an examination of the passage of Title IX and the rise and demise of the Association for Intercollegiate Athletics for Women. The logic and impact of Title IX are discussed at length. We focus on Title IX as liberal legislation and explore the irony of Title IX: spectacular increases in participation for high school and college athletes and dramatic decreases in opportunities for women to coach and administer women's programs. The AIAW/NCAA battle for control of the structure and ideology of women's collegiate sport is also highlighted. The sport studies students could talk about these issues all semester, for they have first-hand knowledge and strong opinions about changes occurring in women's sport in the past ten or fifteen years. For students from other disciplines, this controversial topic provides fairly easy access to a range of contemporary issues in women's sport.

Finally the class explores the rich tradition that now exists, which posits sport as a male preserve. Students invariably have strong reactions to this theme that focuses on sport as a male-defined activity that has not only denied women access to sport opportunities, but also effectively alienated them from the process of sport when they do gain access. As an introduction to this theme, students read accounts from scholars, journalists, humorists, and male chauvinists.

As a transition to contemporary feminist analyses of sport, the class turns to the traditional explanations offered for women's rates of involvement in sport. I characterize these explanations as "deficiency" theories since they subtly but unmistakably locate the problem of women's underrepresentation in sport in women themselves, not in sport and not in the cultural context of gender relations. Willis's (1982) critique of physiological deficiency theories is particularly useful here. We also examine the psychological versions of these theories, particularly the assumptions of role conflict theory.

Finally the class is in a position to examine feminist analyses of sport from an intellectual history perspective (Birrell 1988). It reads some of the early classic statements by Eleanor Metheny (1965), Jan Felshin (1974), and Marie Hart (1981) before it turns to a variety of contemporary feminist analyses. Bryson (1987) provides an accessible preview of important themes further developed in articles by Theberge (1984), Hall (1984), Lenskyj (1986), and Birrell (1984). Two issues of particular interest are drawn out for more detailed analysis: learning gender through sport and the mediation of images of women athletes.

Learning gender through sport is approached from both the traditional socialization perspective and the more recent cultural studies approach. The former is examined as a sociological form of deficiency theory. In the latter context, I have had great success in provoking class discussions with the film *Pumping Iron II: The Women* because the film deals explicitly with the tension between cultural norms of femininity and women's strength. This is an excellent place to discuss issues of sexuality and sport, specifically the ways in which homophobia works to keep women from full involvement in sport, and the way that our culture's strong norms of compulsory heterosexuality redefine the purpose of a woman's increasing interest in fitness from an activity she participates in for her own sake to a means of making herself sexier and more attractive for her man.

The section on media focuses on the representation of women athletes in major media forms such as television, magazines, and newspapers; the depiction of women in sport literature and films (the availability of video cassettes such as *Personal Best* and *The Turning Point* makes this more feasible); and women's place in the process of media production. A prominent theme here is the mediation process itself and how images of active females and women athletes are constructed through media conventions that are often so subtle they elude our immediate detection.

The final section of the course is usually the most provocative. We reexamine sport as a male preserve by reading accounts of resistance to male practices as women attempt to take control of their own sporting experiences and transform them to reflect their own values and interests. There is some excellent work now available on this subject. This topic brings us full circle to a theme introduced early in the semester: if women defined sport, what would it look like? I judge the success of the course not only by how much material about women in sport the students have amassed, but also by how their responses to this question have changed and by their growing ability to envision, appreciate, or critique alternative models of sport.

I have taught the course outlined here for the past seven years, usually at Iowa and for one summer at East Stroudsburg University, and always with the same result. The course is a joy to teach, not because it reflects my own interests, but because the course engages the students in such an immediate and personal way. The reaction of the women who take the course almost approaches gratitude: for the first time they are allowed to focus on *their* place in sport, how sport serves or fails to serve *their* needs, what sport means to *them,* what *they* would like sport to be. I have noticed the same profound reaction in the feminist theory course I teach for the Women's Studies Program. The students' lives have been brought into focus and examined, and their perspectives or perceptions have been rendered legitimate. For some, this is a revelation; for others, a relief; for still others, it is cause for anger at the realization of having been so long dispossessed of knowledge about themselves and their lives. Finally they accept what they already "knew" but were systematically prevented from "knowing": women's lives and women's activities have a logic and dignity to them different from but not inferior to men's. It is an empowering discovery, and it is a privilege to be present when they make it.

APPENDIX I: SYLLABUS

Sociology of Women and Sport
The University of Iowa
Department of Physical Education and Sport Studies
Susan Birrell

COURSE OUTLINE

Introductory material

A. Purpose and content of the course; development of women and sport as a topic of interest.

B. Gender and American society. 1. Sex, gender, and the sex/gender system. 2. Women's place in American society, past and present. 3. Gender role prescriptions in American society. 4. Traditional views of women in sport.

I would like to thank my colleagues who encouraged me in the development of this course and in the preparation of this paper: N. Peggy Burke, Cheryl Cole, Laurel Davis, Bonnie Slatton, and Linda Yanney.

C. Sport in American culture. 1. Differential patterns of sport involvement. (Houzer; Green et al.; Berghorn et al.). 2. Defining sport—the traditional bias (Loy). 3. Dominant values in American sport (Edwards; Eitzen and Sage).

Feminist analysis

A. Basic concepts: equality, discrimination, oppression, patriarchy, sexism, racism, classism, heterosexism.
B. Feminist theories (Jaggar and Rothenberg). 1. Conservatism; antifeminism. 2. Liberal feminism. 3. Radical feminisms. a. Cultural feminism. b. Marxist, socialist, and materialist feminisms. 4. Critiques of women of color (Davis). 5. Feminist cultural studies (Cole and Birrell 1986; Birrell 1987).
C. Feminist critiques of scholarship. 1. Women's place in academia. 2. Correcting substantive omissions. 3. Overcoming methodological and theoretical problems (Ritzer; Birrell 1984b; Hall 1985).

Women's place in American sport.

A. Historical exclusion of women from sport (Lenskyj chaps. 1–4; Lucas and Smith)
B. Recent changes in school sport. 1. The impact of Title IX (Holmen and Parkhouse; Acosta and Carpenter; Boutilier and SanGiovanni). 2. The NCAA/AIAW battle (Slatton; Grant).
C. Sport as a male preserve (Sheard and Dunning; Angell; Keillor; Carroll).
D. Understanding women's place in sport (Birrell, 1988: 459–67). 1. Traditional views of women in sport (Harris; Griffin 1973). 2. Physiological deficiency arguments (Willis). 3. Psychological deficiency arguments (Birrell 1983).

Feminist analyses of sport (Birrell 1988: 467–92).

A. Early feminist work (Metheny; Felshin; Hart).
B. Contemporary feminist theory and sport. (Bryson; Theberge 1984; Hall 1984; Birrell 1984a).
C. Learning gender through sport. 1. The socialization tradition (Greendorfer; Lever). 2. Reproduction of gender relations through sport (Hargreaves; Cole and Birrell 1985; Lenskyj chaps. 5, 6; *Pumping Iron II*).
D. Mediated images of women athletes (Rintala and Birrell; Hilliard; Theberge and Cronk; Griffin 1985; Duncan and Hasbrook).

Feminist resistance and transformation of the male preserve (Dunning; Birrell and Richter; Wheatley; Birrell and Cole; Theberge 1987).

BIBLIOGRAPHY

Acosta, R. Vivian, and Linda Jean Carpenter. "Women in Athletics—A Status Report." *JOPERD* (August 1985): 30–37.

Alexander, Alpha. "The Status of Minority Women in the Association of Intercollegiate Athletics for Women." Masters thesis, Temple University, 1978.

Angell, Roger. "Sharing the Beat." In *Late Innings: A Baseball Companion,* 126–61. New York: Ballentine, 1982.

Barclay, Vranda M. "The Status of Black Women in Sports at Selected Institutions of Higher Education." Master's thesis, University of Iowa, 1979.

Berghorn, Forrest J., Norman R. Yetman, and William E. Hanna. "Racial Participation and

Integration in Men's and Women's Intercollegiate Basketball: Continuity and Change, 1858–1985." *Sociology of Sport Journal* 5 (1988): 107–24.

Birrell, Susan. "Locating Theoretical Absences: Race and Feminist Cultural Studies." Paper presented at the annual meeting of the North American Society for the Sociology of Sport, Edmonton, November 1987.

———. "Studying Gender in Sport: A Feminist Perspective." In *Sport and the Sociological Imagination,* edited by Nancy Theberge and Peter Donnelly, 125–35. Fort Worth: Texas Christian University Press, 1984.

———. "The Psychological Dimensions of Female Athletic Participation." In *The Sporting Woman,* edited by Mary A. Boutilier and Lucinda SanGiovanni, 49–91. Champaign IL: Human Kinetics, 1983.

Birrell, Susan, and Cheryl Cole. "The Body as Political Territory." Paper presented at the Women as Leaders Conference, University of Iowa, July 1986.

Birrell, Susan, and Diana M. Richter. "Is a Diamond Forever? Feminist Transformations of Sport." *Women's Studies International Forum* 10, no. 4 (1987): 395–409.

Boutilier, Mary A., and Lucinda SanGiovanni. "Women, Sport and Public Policy." In *Sociology of Sport: Diverse Perspectives,* edited by Susan Greendorfer and Andrew Yiannakis, 181–91. West Point N.Y.: Leisure Press, 1981.

Brod, Harry. "Philosophy Teaching as Intellectual Affirmative Action." *Teaching Philosophy* 9 (1986): 5–13.

Carroll, John. "Sport: Virtue and Grace." *Theory, Culture and Society* 3, no. 1 (1986): 91–98.

Cole, Cheryl, and Susan Birrell. "Resisting the Canon: Sport and Feminist Cultural Studies." Paper presented at the annual meetings of the North American Society for the Sociology of Sport, Las Vegas, November 1986.

———. "The Challenge of Renee Richards: A Feminist Analysis." Paper presented at the annual meetings of the North American Society for the Sociology of Sport, Boston, November 1985.

Collins, Patricia Hill. "The Emerging Theory and Pedagogy of Black Women's Studies." *Feminist Issues* (Spring 1986): 3–17.

Cully, Margo, and Catherine Portuges, eds. *Gendered Subjects: The Dynamics of Feminist Teaching.* London: Routledge and Kegan Paul, 1985.

Duncan, Margaret Carlisle, and Cynthia Hasbrook. "Denial of Power in Women's Sport." *Sociology of Sport Journal* 5, no. 1 (1988): 1–21.

Dunning, Eric. "Sport as a Male Preserve: Notes on the Social Sources of Masuline Identity and its Transformations." *Theory, Culture and Society* 3, no. 1 (1986): 79–90.

Gerber, Ellen W., Jan Felshin, Pearl Berlin, and Waneen Wyrick. *The American Woman in Sport.* Reading, Mass.: Addison-Wesley, 1974.

Grant, Christine H. B. "The Gender Gap in Sport: From Olympic to Intercollegiate Level." *Arena Review* 8, no. 2 (1984): 31–48.

Green, Tina Sloan, Carole Oglesby, Alpha Alexander, and Nikki Franke. *Black Women in Sport.* Reston, Va: AAHPERD, 1981.

Greendorfer, Susan. "Shaping the Female Athlete: The Impact of the Family." In *The Sporting Woman,* edited by Mary A. Boutilier and Lucinda SanGiovanni, 135–55. Champaign Ill.: Human Kinetics, 1983.

Griffin, Patricia. "R. R. Knudson's Sport Fiction: A Feminist Critique." *Arete* 3 (1985): 3–10.

———. "What's a Nice Girl Like You Doing in a Profession Like This?" *Quest* 19 (1973): 96–101.

Hall, M. Ann. "Knowledge and Gender: Epistemological Questions in the Social Analysis of Sport." *Sociology of Sport Journal* 2, no. 1 (1985): 25–42.

———. *Sport and Gender: A Feminist Perspective on the Sociology of Sport.* CAHPER Sociology of Sport Monograph Series. Vanier City, Canada: CAHPER, 1978.

Hargreaves, Jennifer A. "Where's the Virtue? Where's the Grace? A Discussion of the Social Production of Gender Relations in and through Sport." *Theory, Culture and Society* 3, no. 1 (1986): 109–19.

Harris, Dorothy V. "The Social Self and the Competitive Self of the Female Athlete." Paper presented at the third International Symposium on the Sociology of Sport, Waterloo, Ontario, August 1971.

Hilliard, Dan. "Media Images of Male and Female Professional Athletes: An Interpretative Analysis of Magazine Articles." *Sociology of Sport Journal* 1 (1984): 251–62.

Holmen, Milton G., and Bonnie L. Parkhouse. "Trends in the Selection of Coaches for Female Athletes: A Demographic Inquiry." *Research Quarterly for Exercise and Sport* 52, no. 1 (1981): 9–18.

Houzer, Shirley. "Black Women in Athletics." *The Physical Educator* 31 (1974): 208–9.

Keillor, Garrison. "What Did We Do Wrong?" *New Yorker,* 16 September 1985, 32–35.

Lever, Janet. "Sex Differences in the Complexity of Children's Play." *American Sociological Review* 43 (1978): 471–83.

Loy, John W. "The Nature of Sport: A Definitional Effort." In *Sport in the Sociocultural Process,* 3d ed., edited by M. Marie Hart and Susan Birrell, 21–37. Dubuque Iowa: W. C. Brown, 1981.

Lucas, John A., and Ronald A. Smith. "Women's Sport: A Trial of Equality." In *Saga of American Sport,* 342–72. Philadelphia: Lea & Febiger, 1978.

Murphy, Margaret Diane. "The Involvement of Blacks in Women's Athletics in Member Institutions of the Association of Intercollegiate Athletics for Women." Ph.D. diss., Florida State, 1980.

Oglesby, Carol A., ed. *Women and Sport: From Myth to Reality*. Philadelphia: Lea & Febiger, 1978.

Rintala, Jan, and Susan Birrell. "Fair Treatment for the Active Female: A Content Analysis of Young Athlete Magazine." *Sociology of Sport Journal* 1 (1984): 231–50.

Sheard, Kenneth, and Eric Dunning. "The Rugby Football Club as a Type of Male Preserve: Some Sociological Notes." *International Review of Sport Sociology* 5, no. 3 (1973): 5–24.

Slatton, Bonnie. "AIAW: The Greening of American Athletics." In *The Governance of Intercollegiate Athletics,* edited by James Frey, 144–54. West Point N.Y.: Leisure Press, 1982.

Theberge, Nancy. "Sport and Women's Empowerment." *Women's Studies International Forum* 10, no. 4 (1987): 387–93.

———. "Toward a Feminist Alternative to Sport as a Male Preserve." *Quest* 10 (1985): 193–202.

Theberge, Nancy, and Alan Cronk. "Work Routines in Newspaper Sports Departments and the Coverage of Women's Sports." *Sociology of Sport Journal* 3 (1986): 195–203.

Wheatley, Elizabeth. "Playing, Partying and the Process of Culture Creation: A Subcultural Examination of the Women's Rugby Group." Paper presented at the annual meetings of the North American Society for the Sociology of Sport, Las Vegas, November 1986.

APPENDIX II: SAMPLE EXAM QUESTIONS

1. Before Boutilier and SanGiovanni applied Jagger and Rothenberg's feminist frameworks to sport, Jan Felshin was discussing different positions on women's sport. In what ways are the frameworks as applied by Boutilier and SanGiovanni and as developed by Felshin similar, and in what ways do they differ?
2. Discuss the issue of athletic scholarships for women from the following perspectives:

    conservatism *or* reactionary position

liberal feminism
cultural feminism
material feminism

3. Drawing on Grant and Slatton and any other pertinent readings, discuss the differences between the AIAW and the NCAA. To what extent did the AIAW represent a new model for sport?
4. Discuss the history of women's professional team sport. Why hasn't team sport for women succeeded? What do you predict for the new women's basketball league, and why?
5. How does sport serve as a male preserve? What would sport as a female preserve look like?
6. There is no doubt that passage and implementation of Title IX has had a profound effect on interscholastic and intercollegiate athletics for girls and women. These effects have been both positive (the massive increase in participation opportunities) and negative (the loss of coaching and administrative positions to men). Considering both these trends, what do you project for the future of women in sport as a logical outcome of Title IX?
7. Research cited in class has clearly demonstrated that female athletes are underrepresented in the media, such as television, newspapers, and magazines. What difference does it make how and to what extent women athletes are portrayed in the media? Relate the points you make to other topics discussed in class.
8. In the minds of some, androgyny is the best way to ensure equality for women in society. Discuss the concept of androgyny, the research on androgyny, its implications for sport and its usefulness as a feminist principle.
9. What does research say about the likelihood that inherent psychological sex differences exist? If no inherent sex differences exist, what does that imply for sport? If some inherent sex differences do exist, what does *that* imply for sport?
10. Since the late seventies, a feminist critique of sport has been growing. Discuss the major elements of these feminist critiques. What types of solutions are offered by the authors who launch these critiques?
11. A strong case could be made that women have been excluded from positions of power and profit in sport. Specifically, few women are in positions of control in sport as owners, promoters, sportswriters, or media producers. Choose a feminist perspective from Jagger and Rothenberg and discuss women's place in the economy and media. What changes could be expected for sport if women were in control of such important structures?
12. Sport is an inherently sexist institution that can never be reformed to meet the needs of girls and women. Support or attack this position.
13. Many explanations for women's involvement in sport center upon the concept of role conflict. What is role conflict? How does the concept of role conflict apply to sport? What evidence is there that role conflict explains women's lower rates of sport involvement?

WORKS CITED

Birrell, Susan. 1984. "Separatism as an Issue in Women's Sport." *Arena Review* 8, no. 2: 49–61.

———. 1988. "Discourses on the Gender/Sport Relationship: From 'Women in Sport' to 'Gender Relations.'" In *Exercise and Sport Science Reviews,* edited by Kent Pandolf, 459–502. New York: Macmillan.

Boutilier, Mary A., and Lucinda SanGiovanni, eds. 1983. *The Sporting Woman.* Champaign, IL: Human Kinetics.

Bryson, Lois. 1987. "Sport and Maintenance of Masculine Hegemony." *Women's Studies International Forum* 16, no. 2: 349–60.

Davis, Angela. 1983. *Women, Race and Class.* New York: Vintage.

Edwards, Harry. 1973. "The Dominant American Sports Creed." In *Sociology of Sport*, 103–30. Homewood, Ill.: Dorsey.

Eitzen, D. Stanley, and George Sage. 1986. *Sociology of North American Sport*, 3d ed., 14–15. Dubuque Iowa: W. C. Brown.

Felshin, Jan. 1974. "The Triple Option . . . For Women in Sport." *Quest* 21: 36–40.

Hall, M. Ann. 1984. "Feminist Prospects for Sociology of Sport." *Arena Review* 8, no. 2: 1–10.

Hart, M. Marie. 1981. "On Being Female in Sport." In *Sport in the Sociocultural Process*, 3d ed., M. Marie Hart and Susan Birrell, eds., 450–60. Dubuque Iowa: W. C. Brown.

Jagger, Allison M., and Paula S. Rothenberg. 1984. *Feminist Frameworks: Alternative Theoretical Accounts of the Relations Between Women and Men.* 2d ed. New York: McGraw-Hill.

Lenskyj, Helen. 1986. *Out of Bounds: Women, Sport and Sexuality.* Toronto: Women's Press.

Metheny, Eleanor. 1965. "Symbolic Forms of Movement: The Feminine Image in Sports." In *Connotations of Movement in Sport and Dance*, 43–56. Dubuque Iowa: W. C. Brown.

Ritzer, George. "Sociology: A Multiple Paradigm Science." *The American Sociologist* 10: 156–67.

Theberge, Nancy. 1984. "Joining Social Theory to Social Action: Some Marxist Principles." *Arena Review* 8, no. 2: 21–30.

Willis, Paul E. 1982. "Women in Sport in Ideology." In *Sport, Culture and Ideology.* Jennifer Hargreaves, ed., 117–35. London: Routledge and Kegan Paul.

18
Teaching at the Cutting Edge: Sports-Related Courses and Curricular Legitimacy

NEIL D. ISAACS

A new breed is abroad in academe. Not as numerous as its talent for display would suggest, it nevertheless grows alarmingly. The species is known for separating its professional activities from its classroom chores; indeed, its goal is the non-hour load. But coursework is routinely forsaken whenever a symposium, convention, minigrant, or job interview provides cover for a flight from campus. At end of term, when others are giving their students papers and finals, you will find them giving wine and cheese parties to theirs.

These birds rarely fly high in the firmament of intellectual accomplishment or scholarship of lasting effect. Yet their wings are so gaudily painted with a Day-Glo sleaze and so giddily flapped with the busywork of self-gratulation that they are frequently rewarded with whatever assistance, subvention, and other perks the profession has to offer.

These animadversions are prompted by the canard that sports-related courses are part of the illegitimacy on which that new breed feeds. But academic curricula have always accommodated the timely and the trendy as well as the traditional and the true. The basic distinction that must be made, it seems to me, is between those courses that satisfy the late Myron Brightfield's criterion—if it is a legitimate subject for study, then it may be treated as a subject for study—and those that do not.

In the remarks that follow, I discuss five different sports-related courses I have taught, demonstrating to varying degrees their comfortable place in the embrace of traditional curricula. If I may be indulged in autobiographical allusions, I will also show how research, writing, and other professional activities benefit from and contribute to the courses themselves. It is by the coherence and integrity of this practice, rather than any loftiness of avowed principles, that I claim my distance from that new breed I disparage and disdain.

The courses began, then, with a book. I had proposed to write an illustrated personal essay concerning my life-long love affair with the game of basketball, and one of the publishers who turned it down had counterproposed that I write a history of college basketball. The question of how such a divergent turn in professional life could become confluent with the mainstream of academic performance in general and coursework in particular arose, then, alongside the question of how to organize such a narrative. But the answer to the latter brought with it an answer to the former.

All the Moves ([1975] 1984) had to find a context in the cultural history of twentieth-century America. Finding that I could not tell the story of college basketball without reference to wars, social attitudes and values, economics and nutrition, racism and demographics, education and media developments, I also found my way to the course, "Sports Culture, U.S.A."

The concept was at once simple and grandiose. Taking as a premise that our society's involvement and fascination with sports have enormous, far-reaching, and destructive effects; I sought to prove the case by conducting classroom interviews (followed by questions from the class) with guests from the worlds of law, medicine, politics, foreign service, education, gambling, newspapers, and electronic media on their connections and relationships with the world of sports. The extensive interviewing I did for the book, along with occasional newspaper assignments from the *Washington Post*, provided me with many contacts who were apparently delighted with their visits and contributions to the course.

The students' primary responsibility was to keep a journal in which they recorded responses to the guests, the issues raised, the assigned readings, and the half dozen lectures I gave (mostly providing broad contexts for the particular readings, especially the literary ones). They were also encouraged to talk about their own experience in and with what I had already begun to call the "jockocracy."[1] My model for this pedagogical approach was the Great Issues course for seniors at Dartmouth College (except that the guests in Hanover, as I recall, lectured without the imposition of questions from staff or students). I chose to ignore the common practice at Dartmouth of seniors (especially pre-meds) hiring others to attend lectures and write entries. And I managed to forget that there were many instructors to read and grade the journals.

Triggered by ambivalence (sports-fan-cum-sports-critic) and designed to raise the consciousness of sports-oriented students to a revaluation of how sports inform the values, structures, institutions, and artifacts of our society, "Sports Culture, U.S.A." became a powerful learning experience for me. Even more than the collective impact of the guests, it was reading the nearly two hundred journals that taught the teacher that he had barely scratched the surface in his thinking. But the proverbial success-breeding successes were at their fathering-forth.

All the Moves was a book-club selection and elicited a two–sports book contract. The course experience would elicit a fortnightly column in the *Boston Globe* and *Washington Star* by the same name (shortened later to "Sports Culture") and one of those two books would be *Jock Culture,*

U.S.A. (1978). In an "improved" format, the course was repeated: several graduate assistants led small discussion groups that alternated with lectures, interviews, and films for the whole class. Since the teaching assistants assigned and graded the papers and all I read was the final (essay) exam, I was relieved of much of the pedagogical burden; unfortunately I was also distanced from the heart of the course—the students' experience—and the course lost the coherence of a unifying or at least centering consciousness amid the fragmenting pluralism of my very capable assistants.

Another serious flaw had surfaced—the random, almost hit-or-miss nature of the reading lists. It was at this point that I asked Jack Higgs—who had twice visited the course, gracing it with his prodigious enthusiasm, wisdom, and humor—to collaborate with me on an anthology. The resulting text, *The Sporting Spirit: Athletes in Literature and Life* (1977) owes its continuing success primarily to the devoted, intelligent attention of my collaborator, both in design and execution. In any case, when "Sports Culture, U.S.A." was reconvened, it had two texts, and the course, while retaining the feature of guest interviews, could be organized coherently around the issues that structured the books (a structure determined by the prior experiences of the course; see Appendix I).[2]

In its final incarnation, "Sports Culture, U.S.A." appeared under the rubric of American Studies, where, for a time, under the late Gene Wise, it was arranged that I offer half my courses. That was a suitable send-off, I suppose, because as a product of what I called cultural history, the course had both made its statement and exhausted its audience. But by this time, a number of other ways of relating SportsWorld activities to curricular efforts had suggested themselves.

The first was a traditional "topics" course, offered only twice (including a summer session) because I could not sustain sufficient interest in a fairly limited corpus of material. The limitations will be apparent in the reading list itself. Appendix II presents a schedule for the summer offering. But note the reference to "ideal" conditions for the course: while attractive in the context of an examination of a *topic*, such a syllabus does not hold much promise for several renewals. To make the list challenging and academically justifiable, the readings are sometimes peripheral to the topic, or the topic tangential to central issues in the readings. I have included the final exam in the appendix to indicate how labored the concept seemed finally to be.

In the framework of another course, however, the "topic" of sports worked far more satisfactorily for me. That was a framework called "The Uses of Literature," which I had developed for several purposes: to make the classroom hours a far more *active* experience for students; to build a demand for intellectual engagement, exercise, and growth into the very structure of a course; to demonstrate the significance of literary study (and its potential relevance); to relieve the instructor from the monotony of ever-repeating reading lists and release him from the narrow "field" approach to what I believe should be the broadest, most open-ended of disciplines.[3]

By the time the topic "Sports and Games" was offered, "The Uses of Literature" had looked at "Love," "Madness," "Death and Dying," and "The Drug Experience" with varying degrees of success. If I say that I was disappointed, finally, with the accomplishment of this course, it should be borne in mind that I had very high expectations even though the presence of *sports* in the title is not likely to attract an intellectually ambitious clientele. I had hoped, for example, that game theory would emerge as a topic for exploration; and then, arbitrarily, I had to impose the whole issue of chess and its many literary gambits and analogues.

This group in general had rather limited expectations of simply reading literature "about sports" and had to be pushed, prodded, provoked, and cajoled into reaching beyond a vague overlapping of tastes for books and for games. Once called upon to analyze the elements of their own tastes, however, they were then hard pressed to consider larger matters of structure, symbolism, ritual and mythology, time and timelessness, and to become aware of how our literature and our sports reflect each other and cohere, from anthropological, cultural-historical, and philosophical perspectives. As with the original "Sports Culture, U.S.A.," it was the optional project of a journal rather than a sequence of exams (see Appendix III) that was more likely to be productive in registering genuine growth.

There remain two other courses, in the category of special topics (a.k.a. one-shot spectaculars), and both go back to the reasons for my being at Maryland in the first place. Morris Freedman wanted to bring me here to initiate coursework in the study of film as literature, and I wanted to come for the freedom to design and teach courses that meshed with current interests and professional activities. So, having inaugurated (with Bob Kolker) English 245: Introduction to Film as Literature (and having left it in the capable hands of my dedicated colleague Joe Miller), I was free to offer an occasional film course of my own device.

One such occasion was "The Sports Film." Appendix IV presents as clearly as possible what I am urging as the value of coordinating one's teaching with one's writing. Part I of the appendix is part of my prospectus for a book on the subject; Part II recapitulates the premise and calendar for the course; Part III is a sample approach used for one of the films; and Part IV, the final exam, implies the investigative nature of the course.

The book was never written, but I regard the course as a success. In it, and through the cumulative efforts of sixty students, I concluded that the notion of "sports film" as genre, after the models, say, of Western or *film noir,* did not hold up under careful scrutiny. There were neither the set of characteristic conventions nor the satisfaction of common audience anticipations (what I call "aesthetic prescience"), both necessary for a genuine genre.

Finally, in spring 1986 (during which I predicted a season of 113 wins including NLCS and World Series for the Mets), I offered "The Myth and Legend of Baseball in Fiction and Film." That pretentious title masked a premise that could be reduced to the simple question, Why Baseball?

Since the organization of a Sport Literature Association, under the energetic leadership of Lyle Olsen, and the appearance of the handsome *Aethlon: The Journal of Sport Literature,* it has become increasingly clear that the best writing done on sports, whether journalistic or scholarly, is done on baseball; that the best imaginative works with sports backgrounds use baseball; and that baseball has retained a sometimes shaky claim to being the national pastime because of its firm hold on the cultural imagination, its fine tuning-in to the American psyche.

The point to be made here is the same as in the other courses. There is no baton sinister on their escutcheon; they are the legitimate issue of academic activity. The begats of the courses and the books are a chronicle of that integrity: *All the Moves* begat "Sports Culture, U.S.A.," which begat *Jock Culture, U.S.A.*, which begat "Sports Culture, U.S.A., II," which begat *The Sporting Spirit*, which begat "Jock Lit."

From a collateral line, including scores of papers, articles, columns, and chapters, the idea was generated for *Sentiment in Action: The Sports Film,* which, though never reaching maturity itself, begat "The Sports Film." In the same family was the baseball course, which sought answers to Why Baseball? in several ways (see Appendix V for calendar and paper assignment). In addition to screenings and discussions of readings, there were classroom visits by Tom Boswell, Tony Kornheiser, and Gerry Strine, writers who offered their own answers from their several perspectives.

And at last, when I had gotten it together, taken in the wealth of experience gathered in and for the course, and collected my thoughts; I prepared a brace of lectures called, "Why Baseball? A Cultural Historian Looks at the Phenomena of Literature/Baseball." The first section consisted of definitions. I set up five axes along which cultures may be described: broad/narrow, deep/shallow, still/dynamic, simple/complex, active/passive. I then labeled American culture as broad, shallow(!), dynamic, simple (?), and a mixture of active and passive. Then, in turn, I defined *myths* as formulations of cultural perceptions (examining relations with rituals and institutions), *literature* as formalized expressions of mythic scenarios (briefly discussing conventions and expectations), and then, leaning heavily on Empson, the *pastoral*.

The second section was largely a listing of what I called icons of American culture—the concepts, clusters, and conventions that make up a comprehensive value system. These included Frontier (e.g., the West), Freedom (which, along with the next three, allowed for mention of Puritan Ethic, Capitalistic System, and Free Enterprise), Individualism, Energy, Morality (subsuming Goodness, Rightness, Faith, Law, and Principle), The People (under which the idea of History as Cultural Invention may be discussed), The Land, Nature (with reference to Reaganistic Pastoralism), Technology, Quantification of Values, The New (subsuming both Progress and Youth), Competition, Tradition, and Teamwork. I broke Teamwork into levels of country (patriotism, family), verities, ethnocentrism (our side), and immortality (tribal self).

The third section discussed baseball under three headings: as game; as myth/ritual; and as literary material, with regard both to subject matter and to structure. And this led naturally to the final section, in which the readings for the course were summarily related to the elaborate framework I had erected.

For me this was the highlight of the course, though most of the eighty students were more interested in a field trip to Memorial Stadium. But does it sound like an outline for a book? Watch this space. Birth announcements may eventually appear.

NOTES

1. The term was not original with me, though I cannot cite a source. I'm afraid I am indirectly responsible for its currency, however, because it has been rasped nearly to death by Howard Cosell, who discovered it in the copy of *Jock Culture, U.S.A.* I respectfully presented to him.
2. I have always been uncomfortable with the idea of making money from sales of books to my own students, even when the books are specifically designed for a course. I have resolved this conflict by pledging that, when permission fees and advances are earned back, any royalties resulting from sales to my own classes will be donated to the library of our university.
3. Appendix III should be examined with the understanding that any topic could be substituted, with appropriate changes in predetermined texts. For example, for "Love" I assign Chaucer's *Troilus and Criseyde* and Proust's *Swann's Way*.

APPENDIX I: SYLLABUS

Sports Culture, U.S.A.

The purpose of the course is to examine the thoroughgoing way in which contemporary American culture—its institutions, its artifacts, its values—is informed by sports and sportsmindedness.

TEXTS

Higgs and Isaacs, eds., *The Sporting Spirit*, (SS). Isaacs, *Jock Culture, U.S.A.* (JC).

ASSIGNMENT CALENDAR

Jan. 27: First group of readings—JC I and Shaw, Housman, Hemingway, Huizinga in SS.
Feb. 3: Second group of readings—JC II and Powers, Jarrell, Updike in SS.
Feb. 10: First paper due.
Feb. 17: Third group of readings—JC III and Mishima, Mencken, Schulberg (191), Castiglione, Mailer, Faulkner, Frost in SS.
Feb. 24: Fourth group of readings—JC IV and Owens, Kramer in SS.
March 3: Second paper due.
March 10: Fifth group of readings—JC V and Lardner, Toynbee in SS.
March 24: Sixth group of readings—JC VI and Veblen (2), Runyon, Mumford in SS.
March 31: Third paper due.
April 7: Seventh group of readings—JC VII and Schulberg (55), Nyad, Spino, Weiss in SS.
April 14: Eighth group of readings—JC VIII and Thurber, Tunney, Anderson, Phelps, Roosevelt, White in SS.
April 21: Fourth paper due.
May 5: Final due at 1100 hours.

INSTRUCTIONS FOR PAPERS

Consider these written exercises (of column length, i.e., 800–1,000 words) as ways of *bringing together* the various materials of the course—readings, guest appearances, other experiences in the jockocracy (participation, spectation, media awareness). Your goals should be *coherence* and *pointedness.* I recommend the following strategy. Ask yourself a question that challenges you to bring various materials together. Your answer should then consist of three parts: (1) a *proposition,* in which you assert your point of view, state your hypothesis, or signal your insights; (2) a *demonstration*, in which you illustrate your case or compile your evidence; and (3) an *application*, in which you answer the question "So what?" by considering the implications of what you have to say or by arguing how important it is to recognize the connections you've made or at least by showing why it's significant to you.

The final will be a somewhat longer paper on an assigned topic to be issued no later than April 7. Keep all papers. They should be turned back in with the final at the end of the semester. at that time all your work will be reviewed by the instructor, who will look for ample evidence of familiarity with the several components of the course. In other words, don't focus all your attention for every paper on the same kinds of material (e.g., guests) and neglect the others (e.g., readings from *The Sporting Spirit*).

All papers and finals may be reclaimed, after grades are submitted, up to a year and a day after the end of the course, when those remaining in the instructor's hands will be shredded, mutilated, recycled, or biodegraded in some fiendishly celebratory fashion.

PROCEDURES FOR GUEST APPEARANCES

During the first part of the session, the guest will be interviewed by the instructor, who will try to focus attention of specific issues within the range of the guest's expertise. In the second part, questions will be solicited from the class. The questions should be thoughtful rather than argumentative, but you will be allowed to ask follow-up questions when it seems profitable to pursue a line of investigation.

Questions regarding personal matters or personalities will not be tolerated. I will insist on courtesy to the guests. Proper protocol will be to identify yourself to the guest before asking your question. The instructor regards participation in these question-and-answer sessions as a significant contribution to the course.

APPENDIX II: SYLLABUS

The Literature of Sports (Jock Lit)

The purpose of the course is to examine in a literary context the significance of sports in our culture. After some introductory readings from *The Sporting Spirit*, we will analyze a sequence of longer works of fiction. Ideally, the course would cover thirteen such books in a sequence with the following topics:

1. The sporting event as structure: Norman Mailer, *The Fight.*
2. The sport itself as content: Michael Murphy, *Golf in the Kingdom.*
3. The fan as subject: Frederick Exley, *A Fan's Notes.*
4. The curse of the ex-athlete: John Updike, *Rabbit, Run.*
5. The delayed maturity of the ex-athlete: John Updike, *Rabbit Redux.*
6. Sport as social, ethical arena: Patricia Nell Warren, *Front Runner.*
7. Sport as limited metaphor: Don DeLillo, *End Zone.*
8. Sport as artistic metaphor: Robert Coover, *The Universal Baseball Association.*
9. Sport as archetypal metaphor: Bernard Malamud, *The Natural.*
10. Sport as mythic substance: Philip Roth, *The Great American Novel.*
11. Sport as cultural phenomenon: James Whitehead, *Joiner.*
12. Sport as cultural given (character): Ernest Hemingway, *The Sun Also Rises.*
13. Sport as cultural given (attitude): F. Scott Fitzgerald, *The Great Gatsby.*

Unfortunately, the limitations of time (and the book business) make such a syllabus impossible. The following seems to me the best we can do:

SCHEDULE

Session 1. Powers, "Jamesie"; Hemingway, "The Capital of the World"; Jarrell, 40.
Session 2. Shaw, "Eighty-Yard Run"; Updike, "Ace in the Hole"; Housman, 66.
Session 3. Schulberg, "Crowd Pleaser"; Lardner, "A Caddy's Diary"; Thurber, 41–44.
Sessions 4–5. *Golf in the Kingdom.*
Sessions 6–8. *Front Runner.*
Session 9. Exam 1.
Sessions 10–12. *A Fan's Notes.*
Sessions 13–15. *Rabbit, Run.*
Session 16. Exam 2.
Sessions 17–19. *End Zone.*
Sessions 20–22. *The Natural.*
Session 23. Exam 3.

REQUIREMENTS

The three exams will follow the same format, and each will cover only one third of the readings. Each will consist of a single essay question, selected (or when necessary edited) from three suggested questions submitted by each student. For exams 2 and 3, one additional book each, from the following material will be included:

Numbers 5, 8, 10, 11, 12, and 13 from the "ideal" list above plus Todd Walton, *Inside Moves*; Mark Harris, *Bang the Drum Slowly*; Peter Handke, *The Goalie's Anxiety at the Penalty Kick*; or any suitable substitution approved by the instructor.

Clearly, a wise procedure would be to think, while you are reading the books, about ways to bring them together for discussion around shared central issues or by means of approaches that would illuminate them in common.

JOCK LIT FINAL

(for regular, not summer, session)

Compose a coherent, pointed essay, drawing your examples primarily from the readings for the course (concentrating on the later assignments and on those texts that you have not yet demonstrated familiarity with), in which you discuss the following issues:

1. The reliance of American fiction on the audience's thoroughgoing sports-mindedness.
2. The implications for the literature of that reliance (i.e., how it enriches and/or limits literature).
3. The relationships between form and content evidenced in such a literature.

The choice of emphasis, obviously, must be your own.

If you want to offer an essay on a different (but equivalent and related) topic, you may do so, provided that you clear your topic with me in advance.

This is not to be understood as a research assignment. I do not want use of or references to secondary sources except as the most casual and incidental kind of allusion.

As far as length is concerned, you may take as a minimum what you would be able to write in two full hours of a final exam situation.

APPENDIX III: SYLLABUS

The Uses of Literature: Sports and Games
Fall 1983

The premise of the course is simply this: literature is the way in which mankind records its perceptions about whatever it considers significant. That is not a definition of literature but a partial, telic description.

To test the premise, a significant topic is chosen—in this case, sports and games—and a number of readings treating the topic are examined. The literature should demonstrate both the breadth and depth of treatments of the topic and the value to the literature of such material.

As the course begins, as we discuss in a general way what we are about and arrive at some working definitions and statement of reasonable goals, the primary assignment is to develop a reading list. That may be the most important assignment of all and should be pursued with vigor if not fervor. Lists are due 14 September.

Meanwhile I have chosen the first two texts. We'll begin with Walton's *Inside Moves*, which you should have read by 14 September, and Roth's *Great American Novel*, by 21 September. The third assigned text, Coover's *UBA*, will come toward the end of the semester.

Written assignments will consist of a series of three exams *or* a journal. If you opt for a journal, you may later switch to exams; but you may not switch from exams to the journal option.

Journals should have frequent entries in recording and developing the ideas, insights, perceptions, and conceptions elicited from, suggested by, in opposition to, or taking off from the readings and the classroom discussions and any related experiences. Remember that the subject is literature/sports and games, so that entries should not roam unfocusedly into pure literary exegesis or abstract musings on play. Above all, the journal should chart a learning experience or demonstrate the growth or expanded awareness that comes from your explorations. Journals will be collected and reviewed 28 September, 24 October, and 18 November; they will be discussed in class 30 September, 26 October, and 21 November. Complete journals, including final long entry (see note on finals below), are due 14 December at 1200 hours.

The procedure for the exams is as follows. On 28 September, 24 October, and 18 November, you will each submit three questions. You should design questions that will challenge you to bring together the material of that segment of the course in a coherent, pointed essay of 1,200 to 1,500 words. I will discuss your questions with each of you, and we will agree on an assignment that should then be completed and submitted on 30 September, 26 October, and 21 November respectively.

The final exam (or final long entry in the journal) will be a relatively long essay on an assigned topic to be issued in class no later than 30 November. It will be due, along with all other exams, questions, lists, and journals, on 14 December at 1200 hours.

All submitted material may be reclaimed, after grades are submitted, up to 14 December 1984, when those remaining in the instructor's hands will be shredded, mutilated, recycled, or biodegraded in some fiendishly celebratory fashion.

APPENDIX IV: PROSPECTUS AND SYLLABUS

PROSPECTUS FOR BOOK: THE SPORTS FILM

Of all the staples of motion picture entertainment, one genre has received no critical attention. While westerns and musicals, detectives and monsters have been classified and analyzed to a fare-thee-well, the equally popular material of sports films has been neglected. *Sentiment in Action: A Study of the Sports Film* is conceived as a comprehensive attempt to fill the gap.

I am projecting a book of ten or more chapters designed to cover the field according to various subtypes of the genre. In each case I plan to identify the type descriptively, referring to as many titles as possible, and examine in some detail both an excellent and a failed model.

Two chapters will cover the closely related types of the sports biography and the sports tear-jerker, both of which carry an enormous burden of sentimentality. Whether the subject is Lou Gehrig, Babe Ruth, Babe Didrickson, Jim Piersall, Rocky Graziano, or Wilma Rudolph, an outstanding athlete has been transformed into a figure of pathetic identification. In the tear-jerker, either an incredible comeback against all odds or a "tragic" death is developed around an athlete (or both, e.g., *The Champ*). Sometimes these types overlap (*Brian's Song*), and occasionally one may produce an excellent movie (*Bang the Drum Slowly*).

At the opposite extreme of sentimentality is the cinematic capability for authenticity. A pair of chapters will examine the sports documentary (both the recording of events and the examination of ritual and aesthetic dimensions in sport) and the fiction film that tries to "tell it like it is" (*Fat City*, *Downhill Racer*, *Kansas City Bomber*).

The dark side of sports will be an important chapter because of the fine examples to be discussed, including *This Sporting Life*, *Requiem for a Heavyweight*, and *North Dallas Forty*. Other chapters will deal with fantasy *(Roller Ball, Angels in the Outfield, Here Comes Mr. Jordan, Heaven Can Wait)*, comedy (*Pat and Mike, Slap Shot, Bingo Long, Bad News Bears*) and what I call "the romance of the game"—where the focus is on how it feels to be a surfer (*Endless Summer*) or a bicycle racer (*Breaking Away*) or a pool shooter (*The Hustler*) or an automobile racer (*Winning*), and where concepts of competition and stakes are probed.

Finally, several chapters will examine the use of sports in movies as metaphor, as icon, and as mise-en-scene. One example is *They Shoot Horses, Don't They?* in which a dance marathon serves as a paradigm of the sporting spectacle. Another is *The Goalie's Anxiety at the Penalty Kick* in which the event serves as symbol-in-action for the philosophical thrust of the film. Memorable sequences such as the cricket match in *The Go-Between* or the chariot race in *Ben Hur* or the football game in *All the King's Men* would be grouped in the final category, a look at how sporting fragments supply thematic pointers for whole movies.

CALENDAR

The course is designed to cover the field of the sports film by looking at representative selections of the various subtypes of the genre. Our analysis should produce a rudimentary system of classification.

Ten times during the semester we will screen movies in class. The format for those sessions will be: (1) an approximately twenty-minute introductory discussion, (2) screening, and (3) up to an hour of discussion, as time allows. Schedule for screenings:

Sept. 9: *Pride of the Yankees.*
Sept. 16: *Bang the Drum Slowly.*
Sept. 23: *Kansas City Bomber.*
Sept. 30: *Olympia.*
Oct. 14: *Fat City.*
Oct. 21: *The Hustler.*
Oct. 28: *Junior Bonner.*
Nov. 4: *Requiem for a Heavyweight.*
Nov. 18: *Loneliness of the Long Distance Runner.*
Nov. 25: *They Shoot Horses, Don't They?*

SAMPLE APPROACH

The documentary approach to sporting events proceeds from the premise that the events themselves are intrinsically interesting. Moreover, there is an assumption of inherent aesthetic values in athletics. The good and the beautiful, the heroic and the noble (winners and losers), are viewed in the context of dramatic situations (the events) that can have their elements arranged and emphasized to produce comedy, irony, tragedy, romance, or a mixture thereof. In another sense, the documentary may pose as an objective record of ritual celebrations, with implicit significance. Given these elements and procedures, the documentary film may very artfully communicate whatever the filmmaker wishes.

After viewing *Olympia*, consider the following questions:

How does the movie identify, describe define, and prioritize values (good, beautiful, heroic, and noble.)?
Does it stray from a neutrality of tone? How?
Does it propagandize? How? To what end?

Do any departures from objectivity and neutrality actually effect a presentness of the experience? That is, do you feel that you were there, and if so does any bias deter or heighten that feeling? How? Can you identify any self-conscious or self-reflexive elements? Do they deter or heighten the presentness of the experience? How?

FINAL

Sports films easily engage audiences' attitudes toward heroes, but so do other kinds of movies, for example, westerns. Sports films easily attract audiences' attention to simple, often abstract conflicts, but so do other kinds, for example, detectives. In a pointed, coherent essay of 2,000 to 2,500 words, consider the question of whether there is such a genre as "sports film."

Consider such issues as these: the presence or absence of identifiable conventions and characteristic motifs (that any genre should have); expectations or assumptions you bring to a movie that has been labeled a sports film; ways in which sports films succeed or fail in the cohesion of form and content, structure and texture (material), style and meaning, and the like.

In other words, I am asking you to state and illustrate your own thoughtful conclusions about the experiment that this course has been.

Use *Loneliness of the Long Distance Runner* and *They Shoot Horses, Don't They?* as two of your examples (whatever your position), and range freely among other films in and out of the course. You would be well-advised to touch on those films you ignored in earlier papers.

Thank you and good luck.

APPENDIX V: SYLLABUS

The Myth and Legend of Baseball in Fiction and Film

CALENDAR

Jan. 27: Introductory remarks.
Feb. 4: Screening of *Pride of the Yankees.*
Feb. 11: Discussion of Roger Kahn, *Boys of Summer.*
Feb. 18: Screening of *Bang the Drum Slowly.*
Feb. 25: Discussion of W. P. Kinsella, *Shoeless Joe.*
March 4: Screening of *Bingo Long.*
March 11: Lecture.
March 18: Discussion of Thomas Boswell, *Life Imitates the World Series.*
April 1: Discussion of Robert Coover, *Universal Baseball Association.*
April 8: Discussion of selected readings: James Thurber, "You Could Look It Up"; P. G. Wodehouse, "The Pitcher and the Plutocrat"; J. F. Powers, "Jamesie"; Ring Lardner, "Alibi Ike"; Charles Einstein, "Reflex Curve"; William Heyen, "The Stadium"; Rolfe Humphries, "Polo Grounds"; Richard Eberhart, "Ball Game"; William Carlos Williams, "At the Ball Game."
April 15: Discussion of Daniel Okrent, *Nine Innings.*
April 22: Screening of *The Natural.*
April 29: Paper due.
May 6: Discussion of selected readings: Richard Grossinger, "Baseball Voodoo"; John Updike, "Hub Fans Bid Kid Adieu"; A. Bartlett Giamatti, "The Green Fields of the Mind"; Donald Hall, "Fathers Playing Catch with Sons"; Roger

Angell, "The Interior Stadium"; Mikhail Horowitz, "Howl for Casey"; Gregory Corso, "Dream of a Baseball Star"; Peter Meinke, "Byron vs. DiMaggio"; Marianne Moore, "Baseball and Writing."

May 13: Discussion of Philip Roth, *The Great American Novel.*

REQUIREMENTS

Your performance in this course will depend on your ability to hit the assignments consistently and with power. Each reading assignment will be accompanied by a quiz worth 20 points; after each screening you will be thrown a quiz worth 10 points; the paper will be worth up to 150 points. You could possibly score 350, but it will take probably 315 points to get an A.

The *paper* is perhaps the single most important part of the course. It is worth up to 150 points toward your batting average (grade), and it should reflect both the major thrust of the course itself and the way you choose to showcase your own educational accomplishment in the course. Consider the following guidelines as suggestions. You are free to work beyond these limitations, outside these parameters, but remember that the further you stray from the letter or spirit of the assignment the more important it is to obtain the instructor's explicit approval in advance.

Choose a work of baseball fiction and a book of nonfiction baseball writing not on the required reading list for the course. A list of possible selections, not intended to be complete, will be distributed separately.

Compare and contrast the two books, focusing on the elements of historical and technical realism and accuracy in the fiction, on elements of legend and myth, of symbol and heroism and mystery in the nonfiction. You should pull your paper together with some pointed observations about (1) the nature of the game as it reflects American culture or (2) about American culture as particularly hospitable to the game of baseball, or (3) about the ways in which baseball and writing on baseball interact.

Option A: Substitute a movie (to which you have access for study) for one of the books.

Option B: Substitute movies for both books.

Option C: Analyze in considerable depth and detail the transformation of a baseball book into a baseball movie.

Consider the ways in which the different media foster the treatment of fictional and nonfictional elements (see above). Format: This assignment calls for submission of a piece of formal writing (typed, double-spaced). In part, your performance will be judged on the quality of your writing, so be sure to allow ample time for revision, editing, and proofreading. But most important will be the quality of the thought informing the presentation. There are, then, no quantified standards (no arbitrary word count); this is one aspect of baseball without statistical measurement.

WORKS CITED

Higgs, Robert J., and Neil D. Isaacs, eds. *The Sporting Spirit: Athletes in Literature and Life.* New York: Harcourt Brace, 1977.

Isaacs, Neil D. 1975. *All the Moves: A History of College Basketball.* New York: Harper and Row, 1984.

———. 1978. *Jock Culture, U.S.A.* New York: Norton. 1978.

Contributors

SUSAN BIRRELL is Associate Professor in the Department of Physical Education and Sport Studies at the University of Iowa. She is a feminist teacher and scholar whose work has appeared in journals such as *International Journal of Sport Psychology*, *Sociology of Sport Journal*, *Social Forces*, *Women's Studies International Forum*, and *Urban Life*. She has coedited, with M. Marie Hart, *Sport and the Sociocultural Process,* 3d ed. (W. C. Brown, 1981).

KENDALL A. BLANCHARD is Professor of Anthropology and Chair of the Department of Sociology, Anthropology and Social Work at Middle Tennessee State University. He is the author of *Mississippi Choctaws at Play: The Serious Side of Leisure* (University of Illinois Press, 1981) and coauthor of *The Anthropology of Sport* (Bergin & Garvey, 1985) with Alyce Cheska.

WAYNE A. BURROUGHS is Professor of Industrial/Organizational Psychology at the University of Central Florida. He is coauthor of several books designed for management development and has contributed numerous pieces on leadership, management selection, and sport psychology to management and psychology journals. One recent article is "Visual Stimulation Training of Baseball Batters" in the Fall 1984 issue of the *International Journal of Sport Psychology*. In addition, he has often served as a consultant for such entities as Southern Bell Telephone, the Federal Aviation Administration, and several major league baseball franchises including the New York Mets, the New York Yankees,the Detroit Tigers, the Minnesota Twins, and the Houston Astros.

JOAN M. CHANDLER is Associate Professor of Arts and Humanities and American Studies Program Head at the University of Texas at Dallas. She is well known for her work in sport and the media, most recently displayed in her article, "American Televised Sport: Business as Usual," in *American Sport Culture: The Humanistic Dimensions,* edited by Wiley Lee Umphlett (Bucknell University Press, 1985). The article anticipates her book, *Television and National Sport: The United States and Britain* (University of Illinois Press, 1988).

JAY J. COAKLEY is Professor of Sociology at the University of Colorado–Colorado Springs and the editor of *Sociology of Sport Journal.* He is the author of *Sport in Society: Issues and Controversies,* 3d ed. (C. V. Mosby, 1986).

FRANK COSENTINO is Professor in the Department of Physical Education and Athletics at York University, where he serves as head football coach. He is the author or coauthor of five books on Canadian sport history, including *Canadian Football: The Grey Cup Years* (Musson Book Company, 1969), and he has produced a film strip called *An Audio-Visual History of Canadian Sport.* All this came after a distinguished ten-year career as a quarterback in the Canadian Football League.

JEFFREY H. GOLDSTEIN is Professor of Psychology at Temple University. He is the editor of *Sports Violence* (Springer-Verlag, 1983), and *Sports, Games, and Play* (Lawrence Erlbaum Associates, 1979). A second edition of *Sports, Games, and Play* is in preparation.

ALLEN GUTTMANN is Professor of American Studies at Amherst College. His sport-related work includes the contemporary classic, *From Ritual to Record: The Nature of Modern Sports* (Columbia University Press, 1978), *The Games Must Go On: Avery Brundage and the Olympic Movement* (Columbia University Press, 1984), *Sports Spectators* (Columbia University Press, 1986), and *A Whole New Ball Game: An Interpretation of American Sports* (University of North Carolina Press, 1988).

NEIL D. ISAACS is Professor of English at the University of Maryland. Among his several books are *Jock Culture, U.S.A.* (Norton, 1978) and *All the Moves: A History of College Basketball* (Lippincott, 1975; reprinted by Harper, 1984). He also coedited *The Sporting Spirit: Athletes in Literature and Life* (Harcourt, 1977) with Robert J. Higgs. He is a frequent contributor to *Aethlon: The Journal of Sport Literature,* where one may read his short stories, "Closing Ceremonies" and "Match Points."

J. A. MANGAN is Head of the Education Department at Jordanhill College of Education and the editor of the *British Journal of Sports History.* He is the author and editor of numerous volumes, including *The Games Ethic and Imperialism* (Penguin/Viking, 1985), *Athleticism in the Victorian and Edwardian Public School* (Cambridge University Press, 1981), and, with Roberta J. Park, *From 'Fair Sex' to Feminism: Sport and the Socialization of Women in the Industrial and Post-Industrial Era* (Cass, 1986).

MARY MCELROY is Associate Professor in the Department of Physical

Education and Leisure Studies at Kansas State University. Among her recent articles is "Malamud's *The Natural* and the Appeal of Baseball in American Culture" in the Summer, 1985 issue of *Journal of American Culture,* cowritten with Kent Cartwright, an article that won a Carl Bode Research Award.

KLAUS V. MEIER is Professor of Physical Education at the University of Western Ontario and the editor of *The Journal of the Philosophy of Sport.* A former President of the Philosophic Society for the Study of Sport, he is coeditor of *Philosophic Inquiry in Sport* (Human Kinetics Publishers, 1988) with William J. Morgan.

ANDREW W. MIRACLE is Professor of Anthropology at Texas Christian University. He is coeditor of *Sport and Social Theory* (Human Kinetics Publishers, 1986) with C. Roger Rees and *Studies in the Sociology of Sport* (Texas Christian University Press, 1982) with Rees and Aidan O. Dunleavy.

DON MORROW is Associate Professor of Physical Education in the Faculty of Physical Education at the University of Western Ontario. He has published extensively in Canadian sport history and is coauthor of a forthcoming book, *A Social History of Canadian Sport* (Oxford University Press).

DONALD J. MROZEK is Professor of History at Kansas State University and the author of *Sport and American Mentality, 1880–1910* (University of Tennessee Press, 1983). His summers are spent exploring the Arctic.

CHARLES S. PREBISH is Associate Professor of Religious Studies at the Pennsylvania State University. His piece in *The Antioch Review* (Summer 1984), "'Heavenly Father, Divine Goalie': Sport and Religion," is a portion of a forthcoming full-length study entitled *Sport Religion: The New Nirvana.* He has published four books on Buddhism, the most recent of which is *American Buddism* (Duxbury Press, 1979).

GREGORY S. SOJKA is Academic Dean at the University of Wyoming at Casper. He publishes often on American literature, popular culture, and sport studies. His most recent book is *Ernest Hemingway: The Angler As Artist* (Peter Lang Press, 1985).

DAVID L. VANDERWERKEN is Professor of English at Texas Christian University and the coeditor of *Sport Inside Out: Readings in Literature and Philosophy* (Texas Christian University Press, 1985) with Spencer K. Wertz. He is a former President of the Sport Literature Association.

SPENCER K. WERTZ is Professor of Philosophy and Chair of the Department at Texas Christian University. He is coeditor of *Sport Inside Out: Readings in Literature and Philosophy* (Texas Christian University Press, 1985) with David L. Vanderwerken and the author of numerous articles in sport philosophy. His book, *Talking a Good Game*, is forthcoming from Southern Methodist University Press. He is a former President of the Philosophic Society for the Study of Sport.

Index